THE ART & ARCHITECTURE OF THE AZTEC & MAYA

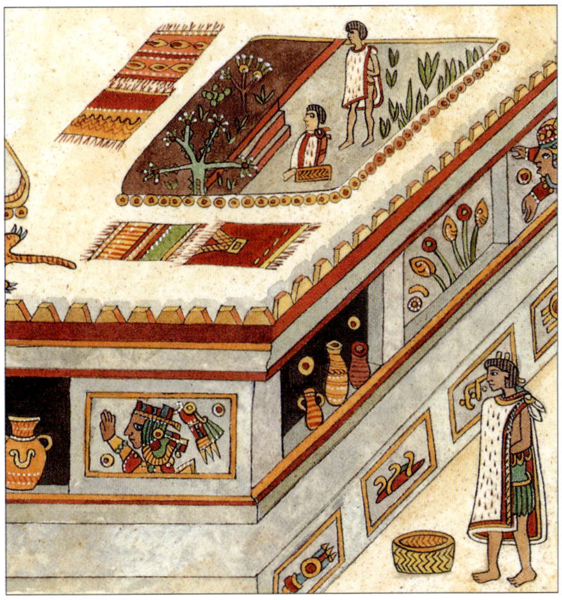

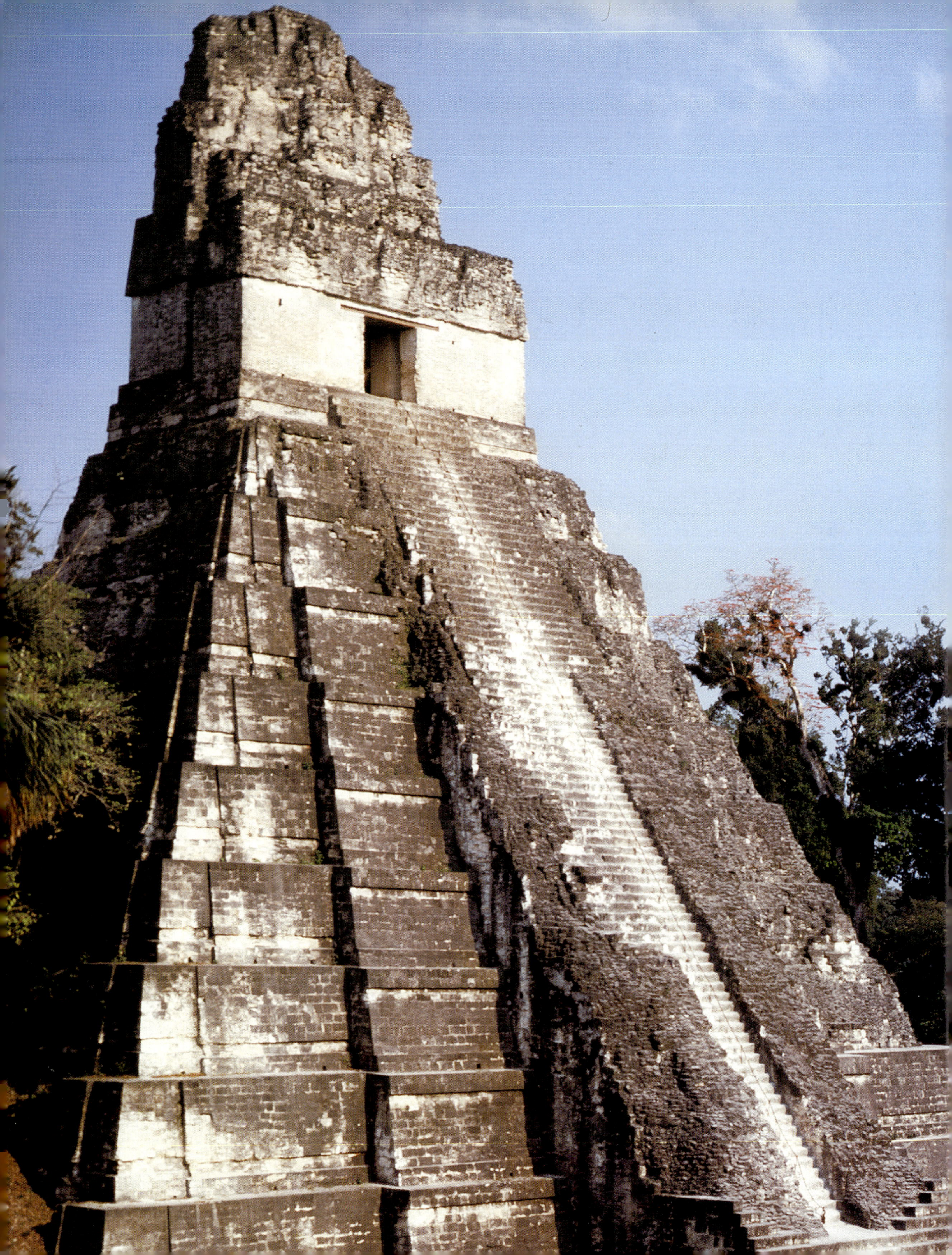

THE ART & ARCHITECTURE OF THE

AZTEC & MAYA

An illustrated encyclopedia of the buildings, sculptures and art of the peoples of Mesoamerica, with over 220 photographs, fine art drawings, maps, diagrams, site plans and reconstructions

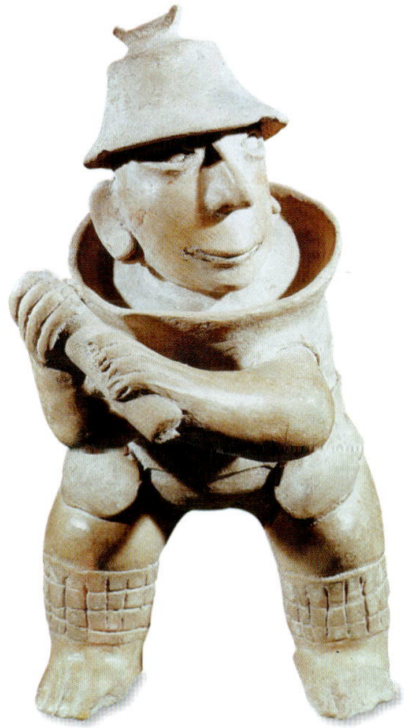

CHARLES PHILLIPS
CONSULTANT: DR DAVID M JONES

southwater

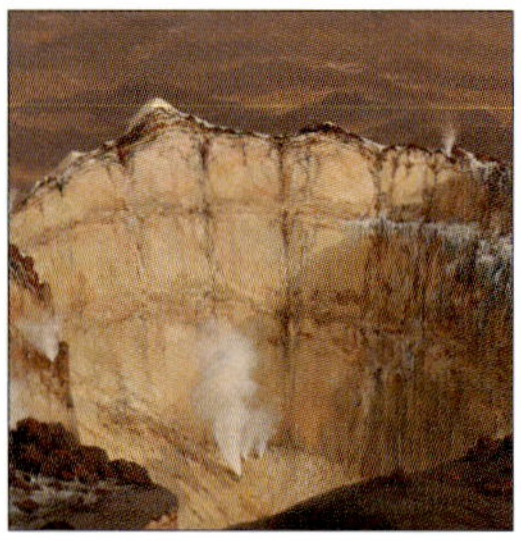

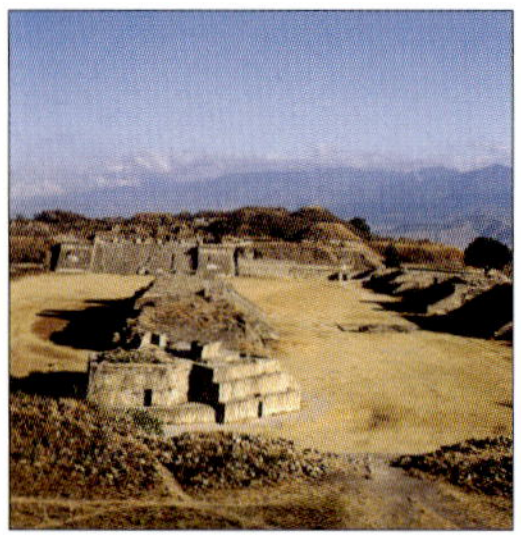

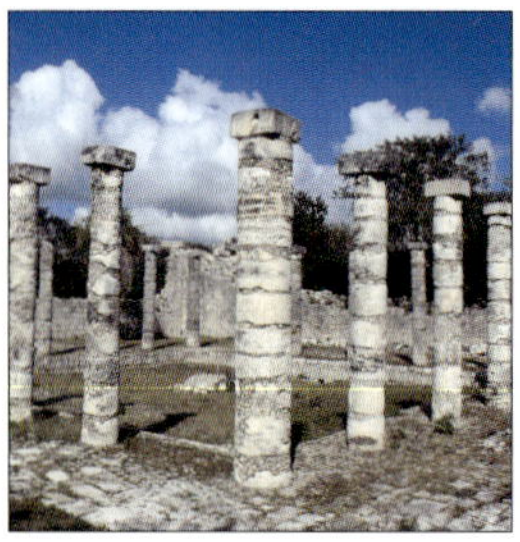

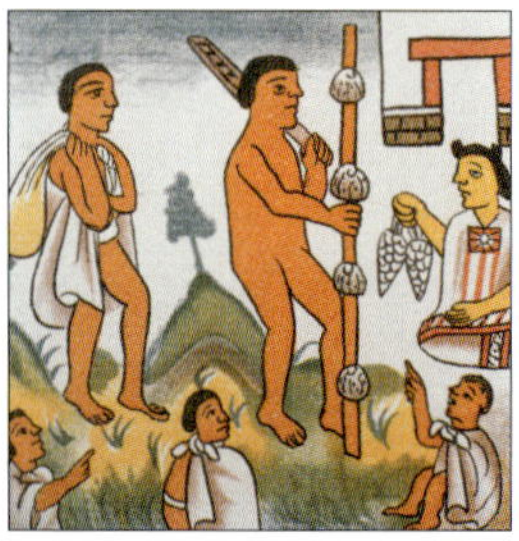

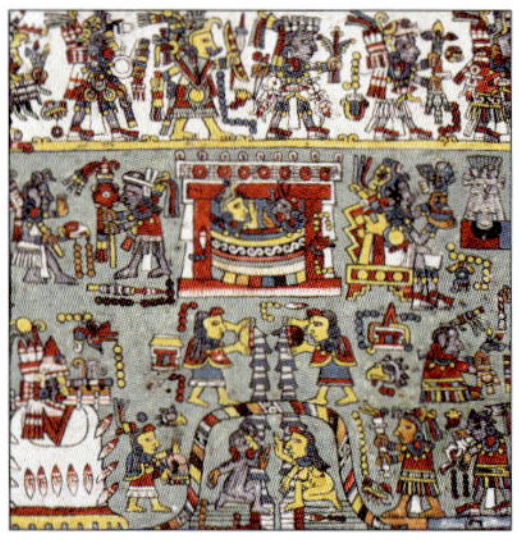

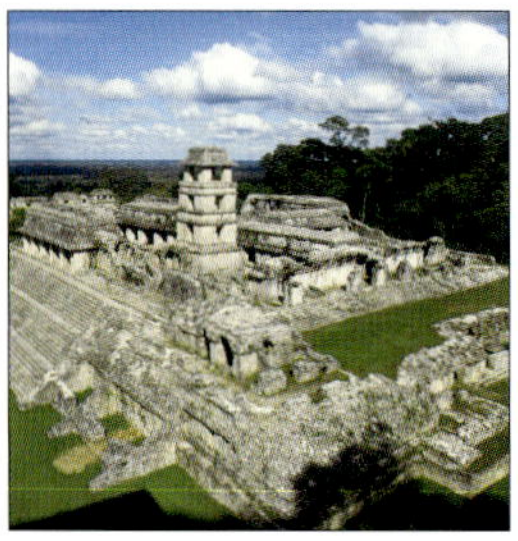

This edition is published by Southwater
an imprint of Anness Publishing Ltd,
Hermes House, 88–89 Blackfriars Road,
London SE1 8HA
tel. 020 7401 2077; fax 020 7633 9499

www.southwaterbooks.com
www.annesspublishing.com

Anness Publishing has a new picture agency outlet for images for publishing, promotions or advertising. Please visit our website www.practicalpictures.com for more information.

UK agent: The Manning Partnership Ltd
tel. 01225 478444; fax 01225 478440
sales@manning-partnership.co.uk

UK distributor: Grantham Book Services Ltd
tel. 01476 541080; fax 01476 541061
orders@gbs.tbs-ltd.co.uk

North American agent/distributor:
National Book Network; tel. 301 459 3366
fax 301 429 5746; www.nbnbooks.com

Australian agent/distributor:
Pan Macmillan Australia
tel. 1300 135 113; fax 1300 135 103;
customer.service@macmillan.com.au

New Zealand agent/distributor:
David Bateman Ltd
tel. (09) 415 7664; fax (09) 415 8892

Publisher: Joanna Lorenz
Senior Managing Editor: Conor Kilgallon
Editor: Joy Wotton
Designer: Nigel Partridge
Illustrator: Peter Bull Art Studio
Production Controller: Wendy Lawson

Previously published as part of a larger volume
The Aztec & Maya World

Page 1: A reconstruction of Moctezuma's palace in Tenochtitlán
Page 2: The Great Jaguar Temple, Tikal
Page 3: Ceramic ball player from Nayarit, Mexico

ETHICAL TRADING POLICY

At Anness Publishing we believe that business should be conducted in an ethical and ecologically sustainable way, with respect for the environment and a proper regard to the replacement of the natural resources we employ.

As a publisher, we use a lot of wood pulp to make high-quality paper for printing, and that wood commonly comes from spruce trees. We are therefore currently growing more than 500,000 trees in two Scottish forest plantations near Aberdeen – Berrymoss (130 hectares/ 320 acres) and West Touxhill (125 hectares/ 305 acres). The forests we manage contain twice the number of trees employed each year in paper-making for our books.

Because of this ongoing ecological investment programme, you, as our customer, can have the pleasure and reassurance of knowing that a tree is being cultivated on your behalf to naturally replace the materials used to make the book you are holding.

Our forestry programme is run in accordance with the UK Woodland Assurance Scheme (UKWAS) and will be certified by the internationally recognized Forest Stewardship Council (FSC). The FSC is a non-government organization dedicated to promoting responsible management of the world's forests. Certification ensures forests are managed in an environmentally sustainable and socially responsible basis. For further information about this scheme, go to www.annesspublishing.com/trees

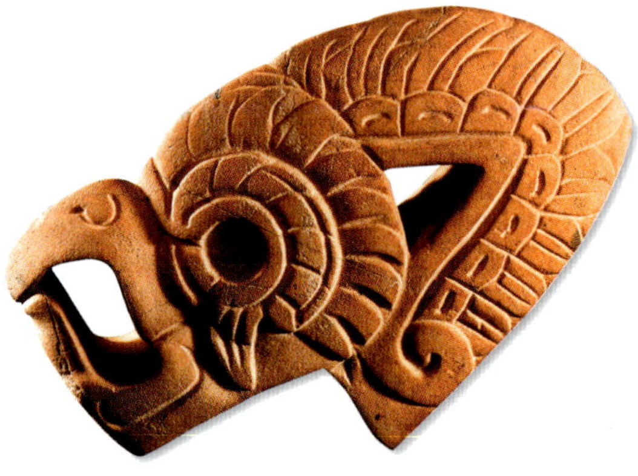

CONTENTS

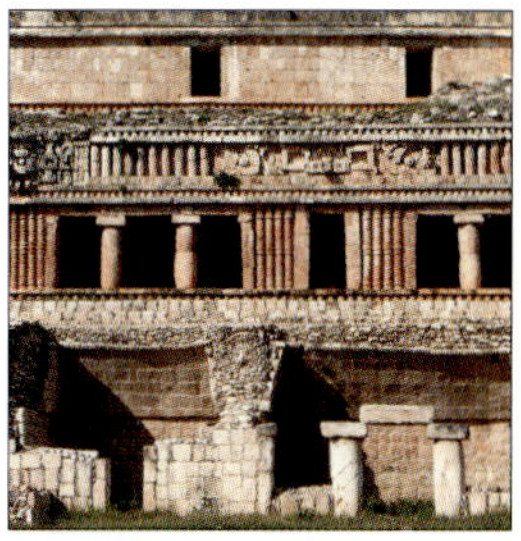

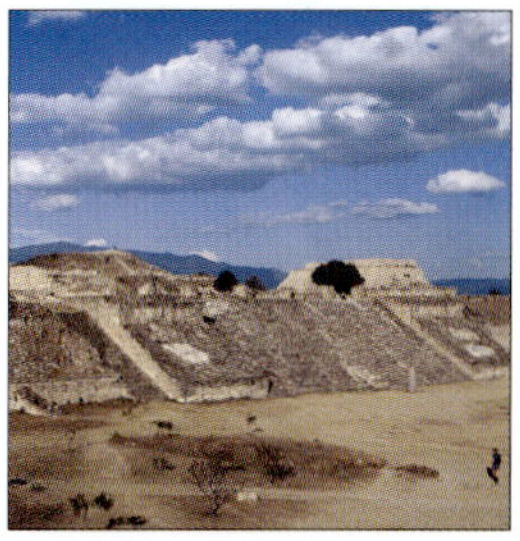

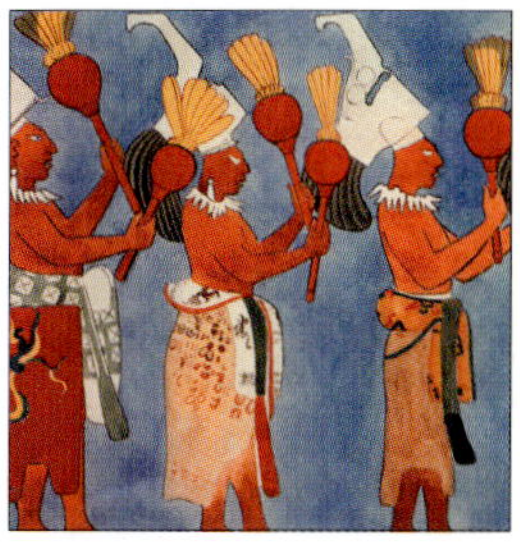

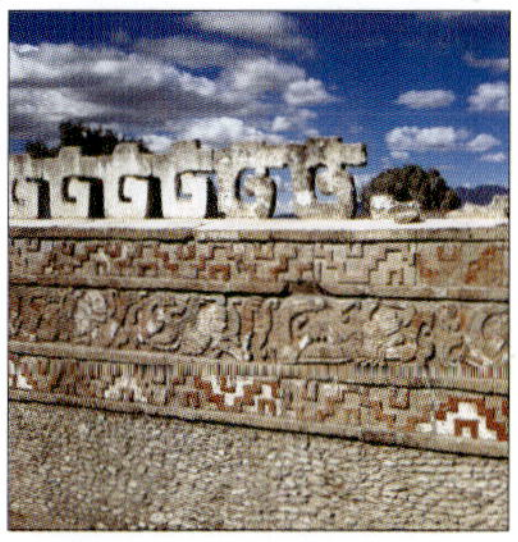

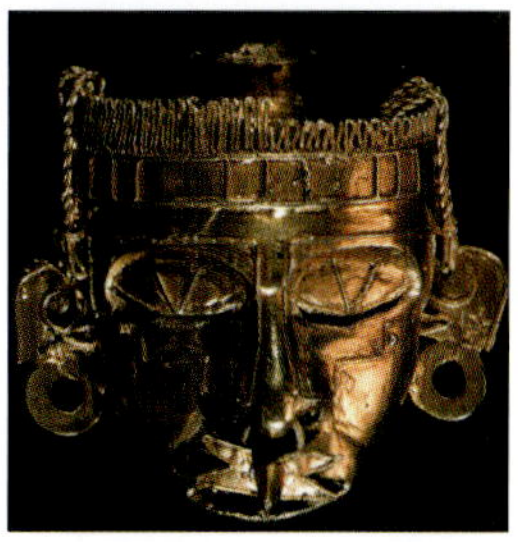

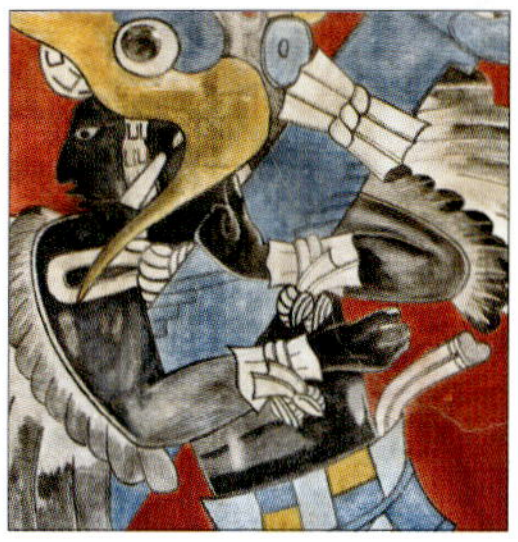

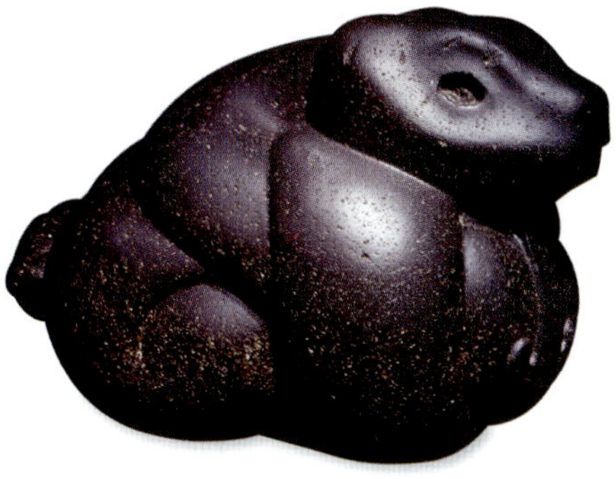

INTRODUCTION

This survey of arts and crafts begins with a discussion of the main styles of architecture and a survey of the great cities. It describes the work of potters, weavers and featherworkers, then looks at stone and wood carving, metalwork, jewellery, mural painting and the production of painted codex screenfold books. It ends with a discussion of Mesoamerican aesthetics.

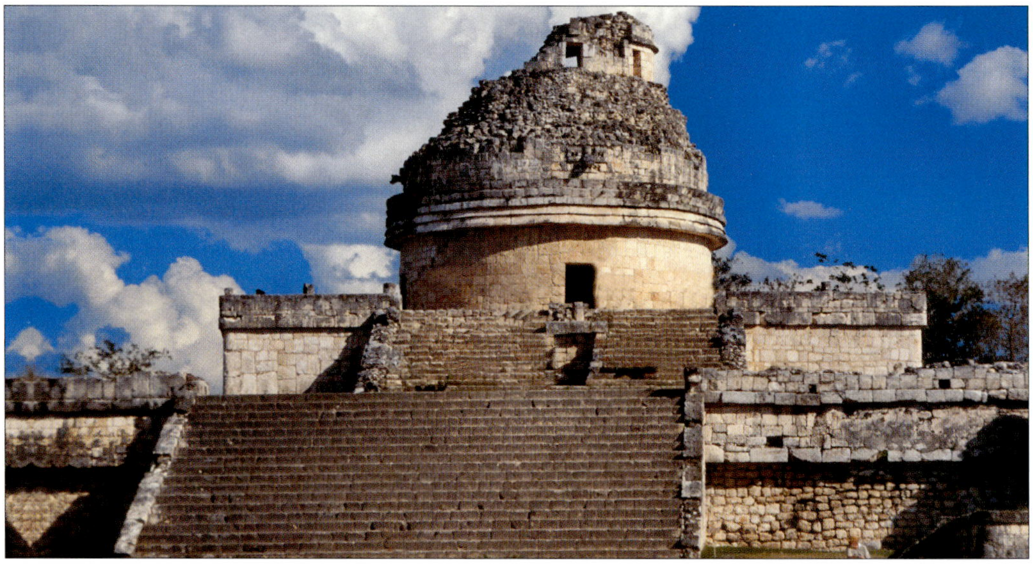

Above: In observatories such as the Caracol at Chichén Itzá, the patterns of the night sky were interpreted.

AN ARTISTIC TRADITION

A carved bone found in the tomb of King Ah Cacau (*r.* AD682–734) beneath Temple I at Tikal depicts the hand of an artist-scribe emerging from a gaping monster's mouth. This monster-mouth was an established Mesoamerican image for the entrance to the spirit realm of the underworld – and the carving indicates that the Maya believed artistic ability and inspiration to have a divine source. Certainly the Maya of the Late Classic Period, in which this bone and the great majority of delicately painted polychrome vases were produced, celebrated their artists as a gifted elite. These exquisite vases – some of the finest produced in any world culture – were often signed by the artists who painted them.

The Méxica/Aztecs, too, revered their artists, whom they called 'Toltecs' after the founders of the city of Tollán/Tula. In the Aztec Nahuatl tongue *tolteca* meant 'artist', and the word for artistic ability was *toltecayotl.* In the years of the Aztec empire, there was no distinction between artists and craftsmen: *tolteca* included artisans such as carpenters and weavers. They were seen as divinely blessed: their task was to seek sacred meaning in their heart and express this truth in their work. If they worked in this way, then they would truly be like the Toltecs, whose city of Tollán was remembered as place of beauty and artistic excellence.

Human activity in the region of Mexico and neighbouring Guatemala dates back 20,000 years or more to when the first hunter-gatherers settled in the area. In the period between then and the height of the Aztec empire in the 14th-16th centuries AD, several civilizations rose and fell in the locality. Among these were the Olmec, carvers of magnificent stone monuments; the Zapotec, builders of Monte Albán, who may have been the first people in the region to develop written communication; and the builders of Teotihuacán, who excelled in the manufacture of masks and the painting of murals.

Other civilizations included the Maya, who raised magnificent temples and palaces in the jungles of Guatemala and in parts of eastern Mexico, *c.*AD250–900, and who continued to thrive until the Spanish Conquest; the Toltecs, who built their capital Tollán north-west of Teotihuacán *c.*AD950; the Mixtecs, who excelled in metalworking and hand-painted screenfold books; the Tarascans in western Mexico, highly skilled metalworkers who forged an empire after 1200; and the Méxica, or Aztecs, who in the years after founding their capital of Tenochtitlán in 1325 built a vast empire.

CULTURE CLASH

On their arrival in 1519, the Spanish encountered certain elements familiar from their own European culture. As in Europe, the warriors' achievements were lauded and military might enforced

Below: Maya sculptors reached great heights of artistic expression. This head represents King Pacal of Palenque in middle age.

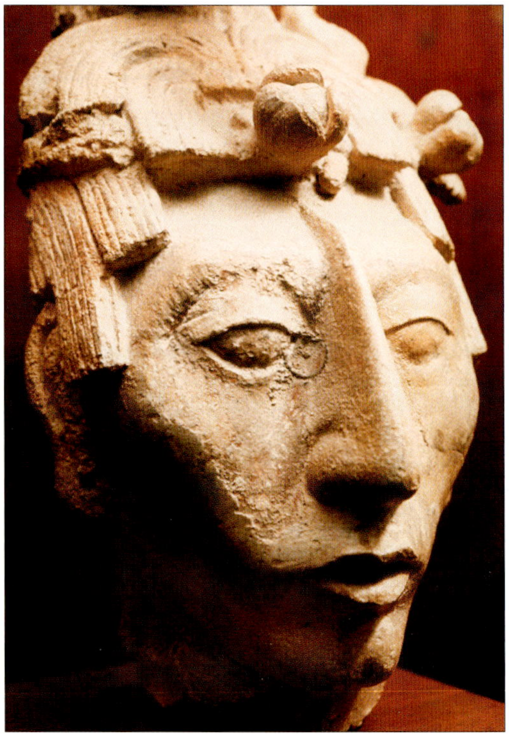

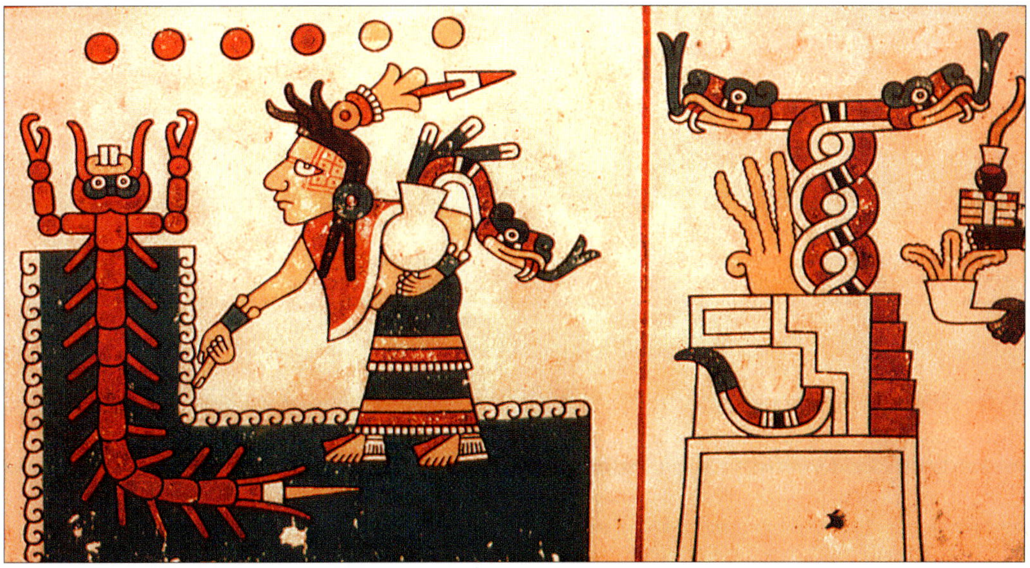

political power, networks of trade and tribute were vibrant and a strong sense of the sacred informed all parts of life. Other elements of Mesoamerican civilization, however, were bafflingly strange or broke European taboos. For example, while the conquistadors were certainly not unfamiliar with torture and slaughter, they were unprepared for the Aztecs' ritual celebration of slaughter, in which human hearts were torn out as a key element of public religious ritual.

CYCLES OF TIME

Another key element of Mesoamerican culture that was immediately alien to the Europeans was the idea that the gods made time move in cycles. The Aztecs believed that the current world was the fifth in a succession of creations and that, within the current world age, events were destined to be repeated in a way which followed large, cyclical patterns.

Mesoamericans had a very deep respect for the past. In both Aztec and Maya lands, worshippers made respectful journeys to the great cities built by their ancestors such as Teotihuacán and Tollán for the Aztecs and Tikal and Chichén Itzá for the Maya. Indeed, the desire to recreate in the present the glories of the past was one of the driving forces behind the Aztec empire.

The Aztecs wanted to honour the achievements of the Toltec founders of Tollán. They were also keen to celebrate the sacred city of Teotihuacán, which they viewed as the birthplace of the gods. Aztec builders and stonemasons made reverent use of architectural and sculptural styles from these ancient cities in creating the sacred precinct of Tenochtitlán. Aztec pilgrims took masks and other sacred items from graves in Teotihuacán and Tollán to reuse them in their own temple offerings in Tenochtitlán. Aztec priests and worshippers enthusiastically practised the rituals of human sacrifice which (although they had ancient beginnings in the Mesoamerican past) had been decisively escalated by the honoured Toltecs. At Chichén Itzá in northern Yucatán, a group of Maya, also influenced by the Toltecs, similarly used *chacmools*, arranged the skulls of victims on skull racks and held vast public rites of human sacrifice.

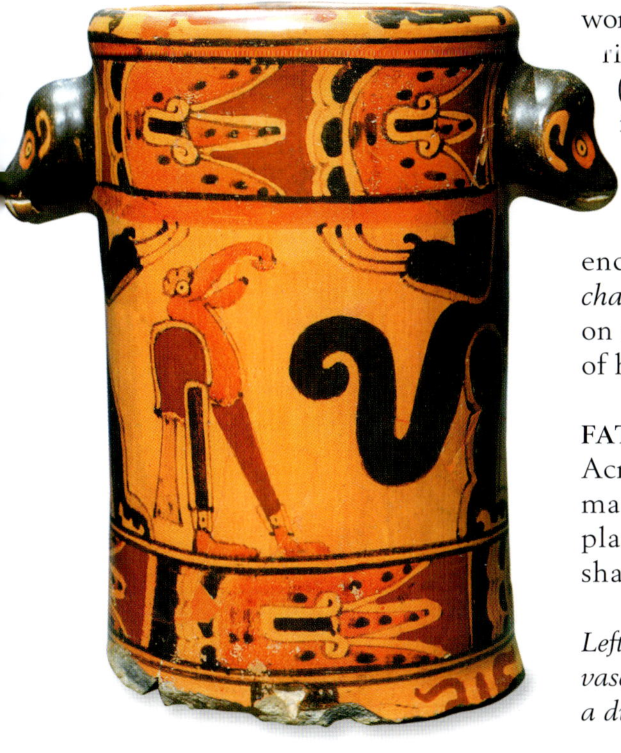

FATE AND FATALISM

Across Mesoamerica, astronomer-priests made observations of the cycles of planets and movements of stars, while shaman-priests interpreted the ritual calendars and performed rites of divination using psychotropic substances. It was believed diviners had the power to identify sacred influences on human activity in the patterns of the sky and in the cycles of time. Some historians argue that beliefs in divination, the power of omens and the inevitability of time's repeating patterns made Mesoamericans more fatalistic.

Left: Sacred symbols in nature. This Maya vase from the Sula valley, Honduras, shows a divine monkey-spider and a bird-man.

Above: Serpent imagery abounds in this Mixtec representation of water goddess Chalchiúhtlicue. The snake was associated with water, fertility and the earth.

The so-called 'Maya collapse' – when in the 9th and 10th centuries AD a series of powerful cities across Guatemala stopped erecting dated monuments to the glory of their kings and fell into rapid decline – had many causes, principally environmental degradation, but may have been encouraged by a fatalistic belief that the decline could be predicted from the patterns of time, that, by the gods' choice, these events mirrored others many centuries earlier and so were not worth resisting.

Equally, there were many practical causes for the defeat of the mighty Aztec empire by a small band of Spanish invaders fighting in alliance with local peoples, but historical accounts reveal that Aztec leaders were aware that the omens were bad and appeared to prophesy their downfall. Some thought Cortés was destined for victory, and some Aztecs even believed that Cortés was the Mesoamerican god Quetzalcóatl making a long-promised return to claim his rightful inheritance in Tenochtitlán.

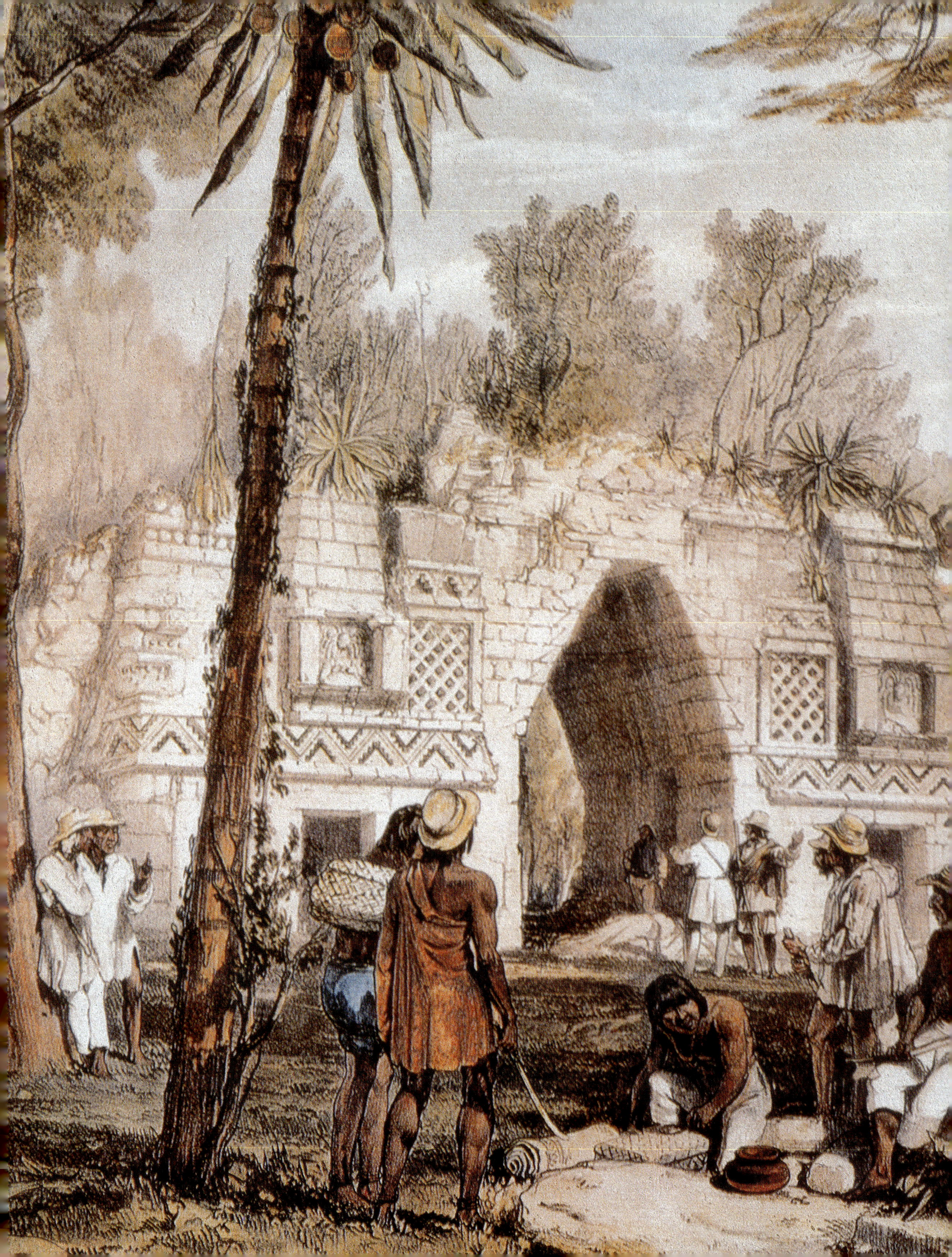

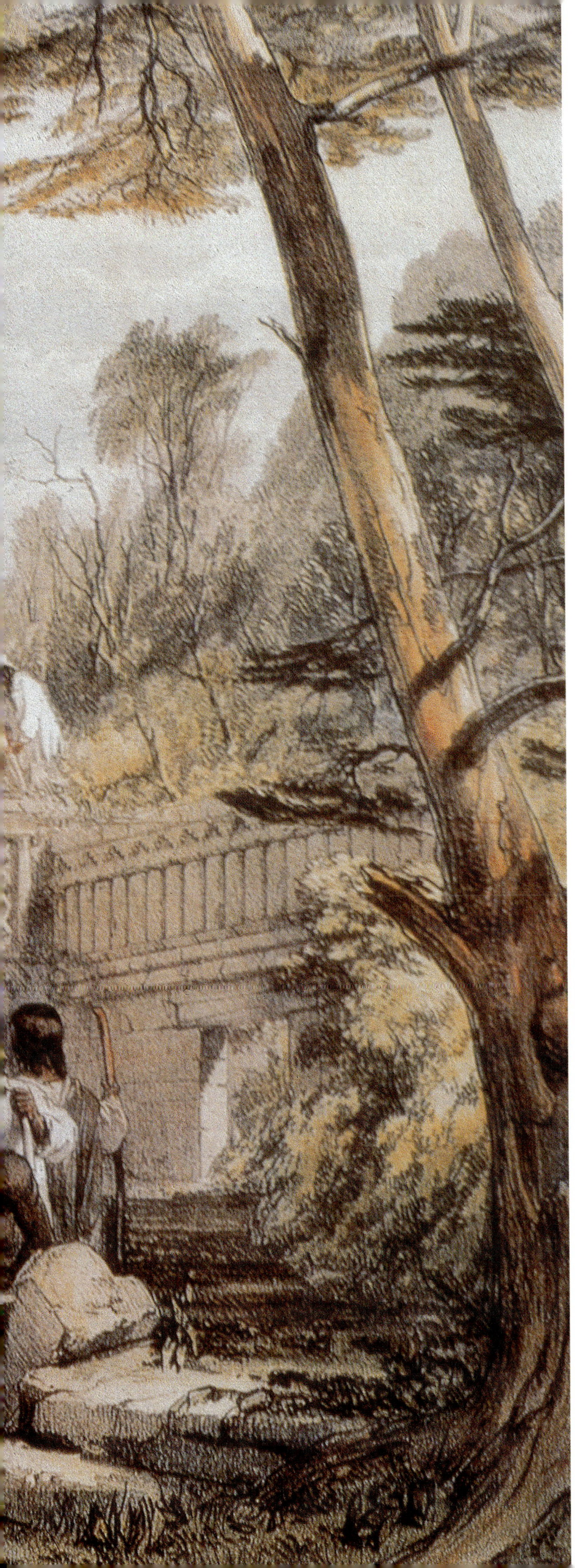

DISCOVERING THE PAST

Mesoamericans themselves were Central America's first archaeologists. The Aztecs and Maya had a deep reverence for their own shared past and the achievements of their forebears, and investigated the evocative ruins of once majestic cities such as Tollán, Teotihuacán and Tikal.

Both Maya and Aztecs engaged with the ruined cities as religious centres rather than as historical sites. They came to satisfy a religious and cultural yearning to touch and be touched by the past. They saw nothing wrong in entering monuments and tombs to gather funerary masks and golden grave offerings for their own religious use, or in adding offerings of their own to a temple cache. The Aztecs carried artefacts back from Teotihuacán and Tula to Tenochtitlán for use as temple offerings in the great Templo Mayor, where later generations of archaeologists would discover them. In Maya lands, pilgrims from Chichén Itzá may have travelled to the ruins of Tikal to perform religious ceremonies; in later times both Uxmal and Chichén Itzá were pilgrimage sites. The Aztecs also carried out sacrifices and sacred rites at the city of Teotihuacán.

The Spanish invaders of the early 16th century treated the great architectural achievements of Mesoamerica with scant respect. They deliberately destroyed the temples and religious statuary of the Aztecs. They erected the capital of their colony, New Spain, atop the rubble and shattered remnants of the Aztecs' great metropolis of Tenochtitlán. It was left to modern archaeologists to rediscover the truth about this ancient past.

Left: This view of the archway at Labná is by English artist Frederick Catherwood who, with American author John L. Stephens, was a pioneer of Maya exploration in the 1830s–40s. It is taken from their 1841 book on Maya ruins.

WONDERS IN THE JUNGLE

The first organized archaeological investigation of Mesoamerican ruins took place in the 17th century. A Mexican Jesuit priest called Carlos de Siguenza y Gongora (1645–1700) led a dig at Teotihuacán which mainly focused on the Pyramid of the Moon, as part of a lifelong attempt to research and write a history of ancient Mexico.

The 18th century saw the modern rediscovery of important Mesoamerican relics and sites, notably of Maya cities that had been abandoned and overgrown by tropical jungle. Palenque, in the densely forested foothills of the Chiapas mountains and overlooking the coastal plain that stretches 128km (80 miles) to the Gulf of Mexico, was rediscovered in 1746 by Padre Antonio Solis.

The first excavation of the Palenque site, which began in May 1786, was carried out by Spanish artillery captain Don Antonio del Río, who had orders from King Carlos III of Spain to search for gold and other valuables. Del Río left with a stucco head, the carved leg of a throne and other pieces of decorative carving, which he sent to Spain by way of Guatemala. Many years later, the captain's report of his excavations was published in English in London in 1822 with copies of del Río's sketches reproduced as lithographs by Johann-Friedrich Maximilien von Waldeck. The book generated interest in further investigation of Maya cities. It was followed by the publication in Paris in 1834 of *Antiquités Mexcaines,* the account of an 1805–6 visit to Palenque by Frenchman Guillaume Dupaix in the company of Mexican artist Luciano Castañeda. Waldeck himself visited the site in 1821 and published his own meticulously rendered images in 1865.

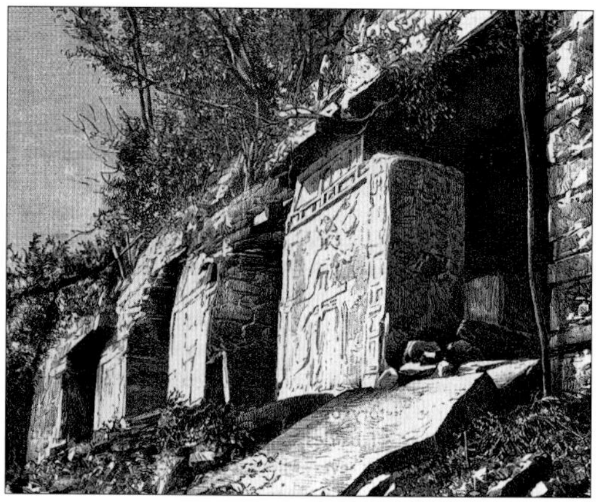

Above: Désiré Charnay, first to conduct archaeological excavations at Tula, made this engraving of Palenque in 1887.

GODDESS IN THE EARTH

An important discovery had occurred at the site of the former Aztec capital Tenochtitlán in 1790. Workmen laying paving stones discovered a 2.5 metre (8ft)-tall stone statue of the Aztec earth goddess Coatlícue, together with a 3.6 metre (almost 12ft) diameter carved stone monument that commemorated the five suns or world ages of Aztec belief (later known as the Sun Stone). The finds were the first evidence of the wealth of archaeological remains that lay directly beneath the surface of Mexico City. The Sun Stone was placed on display on one of the towers of the city's Metropolitan Cathedral, while the statue of Coatlícue was given to the Royal and Pontifical University of Mexico.

THE TREASURES OF THE JUNGLE

In the 19th century, many of the great abandoned cities of the Maya civilization were rediscovered among dense jungle foliage and explored. An important catalyst for the surge of interest in central American ruins was the publication in 1841 of the two-volume *Incidents of Travel in Central America, Chiapas and Yucatán* by American traveller John Lloyd Stephens (1805–52). This work was based on an 1839–40 voyage to Honduras, Guatemala and Mexico, which was undertaken by Stephens in the

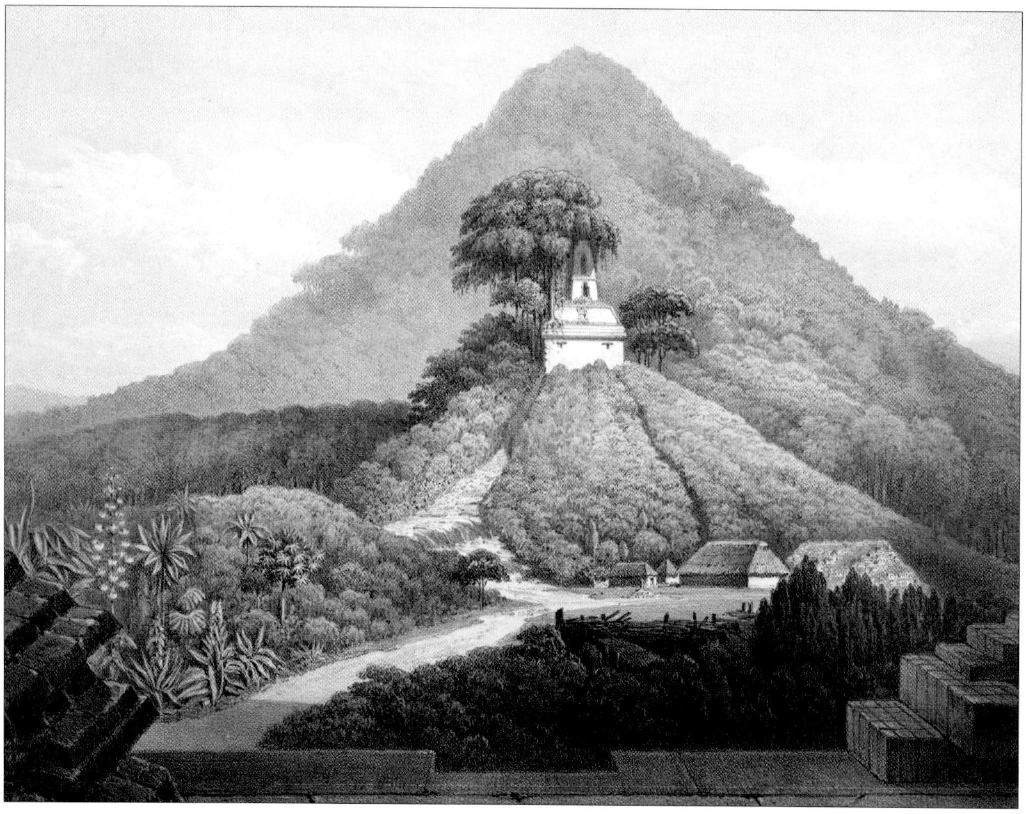

Left: This romanticized view of the Temple of the Cross, at Palenque, was made by Johann-Friedrich Maximilien von Waldeck.

company of English architect and artist Frederick Catherwood (1799–1854). Stephens and Catherwood visited the magnificent site of Copán, which Stephens was able to buy for $50, discovered Quiriguá and also examined Palenque and Uxmal. On a second voyage in 1841–2, the two men explored sites including Chichén Itzá, Cozumel, Tulum, Dzilam, Izamal and Ake. They published another two-volume survey, *Incidents of Travel in Yucatán*, in 1843. Sites they publicized include Copán, Palenque, Chichén Itzá, Tulum, Uxmal and Quiriguá.

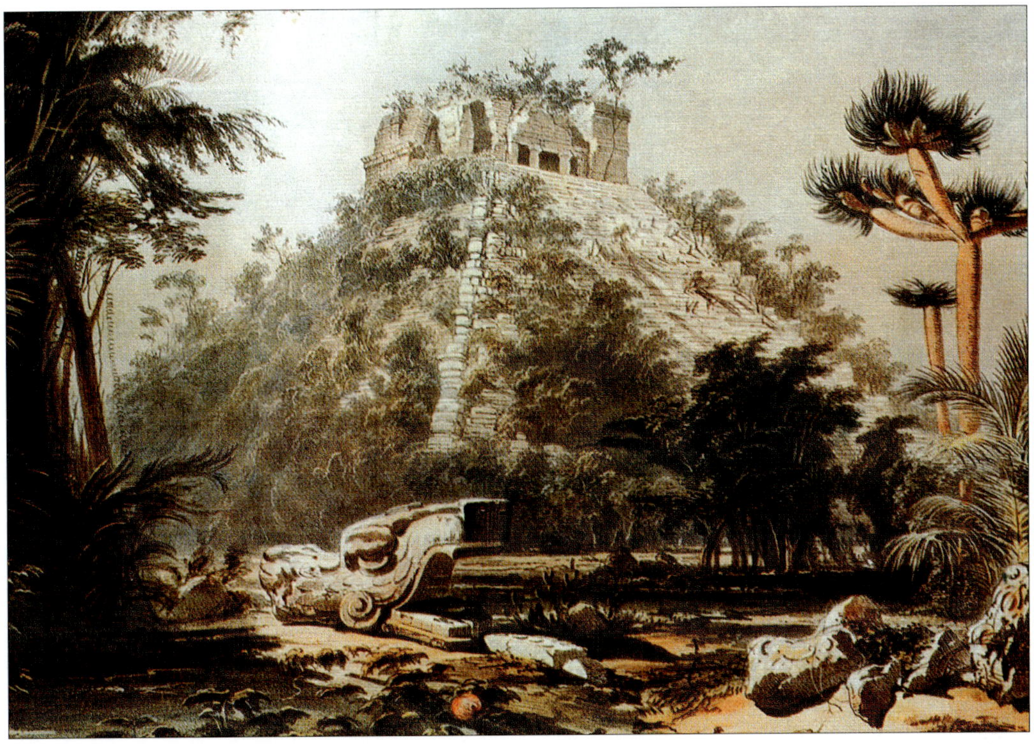

Above: This Catherwood engraving, from the 1841 Incidents of Travel in Central America, Chiapas and Yucatán, *is of the partly overgrown Castillo in Chichén Itzá.*

TOWERS AMONG THE TREES

The remains of the great Classic Period Maya city of Tikal, in the northern part of the Petén region of Guatemala, were also rediscovered in the mid-19th century. They were first noticed by a local gum-sapper named Ambrosio Tut, who saw the roofcombs of the city's soaring pyramid temples while working at the top of a sapodilla tree.

Tut reported the finding to Modesto Méndez, Governor-Magistrate of the Petén region, and a six-day exploratory expedition was despatched by the Guatemalan government under Méndez and Tut in 1848. Méndez's report, with fanciful images by artist Eusebio Lara, was published that year in the Guatemalan newspaper *La Gaceta* and in 1853 in the magazine of the Berlin Academy of Sciences.

Significant later 19th-century expeditions to the site included that of the Swiss botanist Gustave Bernoulli, who removed carved sapodilla-wood lintels from Temples I and IV and carried them off to the Museum für Völkerkunde in Basel. They also included that of the English archaeologist-explorer Sir Alfred Percival Maudslay (1850–1931), who visited in 1881 and 1882. Using recently invented camera equipment, Sir Alfred took the earliest photographs of the city of Tikal's magnificent monuments.

Other cities were being rediscovered in the jungle. In 1882, Sir Alfred led an official Guatemalan government expedition to a major but little known settlement on the Usumacinta river. Then known as Macanche, the riverbank city was later renamed Yaxchilán.

With official approval, Sir Alfred removed the superbly carved lintels from Yaxchilán to prevent their loss to less scrupulous visitors. In the same year, the French explorer and archaeologist Désiré Charnay visited and photographed the site. At Copán, George Gordon of Harvard University's Peabody Museum led a three-year investigation in 1891–4.

In the 1880s, Désiré Charnay also conducted the first archaeological dig at the site identified as the capital of the Toltecs, near the modern town of Tula in Hidalgo State, Mexico. In 1873, Antonio García Cubas, a member of the Mexican Society of Geography and History, had published a written description of the site. Charnay went on to excavate two houses and the structure known as the Adoratorio, in the middle of the main square. Later archaeologists were less than impressed by his unsubtle methods. These included the use of dynamite for clearance. Charnay did, however, also take some of the earliest photographs of ancient Mesoamerican ruins. He also experimented with papier-mâché to make impressions of ancient hieroglyphs.

Below: Beneath ground level in modern Mexico City archaeologists uncover Aztec remains. This is part of the Templo Mayor.

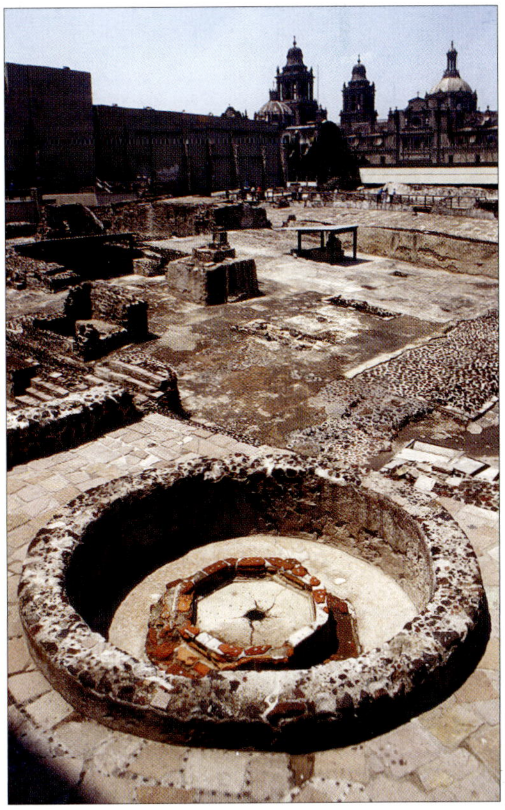

PAINSTAKING EXCAVATIONS

Throughout the 20th century, extensive and painstaking archaeological programmes gradually uncovered more and more evidence of how Mesoamericans lived, fought and worshipped.

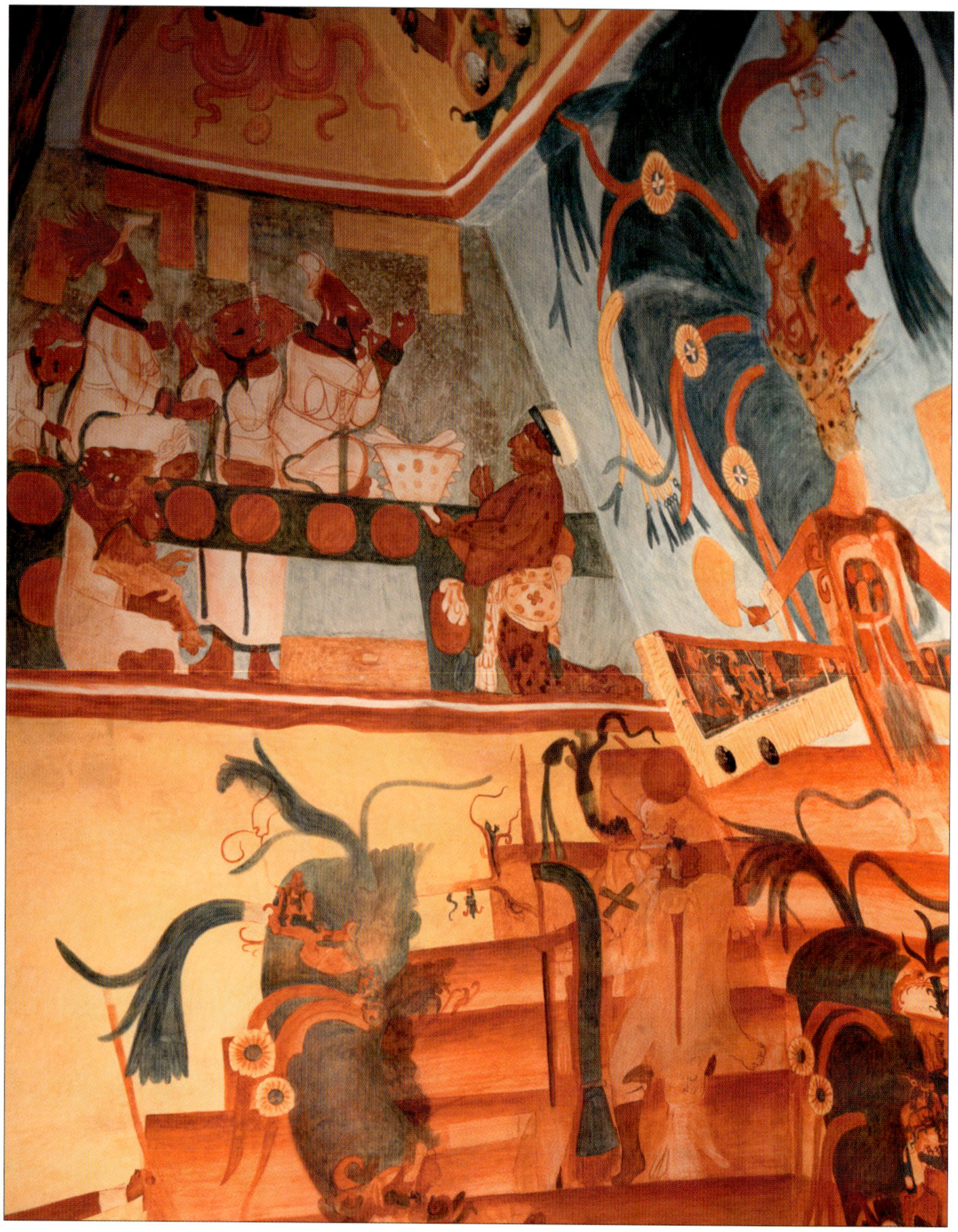

Above: A corner of one of the painted rooms at Bonampak depicts the members of the royal court enjoying a lavish feast.

CARNEGIE EXCAVATIONS

A pioneering archaeological project at Chichén Itzá in north-central Yucatán was led by Sylvanus Morley of the Carnegie Institution, Washington DC, for 20 years from 1924. The project excavated and restored many buildings, in the process discovering beneath them several almost intact constructions. These provided important evidence of the typical Mesoamerican building practice in which new structures were erected on top of their predecessors on sites already sanctified by ritual use. The work led to the scholarly division of Chichén Itzá's buildings into two groups. Those in the local 'Puuc style' from the end of the Classic Period and those exhibiting a Toltec-Mexican influence in the first years of the Postclassic Period.

The Carnegie Institution also conducted archaeological investigation at Uaxactún, 40km (25 miles) north of Tikal, in the years 1926–37. From the calendrical carvings, ceramic remains and buildings at Uaxactún, the Carnegie scholars plotted a chronology of cultural development for the region in the Classic Period that is still widely used by archaeologists today.

NEW MAP OF AN ANCIENT CITY

At Tikal, the combined efforts of Teobert Maler, Alfred Tozzer and R.E. Merwin led to the publication by Tozzer and Merwin of the first map of the site in 1911. Sylvanus Morley made a detailed study of Tikal's monuments and inscriptions on four visits in 1914, 1921, 1922 and 1928, while in 1926, Edwin Shook of the Carnegie Institution found a previously undiscovered group of buildings (now known as Group H) and two *sacbeob* or sacred causeways (now named in honour of Maudslay and Maler). Shook became the first field director of a major 14-year survey, the Tikal Project, which was conducted by the University Museum of Pennsylvania University 1956–70.

Major programmes were also carried out at Tula. In the 1930s, the work of ethnologist Wigberto Jimenez Moreno established that the site excavated by the Frenchman Désiré Charnay in the 19th century was the Toltecs' celebrated city, known also as Tollán. Subsequently, Jorge Acosta of the Mexican National Institute of Anthropology and History (INAH) led a 20-year archaeological programme at Tula in 1940–60, during which his teams

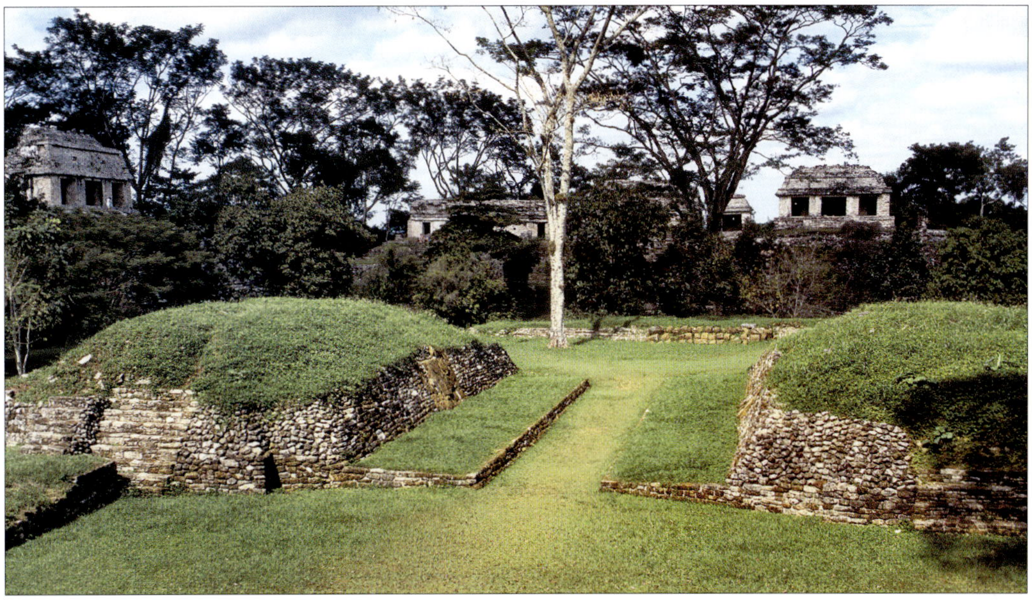

investigated and partly restored one of the site's ball courts (now known as Ball Court 1), Temples B and C, the Coatepantli and the Palacio de Quetzalcóatl. Based on pottery remains, Acosta also worked out a chronology of events and occupying groups for the site. His work was extended through joint excavations by the University of Missouri Colombia (UMC) under Richard Diehl and an INAH team under Eduardo Matos Moctezuma in 1966–76.

The second INAH team conducted a major survey of the surrounding land and restored a second ball court. Together with that of the UMC, their work established that Tula was a large and lively city, at its peak and that, for a period, it was Mesoamerica's prime power.

Above: The ball court at Palenque lies to the north-east of the imposing Palace and the celebrated Temple of Inscriptions.

PAINTED WALLS

About 30km (18 miles) to the south of Yaxchilán, in the densely forested valley of the Río Lacanha in Chiapas state, a Maya site previously known only to locals was revealed to the wider world in 1946. American photographer Giles Healey was on a field trip looking for picturesque ruins when his guides led him to a small settlement they called Bonampak ('Painted Walls'). Healey found a three-roomed building containing vivid, brightly coloured images of court life in a Maya city during the 8th century AD. His report and pictures naturally provoked wide interest and the Carnegie Institute organized an archaeological programme at the site, which also contains an acropolis, a large plaza and a number of stelae. As at some other major Maya sites such as Palenque, there are buildings still unexcavated in the surrounding forest.

PALENQUE'S STEPPED PYRAMID

At Palenque, Sylvanus Morley, Oliver LaFarge, Franz Blom and Edward Seler all carried out work in the early part of the 20th century. In 1952, Mexican architect Alberto Ruz Lhuillier discovered the magnificent royal tomb of King Pacal, Palenque's ruler in the 7th–8th centuries AD, in a crypt beneath the Temple of Inscriptions. Historians had believed that Maya stepped pyramids were used only as temple platforms; that is, to lift their temples above other buildings; Lhuiller's find was the first indication that the pyramids were in some places built primarily as royal funerary monuments.

TENOCHTITLÁN

In the centre of what was once Tenochtitlán, a major excavation of the Aztecs' great temple, the Templo Mayor, began in 1978. The programme was inspired by a chance find, when an electrical company worker digging in central Mexico City uncovered part of a clearly remarkable sculpture. The team of archaeologists who took over to clear away debris uncovered a vast monolith, 3.25m (10ft) in diameter, representing the dismembered form of the goddess Coyolxauhqui who, in Aztec creation narrative, was cut up by her brother Huitzilopochtli in the first moments of his life.

Excavation revealed that the Aztecs built the Templo Mayor in layers, each new construction enclosing an earlier structure. Archaeologists uncovered the successive constructions back to *c.*1390, showing the twin shrines to rain god Tláloc and Lord Huitzilopochtli.

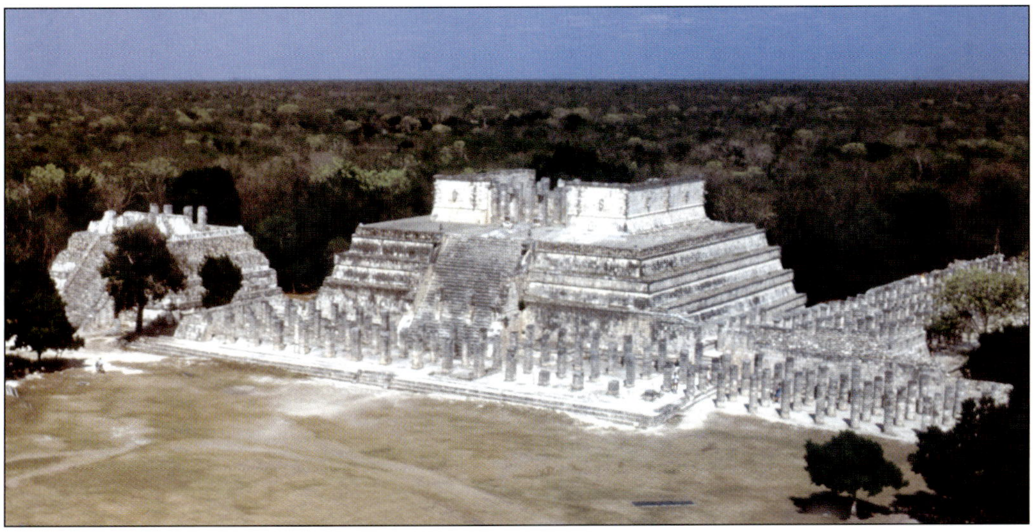

Left: The Group of the Thousand Columns is one of the imposing structures in Chichén Itzá reflecting later, Toltec, influence.

TRANSLATING AN ANCIENT WRITING

The first modern visitors to Maya sites such as Yaxchilán or Copán were enthralled by tall stelae elegantly carved with inscriptions in artistically arranged picture glyphs. Historians were also deeply intrigued by the writing in four surviving Maya codices and by a list of glyphs presented as the 'Maya alphabet' by Bishop Diego de Landa in his 16th-century work, *Relacion de las Cosas de Yucatán*. Historians were frustrated that they could not read this ancient writing and so glean invaluable information about the Maya way of life.

DECIPHERING THE PAST

In the years up to the 1950s, linguists made slow but steady progress in interpreting Maya writing. Figures such as Léon de Rosny, Ernst Förstemann, Sylvanus Morley and J. Eric Thompson catalogued the glyphs and successfully identified some. Förstemann and Rosny, for example, translated the glyphs for 'north', 'south', 'east', 'west', 'zero' and 'twenty'. However, the entire world of Maya scholarship laboured under two misconceptions. The scholars wrongly believed that the inscriptions on Maya stelae contained religious and astronomical information, but no historical facts. Historians were also mistaken in their belief that the glyphs were logographic. The pictures represented whole words or ideas and did not stand for spoken sounds.

The first misconception was removed by the work of Heinrich Berlin and Tatiana Proskouriakoff in the 1950s. Berlin, a German-Mexican scholar, first identified an emblem glyph specific to each of several Maya sites and suggested that it recorded the place name or the name of the ruling dynasty. Proskouriakoff, a Russian-American expert on Maya art, then showed that carved inscriptions on stelae at Piedras Negras celebrated the birth, accession to the throne and other life events of a series of rulers of that city. In her work on Piedras Negras and then Yaxchilán, she identified glyphs for 'was born', 'acceded to throne', 'captor', 'captured' and 'died'.

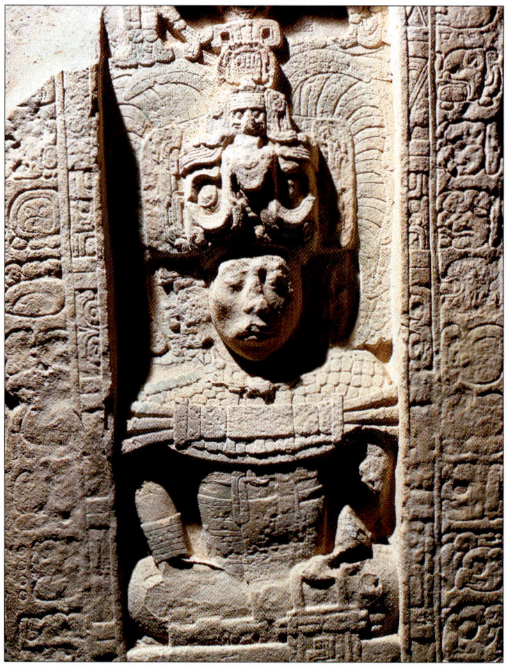

Above: Stela 6 from Piedras Negras shows the king seated cross-legged in a recess with glyphs dating the monument to AD687.

The second misconception was laid to rest, also in the 1950s, by the Soviet linguist Yuri V. Knorosov, who demonstrated that, alongside their function as logograms, the glyphs had a 'phonetic' element; they represented spoken sounds. Working with the de Landa 'alphabet', Knorosov saw that many of the elements of the list were not letters but syllables combining a consonant and a vowel. There were no signs for a single consonant. When writing a word with the pattern consonant-vowel-consonant, he argued, a Maya scribe would use two of the combined signs, consonant-vowel plus consonant-vowel. The vowel in the second sign would match that in the first, but would be read as silent. For example, to write the word *cutz* ('turkey'), a scribe

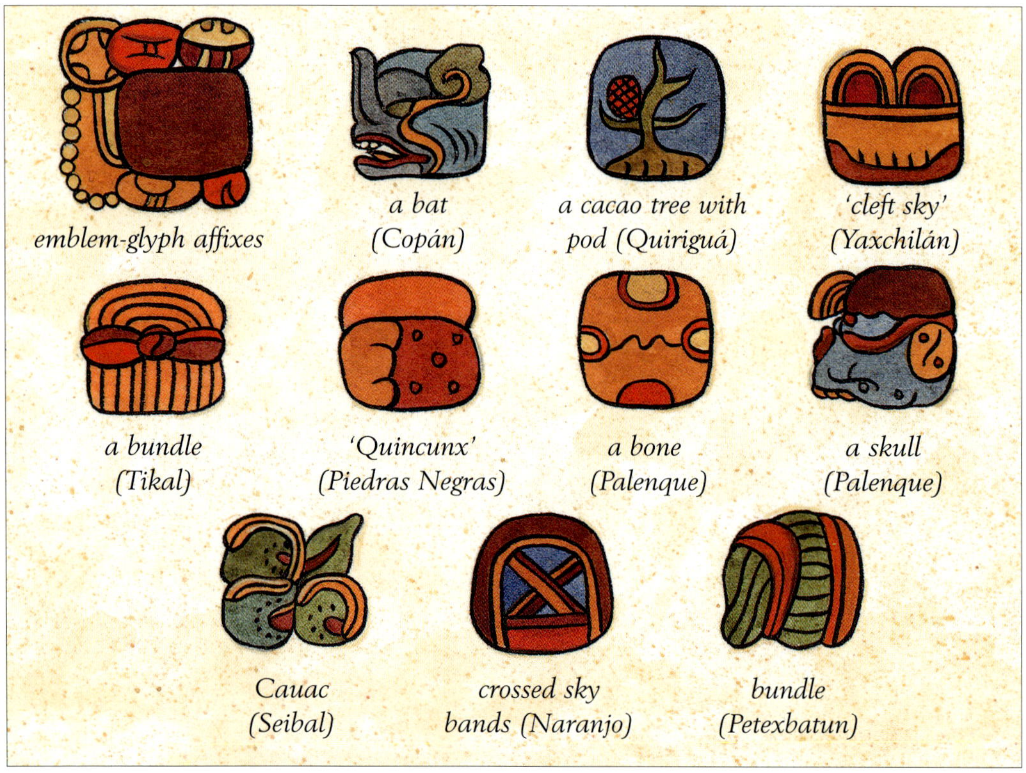

Left: 'Emblem glyphs' specific to particular cities were identified by Heinrich Berlin in 1958. The symbols identifying the cities were written with a pair of affixes (appended signs) meaning 'holy king of'.

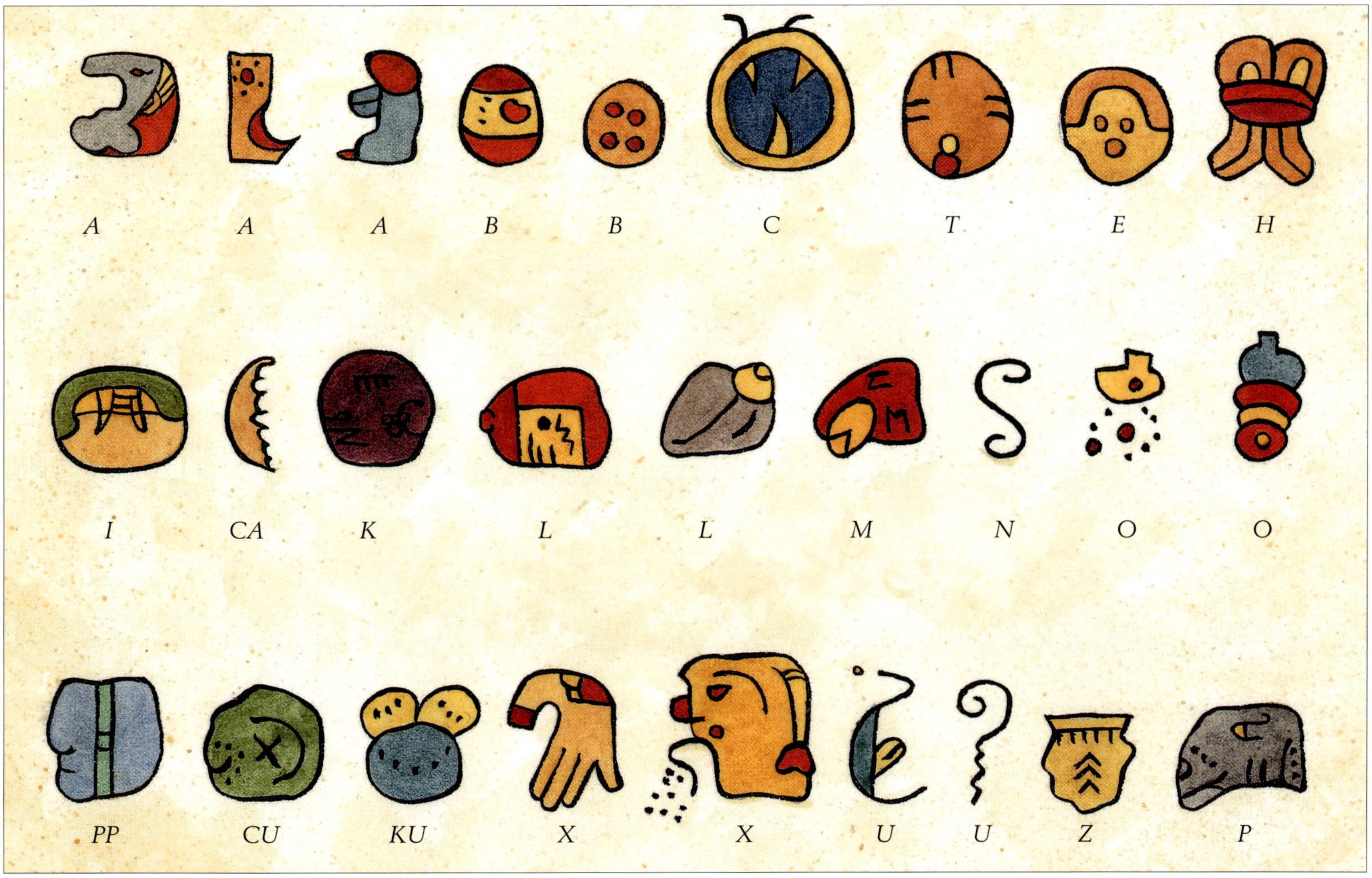

Above: Bishop Diego de Landa's 'alphabet' of Maya writing was dismissed by scholars until linguist Yuri Knorosov showed that it was a list of syllables rather than an 'abc'.

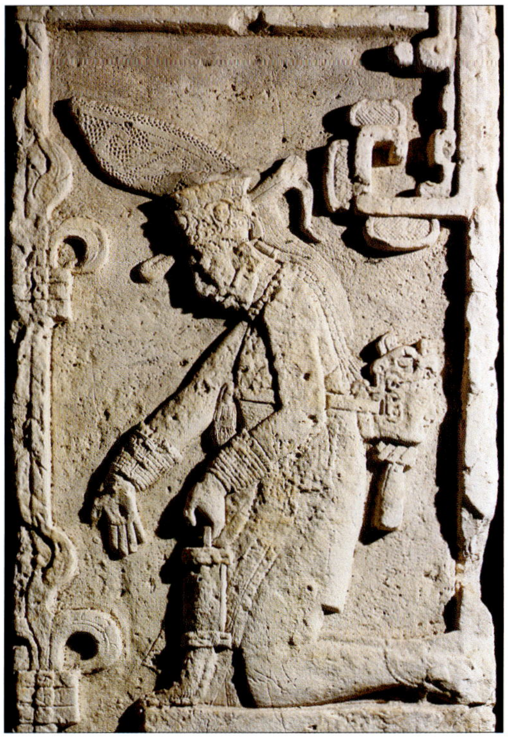

would write the signs *cu* and *tzu*. The two Us would agree, and the word would be read 'cutz' (with the last u silent.) The idea that the vowels would agree was dubbed 'synharmony' by Knorosov.

Knorosov's theory provoked outrage among many Maya scholars, but has proved to be largely correct. As Knorosov argued, Maya script contains both logographs and phonetic elements. The latest thinking is that the script, which was in use for more than 1,500 years, was originally mainly logosyllabic (pictures stood for syllables or words), but over time increasingly included more phonetic elements. However, further progress in deciphering Maya script has partially undermined Knorosov's idea of synharmony. When words were spelled phonetically, they often did not have the matching vowels that his theory suggested they should.

Left: In a detail from Piedras Negras Stela 40, an individual performs a sacred rite of scattering in honour of an ancestor.

REINTERPRETATIONS

Historians have continued to make breakthroughs in interpreting glyphs, often with important implications for our understanding of the Maya. In 1979, Peter Matthews showed that an ear spool found at Altun Ha in Belize was labelled *u tup* ('his ear spool') with the name of the owner. Several other writers have since shown that the practice Matthews termed 'name tagging' was used by the Maya on bowls, plates and carved bones.

David Stuart and Stephen Houston have identified a glyph used to describe the spirit familiar or companion that Mesoamericans believed accompanied each of us. The discovery has led to the reinterpetation of many scenes on Maya pots or stelae, where figures once thought to be gods or rulers can now be positively identified as spirit familiars.

Linguistic work has also revealed that the Maya referred to stelae as 'stone trees' and to the objects historians generally label 'altars' as 'stone thrones'.

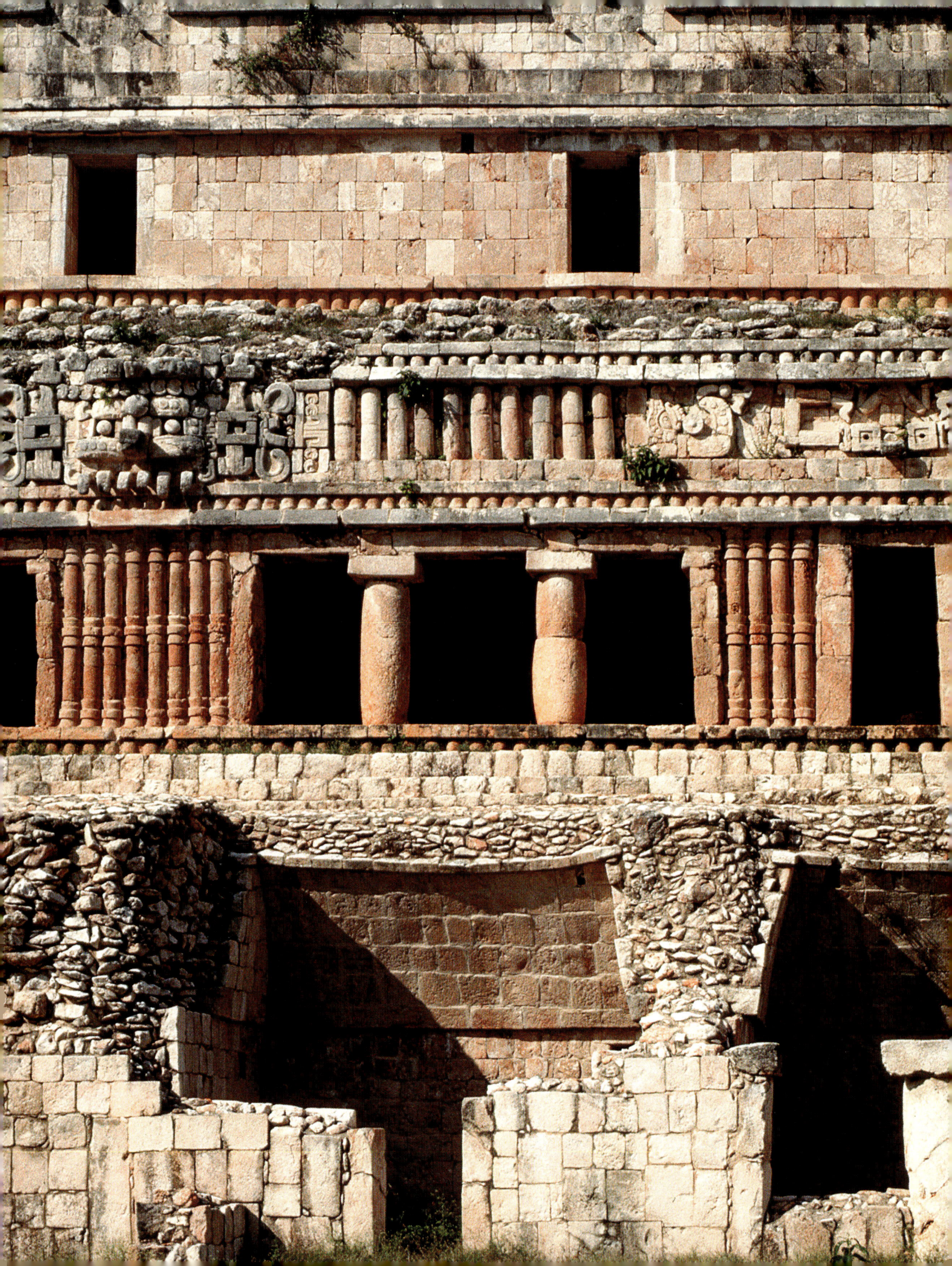

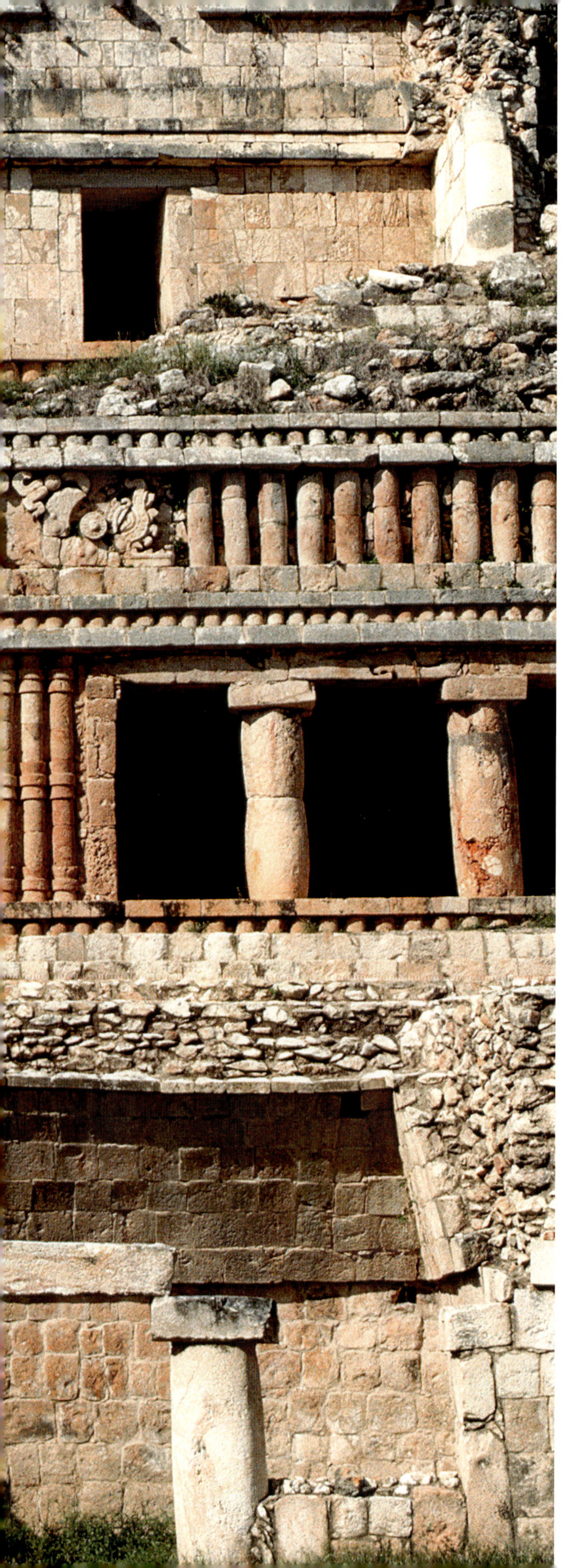

CHAPTER ONE

PALACES, TEMPLES AND SACRED CENTRES

Archaeologists generally distinguish between two types of Mesoamerican public building: 'palaces' and 'temples'. Palaces are usually long, low residential and administrative buildings that contain many rooms, small windows, niches above doorways and carved benches. Temples are usually built on top of tall stepped pyramid-platforms, with very limited interior space, and are topped with tall roof combs masonry structures that support a decorative facade. Scholars see palaces as utilitarian, and temples as sacred spaces reserved for ritual activity.

The distinction is helpful, but must be used with some caution since these words are only labels applied retrospectively by historians. Many palaces were used for administrative functions – such as meetings of council groups, or collection and storage of tribute – in addition to being the residences of kings or leading nobles. They contained shrine rooms and areas used for religious ritual such as autosacrifice – the letting of one's own blood. 'Temples', meanwhile, were used for varied purposes in different places and at different times. Some buildings, such as the five-storey palace in Edzná or the Great Palace of Sayil, appear to have combined sacred and utilitarian functions.

Left: In the middle of the three levels of the Palace at Sayil, a pair of columns divides each of the wide chamber doorways.

FROM HUTS TO TEMPLES

A decorative frieze on the Nunnery Quadrangle at Uxmal gives a stylized representation of a simple hut, the kind of dwelling inhabited by millions of Maya householders. A similar image was carved on an ornate archway leading to a group of palace buildings at Labná and was represented in murals painted at Chichén Itzá. The images depict the front of a single-storey oblong dwelling with a square central doorway and a thatched roof.

The Maya generally erected buildings on raised platforms: even the tall pyramids constructed to support temples can be seen as building platforms functionally. For a simple dwelling, however, the platform was low, built of earth or rubble covered in adobe plaster (a thick mixture of mud and straw). The great majority of Maya houses were built mostly if not entirely of perishable materials and so did not survive to be examined by historians. However, archaeologists can trace the remains of domestic building platforms and so plot the arrangement of houses within settlements. However, the actual building methods used by the Maya to raise their houses remain a matter of educated conjecture, based on the frieze and mural images described above and on the building methods employed today by modern descendants of the ancient Maya.

MAYA BUILDING METHODS

Scholars believe that ancient Maya house builders first set up four sturdy corner posts, then created a lattice of thin sticks between them and covered the latticework with adobe plaster. In hot regions, builders might well have left the walls unplastered, allowing breezes to pass through and cool the inhabitants. The shape of the plot was usually rectangular, but could have rounded ends. In some areas, where building stone was readily available, builders laid stone building platforms for houses, or even built the lower parts of the walls in stone before covering them with adobe or lime plaster.

This tried and tested design was the template for all Maya buildings. Stone temples were more elaborate and permanent versions of the ancestral hut. Elements of the primitive house were reproduced in palace and temple: for example, builders in stone used the same square-shaped door with wooden lintel

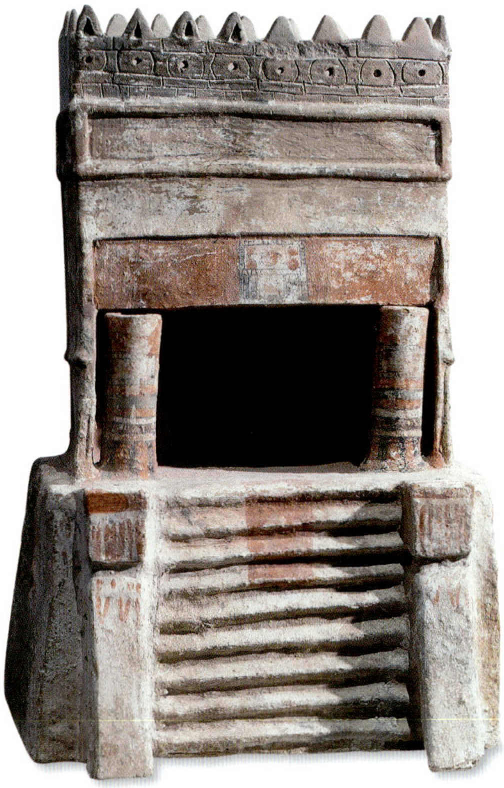

Above: This Aztec terracotta model represents the 'sacred mountain' of a steeply stepped pyramid topped with a temple.

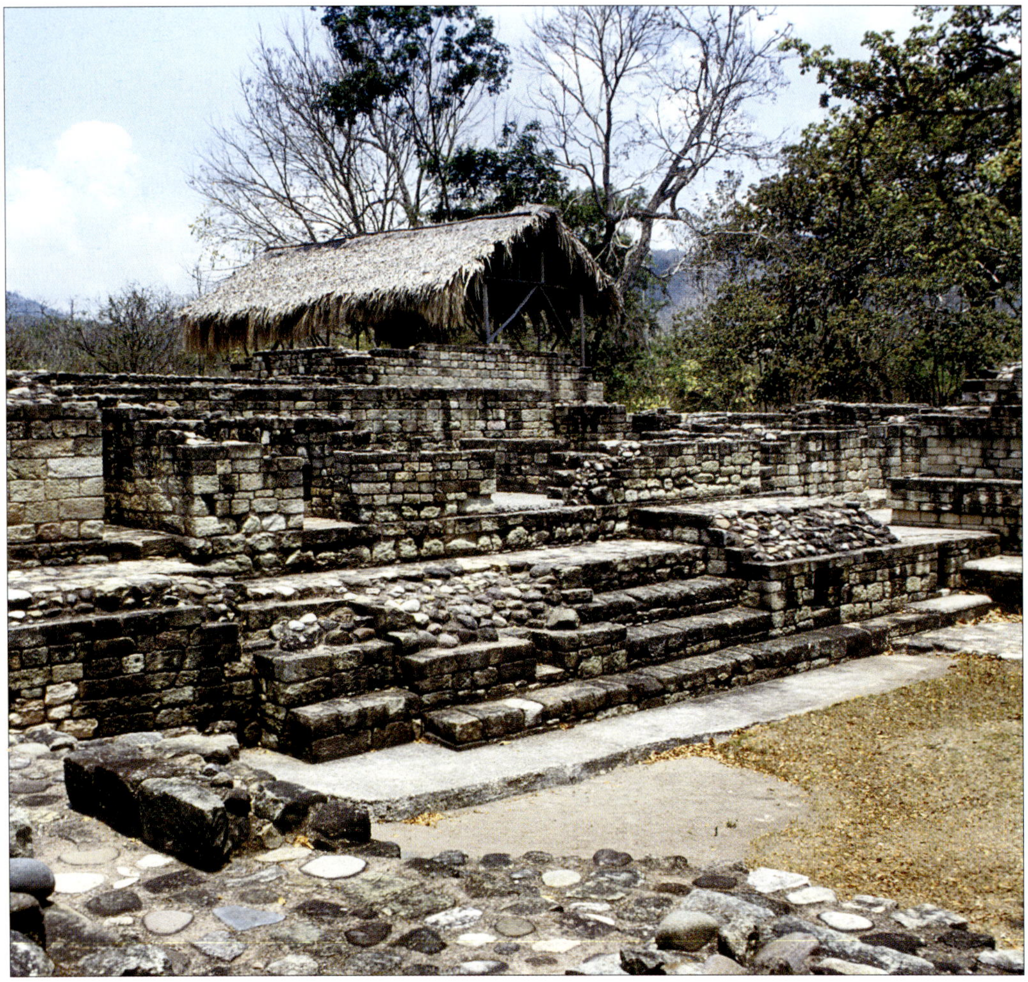

Left: Maya dwellings often consisted of small buildings arranged around a central courtyard. This example is in Honduras.

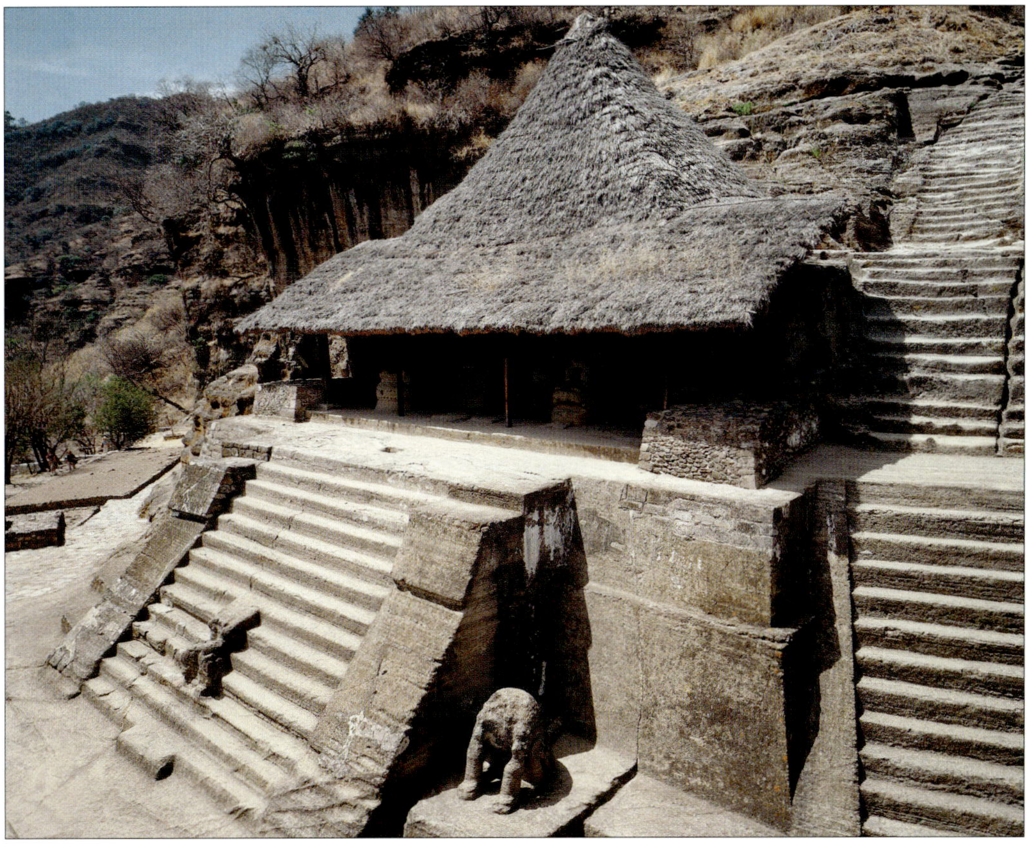

that had been developed over generations by house builders. The sinuous lines of rope or creeper that tied the straw wall-padding in place in the family hut were reproduced in the ornamental carving on the friezes of sacred buildings and palaces.

TEMPLE MOUNDS

The earliest temples, of *c*.2000BC, were probably almost indistinguishable from ordinary dwellings – the gods naturally lived like humans. However, priests and their builders set the gods' buildings apart from village dwellings by raising them on higher platforms than those used for domestic structures. The platforms grew higher and higher over time. The practice of rebuilding temples on the same spot, over and encompassing their predecessors, became a hallowed architectural custom. As the temple mound or platform grew taller and taller, builders had to add a new architectural element – one or more access stairways to enable priests and other ritual contributors to reach the temple at the top of the platform. The temple-platform began to resemble a great hill, entirely appropriate for a people who regarded mountains as sacred.

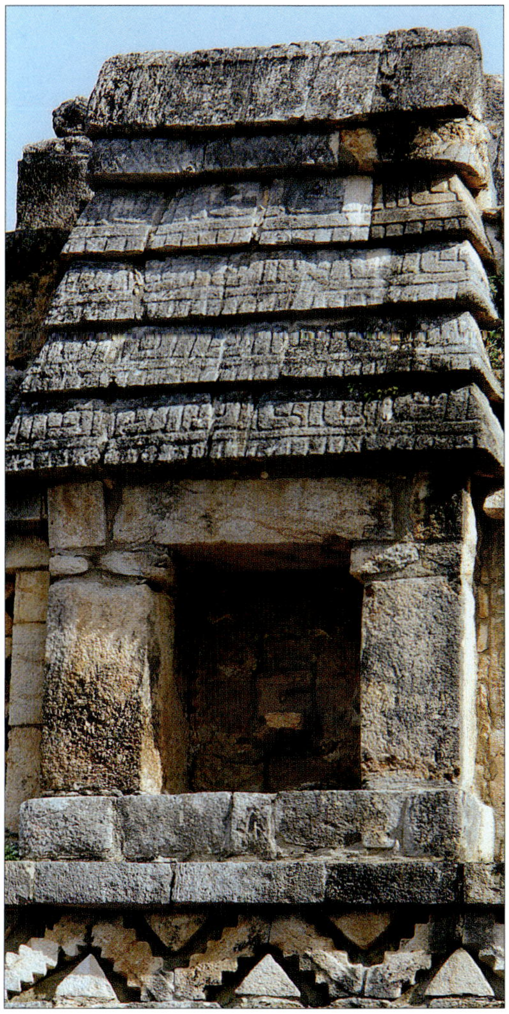

Left: The simple thatched hut occupied by Maya peasants was celebrated in stone in the archway at Labná (c.AD600–900).

AZTEC BUILDING

Houses varied from simple, single-room huts with wooden walls and a straw thatched roof to large and elaborate stone mansions with flat stone roofs supporting herb gardens. Remains indicate that walls were made of wooden planks, latticework plastered with adobe, sun-dried adobe bricks or stone. In the marshy lakeside terrain of Tenochtitlán, even basic houses were often raised on stone building platforms to provide firm foundations

The design of the simplest housing similarly remained the template for palace buildings and the temples atop the steep pyramid-platforms. Images drawn for Friar Bernardino de Sahagún's *General History of the Things of New Spain* (completed 1569) depict an Aztec house made of wood and straw, one built from stone with a straw roof and one built entirely of stone. Another shows a nobleman's house with an elaborate decorated frieze.

Above: The Aztec Temple of the Eagles at Malinalco was cut c.AD1500 from mountain rock near modern Tenancingo.

RAW MATERIALS

Builders made use of locally available stone and other materials. In the southern Maya region, there was generally a shortage of easily worked rock for construction. Even major buildings were often made from adobe blocks, although at Copán labourers quarried and used local trachyte and at Quiriguá they worked with marble, sandstone and rhyolite.

In the central and northern Maya regions, builders had access to large amounts of limestone that was easy to cut into blocks. The limestone could also be burned to produce lime for making plaster.

BUILDING STYLES:
FROM TEOTIHUACÁN TO TIKAL

The architectural style of Teotihuacán was widely influential across Mesoamerica for many hundreds of years. In particular, the city was known for its *talud-tablero* construction, which alternated an upright rectangular section (*tablero*) with a sloping section (*talud*). The *tablero* had a recessed central part.

In Teotihuacán, the style was particularly developed in the Ciudadela or Citadel area of the city, which included the Temple of Quetzalcóatl and 15 other stepped pyramids, as well as two elite residential buildings and an 11-hectare (4.4-acre) open plaza. The Teotihuacános used *talud-tablero* construction only for sacred buildings. At Teotihuacán, the upright *tablero* was always larger than the sloping *talud*, but elsewhere these ratios varied.

Archaeologists do not know for sure where the style originated, although some suggest that immigrants to Teotihuacán from Tlaxcala might have brought a taste for and expertise in this type of building with them. Tlaxcalans, who also brought agricultural expertise in cutting terraced fields and irrigation with dams and canals, were using a form of *talud-tablero* construction in their civic and ceremonial buildings before 300BC, well in advance of the first major sacred buildings at Teotihuacán.

Below: Architectural styles such as 'Puuc', 'Chenes' and 'Usumacinta' take their names from the regions in which they developed. This map also shows the main mining areas for certain raw materials.

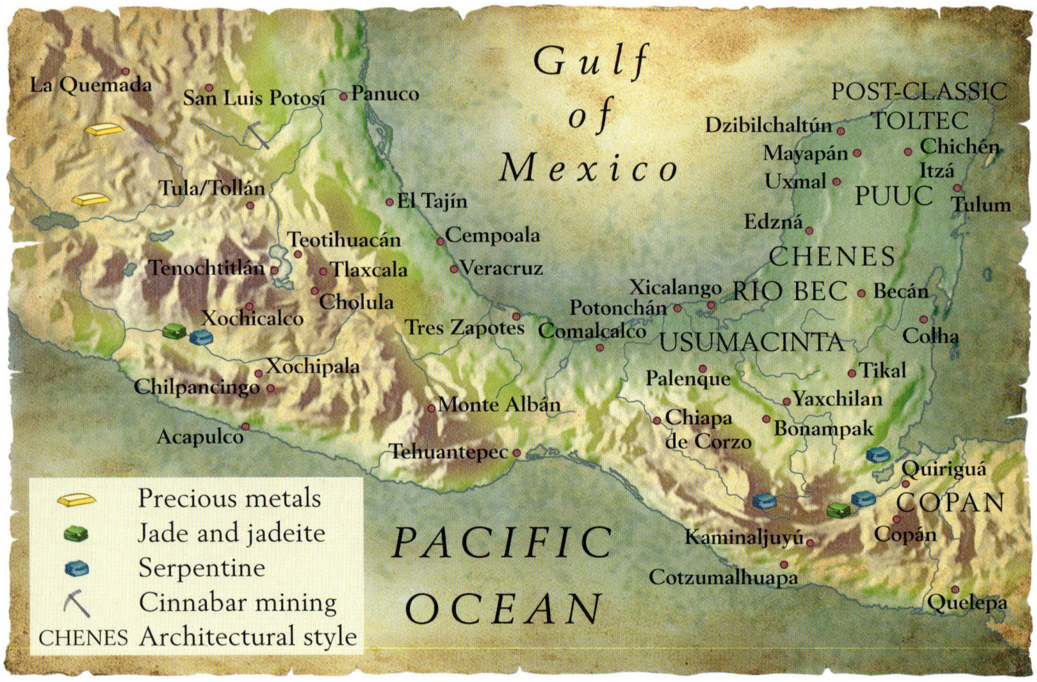

VARIATIONS ON A STYLE

The *talud-tablero* style was used very widely. At Kaminaljuyú *c.*AD200–400 builders either from or influenced by Teotihuacán built a ceremonial centre using *talud-tablero* construction. The style was also used in the Lost World complex at Tikal. At Xochicalco the Temple of the Feathered Serpent played a unique variation on the style by reducing it to the single component of the design: in profile, the temple presents one large sloping *talud* topped with a single *tablero*. Another variation on *talud-tablero* was developed by the builders of the Pyramid of the Niches at El Tajín in Veracruz: there are six *talud-tablero* levels, with each sloping *talud* topped with a vertical *tablero* containing several niches, and at the top of each *tablero* there is an additional 'flying' reverse *talud*. At Tollán the El Corral temple consisted of two *talud-tablero* levels. The style was revived in the Temple of the Feathered Serpent at Chichén Itzá, which has nine *talud-tablero* tiers. The Aztecs built two small *talud-tablero* buildings in their sacred precinct at Tenochtitlán as an explicit tribute to the sacred city of Teotihuacán.

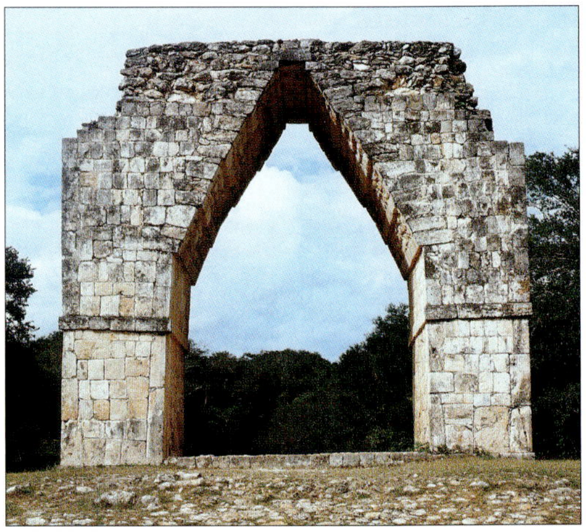

Above: The archway at Kabah, Yucatán, is a good example of the corbelled vault or 'false arch' which looks like an inverted V.

RAISING THE TEMPLE PLATFORM

In Maya lands builders usually constructed pyramid-platforms from earth and rubble and faced them with cut stone. These platforms usually had four faces with either one stairway or four stairways, one on each face, providing access to the temple on the summit. In some sites, several buildings were built on a single platform, in which case archaeologists usually call the platform an 'acropolis'. The platforms rose from generation to generation, for it was customary to build new platforms and temples over and enclosing the existing sacred structures. The roofs of Maya temples were typically decorated with tall facades of stucco

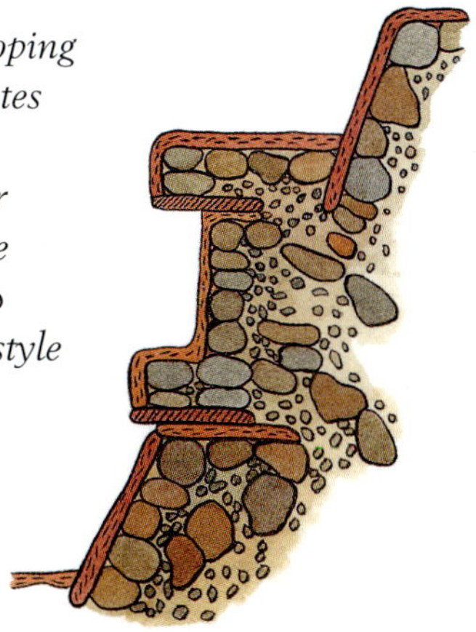

Right: The sloping talud *alternates with the perpendicular* tablero *in the* talud-tablero *construction style perfected at Teotihuacán.*

moulding or mosaic sculpture, usually supported from behind by masonry structures called roof combs. In the mortuary temples of Tikal, the roof comb element contained a portrait of the king buried in a vault beneath the temple platform.

Maya builders of the Classic Period generally relied on the corbelled vault – called the 'false arch' by architectural historians – to support the roof. This structure, which resembles an upside-down V, is created by laying inward-projecting blocks on top of one another: the blocks successively narrow the gap between walls until a single stone can bridge the gap at the top of the arch. (This contrasts with a true arch, whose use was never developed by the Maya, in which the keystone at the top anchors the other stones and creates a structurally much stronger unit.) Corbelled vaults need the support of thick walls beneath them. Maya buildings with false arches had severely reduced interior space given their outer size. Walls were generally made of rubble covered with stone.

BUILDING STYLES

A number of regional styles developed in Maya lands. The sacred buildings of Tikal epitomize the central Petén style, which is characterized by vertiginous pyramid-platforms each topped by a temple with a tall masonry roof comb, a single doorway and thick rubble-filled walls.

At Palenque, Yaxchilán, Piedras Negras and Bonampak the Usumacinta style was characterized by buildings with thinner walls and three or more doorways. At Palenque, for example, builders could erect thinner walls with several doorways

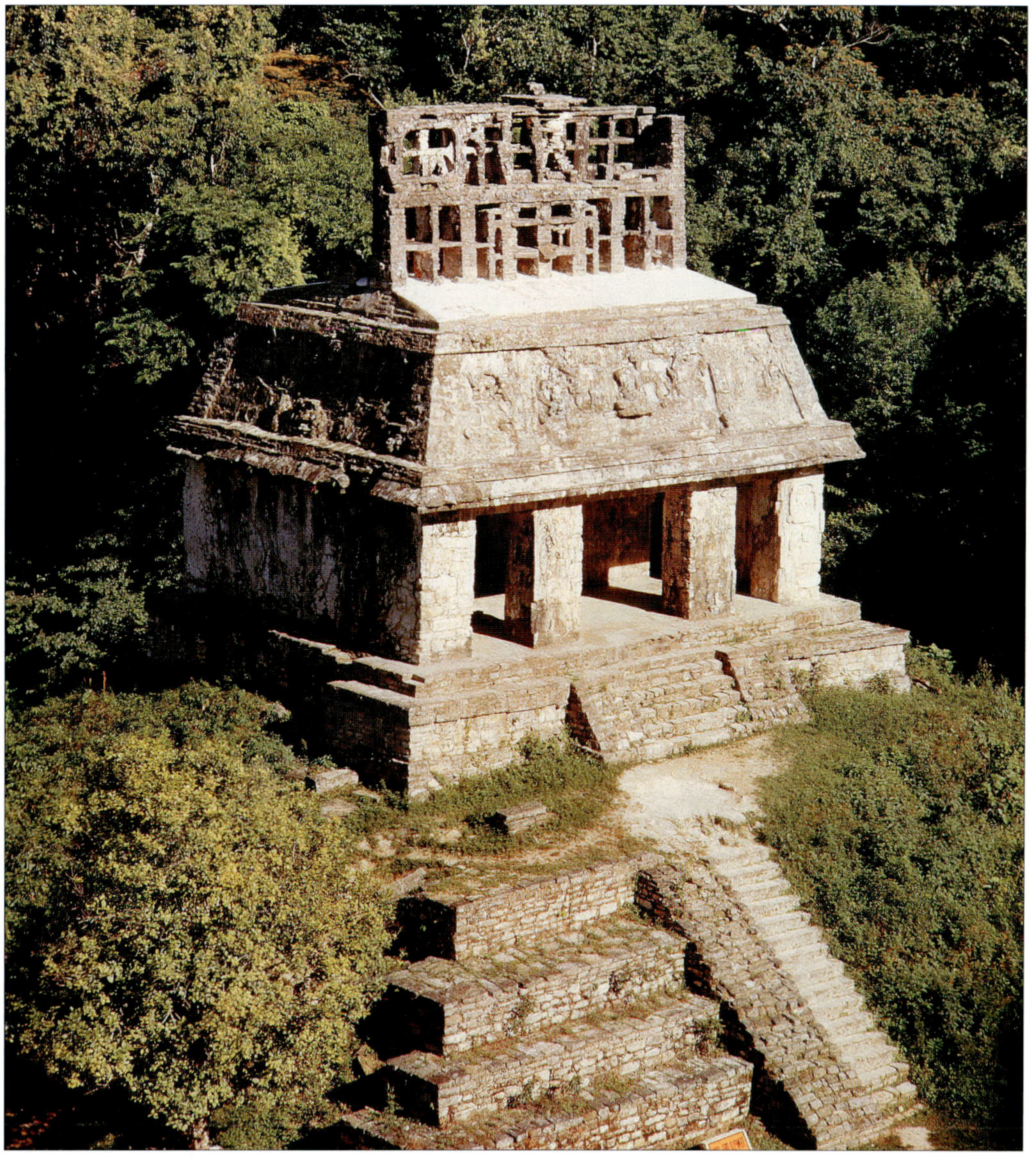

Above: Stucco carving on vertical temple-top roof combs was used to convey dynastic information, as here at Palenque.

because they had replaced the tall vertical facades used in the Petén style with inward-sloping facades that were partly supported by the vaulting of the roof. They also made lighter latticework roof combs rather than the solid masonry ones of the Petén region. Within, the buildings often had two parallel rooms divided by a wall that also helped to bear the roof's weight. A benefit of using thinner walls was that the buildings were considerably lighter and more airy within.

Another regional style of monumental architecture developed at Copán and Quiriguá, where temples, palaces and platforms were decorated with elaborate stucco modelling. A distinctive feature was the building of 'reviewing stands', which were large platforms with wide access stairways. In the reign of King 18-Rabbit (AD695–738)at Copán, artisans began to create carved stone decorative elements in place of stucco; these were generally painted over with plaster.

Below: From the time of the Toltecs onwards, chacmool *sacrificial figures were placed outside pyramid-top temple sanctuaries.*

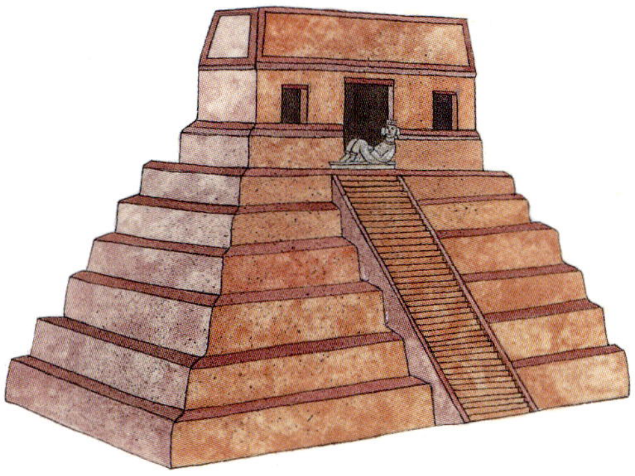

A LOVE OF DECORATION: YUCATÁN

The ornate modelling and façades at Copán had counterparts in styles developed farther north in the Maya region. In the Río Bec style, used in the southern Yucatán peninsula in the late Classic Period, builders put decoration and style before function. They erected vast constructions that were essentially reverent imitations of the great pyramids at sites such as Tikal: lofty towers with non-functional steps, doorways that led nowhere and 'false temples' built of solid rock for appearance only. Their buildings had elaborate façades incorporating mosaic masks, which often featured a long-snouted deity believed to be the rain god Chac.

Examples of the style are found at Becán, Xpuhil and Río Bec, in the region north of Calakmul. For example, the building known to archaeologists as Structure 1 at Xpuhil has towers supporting solid temple-like structures with roof combs. Buildings with the appearance of monumental sacred architecture clearly brought prestige to settlements such as Xpuhil or Becán, even if the temples and pyramids could not be used.

The related Chenes style took decorative elements a stage further, creating building façades dominated by decorative masks. In some of these, the entire façade represented a divine face with the doorway as the god's mouth. Chenes-style buildings were raised in the late Classic Period at sites slightly farther north in the Yucatán peninsula. On the building known as Structure II at Chicanná, the façade represents the face of a god; perhaps the primordial creator Itzamná. The doorway is a serpent mouth, with two stylized eyes and fang-like projections above the opening. The structure gave its name to the settlement, for Chicanná means 'house of the snake's mouth'.

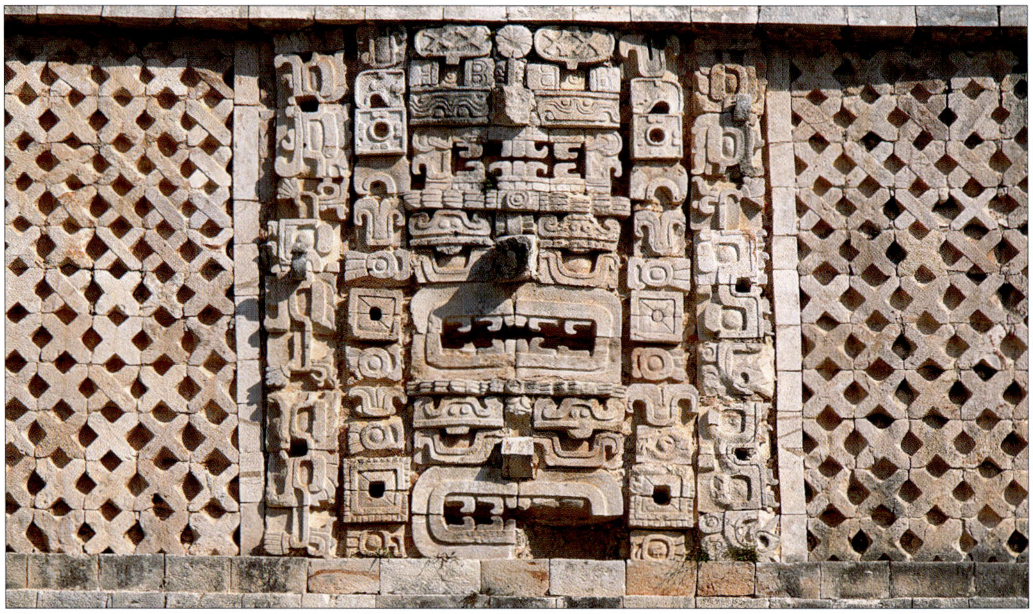

Above: Intricate decorative patterns and masks of the Maya rain god Chac on the upper walls of the Nunnery Quadrangle at Uxmal are typical of the Puuc style.

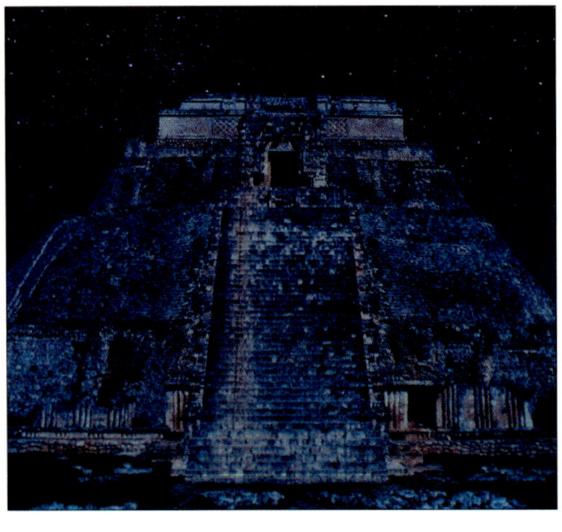

Left: The Temple of the Magician, Uxmal, rises to an imposing height against the night sky. Its western stairway climbs to a sanctuary whose entrance is a god's mask.

PUUC ELEGANCE

Further north again, the Puuc style developed in the Puuc region in north-western Yucatán. Builders preferred to limit decoration to the upper façade and to keep the lower half of walls plain. They built walls of lime concrete and faced the lower part with limestone veneer. Craftsmen applied pre-cut decorative elements to the upper façades in a repetitive pattern, whose elements were sometimes divine masks or serpents, but were more often abstract patterns such as lattices, fretwork and columns. In developing this style, which appeared at the close of the Classic Period (*c.*AD800–1000), Puuc builders may been influenced by the repetitive decorative patterns used by their counterparts at Mitla and other sites in Oaxaca.

Splendid examples of the Puuc style are found at Uxmal in the Governor's Palace and the buildings of the Nunnery

'THE MAYA REVIVAL'

The US architect Frank Lloyd Wright was greatly impressed with the elegance of Puuc structures and applied the style in several public buildings erected in the 1920s. These created a vogue for a Maya Revival movement in architecture that encompassed other architects including Robert Stacy-Judd, Alfred Bossom and Richard Requa. Stacy-Judd used Maya inspiration in building the ironically named Aztec Hotel in Monrovia, California, in 1924–25. Requa's Maya Revival buildings included the Federal Building in San Diego (1935).

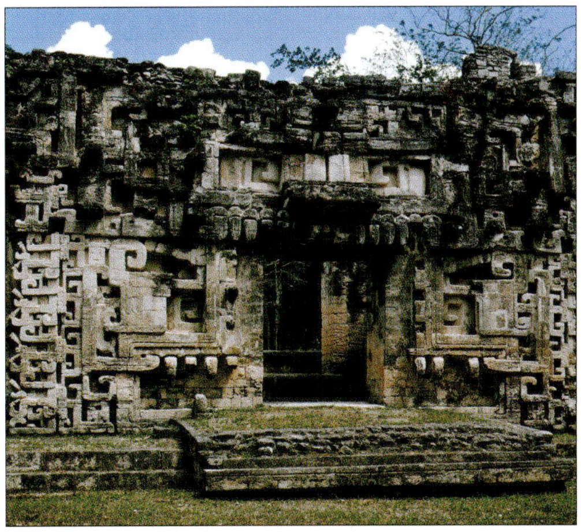

Above: Sacred entrance. The creator god's face – with fangs and eyes above the door – sanctifies Structure II at Chicanná.

Quadrangle, both of which combine a plain lower wall with intricate decorative designs in the upper façade. The city of Uxmal demonstrates that these architectural styles developed alongside one another and were not mutually exclusive, for the shrine on the first terrace of the Temple of the Magician, at the top of a steep west-side storey, presents its west-facing entrance as the mouth of a divine mask in pure Chenes style.

At Kabáh, which was connected to Uxmal by an 18km (11-mile) *sacbé* causeway, the Temple of the Masks uses masks of the rain god Chac as the repetitive element on the façade. The building is identified as Puuc style by archaeologists, although its façade is entirely covered with the pattern of masks and so does not feature the plain lower half and decorated upper half typical of pure Puuc. The Great Palace at Sayil and the Palace Arch at Labná are other fine examples of the Puuc style.

Below: The Castillo and Group of the Thousand Columns typified the Chichén Itzá style copied in later Yucatán cities.

TOLTEC ARCHITECTURE

At Chichén Itzá, archaeologists identify two main groups of buildings, with largely distinct styles. The southern group – which includes the Nunnery buildings, the Akabdzib, the House of the Deer, the Red House and the celebrated circular Caracol – is built largely in the Puuc style. The northern group – which includes the Temple of the Warriors, the Group of the Thousand Columns and the great Castillo or Temple of the Feathered Serpent – pioneered a new architectural style in the Maya region, featuring buildings with colonnades. The style exhibited a strong influence from the monumental architecture of sites such as Tollán (Tula) in highland Mexico.

This style became the prototype for building in the Postclassic Period that followed the collapse of Chichén Itzá. The Chichén Itzá style was influential, for example, in the construction of building at Mayapán and Tulum, although the 'copies' were of much poorer quality than the magnificent originals at Chichén Itzá.

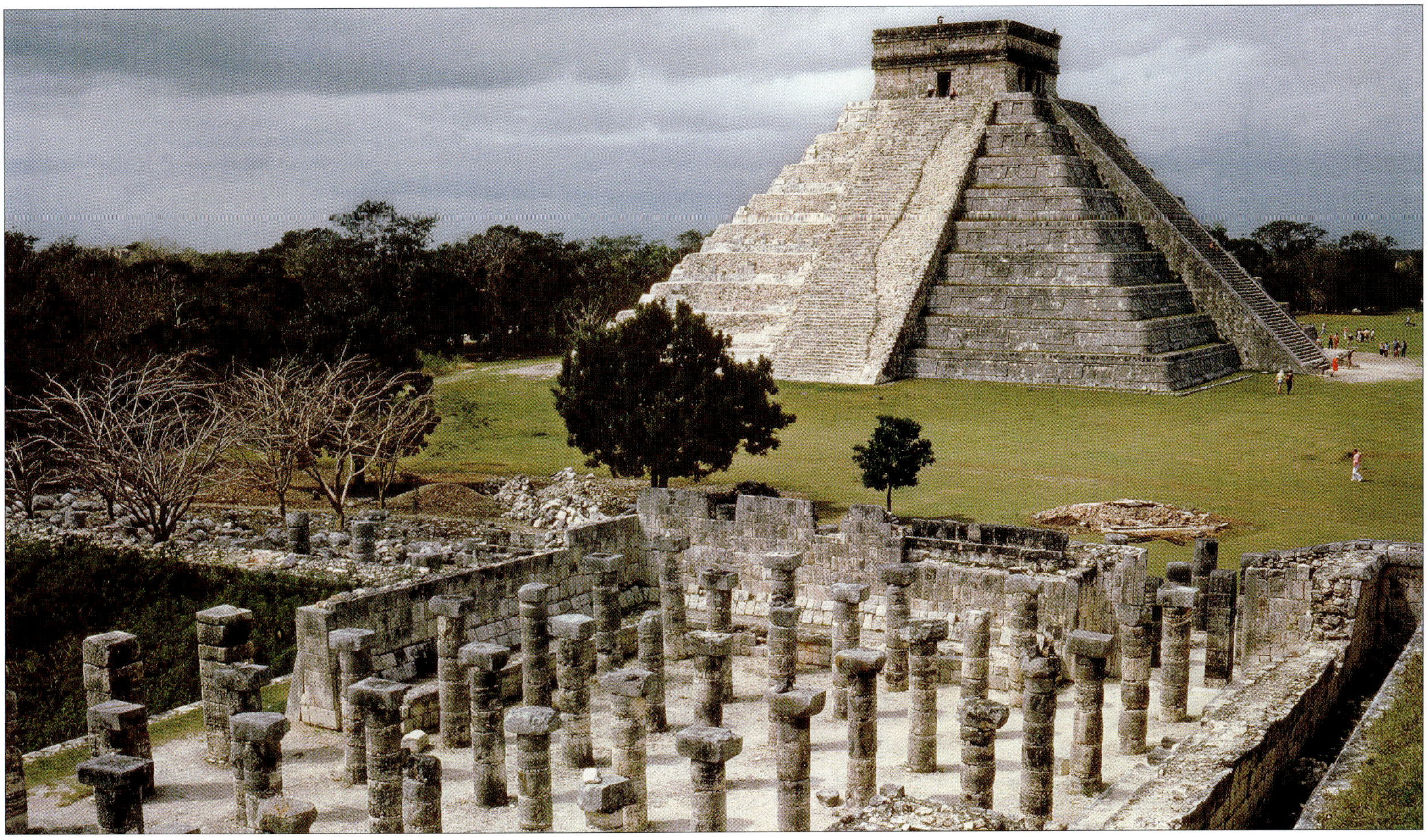

HIDDEN MEANINGS IN SACRED BUILDINGS

At the heart of Tenochtitlán, the Aztecs built up the Templo Mayor over many years on the same sacred site, each new pyramid-temple encompassing its forerunner. The first temple on the site was raised as early as the city's foundation *c.*1325, while improvements and enlargements continued until 1502. This was in line with hallowed Mesoamerican building practice. The great Pyramid of the Sun at Teotihuacán was built in the 1st–2nd centuries AD over a sacred underground cavern and a ground-level shrine, while builders at Tikal, Uaxactún, Chichén Itzá and countless other ceremonial centres followed the same custom, raising their ceremonial structures ever higher, like great mountains, as they built over and on the temples of their ancestors.

In Tenochtitlán, the Aztecs identified the Templo Mayor as a recreation of the holy mountain of Coatépetl on which their tribal god Huitzilopochtli was born. In a number of Maya cities, also, temples were explicitly identified as holy mountains. Stucco masks representing mountains (called *witz*) often flanked the stairways on these structures. Just as a cave in a mountainside was a point of access to the spirit world, so the temple entrance high on a sacred mountain gave access to the supernatural regions.

SACRED TEMPLATE

In Tikal and other cities, architects of ceremonial centres followed a template based on the four cardinal points and three levels of the universe: earth, heaven and underworld. While north was associated with the celestial realm, south was the way to the underworld. East was the place of the rising sun and west, the place of its descent into darkness, represented the earthly realm, governed by time cycles such as the daily pattern of the sun's rising and setting. Buildings in east, west and north were often placed to form a triangle, with the fourth, southern position in the sacred pattern implied.

The scholar Clemency Coggins showed how at Tikal the Twin-Pyramid groups erected to celebrate the end of a *katun* (7,200-day period) were laid out according to this template. These groups consisted of pyramids with four stairways at east and west, with a building containing nine doors lying to the south and a roofless enclosure containing a stela and 'altar' or 'throne' to the north. While the east and west pyramids celebrated the sun's daily cycle, the nine-door southern building represented the underworld, which had nine levels. The northern building was uncovered and so gave access to the sky, the celestial realm of the ancestors. In this place, as if connected to and blessed by his dynastic forebears, the king stood – represented by the stela that named him and the throne stone that celebrated his power.

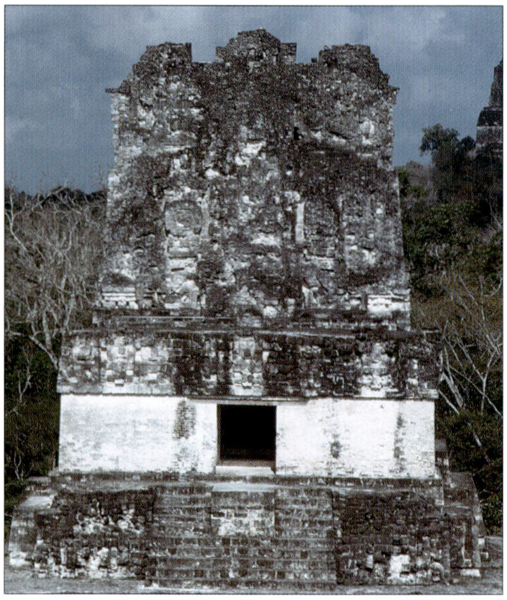

Above: Holy mountain top. Rising 42m (138ft) above the forest floor, Tikal's Temple II outreaches even the towering treetops.

HOLY NUMBERS

The numerical patterning of Mesoamerican cosmology was regularly celebrated in architecture. Just as the southern

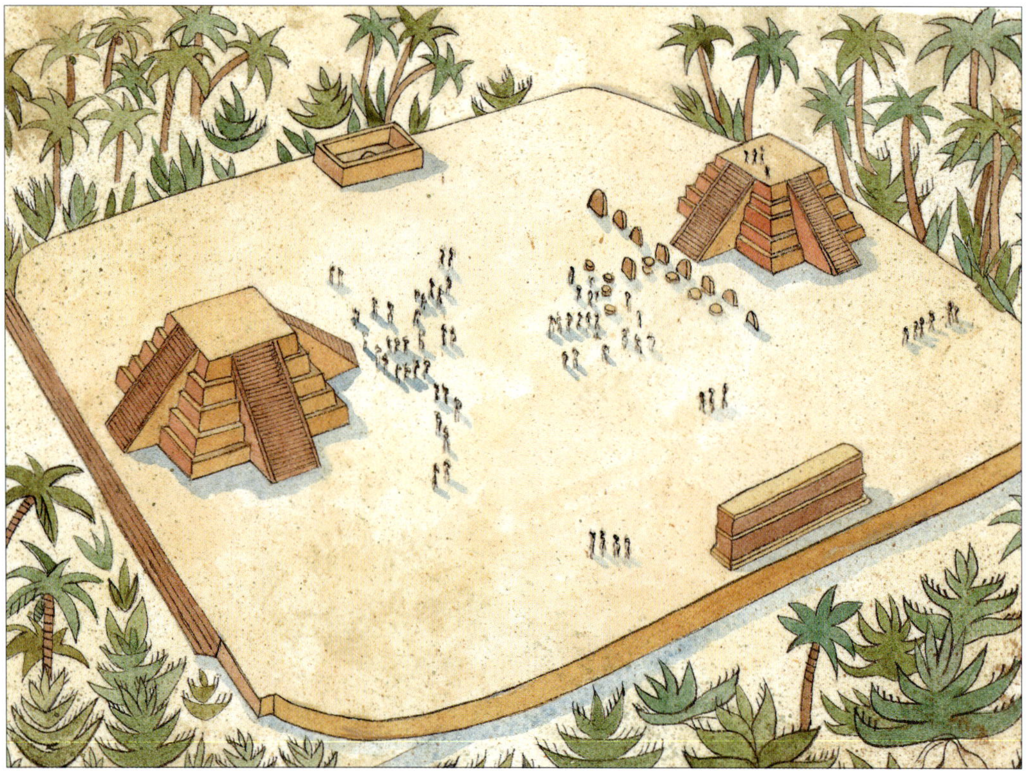

Left: Worshippers gather in the plaza for a katun-ending ceremony at one of the Twin-Pyramid Groups *in Tikal.*

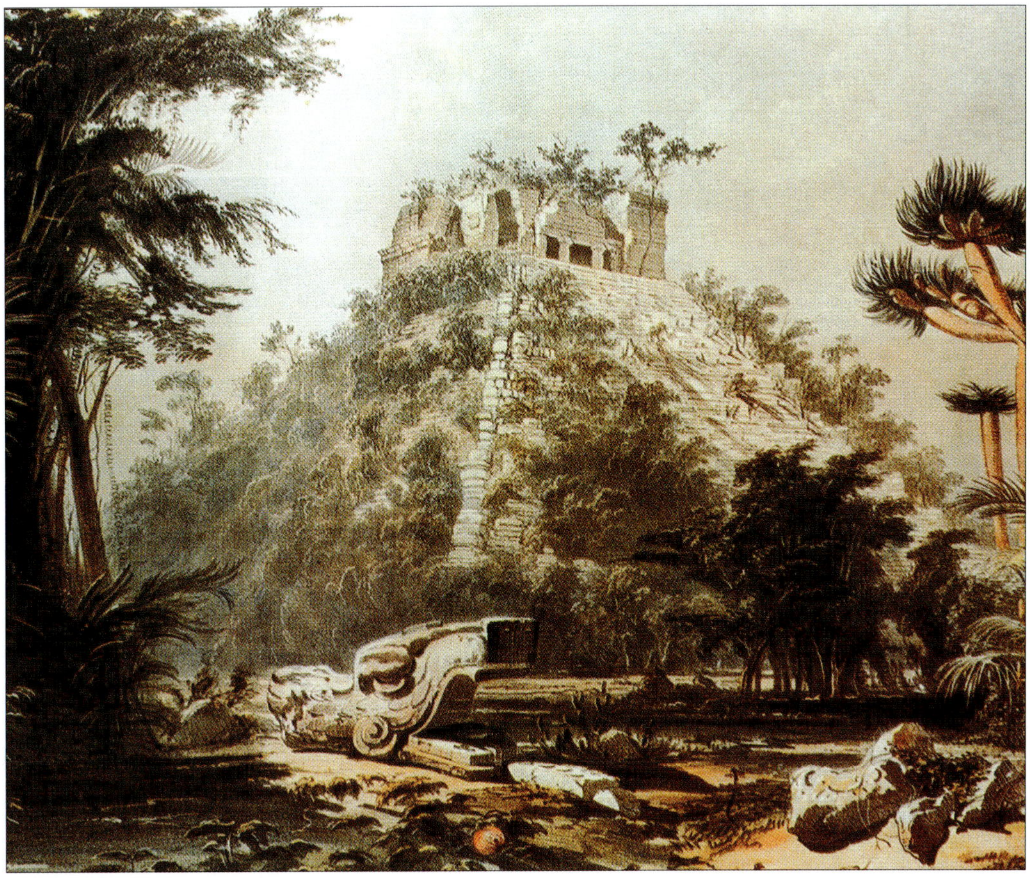

building of the Twin-Pyramid groups at Tikal contained nine doors to represent the nine layers of the underworld, so the 50m (164ft) Temple I at the same site had nine levels. So did the 30m (98ft) Temple of the Feathered Serpent at Chichén Itzá.

The numbers of 365-day and 260-day calendars similarly gave sacred meaning to ceremonial buildings: the Temple of the Niches at El Tajín in Veracruz had 365 niches, while the four staircases of Chichén Itzá's Temple of the Feathered Serpent each contained 91 steps which, when added to the single continuous step at the base, made 365. The Temple of the Masks at Kabah had 260 masks.

Above: In Frederick Catherwood's engraving Chichén Itzá's Temple of the Feathered Serpent is notable mainly for its mountain-like bulk. But archaeological clearing revealed its intricate design, with 365 steps to match the days of the solar year.

RITUAL FURNITURE

In Tollán, Chichén Itzá and Tenochtitlán, adaptations of sacrificial ritual called for specialized pieces of sacred furniture. One was the *chacmool*, carved in the form a reclining figure thought to represent the god Tláloc, with a receptacle on his chest into which a sacrificial victim's heart could be deposited. Another was the skull rack on which the heads of decapitated victims were displayed. These pieces of ritual furniture were used, and might indeed have been invented, by people in the northern reaches of Mesoamerica at La Quemada and Alta Vista in Zacatecas state and at Cerro de Huistle in Jalisco. This people, identified by scholars as belonging to the Chalcihuites culture, built a court with colonnades, using both square and round columns, a plaza with pillars and a very large I-shaped ball court. They carved militaristic images of warriors with shields and weapons and they used skull racks as well as – at Cerro de Huistle – an early form of the *chacmool*.

Scholars believe that the sites predated the rise of Tollán and the Chalcihuites culture might therefore have been the precursor of many of the militaristic sacrificial rituals of the Toltecs and their followers at Chichén Itzá and Tenochtitlán.

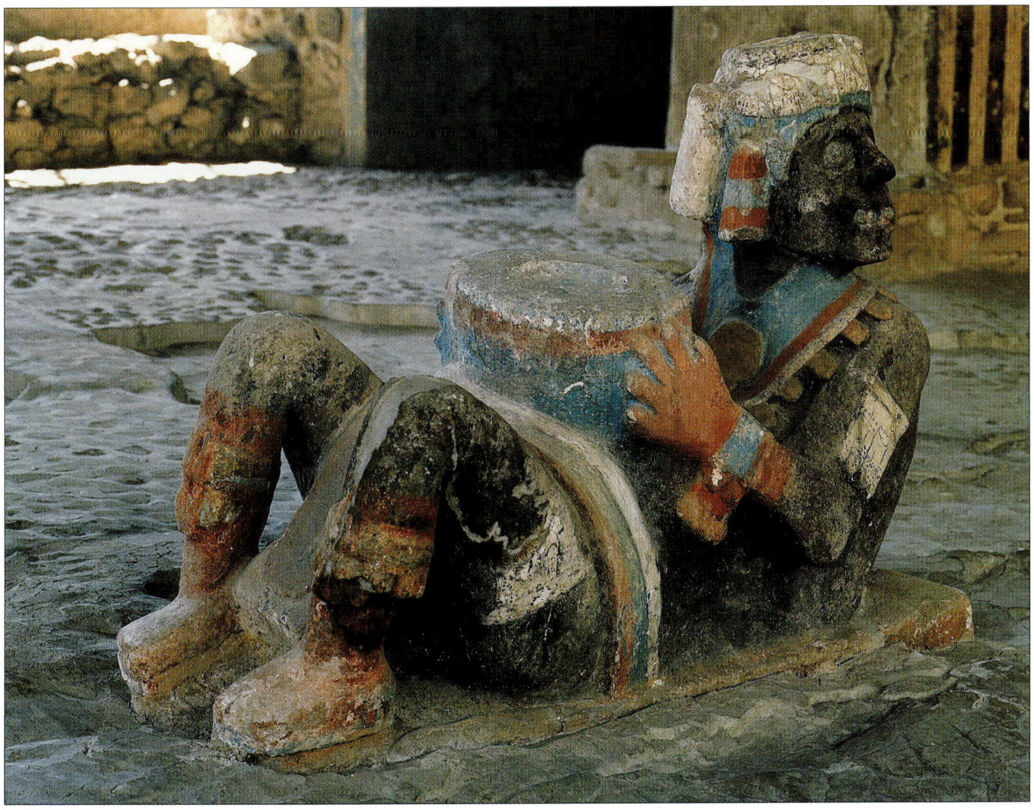

Below: Twin shrines occupied the summit of the Templo Mayor in Tenochtitlán. This chacmool demanded sacrificial blood outside the shrine of rain god Tláloc.

THE IMPACT OF COLOUR AND SOUND

To a worshipper in the Great Plaza of the Citadel in Teotihuacán, the Pyramid of the Feathered Serpent rose vast against the blue sky, presenting a great wall of red, its moulded plaster decoration depicting snakes, feathered serpent heads and goggle-eyed, fanged masks picked out in green, blue and white.

At Tikal, a nobleman in the Great Plaza gazing up at the great temples of the North Acropolis would see towering red-painted buildings adorned with moulded plaster masks. Mesoamerican sacred buildings, which are today remarkable for their size, structure and setting, in their prime also created a major impact with bright colouring and detailed stucco decoration.

The Pyramid of the Niches in El Tajín makes an extraordinary impression because of the contrast of light and shadow in the 365 apertures of the structure. Archaeologists report that its appearance in its prime would have been even more remarkable, for they have found traces of the dark red paint that originally coloured the interior of each niche and of the bright turquoise that bordered each one. Colour played a crucial role in the theatre of the sacred that Mesoamerican ritual centres generated. Priests, and sometimes victims, donned brilliant plumage and costumes. Among the Maya, victims destined for sacrifice were painted turquoise. Their blood splashed brilliant red on the *chacmool* or sacrificial stone.

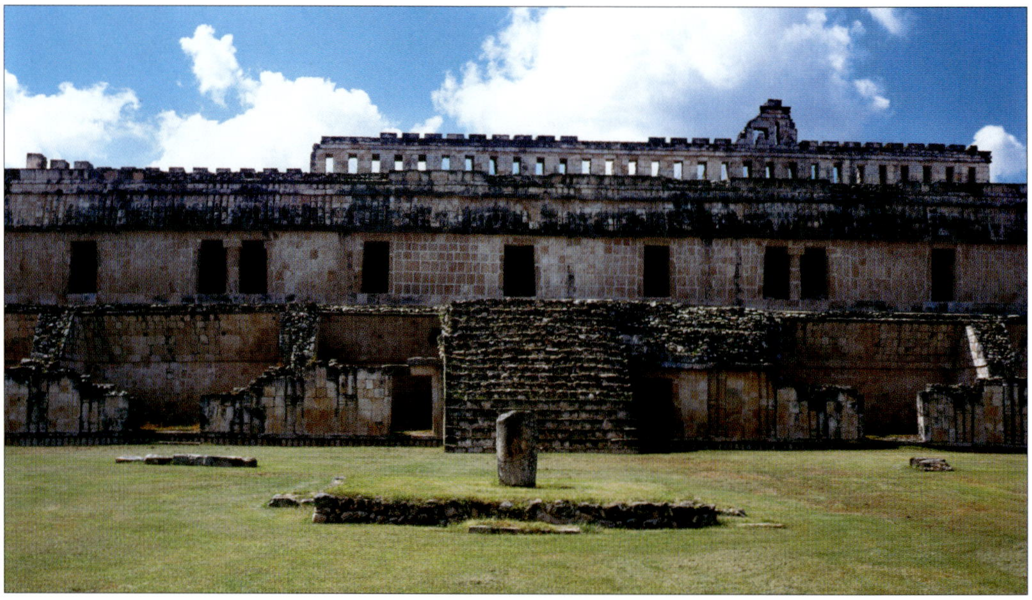

Above: Traces of wall colouring remain on one of the palaces at Kabah. The city was linked to Uxmal by a sacbé *roadway.*

COLOURED MESSAGES

The use of coloured paints enhanced the messages of divine, dynastic or military power represented by sacred and other ceremonial buildings. The twin temples atop the Templo Mayor in Tenochtitlán were painted in bright colours as a way of identifying their divine patrons. The northern shrine to Tláloc was painted blue and white to signify his powers over water, while the southern shrine, to Huitzilopochtli, was red to celebrate his control of war and sacrifice.

At Palenque, the detailed stucco images in the roof comb of the shrine that tops the Temple of the Inscriptions pyramid were painted in bright colours to make them clearly visible to crowds in the plaza below.

At Kabah, near Uxmal, each of the myriad repeating heads of the rain god Chac that adorn the 50m (150ft) length of the Temple of the Masks was originally painted in turquoise, green and red, creating what must have been an overwhelming impression.

At Tollán, the great carved warriors that once supported the temple roof atop the Temple of Tlahuitzcalpantecuhtli were painted in bright colours to emphasize their bulk and power.

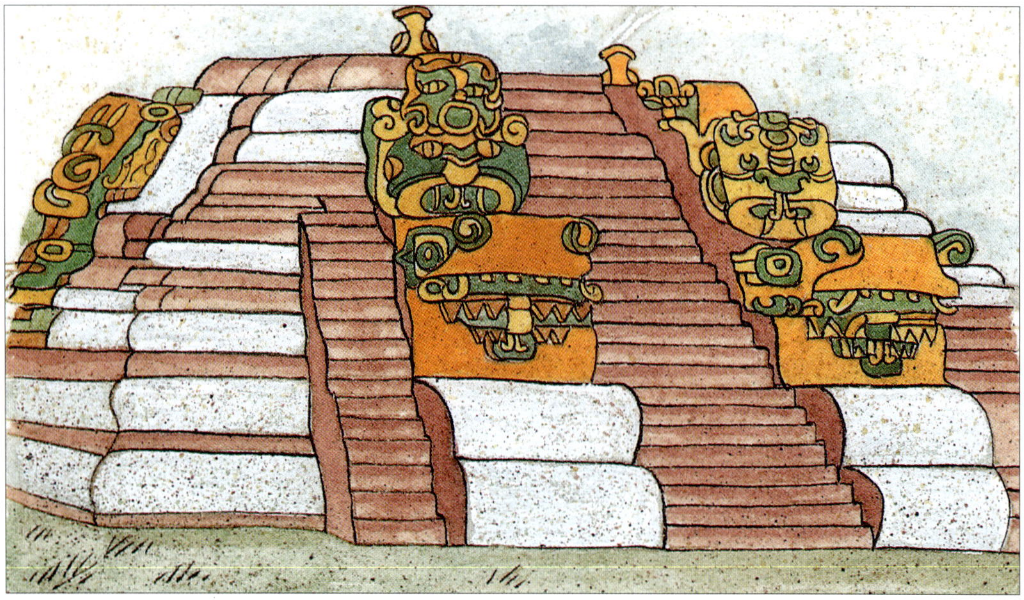

Left: Uaxactún's Pyramid E-VII-sub was originally decorated with red stucco and large masks, perhaps of the underworld god.

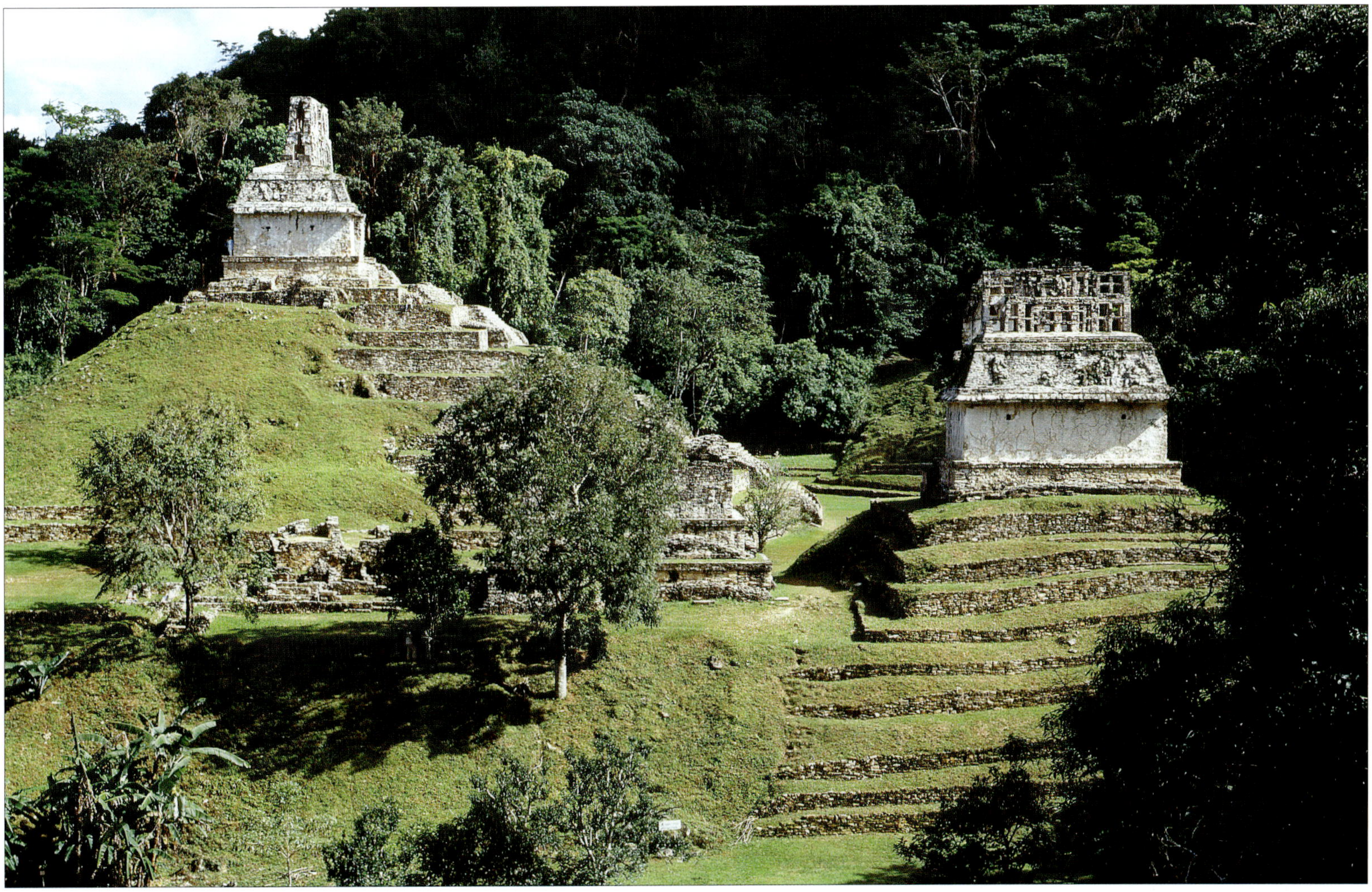

SOUND EFFECTS

Recent scholarly work has suggested that ritual complexes and sacred arenas might have been designed with acoustics in mind. The architecture of the Temple of the Feathered Serpent at Chichén Itzá appears to reinforce the sound of a voice declaiming at the top of the building: a crowd watching and listening in the plaza beneath would have been able to hear the words of a priest making a ritual speech in praise of the gods or celebrating the undying power of the state. If so, the builders would have had knowledge of a building acoustic science that is now lost among architects.

Below: A modern reconstruction of Teotihuacán's Temple of Quetzalcóatl shows the colours that greeted worshippers.

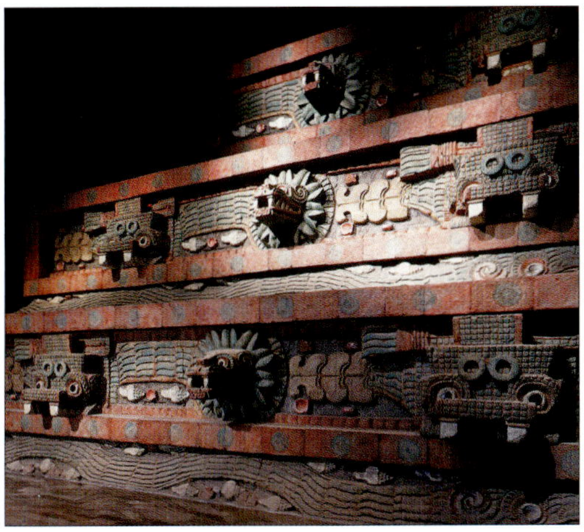

David Lubman has reported that when a person standing in the plaza before the pyramid-temple claps his hands, the pyramid steps reflect back a sound like a descending bird-call – a sound that is a remarkable imitation of the primary call of the sacred quetzal bird. The quetzal was associated with the god Quetzalcóatl/Kukulcán, who is celebrated in the temple. Lubman argues that the steps were carefully designed to produce this echo. The lower steps combine a narrow tread and tall back, making a high-pitched 'chirp' echo, while the upper steps create a deeper echo like a whoop. Together they form a descending sound highly reminiscent of the quetzal's call. Lubman adds that the echo is a little ragged because the pyramid steps are no longer covered with plaster, as they would have been in ancient times. When the pyramid was newly built, the echo effect would indeed have been striking.

Above: Solar blessing. At winter solstice the setting sun's rays lit on dynastic carving in Palenque's Temple of the Sun (right).

LIGHT EFFECTS

The Temple of the Feathered Serpent possessed another remarkable secret. Its builders positioned it so that at spring and autumn equinox, sunlight creates an undulating pattern of light and shadow on the steps, a celebration in light of the divine serpent in whose honour the temple was raised.

Alignments at Palenque produce light effects that celebrated the divine standing of the ruling dynasty. The Temple of the Cross is aligned so that at winter solstice, the setting sun will illuminate carved scenes and appear to bless the dynasty they honoured.

ARENAS FOR A SACRED CONTEST

The magnificent Great Ball Court in Chichén Itzá is Mesoamerica's largest, measuring 68m by 166m (225ft by 545ft) including the surrounding structures. Its pitch is I-shaped, opening out into wider end zones. The playing surface, 36m by 146m (120ft by 480ft), is enclosed by vertical sidewalls 8m (26ft) in height, each of which bears a circular ring halfway up its surface.

Chichén Itzá's Great Ball Court was part of the city's northern complex of ceremonial and sacred buildings, which archaeologists have dated to AD900–1200. The city contained no fewer then 13 ball courts, the largest number at any Maya centre and more even than at the other great Mesoamerican centre of the game, El Tajín in northern Veracruz, where there were 12 ball courts.

As elsewhere, the game at Chichén Itzá had important ritual and sacrificial elements. Relief sculptures on the walls of the court depict a newly victorious ball player who has just decapitated his defeated opponent: he holds the victim's head aloft in triumph, while blood cascades from the headless corpse. The Great Ball Court carvings depict a total of 14 ball players, each with a skull attached to his belt. This iconography identifies them as lords of the underworld, Xibalba, against whom the Hero Twins played ball in Maya religious narrative.

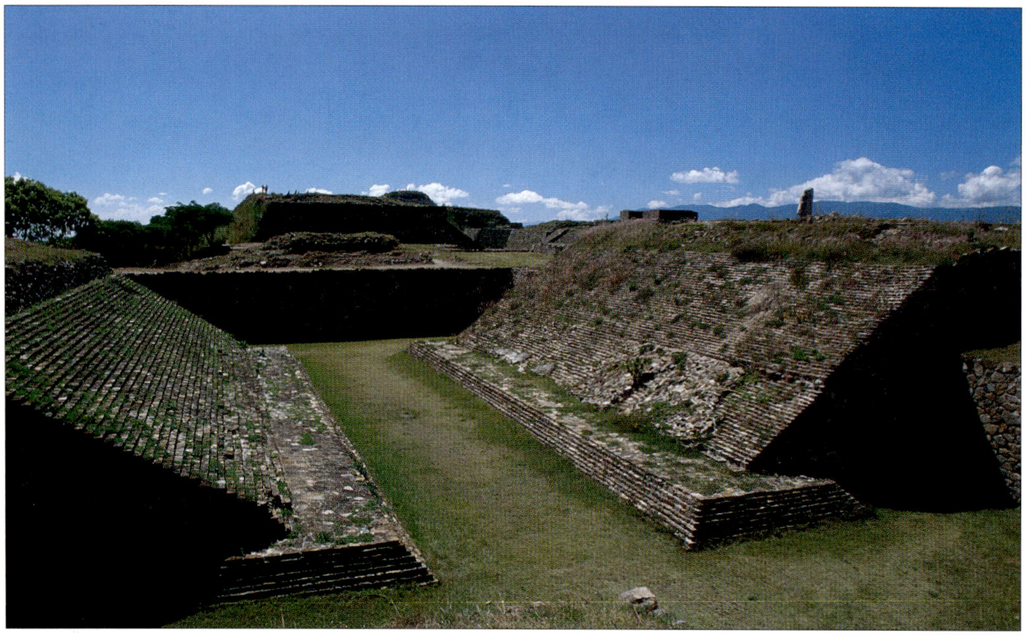

Below: The ball court at Monte Albán is an example of the earlier court design, with sloping sidewalls and without wall rings.

SACRED IMAGES

Similar bloodthirsty rituals were carved in stone at Yaxchilán, where relief images on the steps of the structure known as Temple 33 depict King Bird Jaguar, his father and predecessor Shield Jaguar and his grandfather, another Bird Jaguar, playing the ball game with balls made from the bound bodies of captives. Scholars suggest that the images refer to an ancient Maya religious narrative known as *Ox Ahal* ('The Three Victories'), which told of human heroes who in time immemorial defeated and beheaded three lords of the underworld. The panel depicting Bird Jaguar playing the ball game makes reference to the narrative, which survives in the Quiché Maya *Popol Vuh*. One of the courts at El Tajín had vertical walls carved with a defeated ball player awaiting death, the sacrificial flint knife poised.

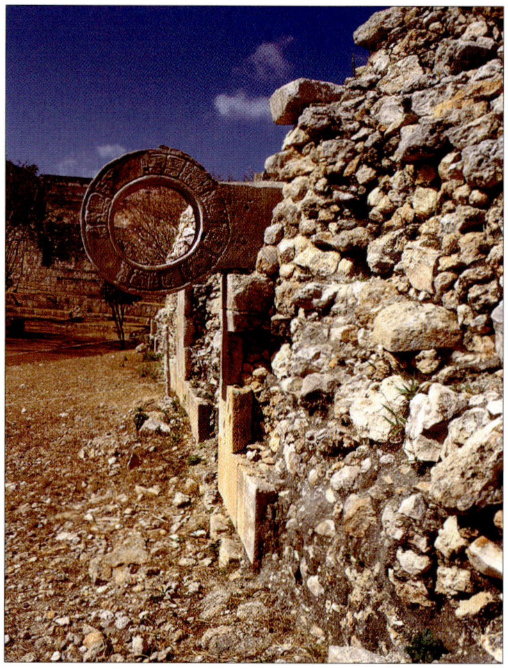

Above: Points were scored by hitting the ball through the ring. This court is at Uxmal, where – as in many cities – it was positioned to connect north and south.

WATCHING THE DEADLY GAME

Ball courts usually provided seating for spectators. The oldest known ball court in Mesoamerica – found in 1988 at Pasa de la Amada in Chiapas, Mexico – had side-banks with benches 30cm (1ft) tall and 2.4m (8ft) deep. Thousands of years later, the Aztecs also built their courts with spectator seating.

Many courts had rings mounted on the walls. Sidewall rings were found on courts at Tollán, and in many highland Mexican sites of the Postclassic Period, including Tenochtitlán. This contrasts with most earlier courts – for example, at Monte Albán, Copán, Cerros and Tikal – that had low sloping sidewalls and no surviving wall-mounted rings.

The earlier courts often had markers indicating the centre of the playing area, so dividing the pitch into two equal halves. Some courts had niches at the ends in diagonally opposite corners. These were found, for example, in the courts at

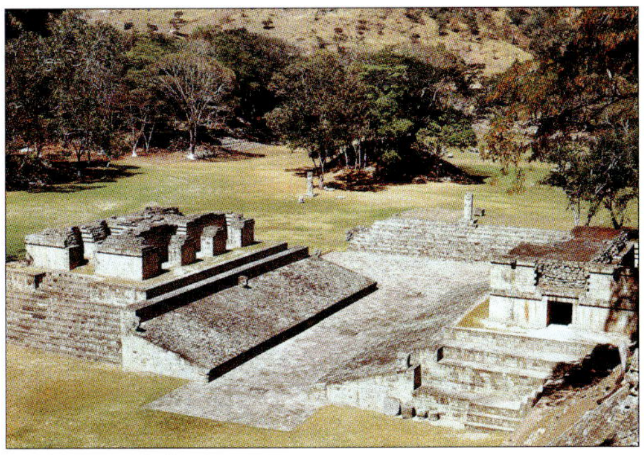

Right: Copán's Great Ball Court – dedicated in 18-Rabbit's reign (AD695–738) linked the Great Plaza to the north with the palaces and temples to the south.

Monte Albán and at Tollán. Scholars are unclear of their purpose. The rules of the ball game clearly varied in different eras and locations. At Chichén Itzá and in other courts of the Postclassic Period, the object appears to have been to score points by driving the ball through the sidewall rings. On other courts, players may have scored points by making the ball bounce in their opponents' endzone.

Below: The Great Ball Court at Chichén Itzá, seen here from the south, was overlooked by the Temple of the Jaguars.

IMPORTANCE OF POSITION

The ancient ball court at Pasa de la Amada was unusual in that it was not linked to a ceremonial centre: it appears to have been built in the heart of an elite residential area with no temples or ritual areas nearby. In many later settlements, the ball court played an important role within the sacred patterning of a city's ceremonial centre. A court was often placed between the northern realm of the celestial ancestors and the southern region associated with the underworld. The court, like the open plaza and the mouth of the pyramid-top temple, represented an entrance to the underworld. A ball court in Tikal's East Plaza performed this function in a three-point north-west-east design based on the North Acropolis and Temples I and II. At Cerros, in Belize, the ball courts (dating to 400–150BC) were positioned to consolidate the north–south alignment of the ceremonial centre.

THREE PARALLEL GAMES

Tikal's oldest ball court, laid out in the Great Plaza's south-east corner, contained a unique triple court, which had three pitches within a single complex. This was built to the south-east of the Great Plaza, beyond a ravine. It stood beside a sweat-bath. These buildings, called *temescals*, were closely associated with the ball game. They might have been used for cleansing rites as part of sacred ceremonial connected with the game.

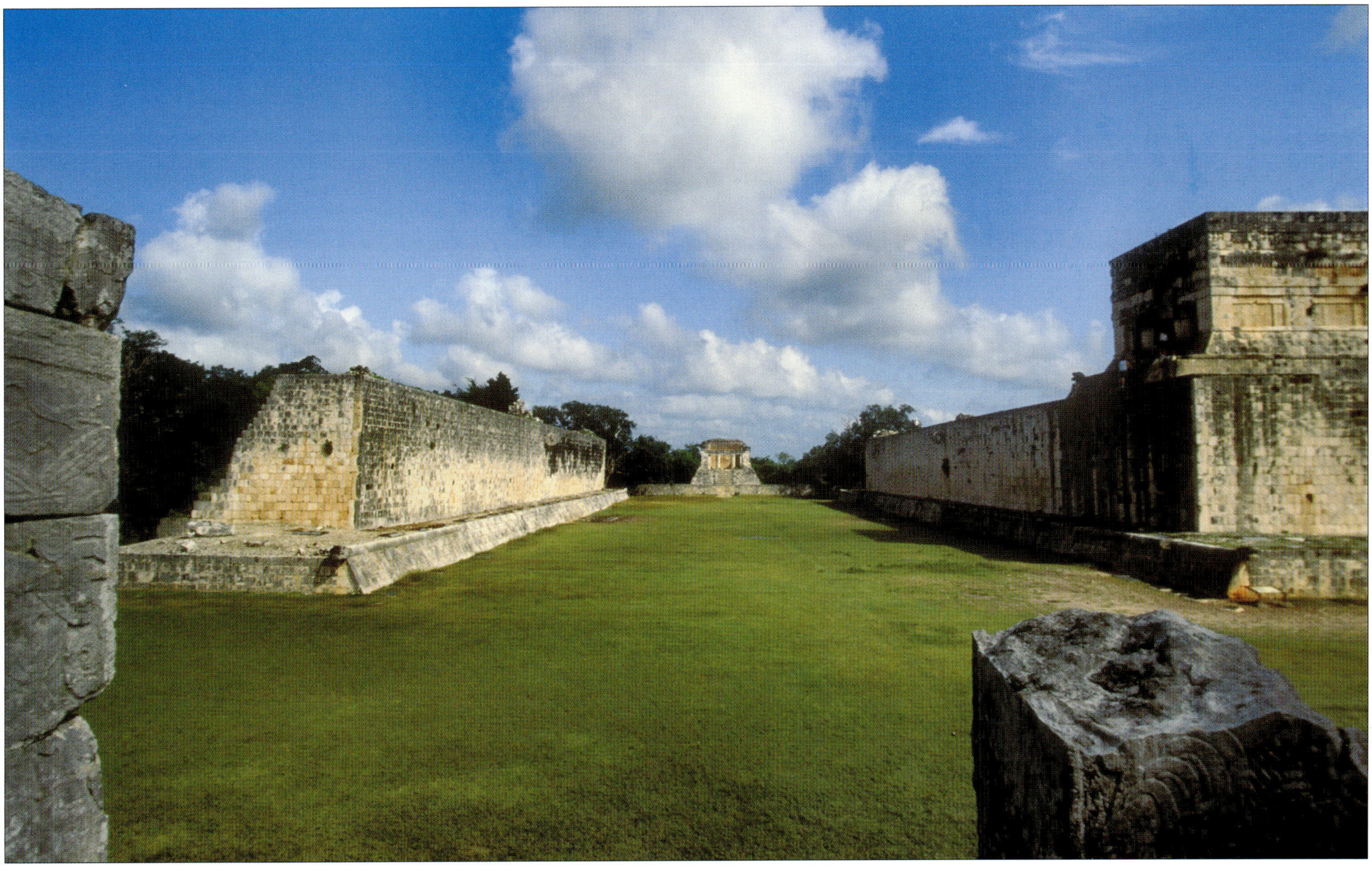

PALATIAL STYLE OF MAYA RULERS

Palenque is unique among the Maya cities of the Classic Period in giving a central position in the city to the royal palace and administrative area. In most cities, the 'sacred mountains' of temple-platforms and mortuary monuments took pride of place, adjoining or enclosing plazas and open spaces that held stelae celebrating the achievements of royal rulers. At Tikal, for example, the central structure was the ceremonial Great Plaza bounded by royal mortuary shrines, to the north in the form of the North Acropolis and, to east and west, in the form of Temple I and Temple II respectively. The palace buildings were situated to the south of the main plaza in the Central Acropolis and farther south again in the buildings known to archaeologists as Group G, which lie alongside the causeway laid to connect the centre to the Temple of the Inscriptions.

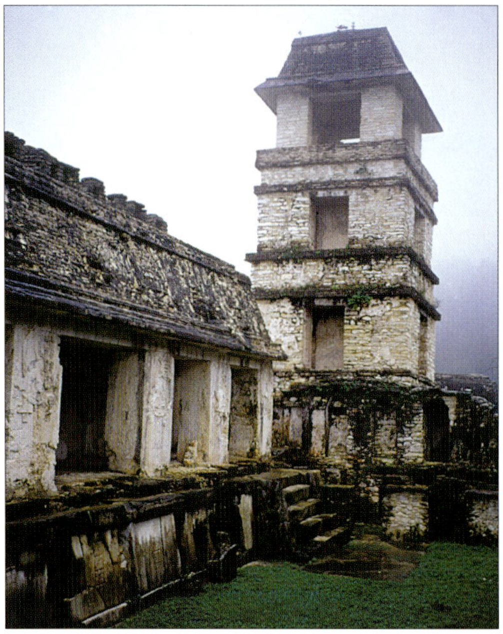

Above: The square four-storey palace tower at Palenque had no counterpart elsewhere in the world of the Classic Maya.

HOME OF A KING

At Palenque, the palace stood on a raised platform, 10m (33ft) in height and measuring 80m by 100m (260ft by 320ft). It commanded views of the city's sacred buildings and ceremonial area and looked beyond them across the river plain of the Usumacinta down to the Gulf of Mexico. The palace was home to King Pacal (*r.* AD615–83), whose ornate tomb was dug beneath his funerary monument, the Temple of the Inscriptions. His accession was marked by a carved panel in the palace representing his royal mother, Lady Zac Kuk, in the act of passing the crown to him.

Pacal greatly expanded and improved the existing palace complex, which had been built by his predecessors from the 5th century onwards. Beginning in AD654, he laid a higher platform in the centre of the palace area and on it erected the structure called House E. This building later served as a throne room, in which three or more of his successors held ritual coronation ceremonies. Pacal constructed House C, to the north of House E, in AD661. Another palace building, House C, rose between two plazas, the East Court and the West Court, in the northern part of the palace. Directly south of the East Court the king raised another palatial dwelling, House B, also *c.*AD661, and directly to the east of the East Court he added House A around seven to ten years later.

Below: King and courtiers enjoyed elegant privacy in the interior courtyards of the palace complex at Palenque. The concrete roof rested on strong beams of sapodilla.

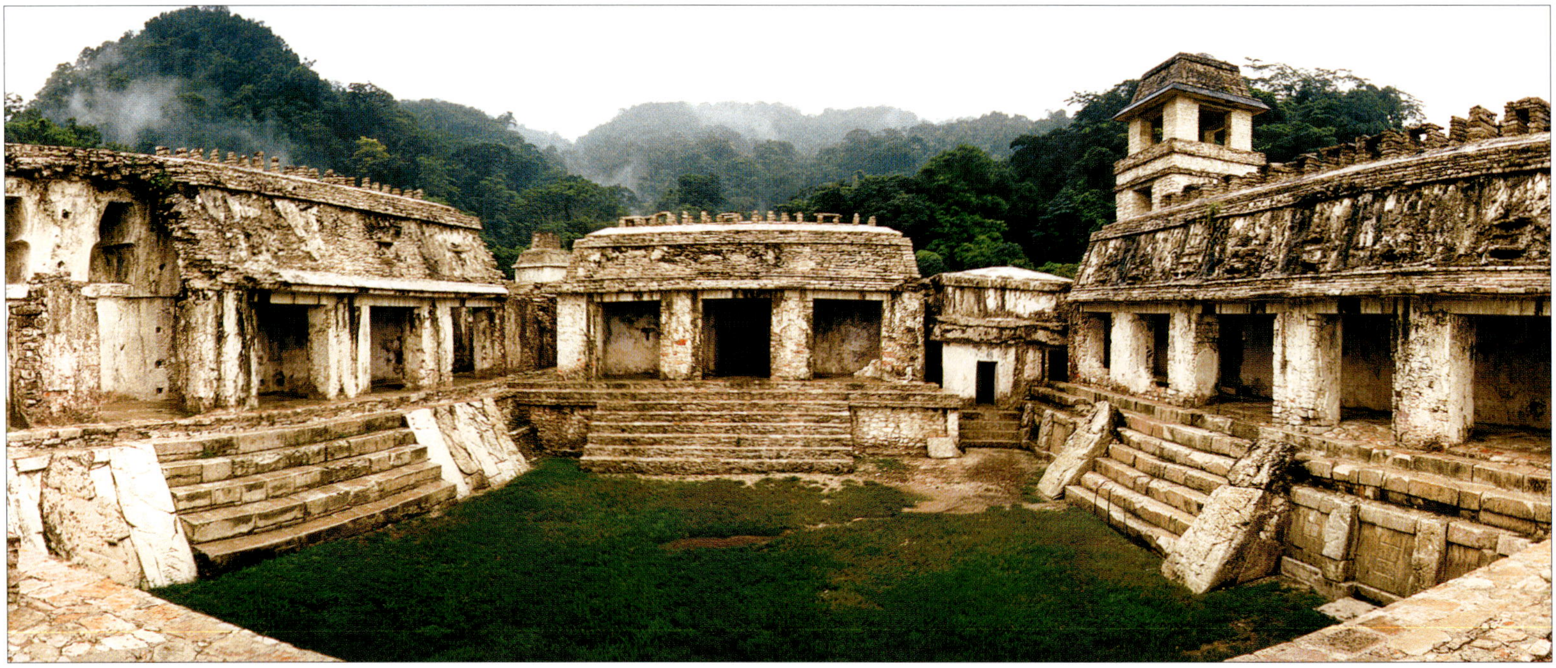

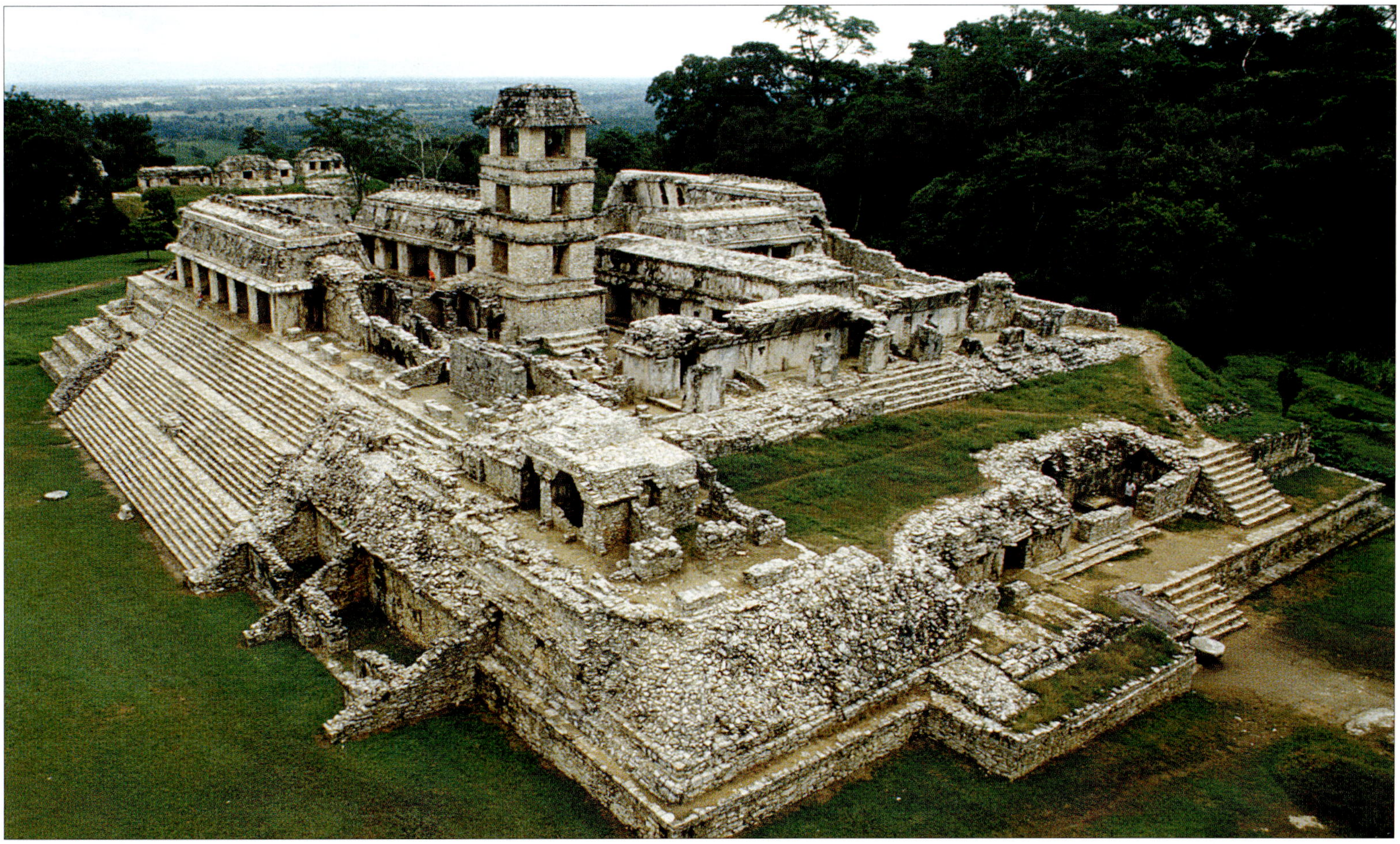

DYNASTIC BUILDING

Pacal's successors continued his work. His son Chan-Bahlum II (AD684–702) might have added Houses A and D at the far eastern and far western limits respectively of the building complex. Another building, House A–D, was probably added at the northern limit of the complex by King Kan-Xul II (AD702–711). He also built the rooms at the southern edge, including the remarkable four-storey tower that may have been an astronomical observatory.

The palace is luxurious throughout. Not only is it decorated with elaborate modelled stucco inside and out, but its builders used a modified arch that allowed spacious interiors , in marked contrast to the corbelled arch and narrow rooms found in many other Maya palaces and cities. When in use, the building was also brightly coloured. House E was painted white and also known as the White House but the other parts of the complex were coloured a dark red with details in blue, green and yellow. The complex contains 85 'windows' in the T-shaped form of a Maya calendrical day-sign that scholars call 'IK': its translation is 'wind-breath' or 'breath of life'. The 'windows' might not have been built for the usual purpose, for they were generally set rather too high in the wall for people to look through them comfortably. Nevertheless, they allowed light to enter and also had a decorative function. In the East Court, the king received ambassadors and fellow rulers. Its walls were decorated with carved inscriptions detailing Pacal's military successes and representing the many foes and rivals he had humbled and made captive.

Right: Carving on the second storey of the Palace at Sayil features monsters and a rare deity known as 'the descending god', found only here and at Cobá and Tulum.

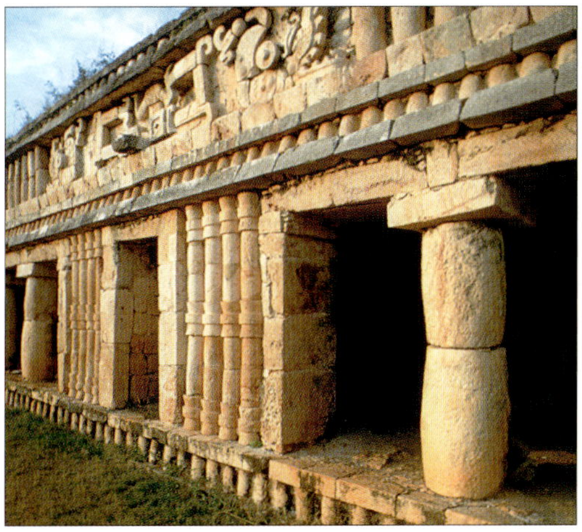

Above: This view of Palenque's palace is from the top of King Pacal's mortuary monument, the Temple of the Inscriptions.

A PALACE-TEMPLE

At Copán, King 18-Rabbit (AD695–738) erected a building that archaeologists believe was a combined palace-temple complex – known to archaeologists as Temple 22 – on the northern edge of the East Court of the Acropolis, the southern part of the city centre. Like many Maya temples, it was adorned with *witz* (sacred mountain masks) at the corners. In the Maya city of Edzná in Campeche, builders raised a pyramid temple platform that was also a palace: the five-storey structure had lower levels designed with many rooms, doorways and windows like a palace, but also a temple building on the flat fifth level that was accessed by a frontal staircase.

THE AZTEC PATTERN OF ELEGANCE

Aztec rulers lived in splendour, at a very great remove from the humble dwellings of their subjects. Their palaces were large and splendid, but took the same basic form as the dwellings occupied by the nobles and the middle classes: several rectangular rooms arranged around a courtyard or patio. They were unusual, however, in having a second floor: only nobles and rulers were permitted to build two-storey dwellings. Palaces contained administrative and storage rooms as well as living quarters for the ruler, his wives, concubines, guards and servants. Royal residential areas in Aztec palaces were generally reserved for the upper storey, while council rooms, courts, war chambers, arsenals, storage rooms and other administrative buildings were laid out on the ground floor. Extensive patios and pleasure gardens, well planted with trees and watered by streams and fountains, stocked with abundant wildlife, covered vast areas.

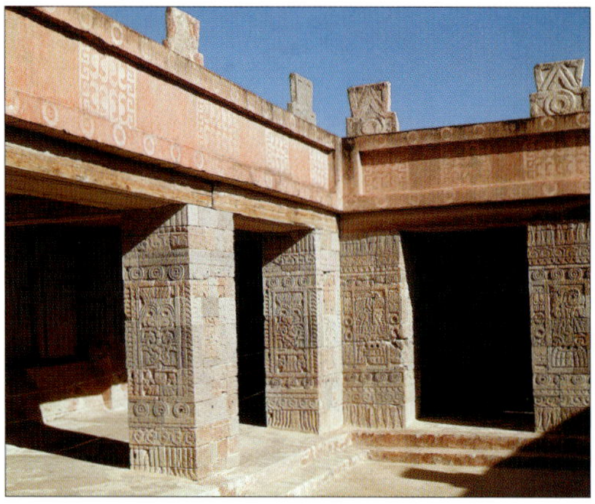

Above: In Teotihuacán the Quetzalpapálotl Palace, at the south-west corner of Plaza of the Moon, may have been priestly quarters.

A PICTURE OF ROYAL LIFE

According to Fernando de Alva Ixtlilxóchitl, writing in the early 17th century, the palace of Netzahualcóyotl, ruler of Texcoco, covered an area of more than 80 hectares (200 acres). A celebrated image from the 16th-century *Mapa Quinatzin* depicts the palace complex in Texcoco. Netzahualcóyotl holds court with his son Netzahualpilli in the throne room overlooking a large patio-courtyard in which several men – either allied rulers or the leaders of Texcoco's communities – are in earnest discussion. Behind them on one side is an extensive network of rooms for storing imperial tribute, while on the other side of the patio are temple rooms containing shrines. On either side of the throne room are administrative chambers, one used for counting and storing military supplies and the other a courtroom for the city's judges.

Opposite these rooms at the far side of the patio is a splendid area for receiving ambassadors from rival and allied cities and a large meeting house set aside for discussing matters of war. This pattern is typical of Aztec-era palaces and similar to the design of Moctezuma's splendid building in Tenochtitlán.

DESIRE FOR PRIVACY

Although an Aztec palace contained many public rooms such as stores and courtrooms that could be accessed even by commoners, the *tlatoani's* own quarters were reserved on the upper storey and contained many secluded outdoor patios and gardens in which the ruler and his intimates could associate with their noble peers in quiet and privacy. The divine aura of the ruler, which dictated that he must eat alone and could not be addressed with full eye contact, needed to be protected.

There were certainly ancient Mesoamerican prototypes in Teotihuacán and Tollán for setting the palace alongside centres of public life such as the marketplace and ceremonial area, but equally in the 'palaces' of Monte Albán, there was a prototype of an elite building with many stairways, corridors and secluded patios – a design intended to safeguard the privacy of rulers and nobles.

Below: Many of Teotihuacán's elite residences were decorated with murals. This owl fresco is from the Tetitla complex.

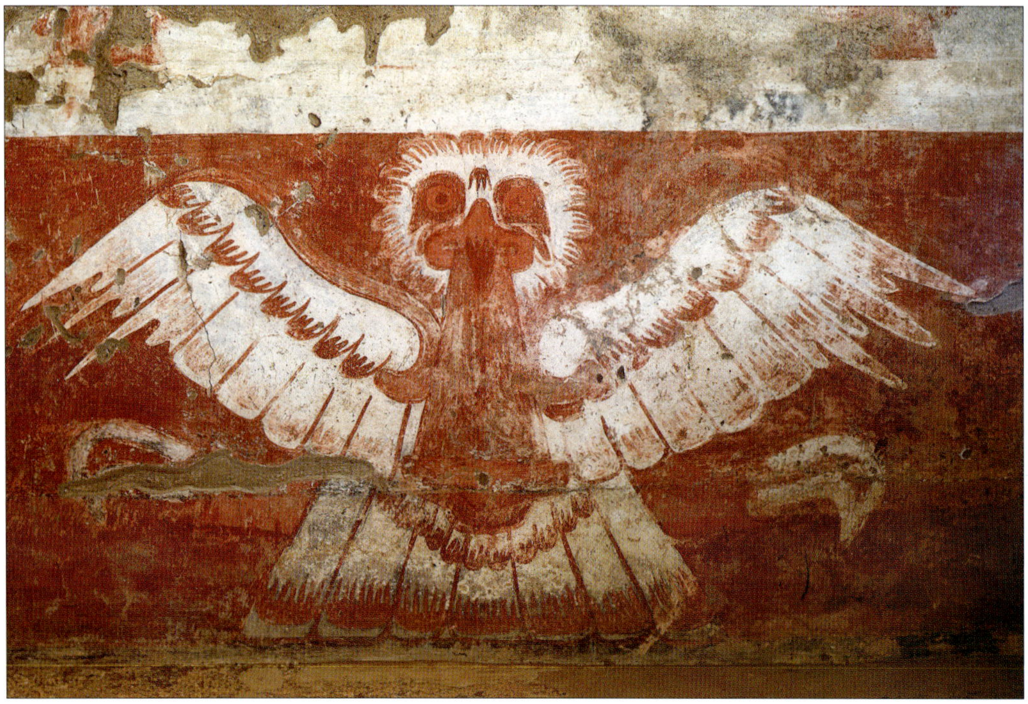

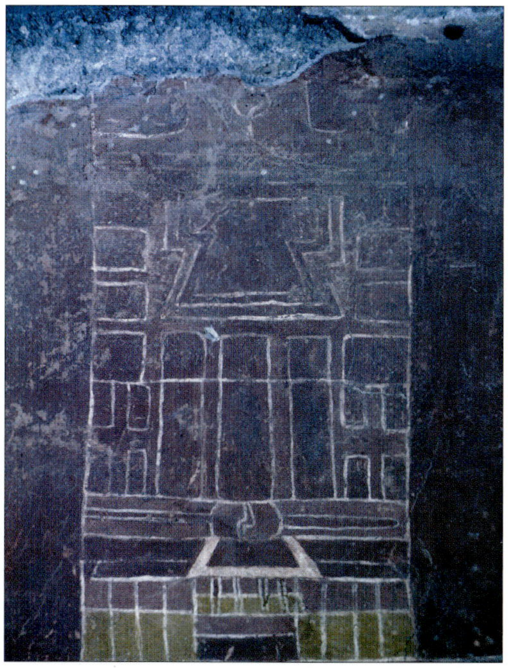

Above: A fresco detail from the Tetitla residence in Teotihuacán contains a floor plan for a palace building.

PALACE PROTOTYPE

The unknown builders of Teotihuacán, who exercised such an enduring architectural influence on later Mesoamericans, constructed a palace compound in the 1st–2nd century AD of the kind built about 1,200 years later by the Aztecs. The palace at Teotihuacán was part of the great Ciudadela or Citadel complex that also contained a vast plaza and the Pyramid of the Feathered Serpent. It lay at the junction of the main thoroughfares that divided the city into four and sat directly opposite a large marketplace. Similarly, in Tenochtitlán the *tlatoani's* palace occupied a position adjoining the main square and temple precinct in the heart of the city.

The Ciudadela palaces lay on the north and south sides of the great Pyramid of the Feathered Serpent. They consisted of groups of low-lying apartment buildings gathered around open patios – the very pattern that Aztec builders would later use in their own designs.

Opposite the Ciudadela, the open space that archaeologists believe was a marketplace was flanked by other low-lying palace-style buildings that were probably administrative buildings needed to monitor and control the vibrant trade on which the city thrived. By the era of Tenochtitlán, the two 'palace' functions – ruler's residence and administrative compound – had been combined.

The monumental Ciudadela complex built *c.*AD100–200 was a new departure for the Teotihuacános, who had previously laid out buildings in groups of three on an ancient sacred pattern. Scholars believe that the new style might have marked the beginning of a new political era, an attempt by a powerful new leadership in the city to distance themselves from a possibly despotic former regime.

The Ciudadela celebrated the authority and power of the state, with its palaces adjoining open spaces for the gathering of residents and centralization of trade. Later Mesoamericans learned a great deal from this association of elite residences with monumental architecture.

THE BURNT PALACE

At Tollán, the Toltecs erected twin palace-administrative buildings adjoining the Temple of Quetzalcóatl. To the east was the Palace of Quetzalcóatl and to the west was a much larger three-halled structure, now known as the Burnt Palace because much of it was lost to a fire. Like its predecessor at Teotihuacán and its successors at Texcoco and Tenochtitlán, the palace building probably hosted meetings, was used to greet notable visitors and was a state storeroom for items of trade and tribute. Once again, the building adjoined both a plaza and a large area that scholars believe was a marketplace.

Below: At Tollán these pillars are remains of the colonnades that once graced the Palacio Quemado or 'Burnt Palace'.

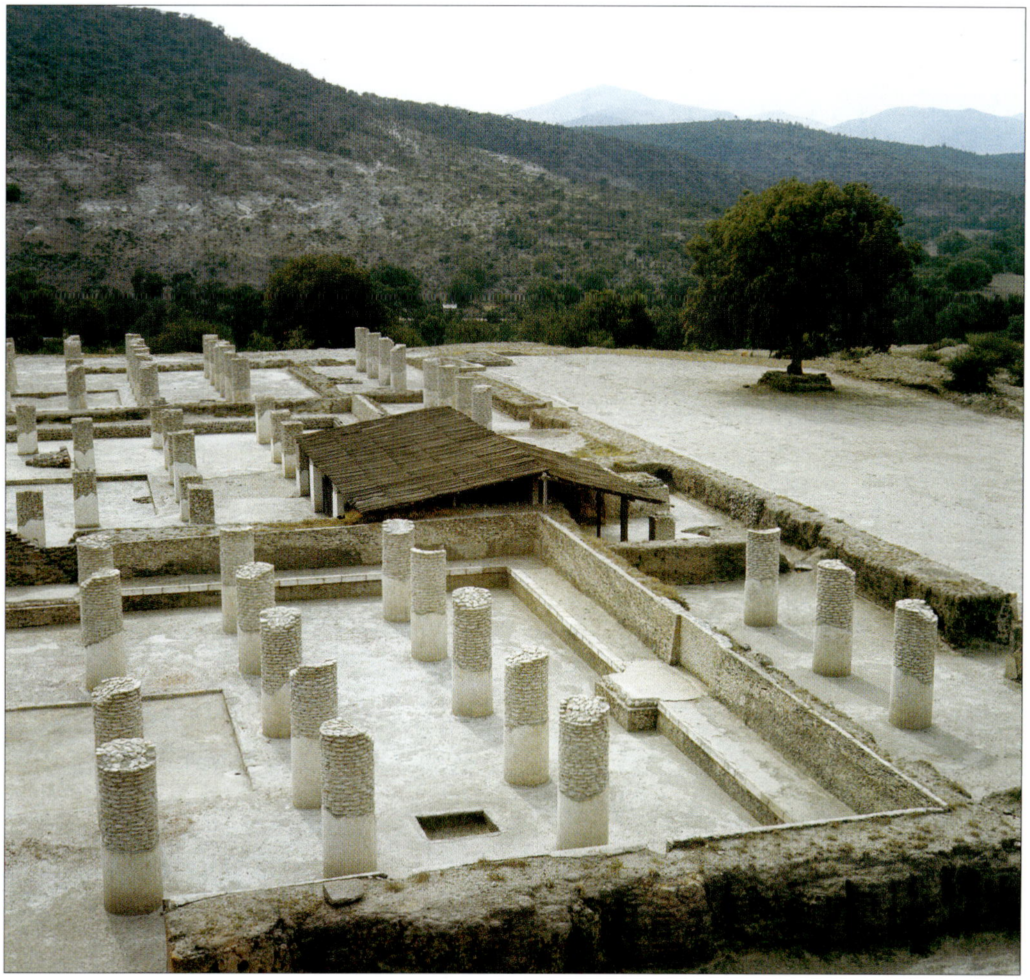

THE MAGNIFICENCE OF MOCTEZUMA

Moctezuma's palace in Tenochtitlán was a statement in stone of the *tlatoani's* divine magnificence. Surrounded by extensive gardens containing ponds, courtyards, an aviary and a zoo, the palace was a residence fit for a ruler so magnificent that none of his subjects were permitted to look him in the eye.

ROYAL CITY WITHIN A CITY

Spanish accounts report that Moctezuma's palace had more than 300 rooms, which were arranged around internal courtyards. Legal documents concerning landholdings suggest that the emperor's city complex covered 4 hectares (10 acres). An administrative building as well as a royal home, the palace contained military council rooms, a throne room and reception areas for greeting ambassadors and political visitors, legal apartments used by judges as courtrooms, two armouries and large areas for storing tribute from around the empire. According to an account by the conquistador Bernal Díaz del Castillo, the palace contained extensive areas for storing cacao, feathers, gold, jewels, cotton and foods that had been received as tribute payments. There were also rooms for accountants managing the wealth generated by tribute and taxation.

The vast building contained libraries, music rooms and areas for craftsmen retained to work for the emperor. There were also permanent quarters for the rulers of Texcoco and Tlacopán, the Aztecs' allies in the Triple Alliance, together with guest rooms for visiting notables from states within the empire. The importance of the lakeside town of Chiconauhtla, derived largely from its control over the straits connecting the lakes of Zumpango and Xaltocán with Lake Texcoco, was reflected in the fact that the ruler had the right to keep an apartment in the imperial palace

The Tenochtitlán palace complex was arranged over two floors, with the *tlatoani's* quarters on the upper floor and state or administrative rooms and servants' living space on the gloomier ground level. An image from the *Codex Mendoza* (*c.*1541) represents the two-storey building with a courtyard and steps leading to an upper-floor reception room in which the dazzling Moctezuma himself sits in state. On either side of his quarters stand apartments for leading allied rulers. Below on the ground floor lie two meeting rooms, in one of which four judges discuss an important case, while the other is kept for councils of war.

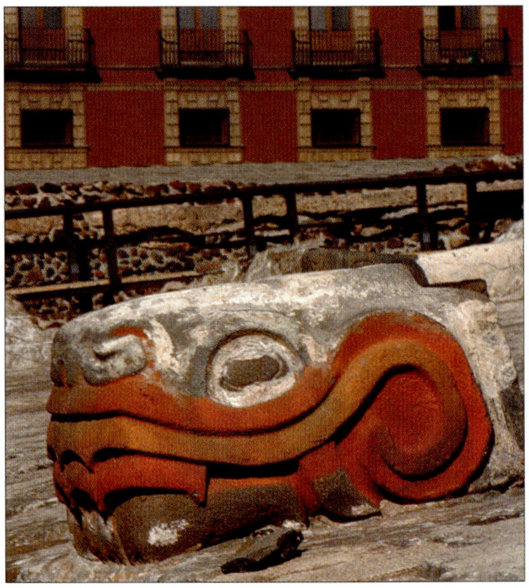

Above: A serpent-head Tenochtitlán foundation stone was uncovered by archaeologists in Mexico City.

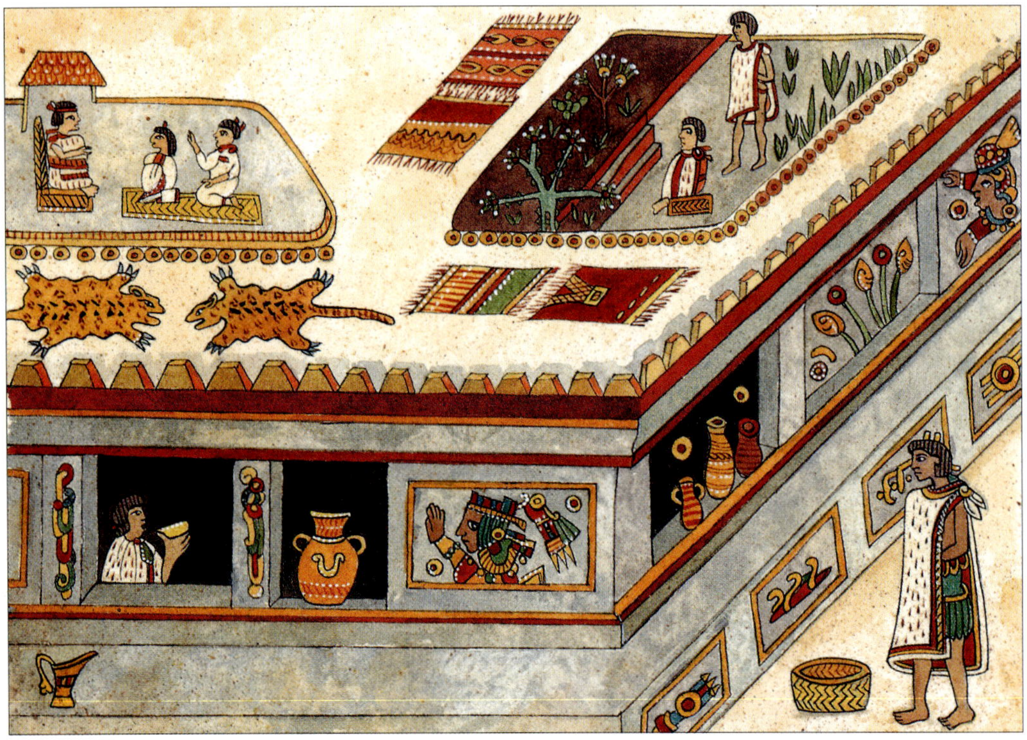

Below: A reconstruction of Moctezuma's two-storey palace in Tenochtitlán reveals extensive courtyards and gardens within.

PALACE COURTROOMS

Friar Bernardino de Sahagún's description of the palace in Tenochtitlán indicated that legal administration worked on three levels for nobles, military and commoners. In one room of the palace court, legal experts heard noble disputes and complaints of wrongdoing. Their sanctions included banning an offender from the palace complex, banishing a person from the city or ordering his execution by stoning, hanging or beating; chopping off the hair was a lesser punishment, but greatly feared because it

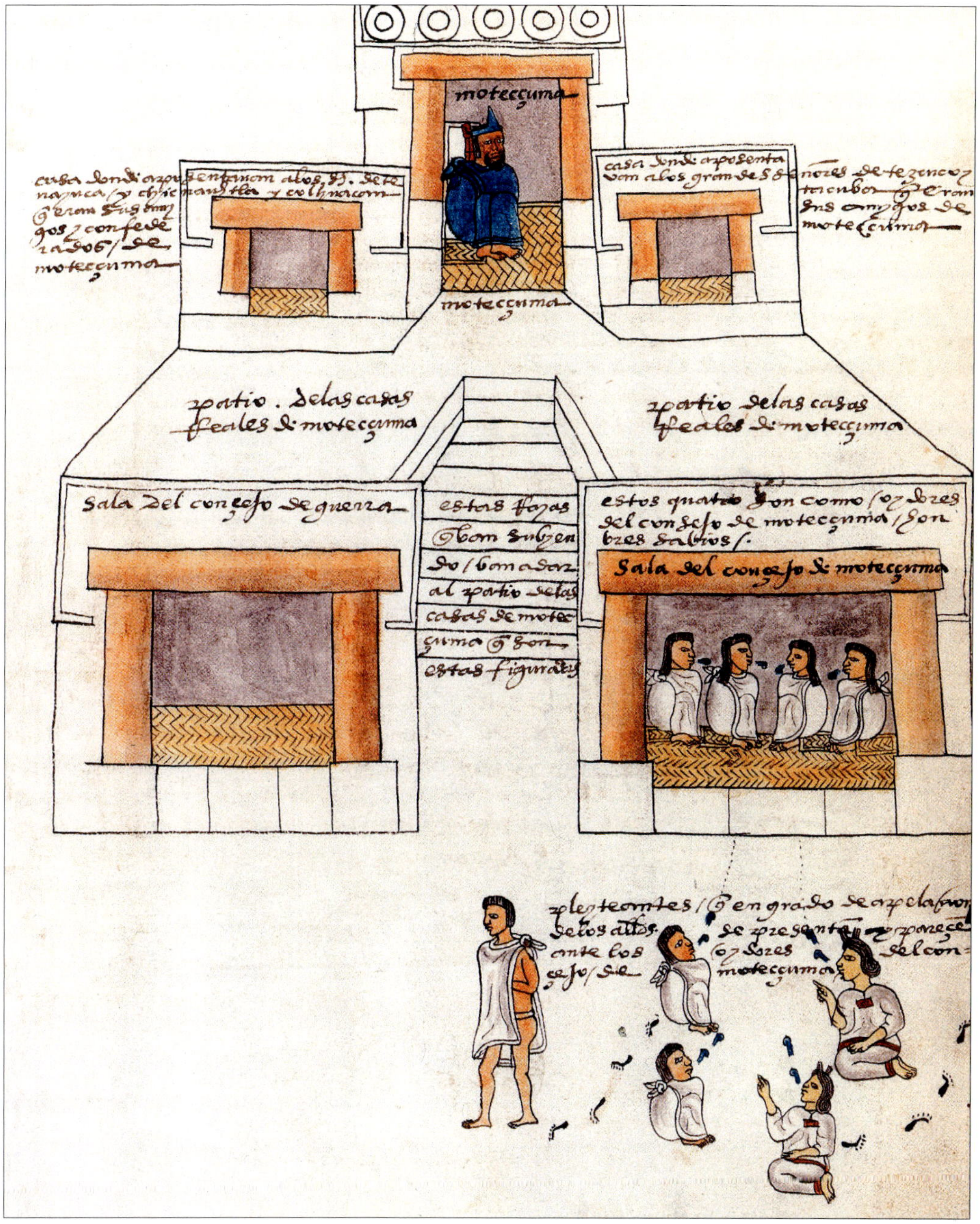

Above: The Codex Mendoza *(c.1541) shows Moctezuma sitting on the upper floor of his two-storey palace, between apartments for visiting dignitaries. Before the building, one man departs while four litigants present a case to the judges in the lower right-hand chamber. The lower left-hand chamber is identified as the war council room.*

would make a leading member of the *pipiltin* nobility look like a shaven-headed *macehual* or commoner.

In a palace room named the *tecpilcalli*, leading members of the military dispensed their own justice. In the *teccalco* chamber, commoners could bring disputes and complaints to judgement. The *tlatoani* himself heard difficult cases and took advice from the three most senior judges or *tecuhtlatoque* before passing judgement. Judges faced the strictest sanctions – including execution – if they were found to be corrupt.

ANCIENT AMENITIES

There were more than 100 bathrooms in the *tlatoani's* palace. Several times a day the ruler washed and changed his clothes: he discarded his garments after wearing them once. He lived in great splendour on the palace's second floor, with his two wives and 150 concubines, together with legions of guards and attendants. His servants were housed in their own luxurious apartments.

A large part of the palace was given over to kitchens and food stores. At every meal some 300 guests were served from an extensive menu designed to stimulating the most jaded palate. Such was the *tlatoani's* splendour that dinner guests were forbidden to watch him engage in activities such as eating: he consumed his food in isolation behind a golden screen. Delicacies to tempt the royal diners included frogs served with green chilli peppers, sage-doused locusts and a helping of prickly pear served with fish eggs from the great lake of Texcoco.

In the patios of the royal palace complex, acrobats and musicians practised. The gardens contained ten pools stocked with waterfowls that feasted on fish. Hernán Cortés wrote to King Carlos V of Spain that these birds were so numerous they required 110kg (250lb) of fish each day. In the zoo, royal jaguars, coyotes and serpents were kept in regal luxury. Some were fed on human flesh carried from the temple complex nearby.

Throughout the palace, servants, guards and administrators burned incense and sweet-smelling woods in their braziers to mask the smell of decaying body parts that the breeze sometimes carried across from the temple quarters.

Below: This stone, once part of Moctezuma's elegant Tenochtitlán palace, shows evidence of having been worked by an Aztec mason.

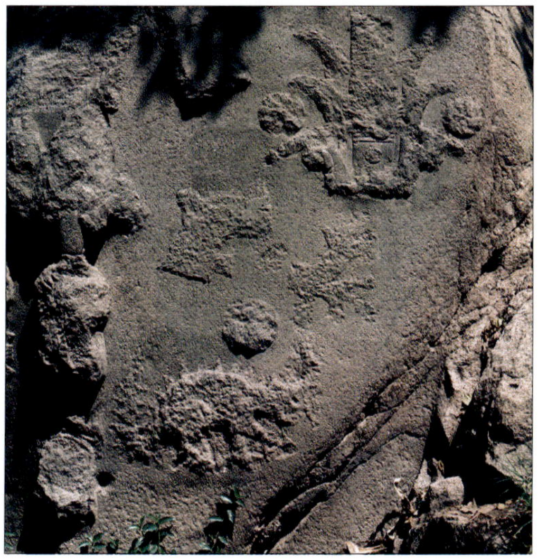

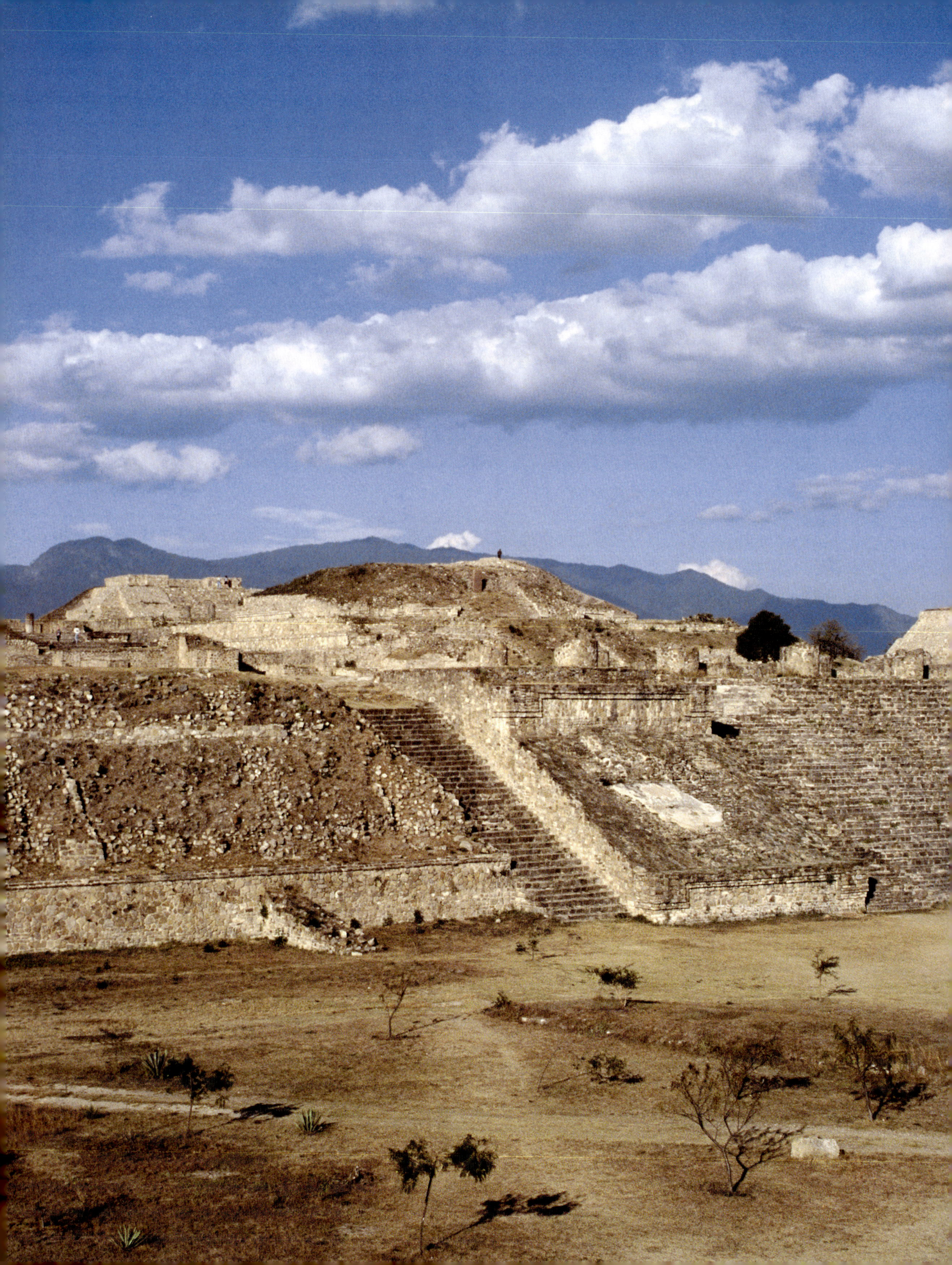

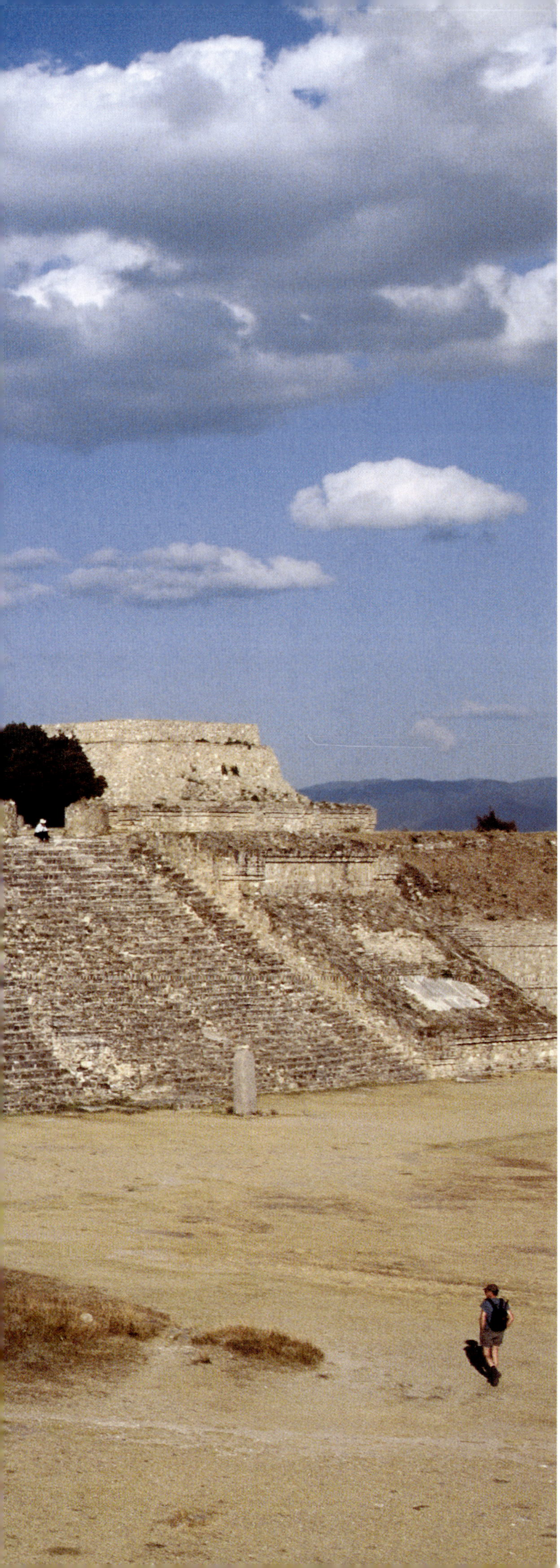

CHAPTER TWO

BUILDING THE CITIES

The builders of great Mesoamerican centres looked for inspiration in the cities and sacred buildings of the past. They paid homage to the achievements of their ancestors by reproducing their styles: Teotihuacáno *talud-tablero* construction spread across Mesoamerica – being used, for instance, in Tikal, Kaminaljuyú, Xochicalco, El Tajín and Chichén Itzá. Great cities of the past were also places of pilgrimage or sacred occupation.

Cities had a unifying function, linking cultures and peoples across centuries, but also connecting people within a region. A city was the focus of its area, providing employment in outlying artisanal areas or an outlet for the excess agricultural produce of the region's farmers. For instance, Tikal provided a means of living for a vast outlying population of some 60,000; Teotihuacán similarly supported a large outer area of rural settlements, some growing food, others working local flint or obsidian; Tenochtitlán was the focus of an extensive area of *chinampa* farmlands.

A city also created connections between areas across great distances: from before the start of the Classic Period, Mesoamerican trade was driven by the needs of wealthy city populations and religious elites for rare or exotic products. Long-distance trade driven by the vast population of Teotihuacán, for instance, forged links across many thousands of kilometres between the Mexican highlands and settlements such as Tikal or Kaminaljuyú.

Left: The North Platform bounds the northern edge of Monte Albán's Plaza, at the heart of Mesoamerica's first true city.

SACRED TOWNS:
SAN LORENZO AND LA VENTA

Settlers first occupied the plateau that became the Olmec centre of San Lorenzo, near the Gulf Coast of Mexico, *c.*1500BC. Their descendants began public building works about 250 years later. A group had grown wealthy and powerful controlling the farming of fertile lands alongside the local Coatzacoalcos and Chiquito rivers and perhaps by managing trade in obsidian, greenstone and basalt from resource-rich uplands nearby. The leader of this group was able to command and reward the labour needed to build a sacred ceremonial centre.

Below: Stela 2 at La Venta shows an Olmec monarch dressed as a player with the bat used in some versions of the game, after c.*1000*BC.

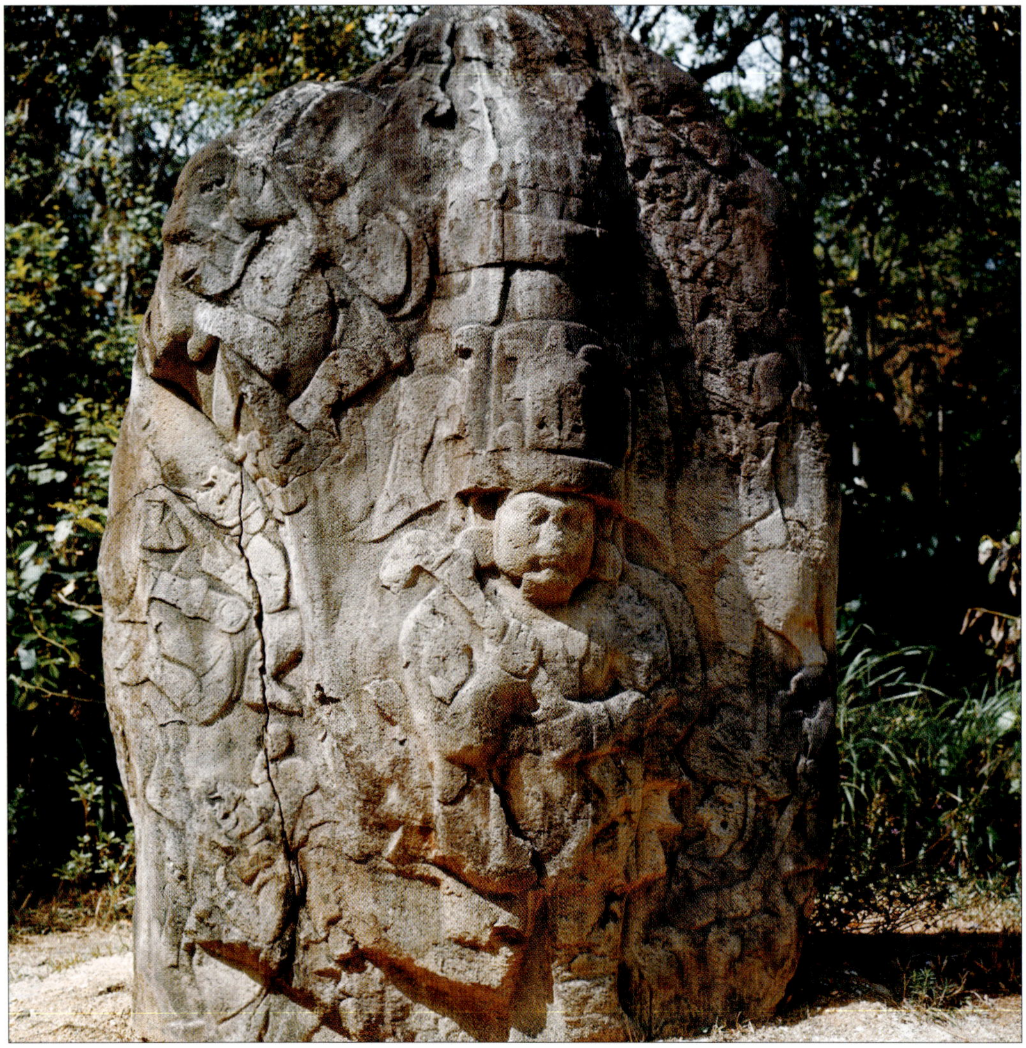

SACRED CENTRE

Beginning *c.*1250BC, hundreds of workers built up and levelled the plateau. On its top, 50m (160ft) above the surrounding countryside, they laid out a series of pyramids and rectangular courts on a north to south alignment, oriented precisely 8 degrees west of true north – probably to line up with the rising of a star or planet at a ritually significant time such as an equinox. They used clay and earth to make these buildings, but imported basalt from the Tuxtla mountains 70km (10 miles) away to line a remarkable series of drains that were connected to fountains and artificial ponds. These were made from skilfully shaped interconnecting pieces of basalt.

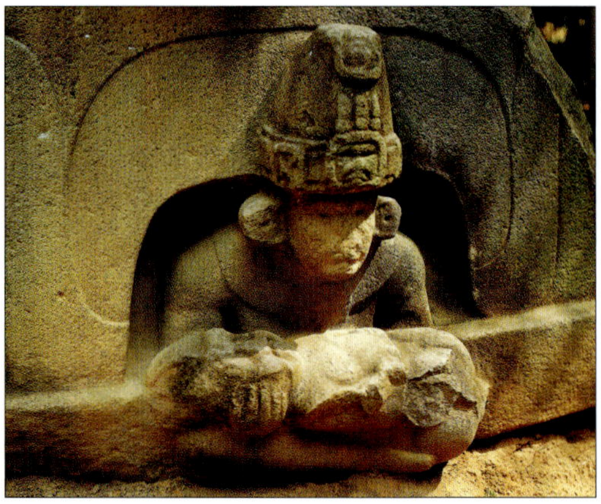

Above: On Altar 5 at La Venta, a king or shaman-priest wearing a jaguar headdress holds a 'were jaguar' baby – an infant with snarling jaguar features.

SACRED FIGUREHEAD

The king may have been worshipped. Eight colossal basalt carved heads erected at San Lorenzo were probably portraits of the settlement's rulers. Some of the heads were more than 3m (10ft) tall and weighed 20 tons. The king's power derived not just from his wealth, but also because he was a sacred figurehead, guarantor of his people's safety and of the

RELIGIOUS PIONEERS IN TWIN OLMEC SETTLEMENTS

Olmec remains at San Lorenzo and La Venta suggest that the inhabitants of these temple towns were pioneers in many facets of Mesoamerican religious life. The Olmec worshipped a feathered serpent deity together with a rain god and revered jaguars and eagles as well as crocodiles and sharks. They also practised the rites of autosacrifice, in which a worshipper expelled his or her own blood: stingray spines and other items – perhaps including shark's teeth – were used to induce blood flow. Generations of Mesoamericans would follow the Olmec lead in these matters.

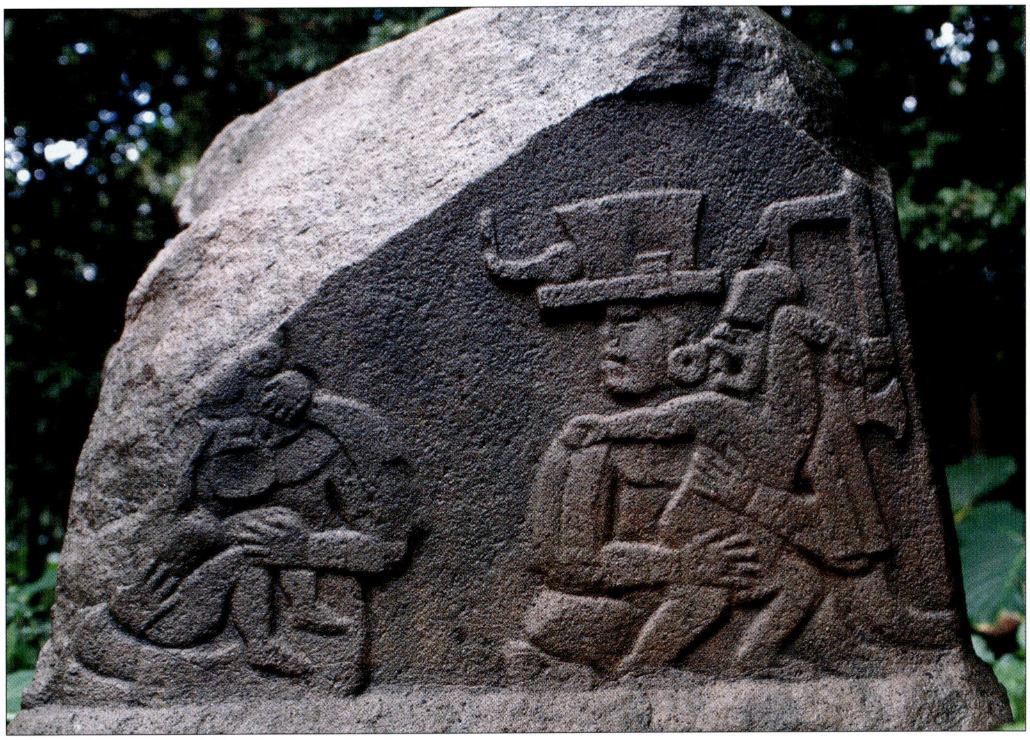

continued fertility of their maize fields. The buildings and monuments of San Lorenzo were erected before 900BC. While the site appears to have been a busy trading settlement after that date, its people did not feel the need to raise further pyramid-mounds or to carve new stone thrones or heads. Some time during the years 900–700BC, axe-wielding men smashed the Olmec heads and thrones of San Lorenzo and buried the remnants in ditches. The violence done to the statues suggests that this was an act of vandalism by invaders, but the careful collection and hiding of the remnants in ditches might indicate that it was a piece of elegiac destruction by Olmec who wanted to set their own age apart from the past.

Pottery remnants from the years after 700BC suggest that at this time San Lorenzo was occupied by people originating in Maya regions of Chiapas and Guatemala. In the years 600–400BC, the inhabitants of the settlement probably built a ball court. Archaeologists have discovered two elongated mounds running in parallel that they believe are the side walls or spectators' stands of a ball court.

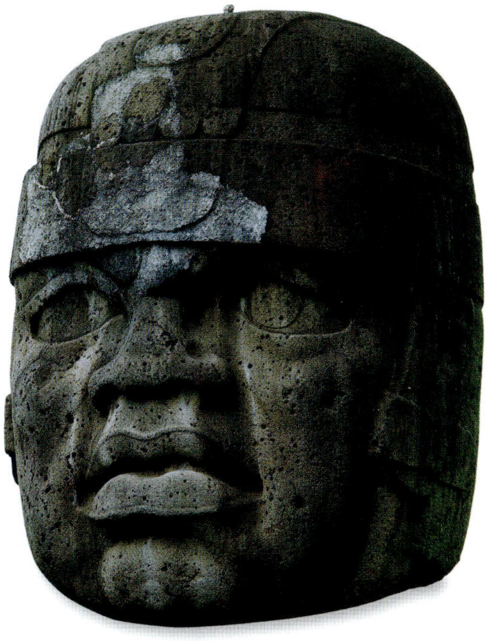

Left: Olmec religious life appears to have centred on worship of the ruler and his ancestors. This colossal basalt head, from La Venta, may represent a departed king.

AMID THE MARSHES: LA VENTA

From *c.*1150BC onwards, Olmec builders constructed another centre at La Venta, about 60km (35 miles) north-east of San Lorenzo and just 12km (7 miles) inland from the Gulf coast. They chose a salt mound amid freshwater marshland, in an area where villagers had already been living for more than a millennium, supporting themselves by fishing, hunting, gathering and growing maize in the fertile soil.

La Venta's builders raised a ceremonial centre of mounds and plazas, aligned like those at San Lorenzo precisely 8 degrees to the west of true north. The tallest of these, called Complex C by archaeologists, is an earthen mound 32m (105ft) high. Some scholars have suggested that it was intended as a recreation of a sacred volcano. Others have likened its shape to that of the pyramid in the Group E complex at the later Maya city of Uaxactún, which may have been structured in four quadrants to celebrate the cardinal points and which was aligned precisely to the sun's rising on sacred equinoctial dates. In front of the mound, running north-west, lay an elongated plaza. Beyond the plaza lay a further sacred arena (named Complex A by archaeologists) containing a court enclosed on two sides by basalt columns, ten further mounds, several platforms and a buried serpentine mosaic pavement measuring 4.5 by 6m (15 by 20ft) and representing the face of a jaguar, beneath which many sacred offerings were laid. Above the pavement, at ground level, lay a sarcophagus of sandstone carved to represent the earth monster in the form of a crocodile floating on water.

Above: The four sides of La Venta Altar 5 are carved with shaman-kings holding 'were jaguar' babies. The 'were jaguar' may have been venerated as an image of the rain god.

Both La Venta and San Lorenzo were relatively small in size. With around 1,000 people resident in each at their peak, the settlements are perhaps better called towns than cities. For many years archaeologists concentrated on the ceremonial role of La Venta and San Lorenzo, but recent work has established that the sites were residential as well as religious centres. At La Venta, living quarters lay to the north-east of the main ceremonial complex. At San Lorenzo the network of drains may have been used functionally by the town's inhabitants, or may have played a role in religious ceremonies celebrating the life-giving power of the waters that fed the maize plants.

CITY OF THE ZAPOTECS: MONTE ALBÁN

An elite group among the Zapotec inhabitants of the highland Valley of Oaxaca founded the settlement of Monte Albán *c.*500BC. It was located in a dominant position on a flattened mountain ridge between two peaks, with good views down all three arms of the valley. In its early years, the settlement consisted of three residential districts and contained up to 7,200 people. The ridge had no agricultural land, and Monte Albán's residents lived on the produce of the three arms of Oaxaca valley: Tlacolula to the east, Etla to the north and Zaachila to the south. Produce was distributed at a market on the flattened ridge. The settlement grew rapidly. Home to 15,000 people by *c.*200BC, Monte Albán had become Mesoamerica's first city.

Major building works had begun about a century earlier, *c.*300BC. An army of labourers flattened the uneven mountaintop and laid out a plaza paved in white stucco.

The Temple of the Danzantes, adorned with carvings of defeated war captives, arose in the south-west corner of the plaza. The city's elite commissioned stone tombs for their burials and builders produced increasingly elaborate masonry graves, some of which were distinguished by corbelled roofs.

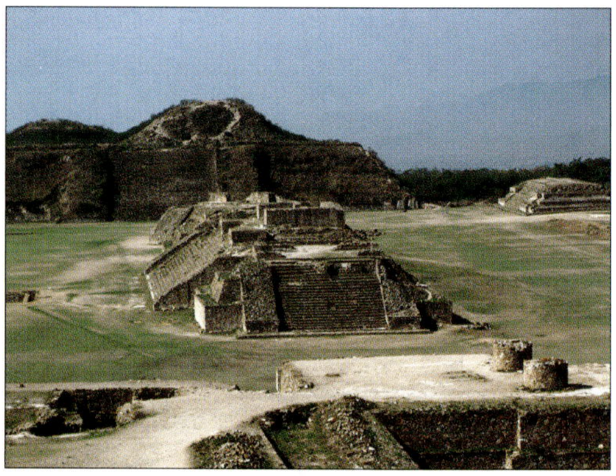

Above: Looking north across the expansive Main Plaza at Monte Albán, Building H looms in the foreground.

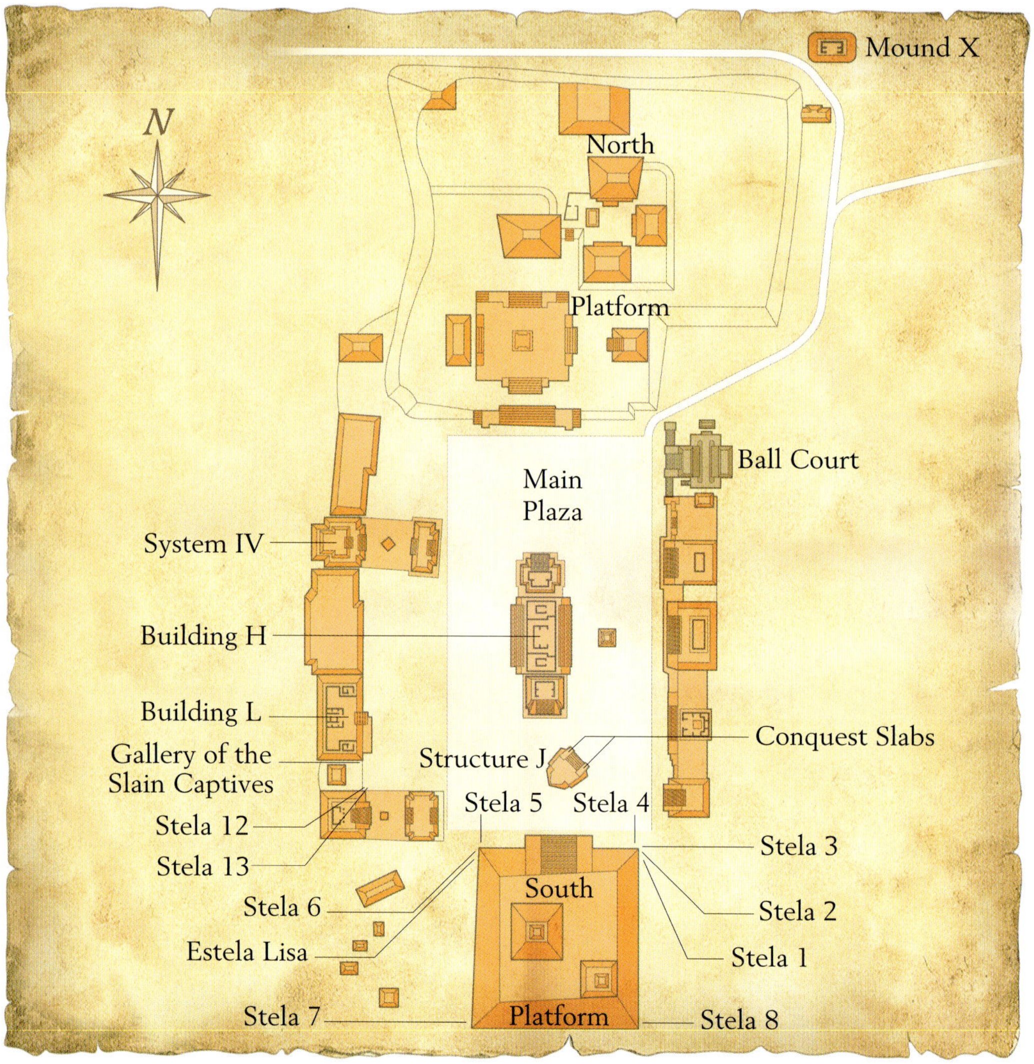

Below: A plan of Monte Albán's Main Plaza. The plaza was laid out and paved in white stucco by Zapotec labourers c.300BC.

A MATURE CITY

Monte Albán was a thriving city for several centuries. In the period AD500–750, its population rose as high as 24,000. The city spread over two adjacent hilltops, covering 6.5km (4 miles), and contained 14 residential areas. Each had its own plaza, while the city's elite rulers and administrators lived in 14 'palaces' arranged around the city's main commercial plaza. In these years, labourers erected a great pyramid 15m (50ft) in height and more than 100m (325ft) in length at the south end of the main plaza. Carved stelae at the four corners appear to commemorate a state visit by emissaries from Teotihuacán, perhaps on the occasion of the building's ceremonial dedication. At the northern end of the plaza, builders constructed a hall with fine colonnades that gave on to a low-level patio backed by tall pyramids.

The city specialized in crafts, making elite produce from obsidian and seashells: The workshops lay to the north-east of the main plaza in an area of noble dwellings. The elite of Monte Albán appear to have valued seclusion and privacy. Noble dwellings were secluded, with central patio areas sometimes accessed by long corridors and through a number of intervening rooms. The main plaza was largely cut off from other parts of the city.

CAPITAL OF THE BALL GAME: EL TAJÍN

The settlement of El Tajín in the Gulf Coast region of northern Veracruz was established in the early Classic Period, when it had trading links with the great metropolis of Teotihuacán. The celebrated remains, which include the Pyramid of the Niches and no fewer than 12 ball courts, date from much later – the 9th–11th centuries AD. These remnants are a small part of the city that once stood here: ruins untouched by archaeologists and so still covered in foliage stretch for 5km (3 miles) into the low hills of the surrounding tropical rainforest.

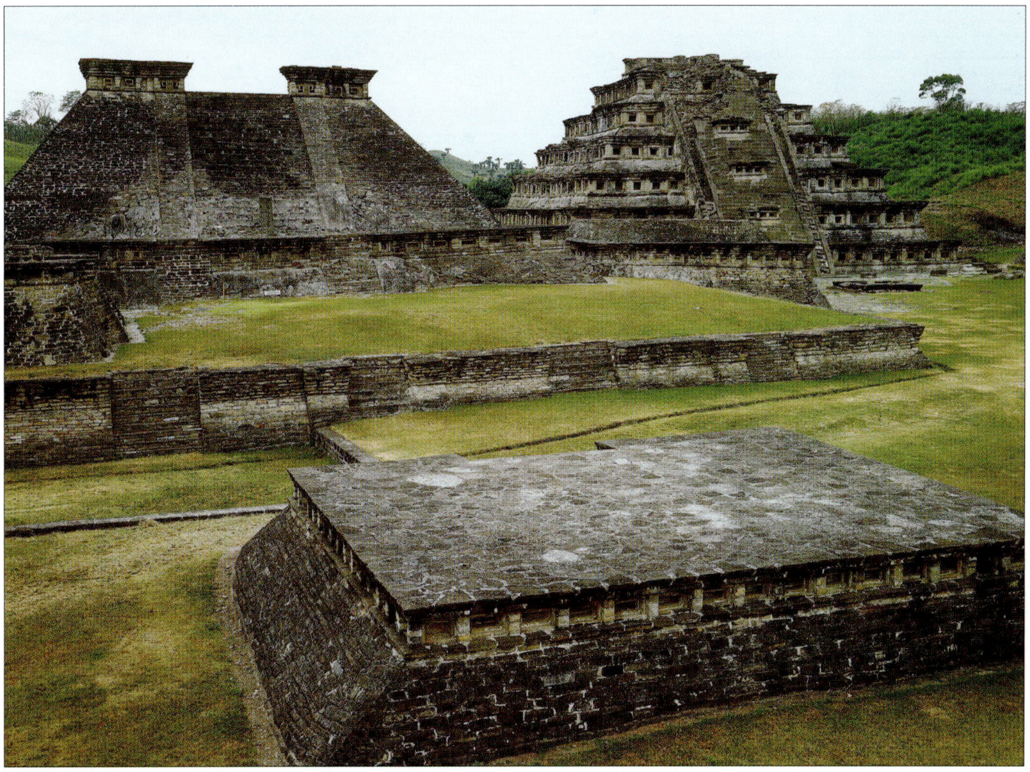

Above: *The buildings of El Tajín were at one time covered with polychrome stucco. The niches of the Pyramid of the Niches were painted red with turquoise borders.*

PYRAMID OF THE NICHES

Builders erected the ceremonial centre that contains the Pyramid of the Niches in the flat southern part of city. The six-tier pyramid supports a temple on its flat top, making seven levels in all, with progressively fewer niches in each level. The bottom tier contains 88 niches, the second has 76, then the levels contain 64, 52, 40 and 28 while the temple has 17 – making a total of 365, one for each day of the solar year. Close by, the builders set out two ball courts. One is decorated with bas-relief carving depicting the sacrificial slaughter of a ball player.

Below: Building 3 stands directly west of the Pyramid of the Niches in central El Tajín. It makes use of niches and Teotihuacáno talud-tablero *architectural elements.*

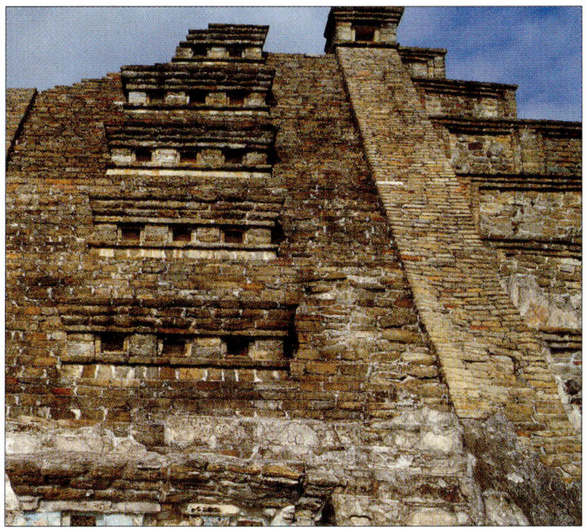

Labourers cut terraces into the small hills to the north of the ceremonial centre and laid out an extensive residential area. They raised elite homes or palaces with colonnades, rooms with corbelled vaults and fine roof combs. They built walls to separate the residential district – known as Tajín Chico – from the ceremonial area to the south and from the king's palace complex to the west.

HOME FIT FOR A KING

Skilled stonemasons cut splendid ornate reliefs in the Building of the Columns, one of the main structures in the royal complex, depicting images of military conquest and sacrificial ritual. The ruler shown most frequently in this area is King 13-Rabbit. Images represent toads as well as sacred serpents and royal jaguars. Glyphs indicate that the people of El Tajín followed the 260-day cycle as well as the calendar of 365 days celebrated in the niches of the main pyramid. The wet season in this part of Mexico hits hard: to prevent flooding and conserve water, builders dug elaborate drains, underground waterways and tanks for storage. The city's 12 ball courts have led scholars to speculate that it might have been a centre for playing the ball game – perhaps a site used for grand enactments of sacred ritual linked to calendrical observations.

CAPITAL OF THE TOTONACS?

El Tajín might have been an early capital of the Totonacs, a people who rose to greater prominence in the Postclassic Period in Veracruz and the northern part of Puebla. In the 16th century, the Totonacs – who by then had their capital at Cempoala, some 150km (90 miles) south of El Tajín – had the distinction of becoming the first Mesoamerican people to join Hernán Cortés in his military action against Tenochtitlán.

THE PLACE OF THE GODS: TEOTIHUACÁN

The great city of Teotihuacán – named 'the place of the gods' by the Aztecs – was laid out from *c.*100BC onwards, on an ancient sacred site in a region of highland Mexico where villagers had been living since *c.*900BC. Builders erected the first buildings in an area now called Oztoyahualco ('Old City'), in the northern part of the valley about 1km (5/8 mile) to the west of the land on which the Pyramid of the Moon was later built. They chose the Old City site, which had little water, because it gave access to a network of sacred caves and tunnels.

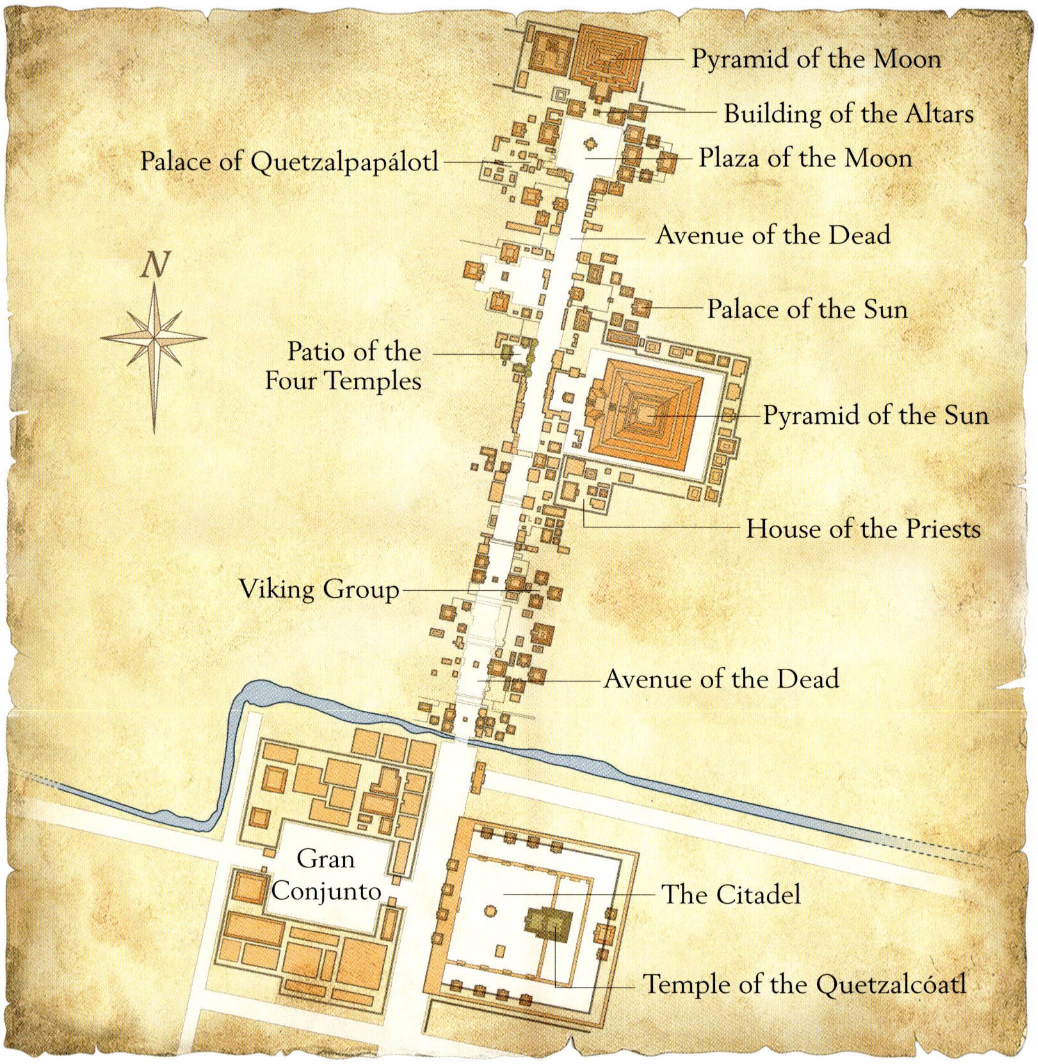

UNDERGROUND RITUAL

In the period AD1–150, the city's builders reverently enlarged a natural cave beneath the ground on which they would later build the Pyramid of the Sun. They created an underground ritual site 100m (325ft) long, with basalt roofing, walls covered with mud plaster and water channelled in for ritual use via a covered drain made of stone. It led into four small chambers. Next they built a small shrine of stone and adobe bricks at ground level.

In the northern, original area of the settlement, the builders laid out a series of small plazas, each enclosed by three temples. Archaeologists report that these sacred constructions were associated with access to caves and suggest that a series of plaza-temple complexes, running roughly south–west, probably followed the line of the ancient subterranean caverns and tunnels. In all there are 20 of these plaza-temple units, which have been left largely untouched by archaeologists. Each might have been the original settlement of 20 tribal or kin groups who possibly united to found the city. In the same period (AD1–150), farmers dug the city's first irrigation system, a network of simple canals excavated to spread the waters of the Barranca de Cerro Colorado among the farmlands at the western perimeters of the expanding settlement.

Below: Looking south from the Plaza of the Moon, the Pyramid of the Sun rises on the east side of the Street of the Dead.

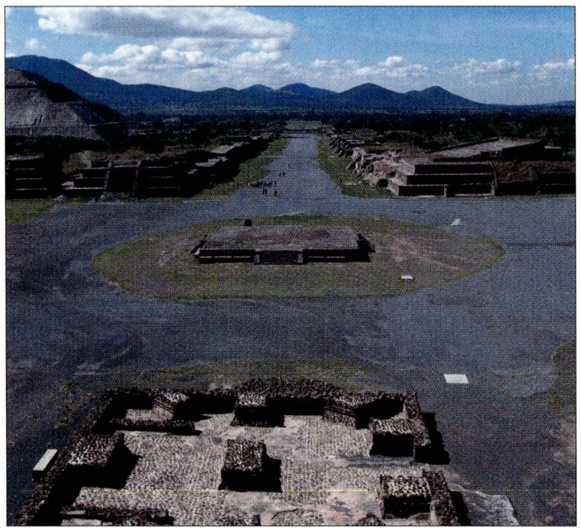

Above: The city's axis, the 2.4km (1.5-mile) Street of the Dead, runs 16 degrees east of true north, linking the Pyramid of the Moon and the Ciudadela complex in the south.

CITY PLANNING

From the start the city was laid out according to a clear design, divided into quadrants by wide thoroughfares running roughly north–south and east–west. The north–south axis was oriented 16 degrees to the east of north to align both with the peak of Cerro Gordo and, according to some scholars, with the point at which the Pleiades set at that time. The Pyramid of the Sun, located on the east side of this north–south line, was the first sacred building erected in Teotihuacán, in the 1st century AD. The original structure was later rebuilt, but archaeologists report that in its first version the pyramid was very nearly as tall as the majestic final building, which rose to a height of 66m (216ft). The original pyramid might have supported twin temples, as did the pyramid built at Cuicuilco, also in the Valley of Mexico, and many later Mesoamerican pyramid/temple-platforms.

The city grew very fast. In AD150 it was home to as many as 80,000 people and covered 20sq km (7sq miles). The population continued to grow – reaching a peak of 100,000–200,000 by AD500 – although the city did not expand far beyond this ground area. Large numbers lived in and farmed outlying rural areas beyond the city limits.

When finished, the north–south thoroughfare was 40m (130ft) wide and 2.4km (1½ miles) long. It was lined on both sides with low-lying buildings identified by archaeologists as elite residences or palaces, but which the Aztecs believed were the tombs of their ancestors – leading them to call it the Street of the Dead. At the northern end of the street lay the Pyramid of the Moon, 43m (140ft) in height. It faced and gave on to an open square known as the Plaza of the Moon. In its south-west corner the elite residential building known as the Palace of Quetzalpapálotl was built in AD500–750. One of Teotihuacán's plaza-temple groups, the Plaza of the Columns, lay to the west of the Street of the Dead, a little to the north and on the opposite side to the imposing Pyramid of the Sun. Both the Sun and Moon pyramids were flanked by smaller pyramids and gave on to plazas, which might also have been intended to form plaza-temple groups of the kind typical of Teotihuacán.

Heading south, the street is flanked by palace buildings and sacred structures and gives access via side streets to areas of residential apartment buildings. An extensive collection of apartments, temples, plazas and platforms on both sides of the street is known as the Street of the Dead Complex. These were magnificent buildings, constructed of the finest materials and provided with mica floors.

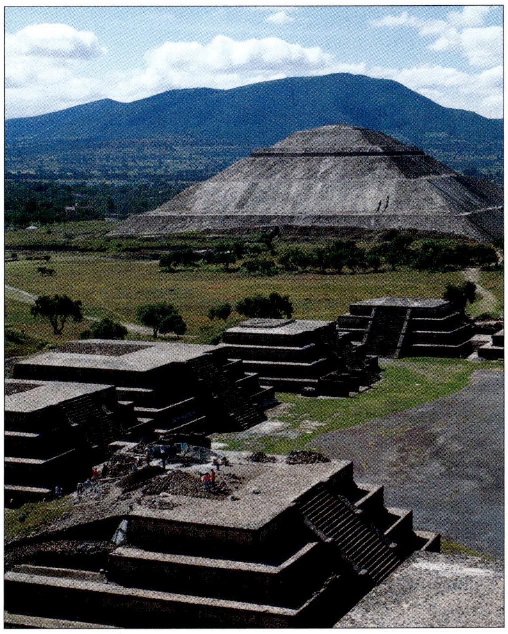

Below: The small stepped pyramids flanking the Plaza of the Moon are dwarfed by the 66m (216ft)-tall Pyramid of the Sun.

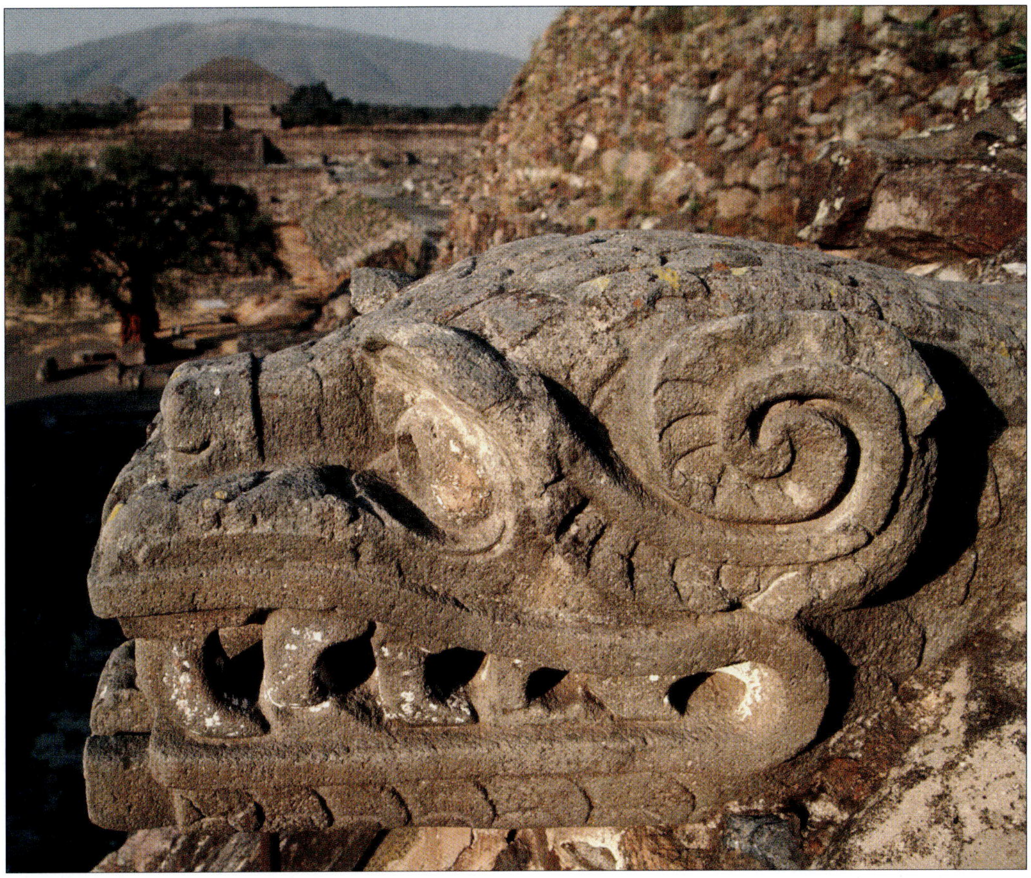

Above: At the southern edge of the city centre, a serpent's head honours the Feathered Serpent Quetzalcóatl on the god's temple in the Ciudadela complex.

IN THE CITADEL

Further south, the Street of the Dead gave to the east on to the city centre, the Ciudadela, a vast, enclosed square structure of platforms, roughly 400m (1,300ft) square and incorporating 15 pyramids, two palaces, an 11-acre (4.4-hectare) plaza and the magnificent stepped pyramid-platform Temple of Quetzalcóatl. Opposite the Ciudadela, on the west side of the Street of the Dead, was another vast enclosed area called the Great Compound that was probably the city's main marketplace. Its northern and southern edges consisted of long platforms supporting apartment buildings thought to have been the homes of the city's administrators and bureaucrats. The large western avenue led directly out of the compound heading west, while the eastern avenue began at the eastern edge of the Ciudadela, behind the Pyramid of Quetzalcóatl. The Street of the Dead continued southwards beyond the Ciudadela and the Great Compound for 3km (2 miles).

TOWERING MONUMENTS: TIKAL

In the dense jungle of the Petén region, Tikal began to expand from a village c.500–300BC. By 300AD it was a major city, celebrating in stone the achievements of a great dynasty of kings. At its greatest extent in the 8th century AD, the city – with extensive environs covering about 16sq km (6sq miles) – was home to a population of 60,000.

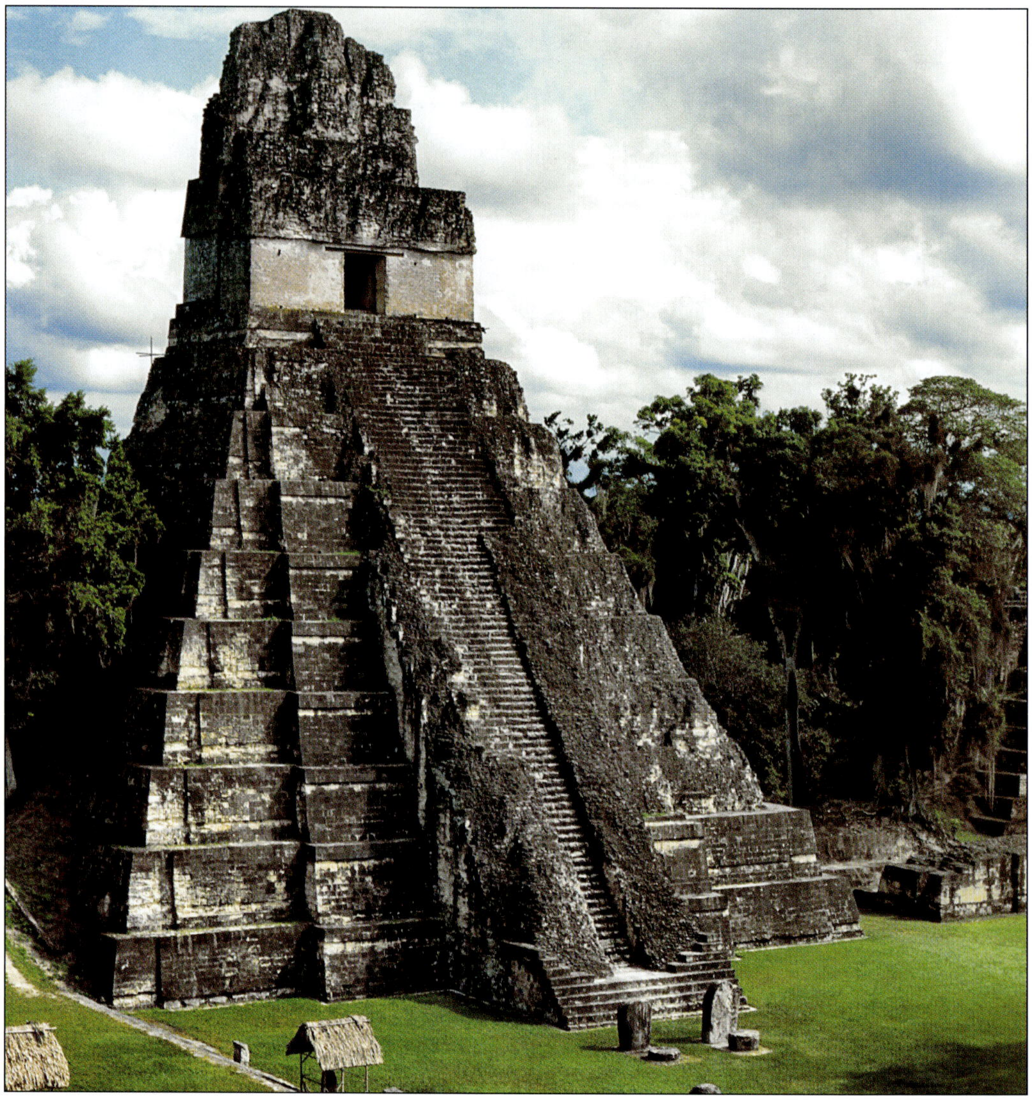

Above: The stairs leading to the summit of Temple I rise at an angle of more than 70°.

CYCLICAL REBUILDING

The building of Tikal was a massive feat of construction. The main temples, tombs, ceremonial buildings and elite residences covered 2.5sq km (1sq mile). Moreover, most of the city's main buildings were refashioned and reconstructed many times. By Mesoamerican tradition, new structures were erected directly above and encompassing their predecessors. In Tikal, the building of the North Acropolis, a collection of pyramid temple-tombs, began as early as 250BC. Over the centuries the Acropolis floor was re-laid 20 times, so that the final layer was a full 10m (33ft) higher than the first. Scholars believe that the city must have supported a full-time force of stonemasons, sculptors, painters and labourers to carry out this cyclical building and rebuilding.

The centre of the ceremonial complex was the Great Plaza. To its north lay the North Acropolis, burial ground of kings. Many times rebuilt, it consisted in its final form of a large rectangular platform, 100m by 80m (325ft by 260ft), supporting eight royal temple-tombs built c.AD250–550. Subsequently, four further temples were built on a second platform along the southern extremity of the North Acropolis, giving via stairways on to the Great Plaza.

TWIN MORTUARY MONUMENTS

Facing one another on the eastern and western sides of the Great Plaza rose Temple I and Temple II. Temple I, which climbs in nine terraces to a height of 50m (164ft) on the eastern side, was built as the funerary temple of King Ah Cacau (AD682–734). He was the first member of Tikal's dynasty to be buried outside the North Acropolis. Temple II, rising in three levels to a height of 42m (138ft), supports a sacred building that might have been set up to honour Ah Cacau's queen: the remains of a wooden lintel from this temple bear a portrait of a royal woman.

To the west and east of the Great Plaza lay other plazas. Behind Temple I lay the East Plaza, containing a ball court and a rectangular collection of buildings thought to have been used as a market. From the East Plaza, a *sacbé* known to archaeologists as the Mendez Causeway led south-east past a collection of palaces now called Group G for 0.5 km (0.3 miles) to Temple VI. This temple is also known as the Temple of the Inscriptions because stonemasons carved a record of Tikal's dynastic history on the rear and sides of the roof comb that rose above its summit temple. Labourers built Temple VI during or just after the reign of Ah Cacau's son, Yax Kin (AD734–46). A stela celebrating Yax Kin's accession was erected at the foot of the great pyramid. South of the East Plaza was the Central

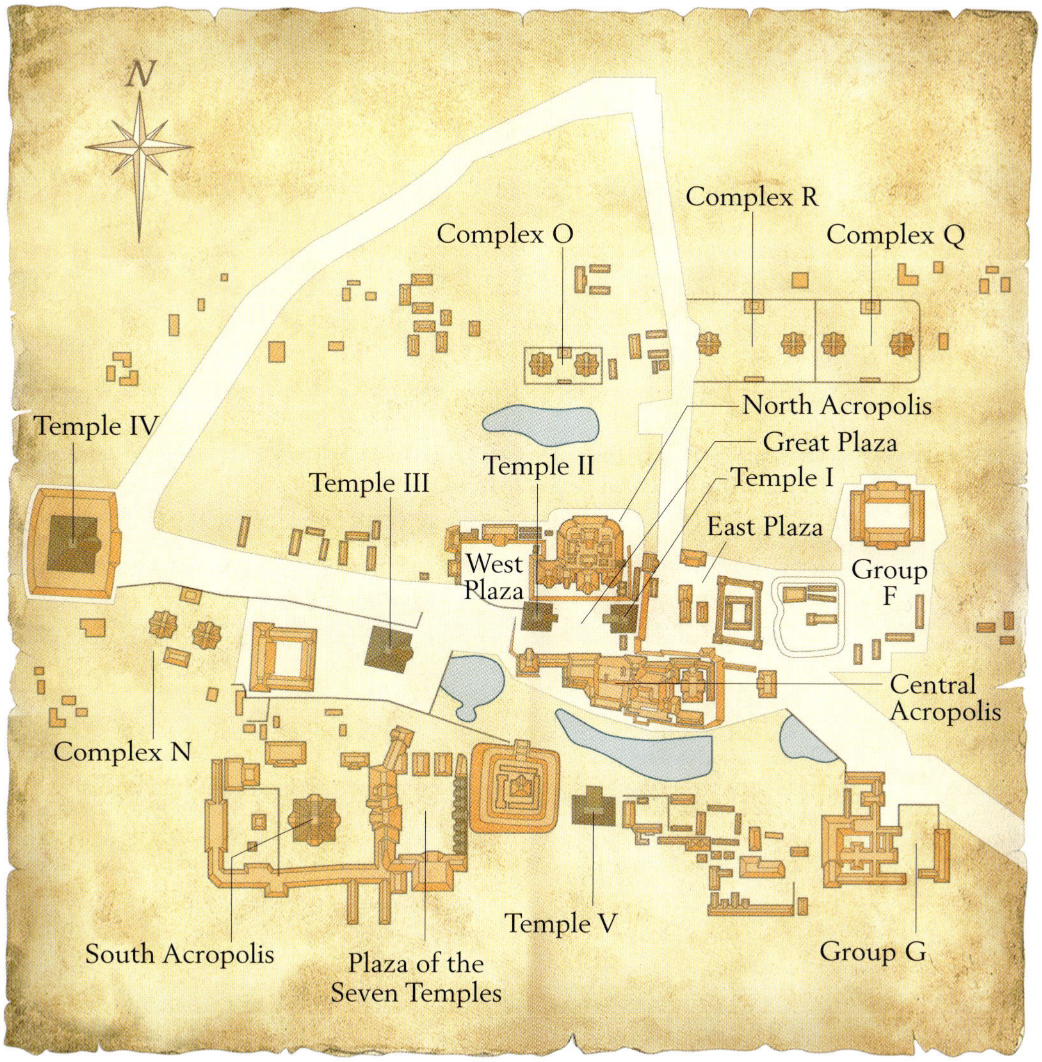

Above: Four sacbeob *(causeways) link groups of sacred buildings in central Tikal.*

Acropolis, a vast palace containing buildings arranged around courtyards. This was probably the official residence of Tikal's ruling dynasty. Farther south beyond one of the city's many reservoirs rose Temple V, Tikal's second tallest structure at 57m (185ft), the temple-tomb of an as yet unidentified ruler. This southernmost region of the ceremonial centre also included another area of royal tombs, the South Acropolis, and the Plaza of the Seven Temples, which in addition to seven temple-shrines gave on to numerous palaces to south and west. It contained a triple ball court, with three pitches, which is unique in Mesoamerica. Beyond this plaza to the west, labourers built the Lost World complex, which contained a platform on its western edge and three platforms on its eastern side aligned with equinoctial sunrises – like the Group E arrangement of pyramids in the Maya city of Uaxactún.

Behind Temple II, a *sacbé* now known as the Tozzer Causeway led westwards to Temple IV, 70m (230ft) high and the tallest building in Tikal. This structure was built for King Yax Kin (AD734–746). Two surviving wooden lintels above the doorway to the temple-shrine on the summit of the artificial mountain record the date 9.15.10.0.0. in the Maya Long Count (AD741). A *sacbé* now called the Maudslay Causeway ran north to a collection of twin pyramid groups.

Below: This view of the North Acropolis is from the heights of Temple I.

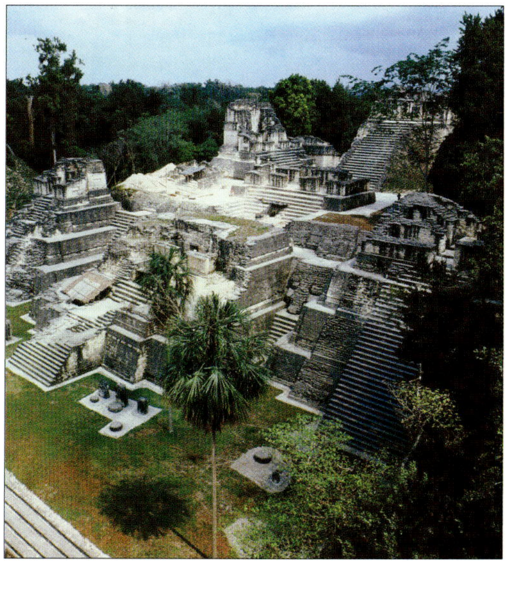

Temple III, which lay to the south of the Tozzer Causeway, was the last pyramid temple erected at Tikal. It was probably the mortuary shrine of King Chitam (AD768–794). A stela erected at its base was carved with the date 9.19.0.0.0. (AD810). Only one later dated monument was raised at Tikal, a stela of 10.2.0.0.0. (AD869) in the Great Plaza. By the end of the 9th century the city had been abandoned to the encroaching vegetation and to groups of squatters.

TWIN PYRAMID GROUPS

At Tikal, several rulers erected twin pyramid groups to mark the close of a *katun* or period of twenty 360-day years (a total of 7,200 days). The groups consisted of two pyramids, each with a flat top and four access stairways, symmetrically arranged on the west and east edges of a plaza, with an enclosure containing an altar and a stela on the plaza's northern edge and a building with nine doorways on its southern edge. These groups have been found only at Tikal, save examples at Yaxha and Ixlu. The first at Tikal was erected in the early years of the 6th century AD in the East Plaza and reused several times. In the late 7th century AD, King Ah Cacau (AD682–734) erected a twin pyramid group to celebrate the end of the first *katun* following his accession. Its altar was marked with the date 9.13.0.0.0. (18 March AD692). From this occasion until AD790, a new group was erected for each *katun*-ending. The largest (known as Twin-Pyramid Group 4E-4) was built in AD771 by King Chitam.

PACAL'S GLORY: PALENQUE

The city of Palenque at the northern edge of the Chiapas highlands in Mexico, site of the ornate 7th-century tomb of King Pacal that is one of the glories of Mesoamerica, was distinctly different from Tikal and other great Maya cities of the Classic Period.

It contained no forests of carved stelae, no wide ceremonial plazas, no great *sacbé* or causeways, no acropolis of royal tombs. Its buildings were adorned with stucco sculpture and carved reliefs that pioneered naturalistic portraiture of royal figures. It gave pride of place at the centre of the city to the royal palace, home of the living king, rather than – as at Tikal – to temple-tombs housing the remains of divine ancestors.

Palenque appears to have risen to a position of power in the reign of King Pacal (*r.* AD615–83). Most of the surviving parts of the city date from his reign or later and the oldest surviving use of the city's emblem glyph was cut during his time.

PACAL'S PIONEERS

Pacal began a major programme of building in AD647, raising the temple Olvidado ('Unnoticed Shrine'), around half a kilometre to the south of the palace in the city centre. His architect-builders pioneered the use of the thin walls and numerous wide doorways that would become a distinctive feature of Palenque architecture. The temple, standing on an escarpment and reached by four stretches of stairs linked by platforms, had three doorways giving on to two inner rooms. Inscriptions on the north façade, carved within round cartouches, identified the king as the son of his father, Kan-Bahlum Mo', and of his mother, Lady Zac-Kuk.

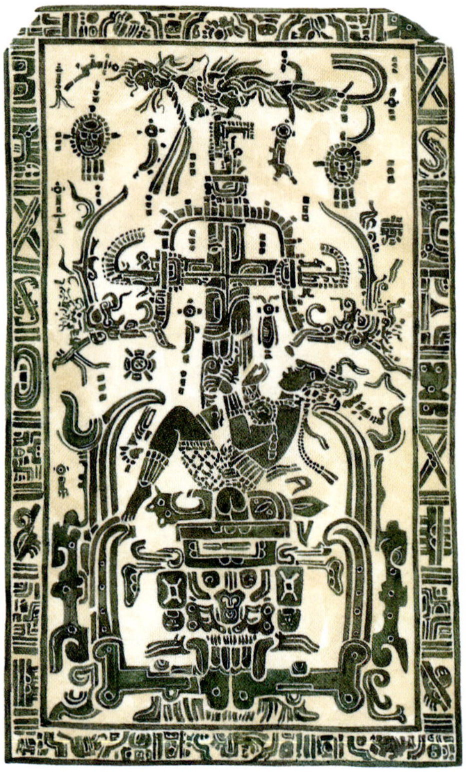

Above: The lid of Pacal's sarcophagus shows the king falling down the cross-shaped Tree of Life into the underworld.

THE KING'S PALACE

Pacal proceeded to develop the palace complex. On the large palace platform originally constructed by his predecessors, he built the royal residences identified as Houses E, C, B and A and laid out the expansive East Court. He commissioned sculptors to decorate the palace walls with stucco portrait masks, hieroglyphs, supernatural symbols and sacred scenes. To the south he began work

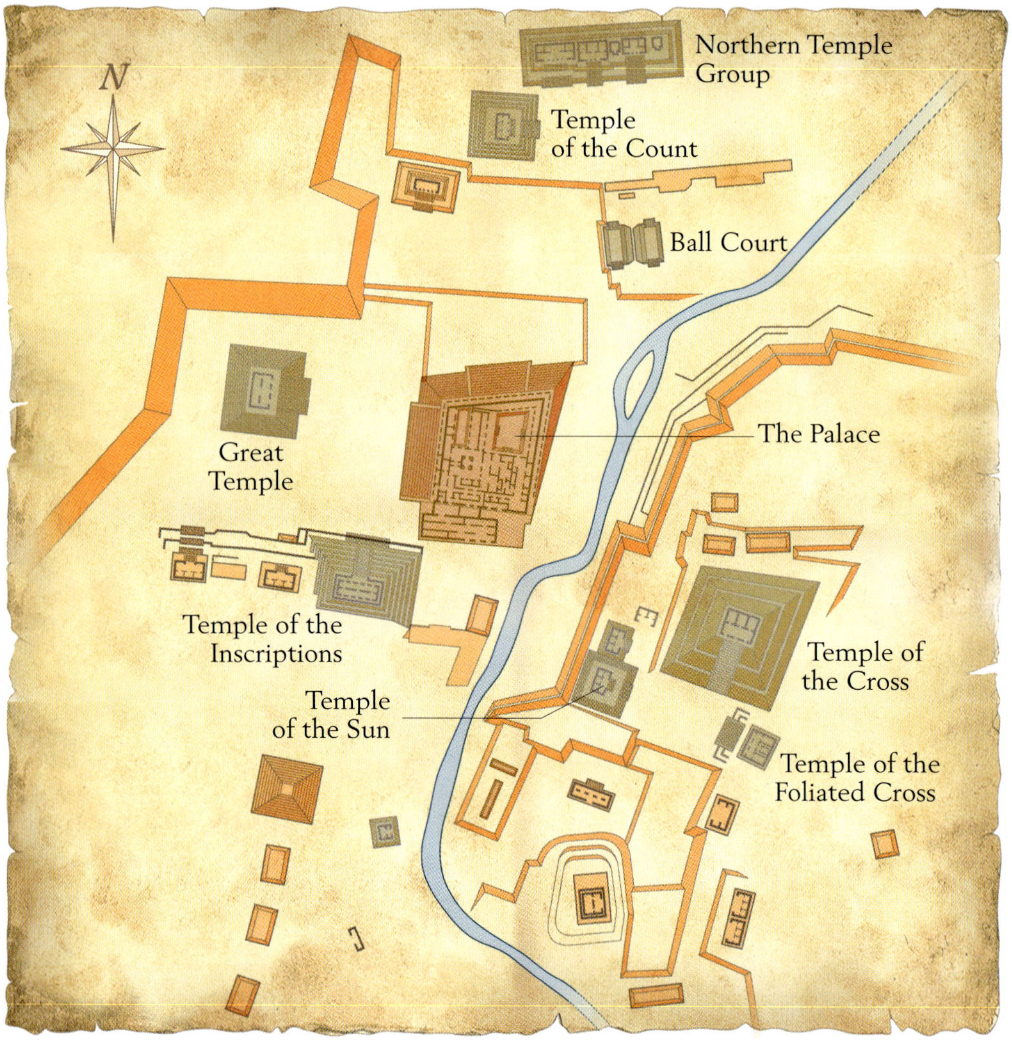

Left: In the eastern part of the city centre, the temples of the Cross, the Foliated Cross and the Sun celebrated Pacal's dynasty.

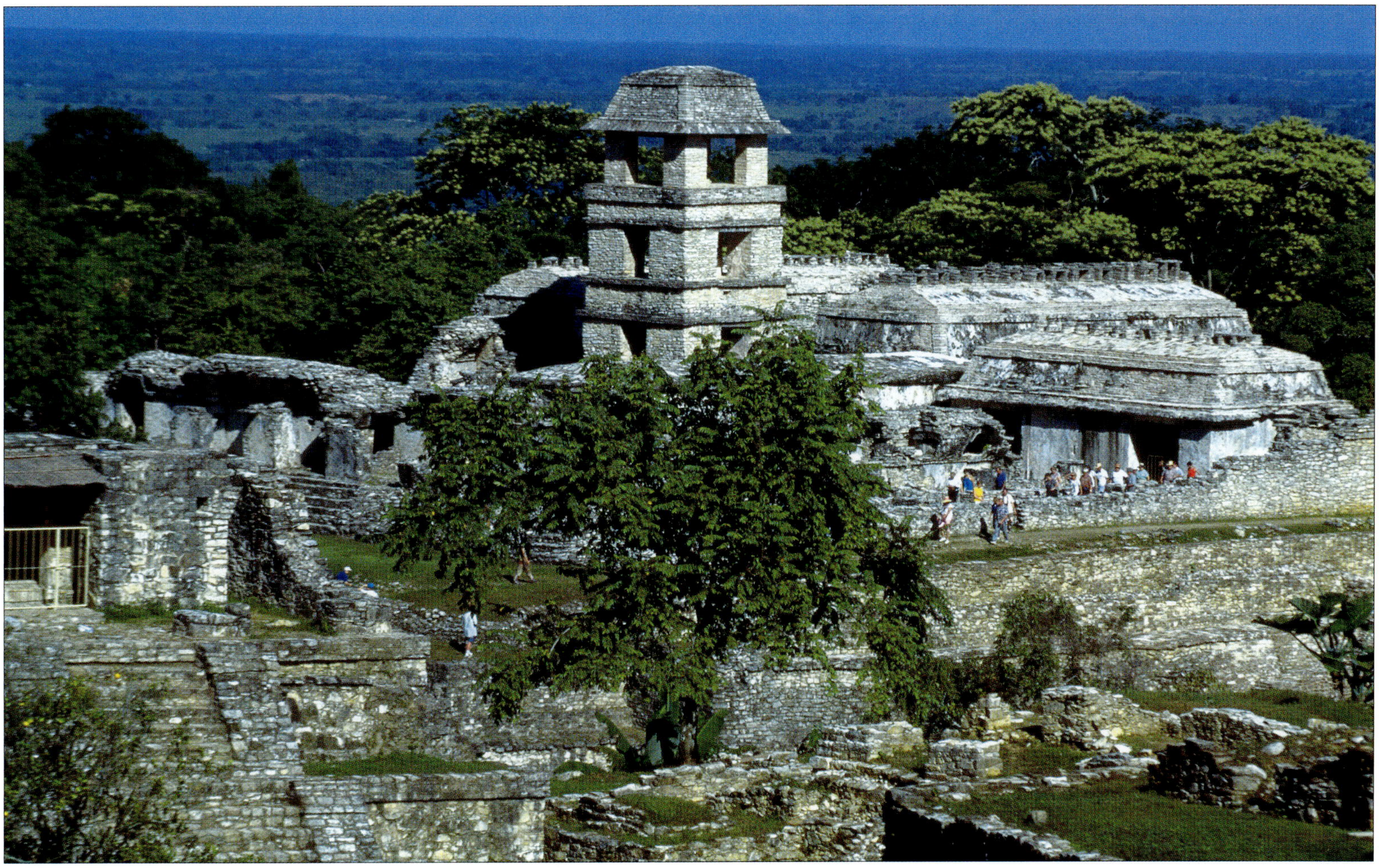

Above: The Palace tower at Palenque commands wide-ranging views of the green Chiapas countryside.

on the great Temple of the Inscriptions, beneath which his tomb was prepared, ready for his eventual death in AD683.

Pacal's son Chan-Bahlum (*r.* AD684–702) completed the Temple of the Inscriptions, which rose to a height of 25m (82ft) and was topped with a temple containing five wide doorways and a roof comb. The portions of the temple facing the court were decorated with painted stucco reliefs that depicted the new king receiving his divine sanction to rule from great Pacal.

POWER OF THE ROYAL LINE

Next, Chan-Bahlum erected three shrines – the Temple of the Cross, the Temple of the Foliated Cross and the Temple of the Sun – facing one another across a plaza in the eastern part of the city centre. They each represented one of the three levels of the Maya universe. The Temple of the Cross, situated in the north, was linked to the heavens; the Temple of the Foliated Cross, in the easterly direction of the rising sun, was associated with the earth; and the Temple of the Sun, in the westerly direction of the setting sun, was identified with the underworld. They contained carvings celebrating Chan-Bahlum's links to his divine father.

A panel in the Temple of the Cross showed Pacal and Chan-Bahlum on either side of the ceiba world tree that the Maya believed connected the three levels of the universe. The carving in the Temple of the Foliated Cross depicted the pair on either side of a giant cob of maize bearing human heads, a reference to the Maya creation myth in which the gods Huracán and Gucumatz made the first humans from maize. The image in the Temple of the Sun presented Chan-Bahlum and his father adopting a martial pose, one to each side of a battle shield adorned with spears and the jaguar god of the underworld.

Archaeologists have not found Chan-Bahlum's tomb, but many believe it may lie beneath the Temple of Cross since this was the northern member of the group and burials were generally laid in the direction of the north.

Chan-Bahlum II's brother, Kan-Xul II, rebuilt the palace complex and may have erected the curious four-storey tower that was probably an astronomical observatory. This structure has no counterpart anywhere else in the Maya realm. Scholar Linda Schele has suggested that the tower was built as a tribute to King Pacal. An observer standing at the top of the tower at the winter solstice would see the sun set directly on to the Temple of the Inscriptions, thus going down into the underworld by way of Pacal's tomb.

With Kan-Xul II's reign the great building work of Palenque came to a close: the king was captured in AD711 by the rival city of Toniná and, after a long captivity, was beheaded there. Before the century was out, Palenque became one of the first Maya cities to cease cutting dates in inscriptions and so enter the historical silence of the celebrated collapse of the 8th and 9th centuries. The last inscribed date at Palenque was AD799.

CITY OF THE JAGUAR KINGS: YAXCHILÁN

Yaxchilán was built on a hill overlooking a bend in the Usumacinta river in Chiapas, Mexico. The city's origins lie in the 4th century AD, when it may have been founded as a satellite of Tikal, but it was developed primarily by two kings of the 8th century: Lord Shield Jaguar (*r.* AD681–742) and his son Bird Jaguar (*r.* AD752–68). From the date of its investigation by Sir Alfred Maudslay, the British gentleman-scholar hailed as the 'father of Maya archaeology', Yaxchilán has been celebrated for its magnificently carved door lintels, some of which have been on display in the British Museum in London since Maudslay had them shipped to Europe in 1882.

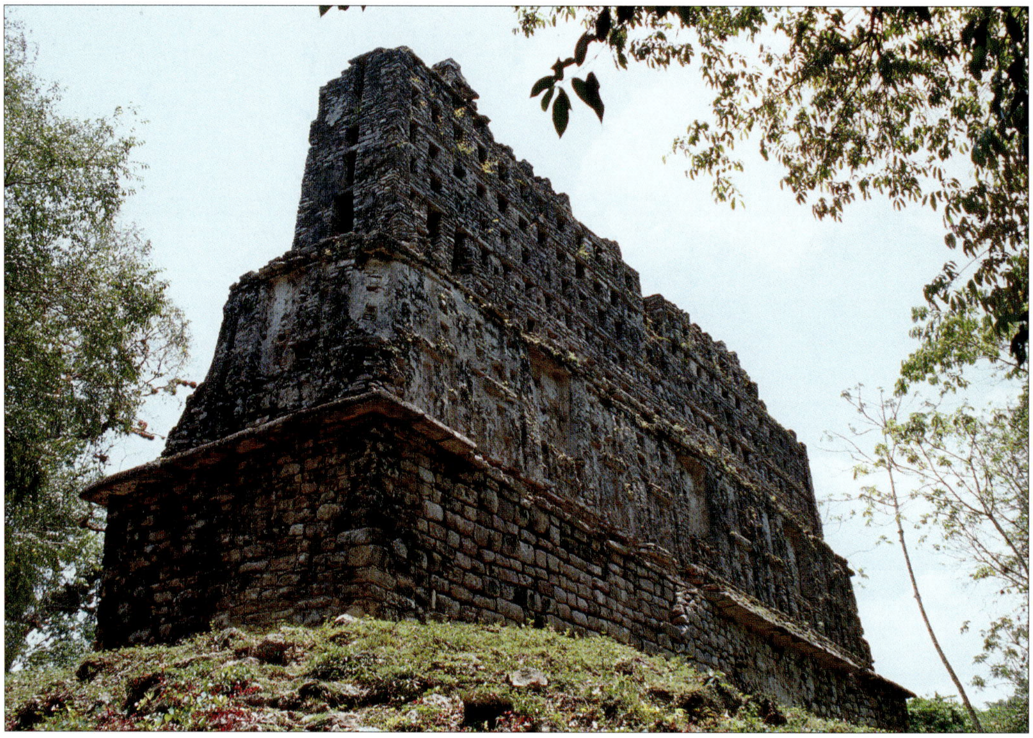

Above: Stucco sculptures once decorated the roof of Temple 33. Standing on high ground, the vast temple dominates the city centre.

TOMB FOR A QUEEN

The city's main ceremonial area lies on an artificial terrace above the Usumacinta. The large plaza runs parallel to the river. On its south side, Lord Shield Jaguar built a structure known to archaeologists as Temple 23, or the Queen's House, that was dedicated to his principal wife, Lady Xoc, in 9.14.14.13.17 (726AD), the 45th year of his 61-year reign. This building contains celebrated door-lintel carvings of Lady Xoc performing rites of ritual bloodletting by running a spiked cord across her tongue; of Lady Xoc having a sacred experience through the Vision Snake of King Yat Balam, founder of the dynasty; and of Shield Jaguar, accompanied by his wife, donning battle garb as he prepared to set out in search of sacrificial captives. Temple 24, erected on the western edge of the Queen's House, recorded her death in AD749 and almost certainly contains her grave.

Below: A detail shows the stone lintels of Yaxchilán's palaces. The remains of a stone throne lie before the building.

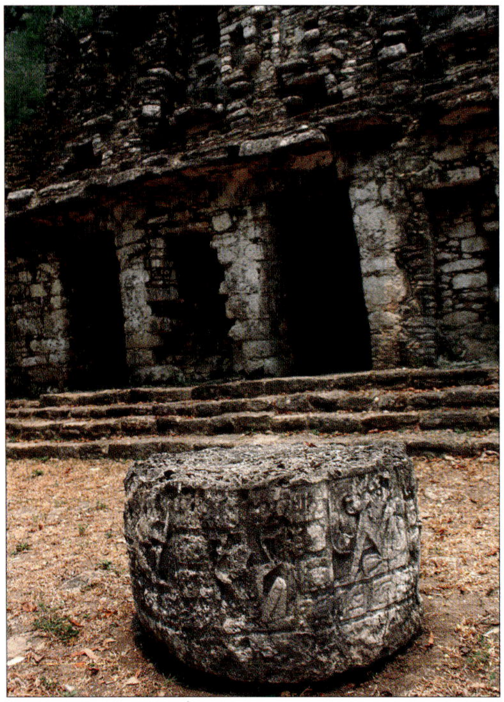

Earlier, in AD732, the king dedicated Temple 44, also known as the War Memorial as it commemorated a series of noble captives taken by Lord Shield Jaguar. Among other sacred structures erected by Shield Jaguar was Temple 41, at the summit of the hill that rises behind the ceremonial terrace. This structure commemorated celebrations of a sacred solstice in 9.15.9.17.16 (AD741).

STRUGGLE TO SUCCEED

Lord Shield Jaguar was succeeded by his son Bird Jaguar. The succession was not without its difficulties. Bird Jaguar was not the king's son by his principal wife, Lady Xoc, but by another royal bride, Lady Evening Star, who is thought by scholars to have come originally from Calakmul. Whether because the succession was contested by a son of Lady Xoc, or because Bird Jaguar's connection to the royal line of Calakmul made him unpopular, there was a gap of ten years between the death of Lord Shield Jaguar in AD742 and the coronation of Bird Jaguar in AD752. Afterwards these difficulties contributed greatly to construction in Yaxchilan's ceremonial quarter: Bird Jaguar erected many buildings and stelae promoting his right to the throne and, once his position was secure, poured his construction efforts into securing the succession of his son Chel Te.

In the course of these projects, Bird Jaguar III rebuilt most of the ceremonial centre and also extended the city to the south-east. Before his time the main plaza was crossed by gullies, but he had the area flattened and smoothed. In a reign of 16 years, he built 12 sacred buildings and raised 33 monuments. Much of the work complemented that of his father. He built a new hilltop structure, Temple 40, alongside Shield Jaguar's Temple 41 and in front raised a carved stela that celebrated both his father and mother and made reference to the solstice celebration of AD741 in which, as a prince, Bird Jaguar had shared duties with his father. Alongside Temple 23, which his father had built to honour Lady Xoc, Bird Jaguar erected Temple 21, which was adorned with lintels representing Bird Jaguar and his wife enacting the same scenes celebrated in the lintels of the earlier temple. One showed Bird Jaguar watching a wife letting blood from a tongue, another showed a wife encountering the Vision Serpent and a third showed Bird Jaguar in his military glory.

Below: Bird Jaguar wears an elaborate costume and headdress and holds the manikin *sceptre, symbol of royal authority.*

LINTEL RECORDS

Behind Temple 23, Bird Jaguar built another sacred building, known as Temple 33, where the steps were carved with scenes of rituals involving the ball game: one showed Bird Jaguar enacting a sacrifice with noble victims bound in the form of balls from the ball game. On the lintel above the temple doorway, Bird Jaguar rose in his full glory at his accession, dressed in the costume of a Maya king and holding the *manikin* sceptre. Other lintels at the temple depict Bird Jaguar and his son performing a ritual and Bird Jaguar again in the company of a leading noble. Many of the nobles of Bird Jaguar's reign are represented in door-lintel carvings and on stelae: scholars suggest that the king may have needed support in order to consolidate his position and so was forced to share status with these lords by including them in the historical record.

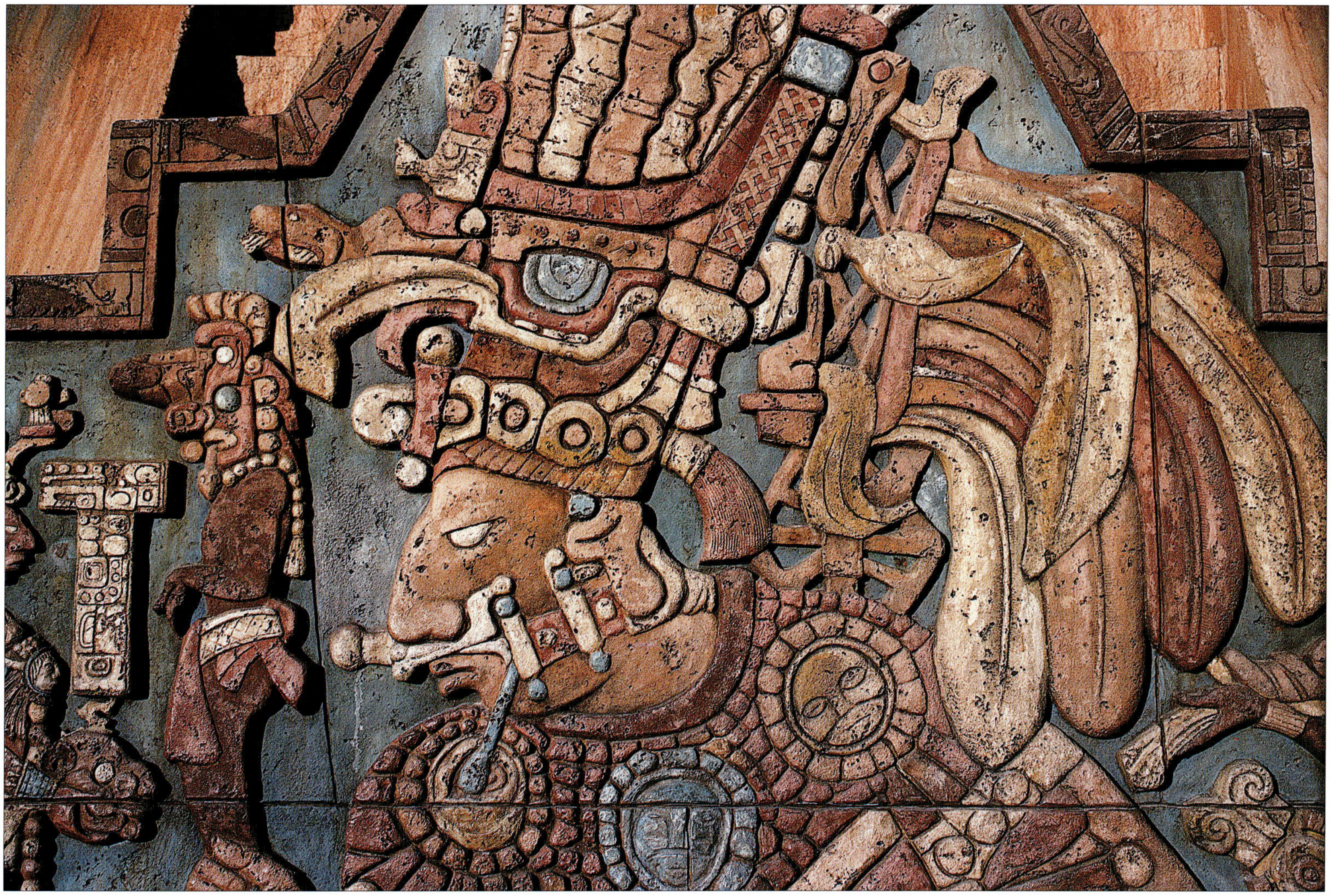

THE ELEGANT CITY:
COPÁN

The great Maya city of Copán in western Honduras – celebrated in particular for the ornate, almost florid style of its sculpture – lay at an altitude of 700m (2,296ft) in a river valley surrounded by mountains. This attractive, well-watered, fertile spot alongside the river Copán was the site of villages from at least 1000BC.

FIRST STAGES OF THE ACROPOLIS

The city developed and rose to prominence in the 5th–8th centuries AD, when it became capital of the most powerful state in the south-eastern Maya region.

Below: The city's extensive ceremonial centre was laid out on a north–south axis on the west bank of the River Copán.

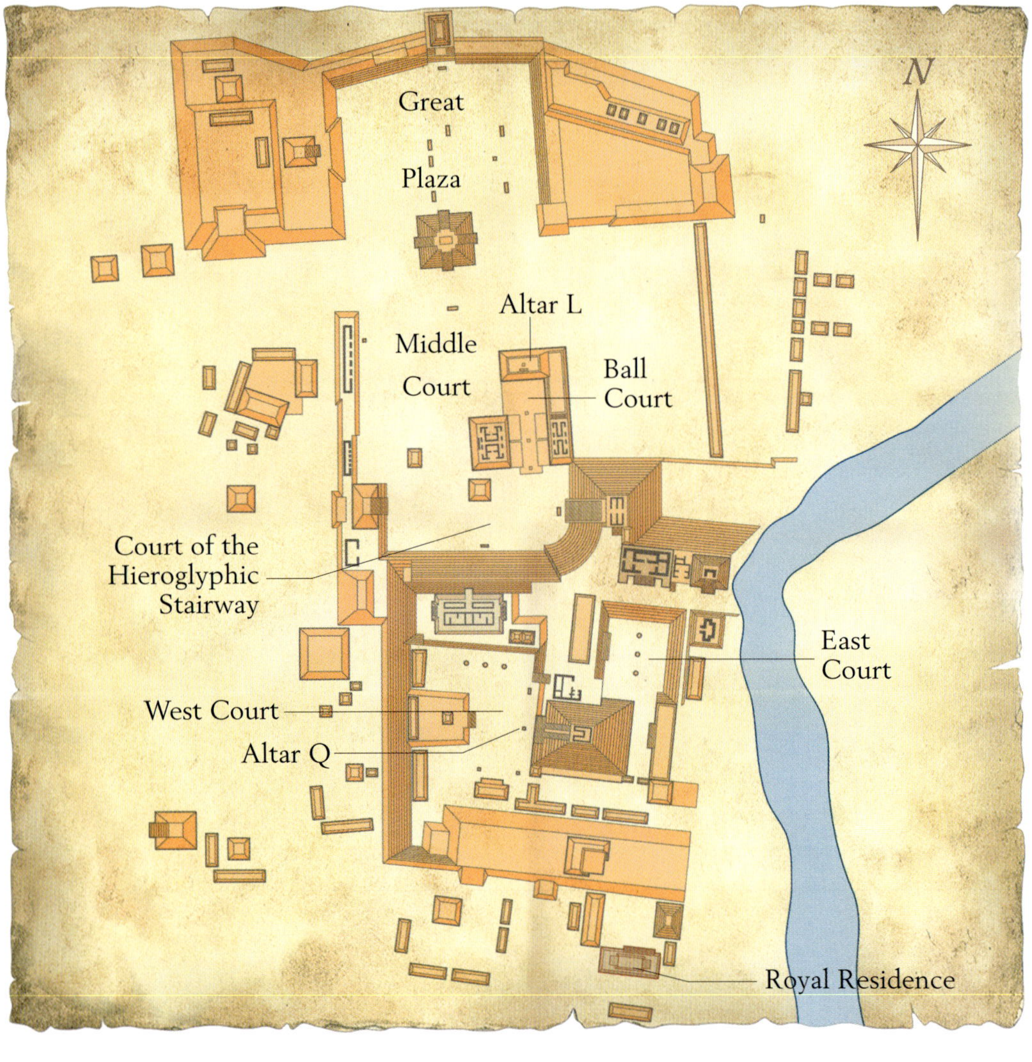

The ceremonial and sacred centre of the site measured some 300m by 600m (984 by 1,968ft). In the southern half was a raised platform known to archaeologists as the Acropolis, built up over generations and incorporating two great courts and a number of temples. In the northern part lay a ball court, a celebrated stairway carved with hieroglyphs detailing dynastic history and the vast Great Plaza, site of numerous stelae and carved 'altars' or thrones. *Sacbé* or causeways left the great plaza running north–east and west: to the north-east lay an elite residential area known to archaeologists as Las Sepulturas.

Copán's kings in the 8th century claimed to be part of an unbroken dynastic succession of 18 monarchs running back to the founder they identified as Yax Kuk Mo' (*c.*AD426–37). In his reign, the buildings of the Acropolis structure – first laid out before AD400 – were added to and expanded.

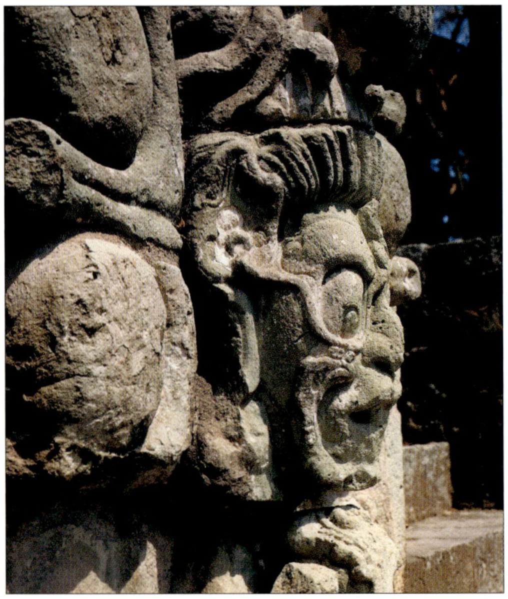

Above: A decorative mask, perhaps of the sun god, adorns the Stairway of the Jaguars (AD200–900) in the East Court.

SHRINE TO THE CITY'S FOUNDER

One of the Acropolis buildings, subsequently built over and called the Papagayo, appears to have been a shrine to Yax Kuk Mo': it contained a stela that identified the dynasty's second king as the son of the founder and recalled rites performed by Yax Kuk Mo' on an auspicious date in 9.0.0.0.0. (AD435). Contemporary with the Papagayo structure, the first of several version of the Copán ball court was laid out to the north of the Acropolis.

The Acropolis was established at its final size by as early as *c.*AD450–500. At this time, a higher platform occupied the south-eastern quarter of the Acropolis, while the northern part consisted of a lower area of elite residential and administrative buildings arranged around three adjacent courtyards.

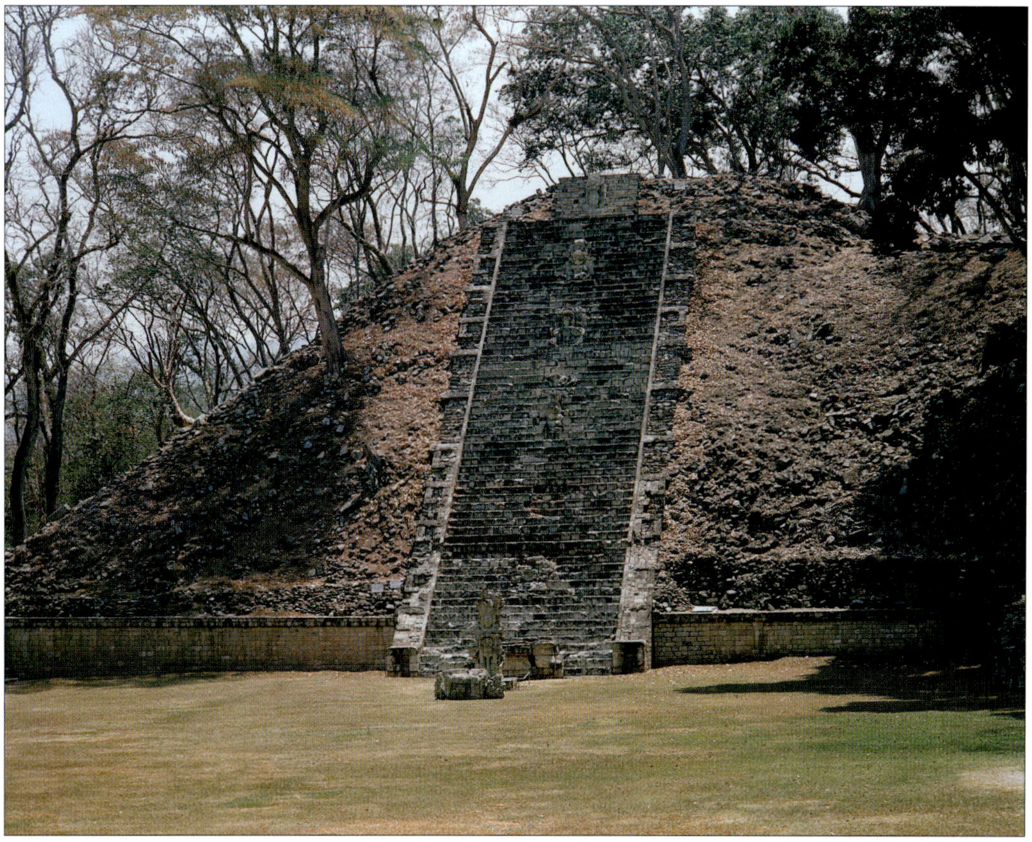

The seventh king of the dynasty, Waterlily Jaguar, may have built a two-level platform that arose in the mid-6th century AD at the eastern edge of the Acropolis's East Court. Hieroglyphs on one of its stairs named the king and reported that he built a palace, called the House of Mah Kina Yax Kuk Mo, on the southern edge of the Great Plaza.

Also around this period, builders on the Acropolis raised a two-storey temple with many rooms known to scholars as Rosalila. Its façade was covered with brightly painted stucco carving of birds and the god Itzamná.

Almost the whole of the 8th century AD was taken up with the reigns of two kings, Butz' Chan (AD578–628) and Smoke Jaguar (AD628–95). In their reigns, Copán developed into a powerful city state with wide influence.

Smoke Jaguar may have begun the final restructuring of the Acropolis. To celebrate the calendar period-ending of AD652, he erected a series of stelae at both the eastern and western limits to the valley of Copán. These may have been intended to mark the limits of his territories or may have been aligned with astronomical events.

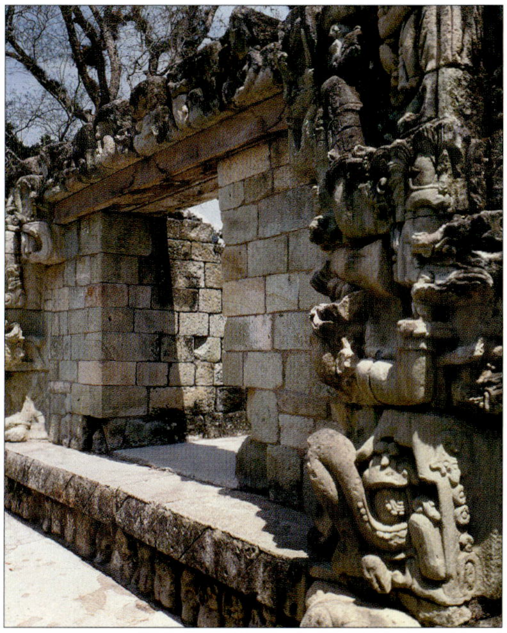

CLAIM OF GREATNESS

Smoke Jaguar's successor King 18-Rabbit (AD695–738) carried out a great deal of construction work in the central part of the city. King 18-Rabbit erected a great temple-palace, identified by *witz* ('sacred mountain') masks in its decorative carving as a holy peak, on the northern edge of the Acropolis East Court. This was the last of several royal structures on the site. He laid out a series of stelae bearing his portrait in the Great Plaza. One of these, Stela A of AD731, was inscribed with the emblem glyphs of Tikal, Calakmul and Palenque as well as that of Copán and has been interpreted as a statement of Copán's status as an equal among these illustrious states.

King 18-Rabbit also built or completed the building of the Great Ball Court, the final version of several courts constructed on a site north of the Acropolis. An inscription on its eastern wall recorded the ball court's completion as 9.15.6.8.13 – a day in AD738. Just 113 days after this date, the king was captured and executed by King Cauac Sky of Quiriguá. The scholars Linda Schele and David Friedel have suggested that 18-Rabbit probably met with disaster during a campaign intended to furnish him with sacrificial victims for the ritual dedication of the ball court.

Left: Temple 22. The main door was carved to represent the mouth of the Witz or sacred mountain – and so was seen as an entrance to the spirit realms of the underworld.

Above: The Hieroglyphic Stairway contains 63 steps carved with 2,500 glyphs recording the history of Yax Kuk Mo's dynasty.

To the south of the ball court, the later King Smoke Monkey (AD738–49) began the Hieroglyphic Stairway that recorded the kings of the dynasty to that date. He also built a council house, believed to have been used for meetings of lineage officials, which was dedicated in AD746. His successor Smoke Shell (AD749–63) completed and dedicated the Hieroglyphic Stairway in the first year of his reign.

The 16th king Yax Pac (AD763–820) commissioned and dedicated the monument known as Altar Q, which bore the images of all 16 kings of the dynasty and featured the first king, Yax Kuk Mo' handing the sceptre of power to Yax Pac. He also built the structure known by archaeologists as Temple 11 facing north across the plaza bounded by the Hieroglyphic Stairway towards the Great Plaza.

PRIDE OF THE TOLTECS: TOLLÁN

The celebrated home of the Toltecs was an extensive city encompassing some 13km (8 miles). Its population of up to 60,000 was spread out in outlying areas and lived by farming, mining basalt, making chert tools and working obsidian. The ceremonial area at the centre was precisely laid out 18 degrees east of north. It contained two pyramids, two plazas, a council hall and two ball courts.

The most important structure, facing on to the main plaza from its eastern edge was the one known as Building C. This was once a pyramid temple platform, but Aztec pilgrims dismantled the temple and removed the stone facing. All that remains is the small mountain of rock and earth that formed the core of the pyramid, together with a few pieces of carved stone. Scholars believe that the temple would have been a modest two-room building with an antechamber and a shrine, but do not know which god was honoured there.

Below: Sacred snakes feast on human skeletons on the coatepantli *or serpent wall that runs along Building B's north side.*

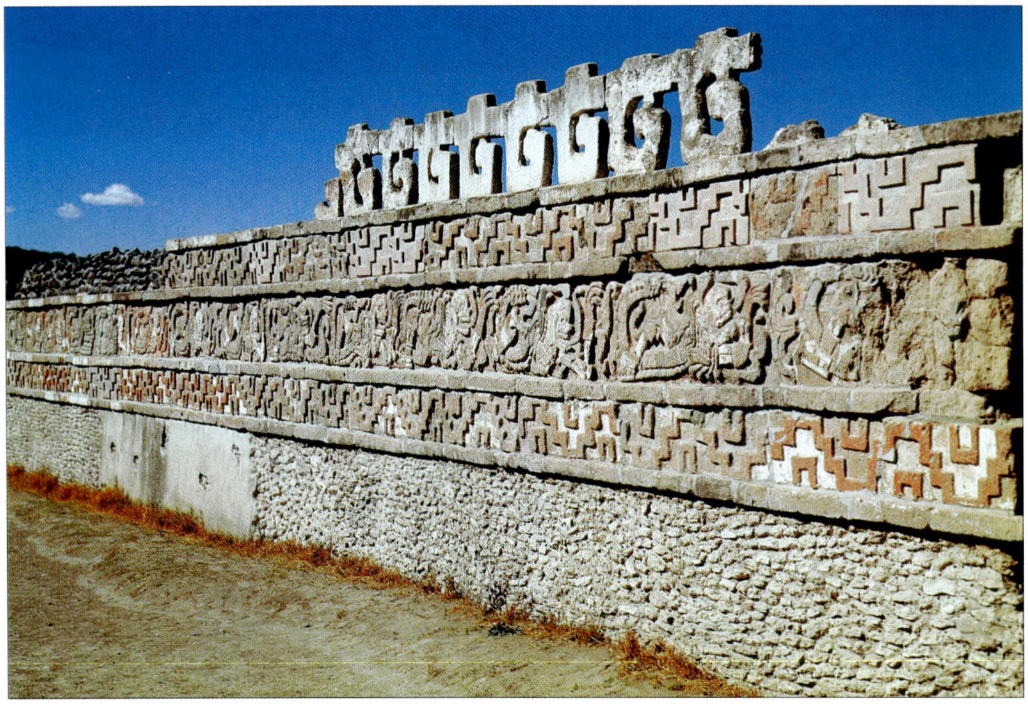

IN QUETZALCÓATL'S HONOUR

To the north of the plaza, Toltec builders erected a five-stepped temple pyramid sacred to Quetzalcóatl. On the top of the pyramid the temple roof was supported by columns, some in the shape of warriors 3.5m (11ft) tall. Before the temple, a reclining *chacmool* would have been placed. The warrior figures were broken up and cast into a ditch, perhaps by looters, but have been reassembled and returned to their place of duty on the top of the pyramid.

Stonemasons cut panels to face the tiers of the pyramid. They represented a human head emerging from a monster's jaws, an image tentatively identified as Quetzalcóatl Tlahuizcalpantecuhtli, the god in his form as Venus the Morning Star. They also showed eagles, jaguars and coyotes consuming human hearts. Traces of paint sometimes show that these would have been painted bright colours.

THE BURNT PALACE

To the east of the temple lay a secular building that archaeologists call the Palace of Quetzalcóatl or Edificio 1, while to the west was a vast building measuring 59m by 91m (200ft by 300ft) and called the Palacio Quemado – or 'Burnt Palace', because it was largely consumed by flames. Its builders set it out in three halls with colonnades that face south on to a long gallery. The Burnt Palace was probably an administrative building used for meetings, receptions and storing trade and tribute items. Gamblers would have gathered there to play *patolli*: three boards for the game are marked on the floor.

In the west of the central area lay a ball court and the space between the main plaza and the court was probably the marketplace. In the centre of the main plaza stood a square shrine around 1.7m (5ft 6in) tall, built in the *talud-tablero* style of Teotihuacán and with one staircase on each of its four sides.

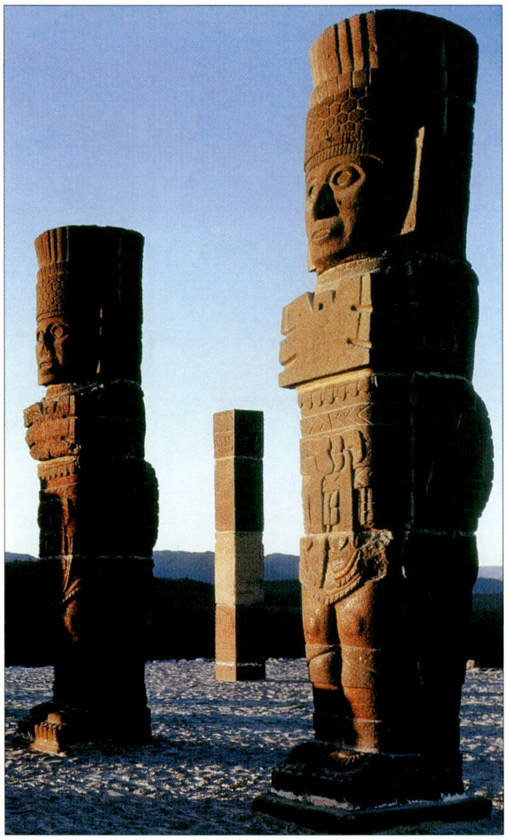

Above: Atlantean figures on the Temple of Quetzalcóatl. Their eyes and mouths were probably inlaid with obsidian or shell.

TWIN STYLES:
CHICHÉN ITZÁ

The main buildings of Chichén Itzá were laid out in two styles in different areas of the city. Three structures, mainly in the Puuc architectural style, later called the Nunnery, the Annex and the Iglesia occupied the southernmost part of central Chichén Itzá. The Akabdzib, a building in similar style to the east of this group, has been dated to *c.*AD869. To the west lay the Casa Colorado or 'Red House', with a frieze commemorating noble bloodletting ceremonies in AD869 and AD870.

North-east of the Nunnery group, lay the curious circular building later called the Caracol (from the Spanish for snail) because the spiral staircase within it was held to resemble a snail's shell. A stela found on the building's upper platform dated it to AD906. It may have been a circular temple or an observatory.

THE NORTHERN COMPLEX

A *sacbé* ran northwards from the Caracol to the northern group of buildings, comprising the Temple of Kukulcán, the Temple of the Warriors, a ball court and the Group of the Thousand Columns. The complex was arranged precisely 18 degrees east of true north.

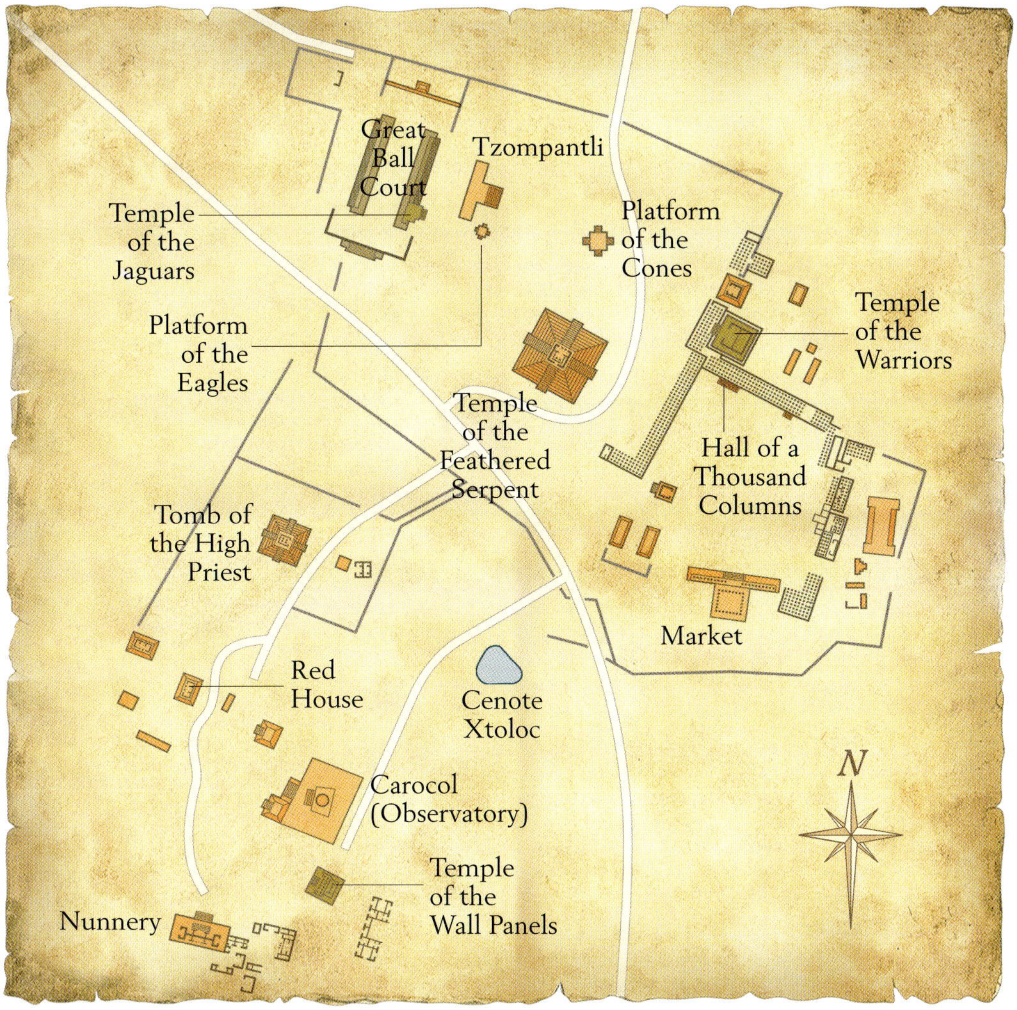

Above: Puuc-style buildings were in the south, Toltec-style structures in the north.

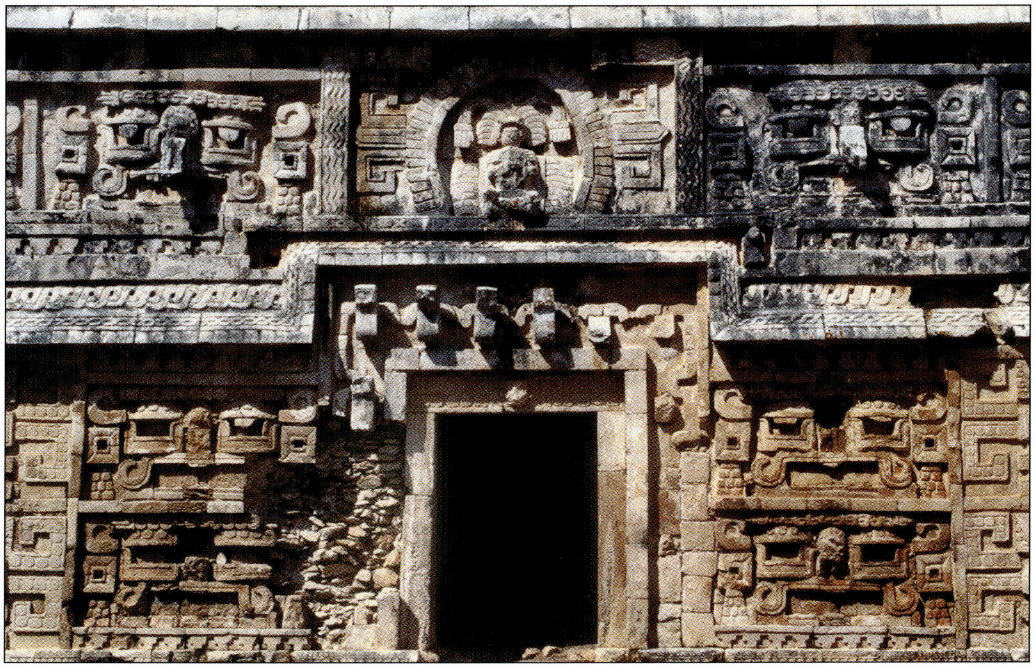

HOLY WATERS

The city made use of two major *cenotes* or natural wells formed when the limestone rock in the area collapsed to reveal water gathered beneath. One, the Xtoloc *cenote*, lay in the centre of the city, to the east of the causeway linking the Caracol to the northern platform. The second, the *Cenote* of Sacrifice, was the site of human sacrifice and other ritual offerings and lay to the north of the northern platform.

Left: Puuc-style carving on the facade of the Nunnery represent the the earth monster and the long-nosed rain god Chac.

HILL FORTS:
CACAXTLA, XOCHICALCO AND TEOTENANGO

In the central highlands around the Basin of Mexico, three fortified hilltop settlements flourished from the 7th and 8th centuries AD onward, at the time that Teotihuacán and Monte Albán were in decline. Historians believe that as the powers of Teotihuacán and Monte Albán waned, the highland cities began to reassert their influence. The cities of Cacaxtla, overlooking the Tlaxcala valley, Xochicalco in western Morelos and Teotenango in the Toluca valley exhibited a common style in the use of glyphs and counting systems. The first two cities largely faded from prominence after AD900, but Teotenango was an important independent centre until its conquest by the Aztec *tlatoani* Axayácatl in 1476.

CACAXTLA

Celebrated for its mural paintings, Cacaxtla rose to prominence after *c.*AD650 in a well-appointed hilltop location that had been occupied since the Preclassic Period. The hill on which Cacaxtla stood would have been an obvious choice for settlement, for it enjoyed a plentiful water supply from its own springs and was an easily defended position commanding views of the Tlaxcala valley and beyond.

Archaeologists have discovered that there were at least five stages of construction at Cacaxtla. Its builders laid out the ceremonial site on the hilltop on a rough north–south axis. They erected a palace, temple-shrines, altars and several corridor-like structures. The corridors were part of a distinctive construction thought to be associated with the system of defences: a series of long, low buildings arranged around patios over several levels and joined by staircases, which would have been easily defended in times of conflict.

Cacaxtla's patios and doorways were the sites of human offerings, mainly of babies and children: 208 skeletons have been found, including those of 199 infants. These scores of young lives were probably offered as dedication sacrifices when the buildings were completed. In the sacrifices the bones were scattered randomly, together with obsidian points and scrapers, shells, figurines of animals, bone needles and jewellery such as ear spools and nose plugs. From the main patio of the ceremonial area, steps led up to an elongated chamber with seven entrances painted with vividly coloured murals depicting battle scenes. The conflict might portray a ritualized bloodletting. Warriors wearing Teotihuacán-style outfits defeat others identified as Maya by their deliberately deformed heads. Some of the Maya are naked and painted turquoise blue, the traditional colour of sacrifice.

A stairway from the chamber led to a structure now called Building A by archaeologists, which was dominated by four large painted figures on either side of the doorway. One figure, believed to represent the moon, is depicted as a jaguar-man releasing drops of life-giving water from a sceptre on to the prone body of a jaguar-serpent. Another figure, in similar costume, pours water from a pot marked with symbols of the rain god Tláloc.

In the south-west of the ceremonial centre builders erected what appears to be a temple to Venus the Morning Star (Tlahuizcalpantecuhtli). On either side of a doorway artists painted two large figures, each wearing a five-pointed half-star that was a well known symbol of Venus.

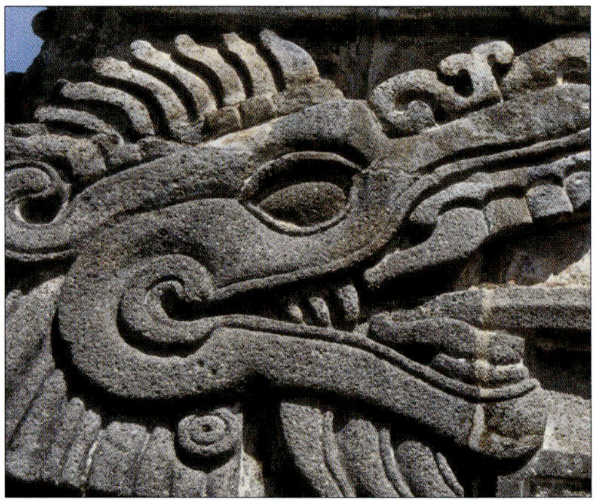

Above: On Xochicalco's Temple of the Feathered Serpent, Quetzalcóatl is represented with consuming jaws.

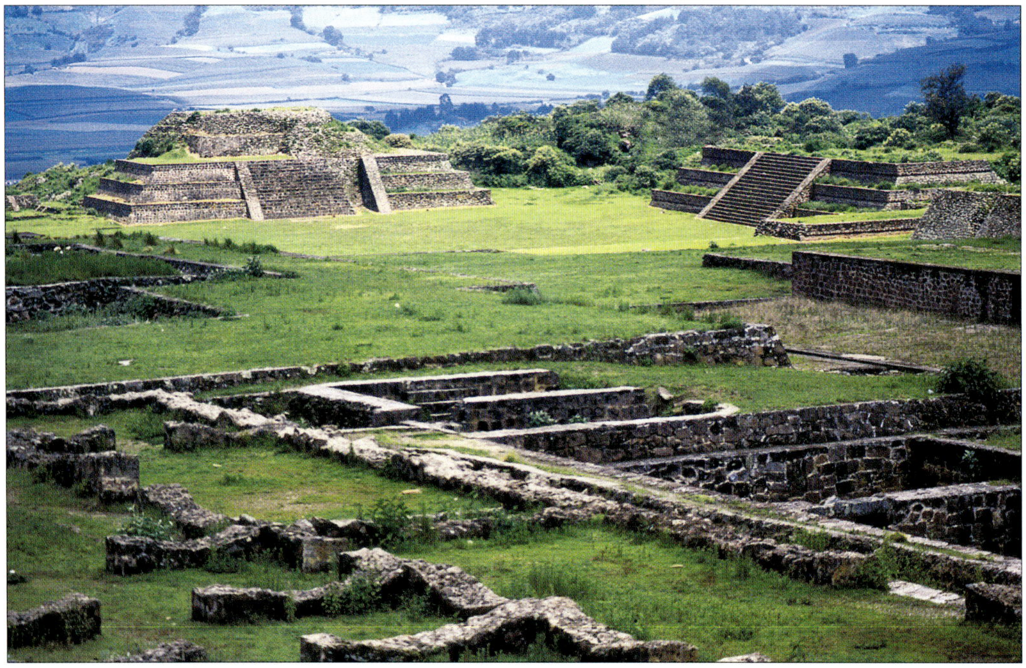

Below: The South Plaza at Teotenango appears to have been laid out as a homage to the Ciudadela or Citadel in Teotihuacán.

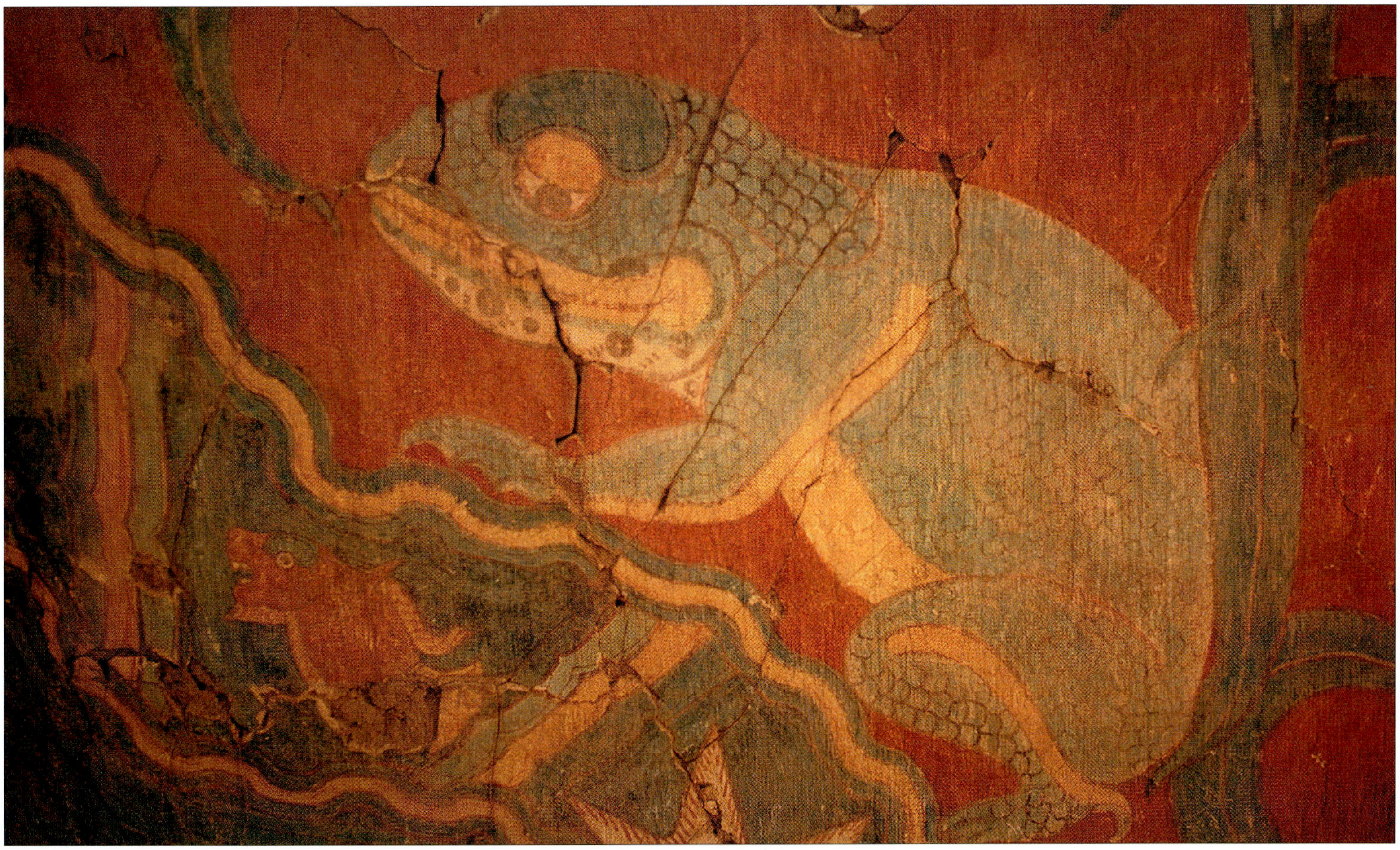

Above: This blue-skinned toad appears in Cacaxtla's Red Temple. The plant behind him bears 'fruit' of human heads.

XOCHICALCO

At Xochicalco, builders cut deep ditches, walls and ramps to fortify much of the lower part of the hill and laid out the residential and ceremonial areas of the settlement on terraces cut into the upper slopes. They built causeways to connect areas of the site and to link the city to nearby settlements. One connected the ceremonial and residential hilltop to the ball court, which was laid out on the lower hill with rings on the side walls.

In the main ceremonial area, artisans carved the Pyramid of the Feathered Serpent with images of high-ranking warriors and lists of places that paid tribute to the city's military hierarchy, together with Feathered Serpent reliefs and glyphs relating to fire ceremonies and to the ritual calendar. About 30m (100ft) south of the pyramid, workers built a sacred structure now called the Temple of the Stelae, because it contained three expertly carved stone posts, each bearing a human face and a set of glyphs. Scholars still debate the meaning of these stelae. Some suggest that they represent sky and fertility deities and were used in agricultural rites. Others claim that they were, like the carving on the pyramid, a celebration of Xochicalco's military might. The stelae were deliberately damaged and broken, then buried in pieces, but scholars have gathered the fragments and put them back together.

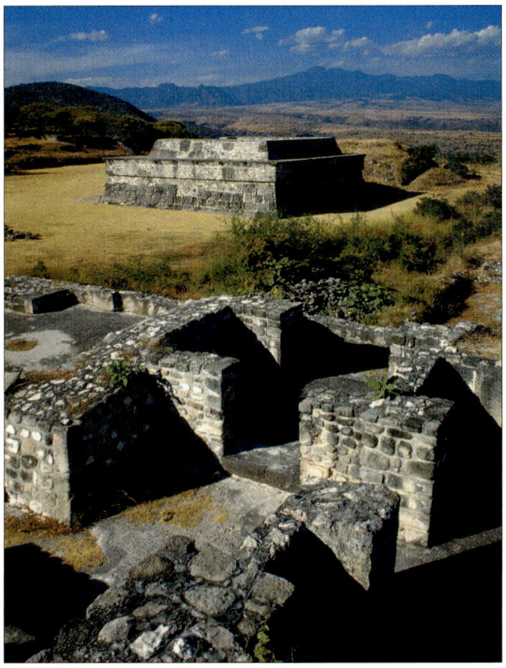

Left: The Temple of the Feathered Serpent stands in the centre of the main square in Xochicalco, laid out on a terraced acropolis.

TEOTENANGO

At Teotenango the land falls away sharply from the hilltop on three sides, while on its northern edge labourers erected a vast defensive wall. On the hilltop, from about AD750 onwards, settlers laid out a large ritual and civic area with a number of plazas, altars, temple platforms, a ball court, residential areas, streets and markets. The builders were clearly influenced by Teotihuacán and paid tribute in their own construction to the architecture and sculptural achievements of that great city. In particular, the South Plaza at Teotenango, enclosed by low buildings with stairways, appears to be a reproduction of the great Citadel at Teotihuacán. Teotenango's highest building was the Temple of the Serpent, adorned with serpent carvings.

TARASCAN STRONGHOLD: TZINTZUNTZAN

The Tarascans laid out their capital, Tzintzuntzan, beneath wooded highlands on the shores of Lake Pátzcuaro in Michoacán, western Mexico, at an altitude of 2,130m (7,000ft). An army of labourers, probably prisoners or workers provided as tribute by peoples humbled in the course of the Tarascans' empire-building wars, created a vast east-facing terrace measuring 440m by 260m (1,440ft by 850ft). Here they built, in line, five temples on terraced circular platforms. The temples have been destroyed but the platforms, called *yácatas*, remain. They were faced with great slabs of stone.

Nearby, the Tarascans' labour force raised a building now known as El Palacio, with many rooms arranged around a patio together with a roofed, narrow gallery defined by rectangular pillars. This might have been a royal palace or a residential area for elite priests, conveniently situated close to the temples supported by the *yácatas*.

A KING'S TEMPLE BURIAL?

The *yácata* temple mounds might also have been mortuary monuments. Archaeologists found graves they believe to be sacrificial burials of servants in the mound they call Yácata V. One grave, in the south-east corner, contained five women, buried with copper ornaments, bells and ritual vessels. Another, in the north, contained nine women buried with arms linked together and accompanied by rich deposits including obsidian lip plugs, turquoise ear plugs, silver tweezers and gold earrings, along with copper bells and axes. The burials might have been made to accompany one of the Tarascan kings on his voyage into the afterlife. The royal grave probably lies nearby, but has not yet been found.

Below: The yacátas *were faced with stone veneer, which does not survive here. Some 40,000 people once lived in Tzintzuntzan.*

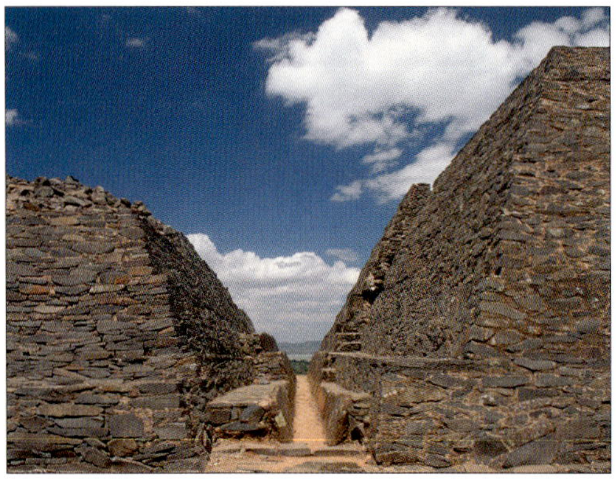

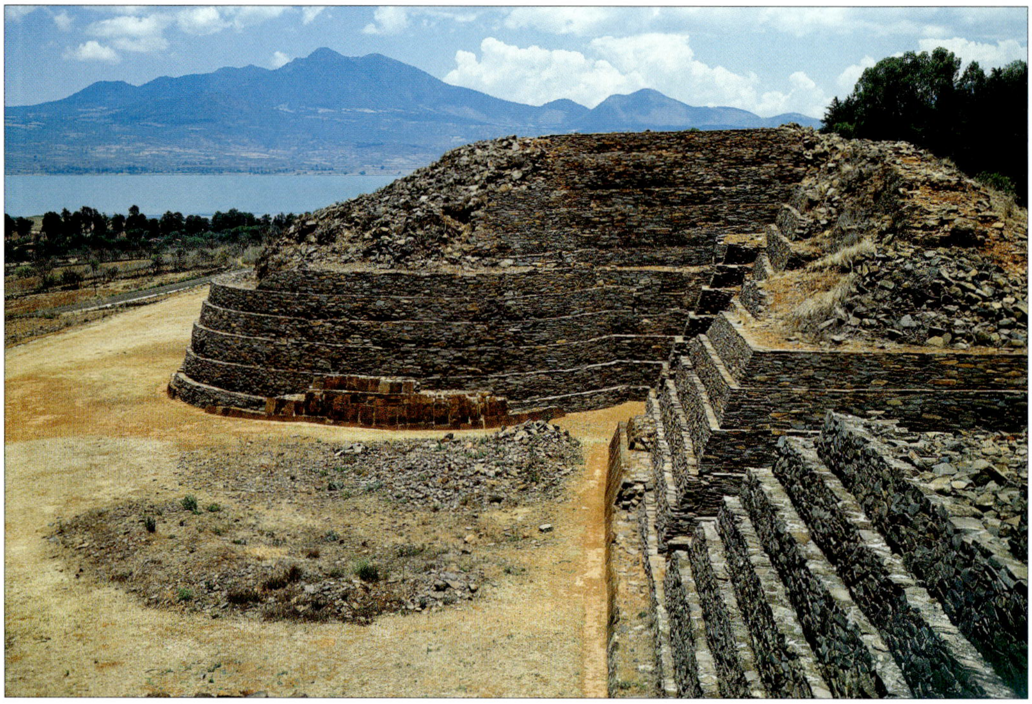

Above: Circular platforms or yacátas *survive at Tzintzuntzan without the temples that once stood on top of them.*

HOME OF THE HUMMINGBIRDS

The Tarascans were skilled producers of gold and silver jewellery and of copper axe heads. They and their predecessors in western Mexico were the pioneers of metalworking techniques in Mesoamerica, using knowledge and skills passed along trade routes into western Mexico from Colombia and Peru. They were the only Mesoamericans to use metal weapons.

The Tarascans were also known for their high level of skill in weaving, in particular for making mosaics of feathers using the plumes of local hummingbirds. Their capital's name, Tzintzuntzan, meant 'home of the hummingbirds'.

TARASCANS DEFEATED

Tarascan skill in making weapons, together with great martial spirit, kept all-comers at bay. Even the imperial Aztec army in the reign of Axayácatl (1469–81) did not succeed in defeating the people of Tzintzuntzan in 1479. However, in 1522 the Spanish adventurer Captain Olíd, who had served under Cortés in the siege of Tenochtitlán, took the Tarascan capital without a struggle.

When Cortés had been marching on Tenochtitlán in 1519 he had sent emissaries to Tzintzuntzan asking for military help. Rather than send a reply, the king ordered his priests to sacrifice the Spaniards to the gods. However, the Europeans had unwittingly brought a hidden weapon, for a smallpox epidemic swept through the ranks of the Tarascans and carried off the king. When the Spanish returned three years later, the new king did not dare to fight the soldiers who had brought down the Aztecs.

CITY OF PRIESTS:
MITLA

The elegant palaces of Mitla, which lie at an altitude of 1,480m (4,855ft) on the eastern edge of the Tlacolula valley in Oaxaca, were built on an ancient settlement inhabited by Zapotecs from as early as 1200BC. Mitla rose to prominence in the Postclassic Period following the decline of nearby Monte Albán. From *c.*AD900 the Mixtecs left their mark on the site. Archaeologists have found numerous Zapotec tombs at the site, which they believe was a sacred burial place. Its Zapotec name was Lyobaa ('Site of Burials'), while the name of Mitla was Nahuatl for 'Realm of the Dead'.

A CITY LAID OUT

The city was laid out in five groups of thin, elongated structures arranged around rectangular courtyards. Beneath the South Group, which was on the southern bank of the Rio Grande de Mitla, archaeologists found a collection of cruciform tombs with elite burials in them. The other buildings were arranged on the rocky hillside opposite. To the west lay the Arroyo Group and the Adobe Group, while the Group of the Columns sat in the east and the Churches Group occupied the north-east of the settlement. Gravediggers laid out more tombs beneath the Group of the Columns.

Below: The Hall of the Columns still bears traces of its original colour. It takes its name from the stone pillars standing within it.

INFLUENTIAL MOSAICS

At Mitla, Zapotec craftsmen arranged cut stones in a mosaic to form a decorative fretwork and other geometric patterns on façades and door frames. Architectural historians believe these designs might have been influenced by the development of geometric decoration patterns in the Puuc style of north–central Yucatán.

The Zapotec builders used beams to support the roofs, which were gently sloping, so that rainwater would drain off into the courtyards. They made the walls of mud and stone and covered them with plaster or trachyte.

The Group of the Columns was divided into north and south courtyards. From the North Court there was access through a hall named for its six huge columns to an enclosed courtyard surrounded by four rooms. Historians believe this was the residence of Mitla's priestly elite. The courtyard decorations represent Quetzalcóatl in the form of a stylized celestial serpent. Some of Mitla's rooms were decorated by Mixtec painters.

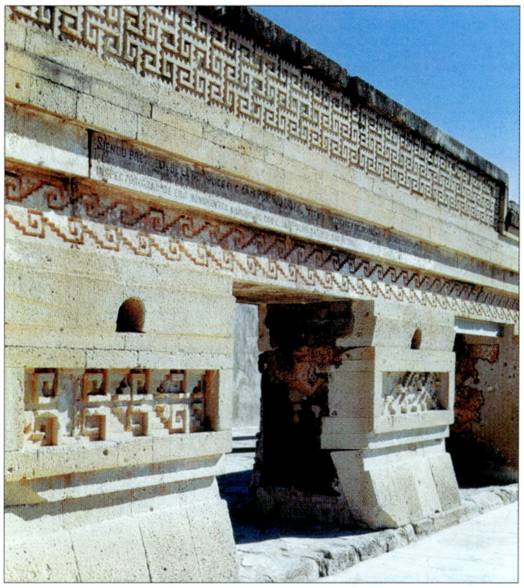

Above: The intricate geometric carving on the outer walls of the Hall of the Columns is remarkably well preserved.

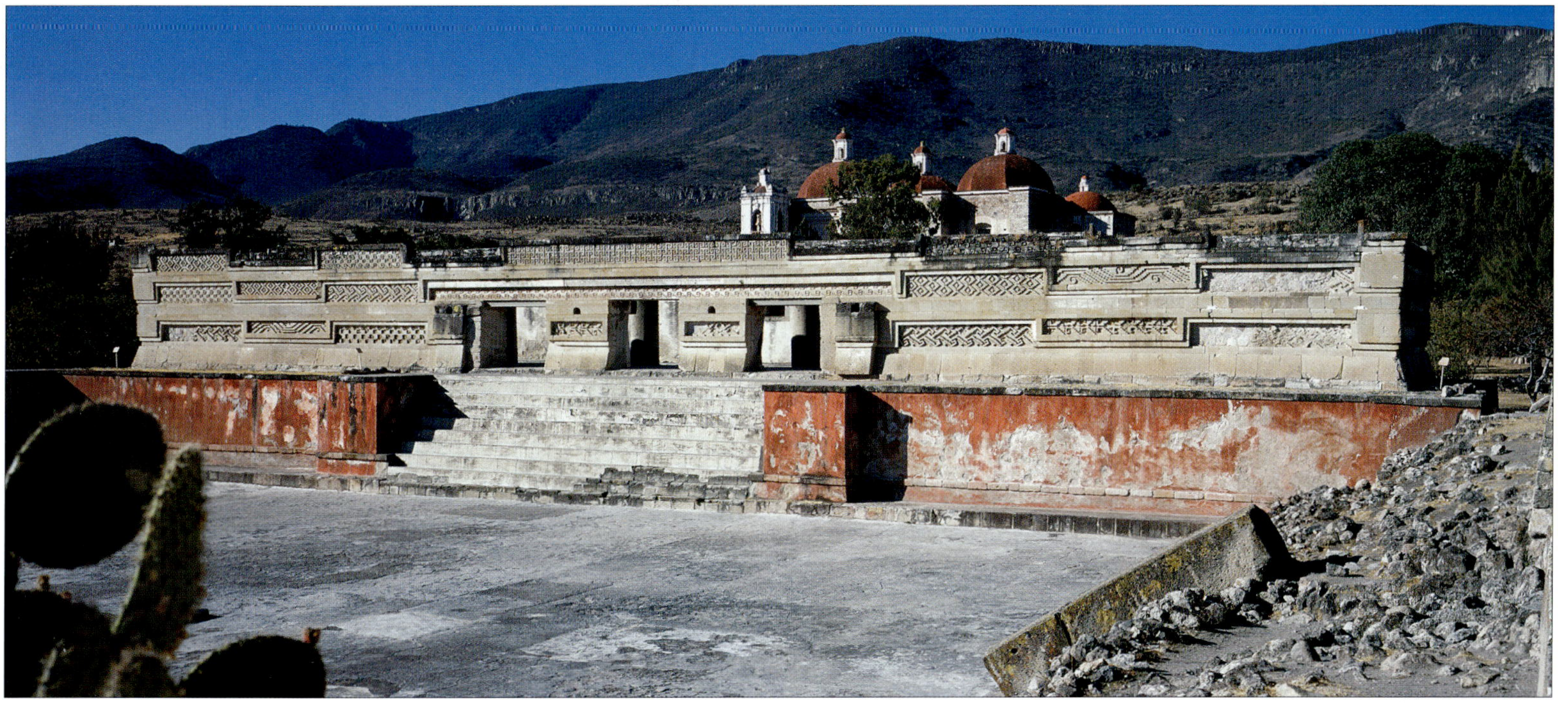

CENTRE OF THE WORLD: TENOCHTITLÁN

Like the Teotihuacános before them, the Aztecs laid out their capital in four quarters – according to legend, on the command of the tribal lord Huitzilopochtli himself. At the centre stood the vast ceremonial precinct containing the Templo Mayor. Nearby was the great imperial palace and the vast market square of Tlatelolco. Causeways 3.5m (12ft) in width left the island city to north, west and south, connecting the mainland. On the island the causeways became great thoroughfares that terminated in the sacred complex at the city's heart. Fresh water was carried into the city by aqueduct from Coyoacan.

Each of the *capultin* or tribal groups had its own land, with sacred precincts and temple. There were 12–15 *capultin* in each of the four quarters. Major rites and important celebrations were held in the main ceremonial precincts. People moved about on foot or by canoe along the canals that crisscrossed the city.

THE TEMPLE GROUNDS

The sacred quarters of Tenochtitlán were enclosed by a wall in a large square area about 365m (1,200ft) on each side. The wall was known as the *coatepantli* ('Serpent Wall'), because its outside was carved with snake images. At the eastern end the Templo Mayor rose to a height of 45m (150ft), supporting twin temples. On the northern part of the temple platform stood a shrine to Tláloc, with a *chacmool* before it, while on the southern part was the holy place of Huitzilopochtli, before which stood a blood-drenched sacrificial stone.

THE IMPORTANCE OF CLEANLINESS

Aztec cities were kept extremely clean. In Tenochtitlán no fewer than 1,000 workers swept the city's public places daily and public toilets were built on the impressive causeways that led into the city. Aqueducts carried clean drinking water into the teeming capital from springs in the hills around. The Aztecs took a bath every day – which would have been unheard of in Europe at the time – and used herbal preparations as deodorants and to sweeten the breath. At every meeting with the conquistadors, the *tlatoani's* courtiers sprinkled the Europeans with incense – which the Spaniards took as a mark of respect, but which might have been a way of fumigating the air. Richer inhabitants of Tenochtilán had their own steam bath in or alongside their home, and there were many public steam baths for poorer citizens.

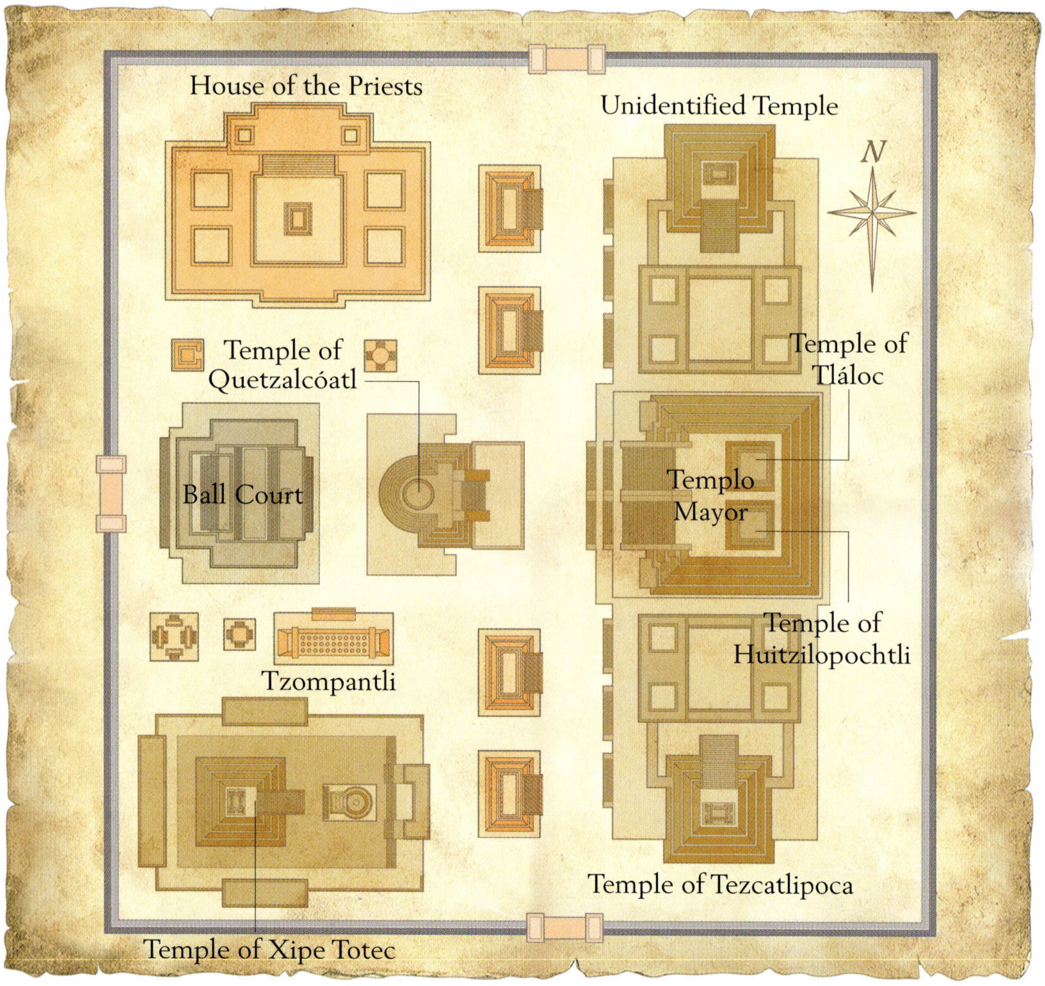

Climbing towards these temples from ground level, a priest first took a staircase decorated with painted stucco designs honouring the Feathered Serpent Quetzalcóatl and with frogs, which were symbols of Tláloc. The steps led him to a lower platform, on which a vast stone carving of moon goddess Coyolxauhqui was set in the floor before the steps to the Huitzilopochtli shrine. From this place steps rose steeply to the temple above. When a victim's body was cast down from the shrine of Huitzilopochtli, it would fall on the features of the god's mother, Coyolxauhqui. The Templo Mayor was flanked by other sacred structures. To the north were the military

Left: Scholars now believe the temple north of the Templo Mayor to have been the warriors' quarters, the House of Eagles.

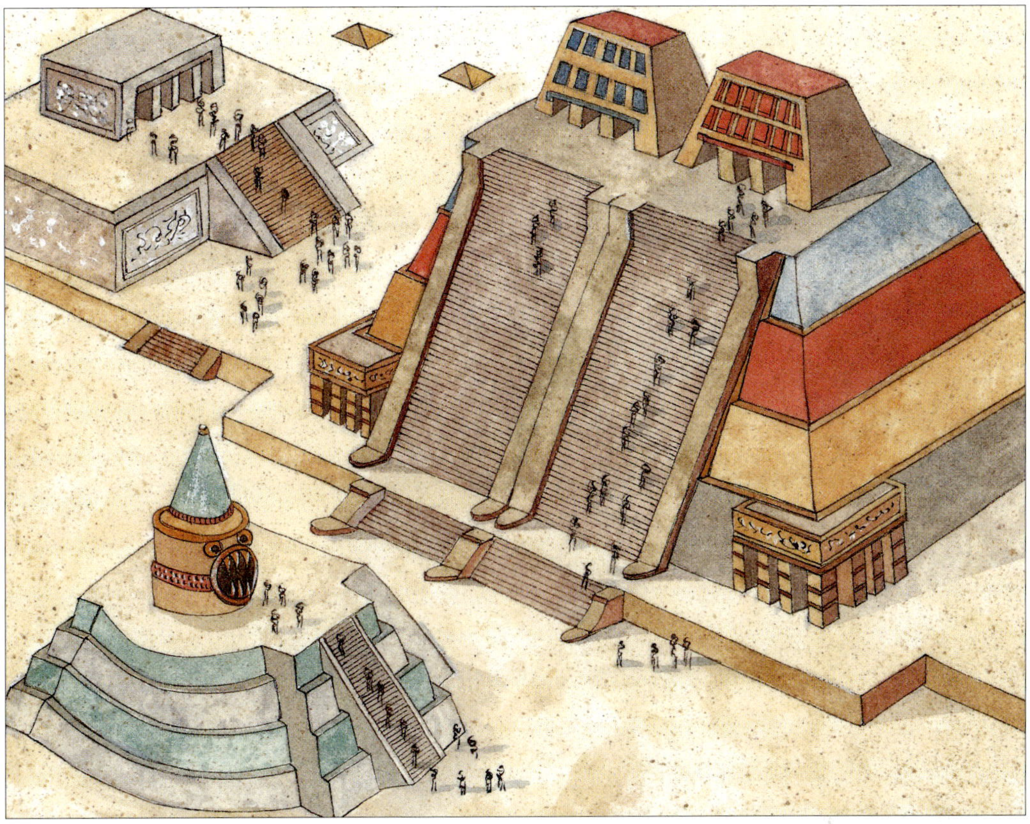

Above: The vast Templo Mayor, 45m (150ft) tall, dwarfed the rounded temple of Quetzalcóatl-Éhecatl that stood before it.

quarters of elite warriors, called the House of Eagles, while to the south rose a temple to Tezcatlipoca. West of the Templo Mayor stood a circular temple holy to Quetzalcóatl in his guise as wind god Éhecatl and beyond that, at the western limit of the ritual enclosure, was a ball court.

THE TEMPLO MAYOR OVER TIME

The first temple was built *c.*1325, the year of the city's establishment. According to the foundation legend, the Méxica/Aztecs built a rudimentary platform and temple from wattle and daub to honour Huitzilopochtli in the very spot at which they saw an eagle consuming a snake on a cactus, in fulfilment of a divine prophecy. Archaeologists have not been able to uncover evidence of this lowest-level structure. They do know that by *c.*1390, a temple building about 15m (50ft) tall stood on the site. It already supported twin temples to Huitzilopochtli and Tláloc, approached by twin staircases.

Around 1431, three years after the foundation of the Triple Alliance of Tenochtitlán, Texcoco and Tlacopan, the Aztecs built a much larger temple on the same site, entirely enclosing the previously existing structure.

They made further improvements in 1454, under the rule of Moctezuma I (1440–69), adding decorative elements and making many offerings. In particular, builders added a new staircase to the western face of the pyramid and skilled craftsmen laid a greenstone sculpture of Coyolxauhqui at its foot. This was the forerunner of the celebrated Coyolxauhqui stone, which artisans carved in 1469 under the rule of Axayácatl (1469–81).

Later rulers Tizoc, Ahuítzotl and Moctezuma II demonstrated their devotion by making improvements and additions to the temple in 1482, 1486 and 1502 respectively.

A SACRED SPOT

The Méxica/Aztecs built up their capital in a sanctified setting on twin islands in Lake Texcoco. Setting the city on an island had great religious significance, for it made Tenochtitlán a recreation of the Méxica/Aztecs' legendary northern place of origin, Aztlán, which they believed was land surrounded by water. It also meant that the city was a microcosm of the earth itself, a tribute to the gods' creation, for in Aztec cosmology, the earth was surrounded, like a great island, on all sides by water.

WATERWORKS

Tenochtitlán's development was due in no small part to their success in reclaiming the marshy shallows of western Lake Texcoco for *chinampa* fields, and later taking control of the established fields in the southern lakes of Chalco and Xochimilco. In the reign of Moctezuma I (1440–69), labourers built a vast 15km (10-mile) dyke to prevent the salt waters of the northern and eastern part of Lake Texcoco from polluting the freshwater areas that they were farming.

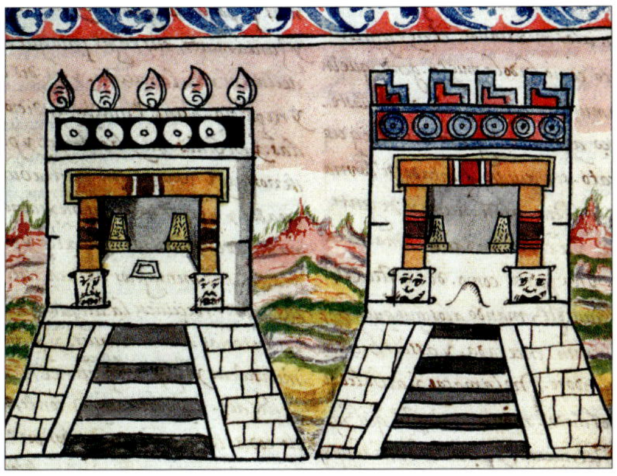

Left: The Codex Durán *represents the twin shrines, to Tláloc and Huitzilopochtli, that occupied the top of the Templo Mayor.*

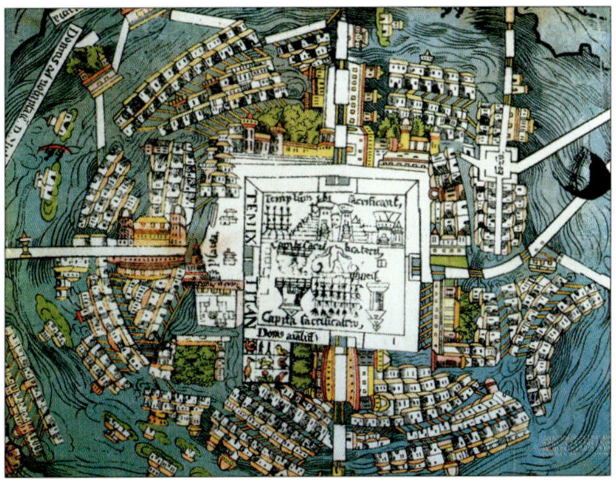

Right: Sacred precinct in the heart of the city. Hernán Cortés drew this map of Tenochtitlán to send to Charles V.

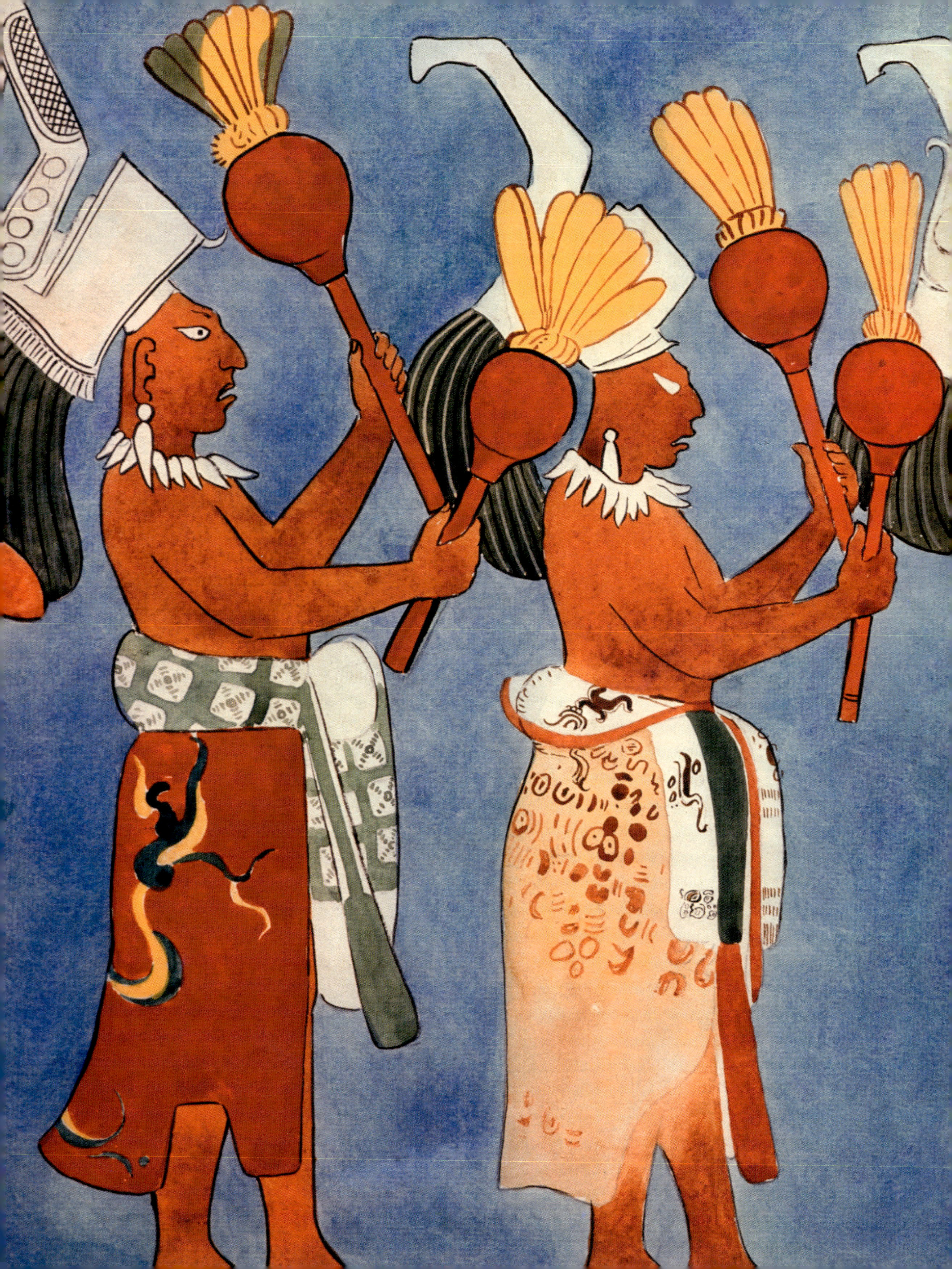

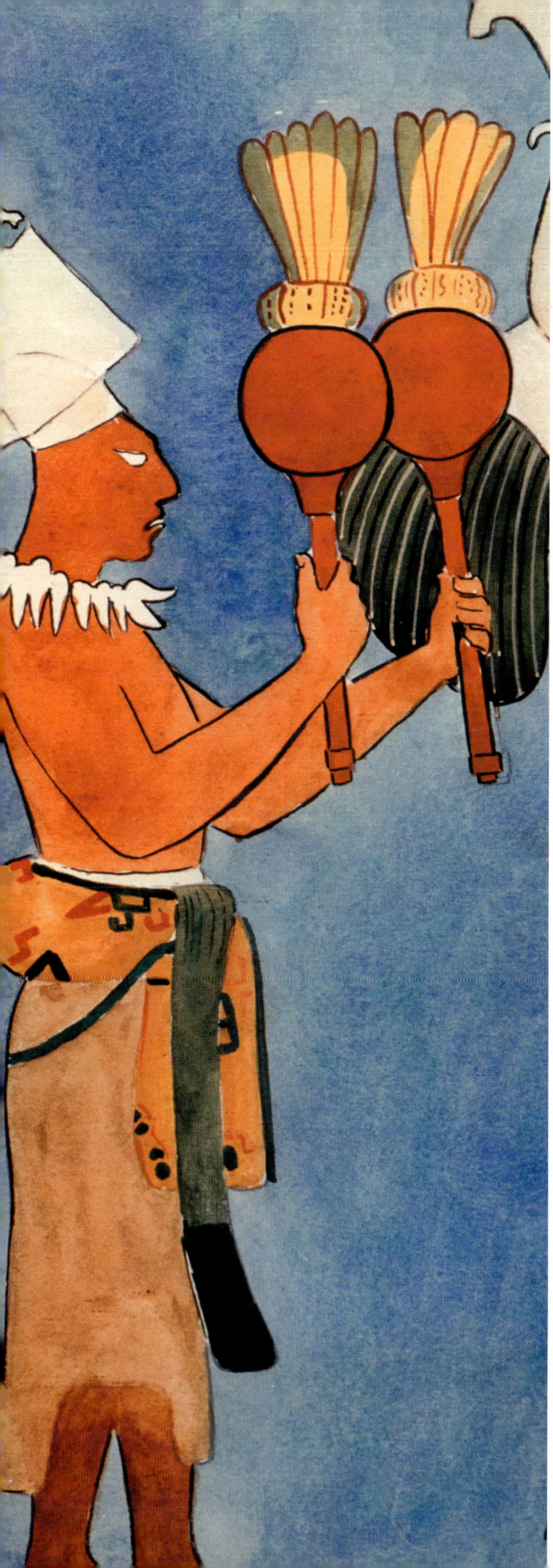

CHAPTER THREE

POTTERS AND WEAVERS

As royal wife Lady Xoc knelt before her kingly husband Shield Jaguar, drawing a spiky rope across her tongue to make a sacred offering of her blood, she wore an exquisitely decorated *huipil* cotton garment. The carver of this celebrated 8th-century scene on a limestone door lintel from Temple 23 in Shield Jaguar's city of Yaxchilán paid great attention to detail – and gave a tantalizing glimpse of the highly developed art of Maya weaving.

Of the work of Mesoamerican potters, weavers, basket-makers, mat-makers and feather-workers covered here, only pots survive in large numbers. This is partly because woven textiles and basket-work naturally decay while ceramic products survive unless smashed, but also because many pots were saved from everyday breakage by being put to sacred use as temple or tomb offerings. Yet although most Maya and many Aztec creations in cloth and basketwork have not survived, we know that they were intricately made and decorated. We have evidence of carved and painted images – both of people wearing woven textiles and of decorative schemes derived from textile and basket patterns. A basket shown in a mural in Chichén Itzá's Temple of the Jaguars, for example, was highly elaborate in construction and decoration. Clothes represented in carvings on Classic Period Maya stelae, in the Bonampak murals, on painted Maya pots, in Aztec statuary and in painted codices give an idea of the range and quality of Mesoamerican woven materials.

Left: The musicians shown taking part in a procession at Bonampak wear elaborate headdresses and costumes.

MILLENNIA OF POTTERY

Mesoamericans produced pottery for 4,000 years, from the beginnings of settled life in villages *c*.2500–2000BC until the Spanish Conquest of 1519–21. They made a variety of wares in many different finishes, reaching the apogée of their craft in the delicate portrait plates and vases made in the Maya cities of the late Classic Period. As Mesoamerican artisans produced such a range of pots, plates, cups, vases and ritual vessels, this survey is only able to select a few highlights and distinctive developments.

*Below: Sea hunter. A cormorant closes in on a fish in the decorative scheme of this Maya cylinder vase (*c.AD*700–900).*

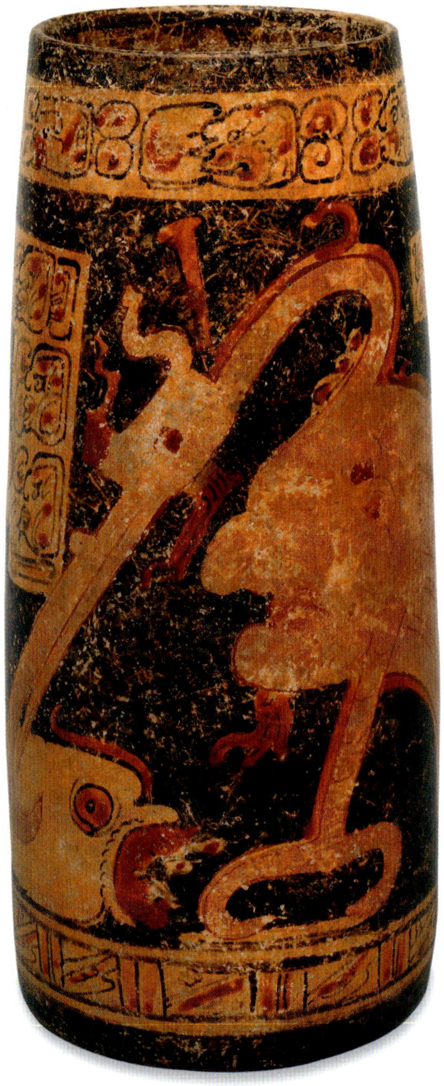

BEGINNINGS

The first Mesoamerican potters might have picked up the necessary skills from South American incomers, for people in Ecuador and Colombia were making ceramic pieces about 1,000 years earlier than their counterparts in Mexico and Guatemala.

Early potters might have taken their basic forms from those of everyday containers . For example, neck-less jars with wide, globular bases were probably based on the shape of gourds.

From these first days in *c*.2500–2000BC (during the early Preclassic Period), Mesoamerican potters experimented with decoration. They added colour-slips (additional layers of clay) and polished the surface. They made incised patterns of dots and lines and used hand-modelling, adding faces or heads to the shoulders of jars. They experimented with painting pottery and using 'resist' or negative patterns to provide a contrast to the main colour and they tested the effects of different firing techniques.

In these early times, potters began to make anthropomorphic figures that probably represented the gods in rites at the household shrine. These figures were produced in considerable numbers right through to the Spanish Conquest.

A DEMAND FOR RITUAL WARES

By *c*.1000–400BC (the middle Preclassic Period), potters were producing tripod bowls, spouted vessels, tall-necked jars sometimes bearing handles on the neck, and cylindrical incense burners.

Artisans first produced polychrome (many-coloured) vessels by applying coloured paints in yellow, red, white and black after the vessels had been fired. They also used bichrome (two-coloured) slips or additional layers of clay on vessels. Incense burners were the first Mesoamerican ceramics to have a specialized ritual function.

Around 400BC–AD250 (the late Preclassic Period), pottery decorated with sinuous parallel lines negative to the main colour – known as Usulutan ware – was popular in Maya lands. Artisans made the pattern by applying parallel lines of wax to the pot. These melted away during firing to reveal a secondary colour beneath. Potters further developed the use of modelled decorations on vessels and their handles, particularly on incense burners. Bowls with toad decorations and clay models of mushrooms are identified by scholars as celebratory of mind-altering substances ingested by shamans, who valued a secretion of toad glands as well as certain mushrooms for their capacity to

METHODS OF PRODUCTION

From the first days of Mesoamerican pottery onwards, many householders who lived by farming probably made simple pots for their own use at home. If they developed their skills, they may have produced extra pots or plates to be sold at market. Around 250BC–AD1, towards the end of the Preclassic Period, some of these home potters began to specialize in particular forms such as vases, plates or pots. By the start of the Classic Period *c*.AD250, certain skilled artisans had become specialist potters who, while working from their home, made their living entirely by ceramic production and no longer worked the land. Soon after this time, elite groups appear to have established workshops of potters in cities, to supply wealthy and royal circles with the elegant handmade pottery they admired. From *c*.AD800–900 onwards, light-industrial centres were established to produce wares using moulds for distribution across wide areas. All these methods of production coexisted.

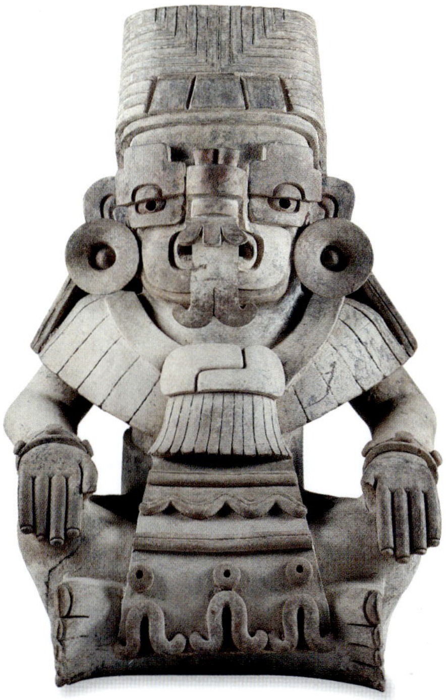

Above: Rain and lightning god Cocijo was a favourite subject for ceramic funerary urns among the Zapotecs who worshipped him.

transform consciousness during spirit adventures and acts of divination. During the years *c.*AD250–550 (the early Classic Period), polychrome decoration became dominant in Maya lands. Artisans used geometric designs or bands of diminutive images in red and black on an orange/cream background. The potters of Teotihuacán were influential at this time: their small containers and brightly painted cylindrical pots with tripod legs were widely traded and copied.

PORTRAIT PLATES AND VASES

Around AD550–800 (the late Classic Period), potters and scribe-artists in city workshops of the central Maya region produced justly celebrated vases, tripod dishes, cups, pots and incense burners painted with portraits, scenes of court life and glyphs. Then in AD800–900 the spread of militaristic Putún Maya merchants from their homeland in Tabasco was accompanied by the fine-grained pots known to historians as Fine Orange Ware.

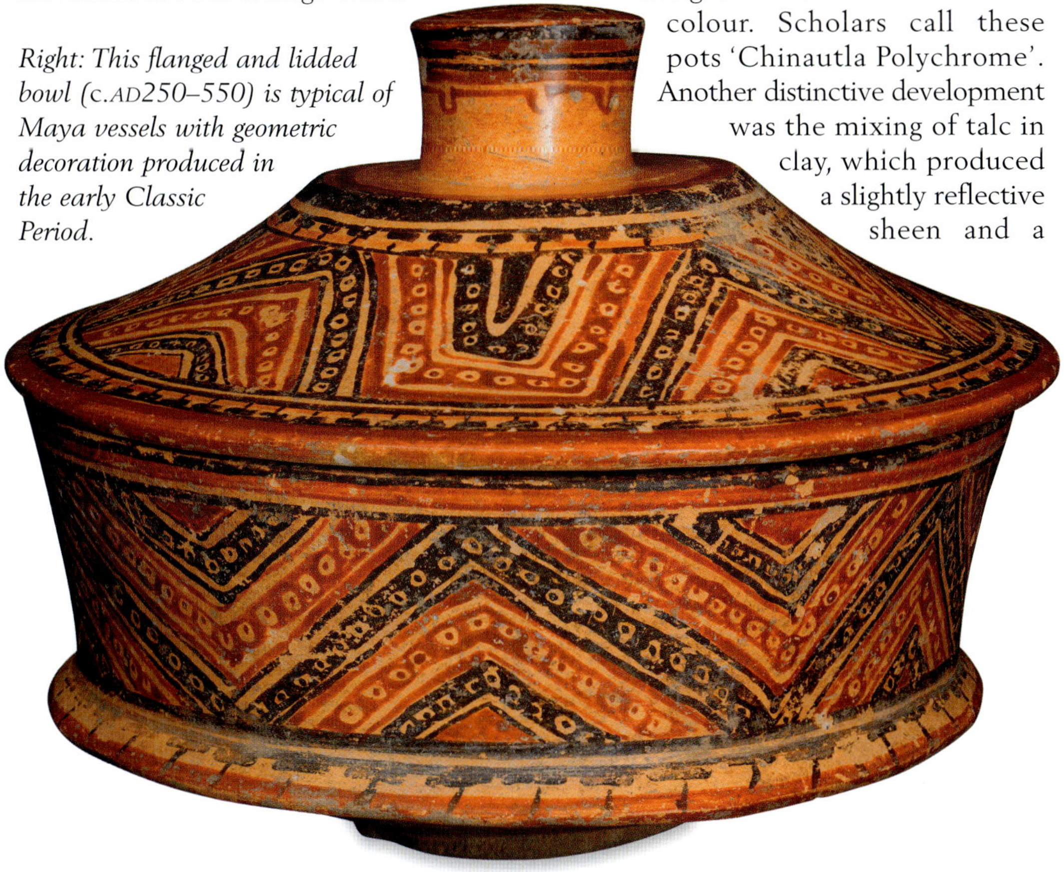

*Right: This flanged and lidded bowl (*c.*AD250–550) is typical of Maya vessels with geometric decoration produced in the early Classic Period.*

These appear to have been early examples of light-industrial production, for they came in standard sizes and with decoration produced using moulds.

In AD900–1250, artisans in the Pacific coastal regions of south-western Guatemala began to fire pots in pit kilns that were able to generate high enough temperatures to produce a glazed finish. The pots, decorated with moulding and carving, are known by historians as Plumbate Ware. They were the only glazed pots produced in Mesoamerica, although from the Classic Period on, potter-artists in Maya cities had been able to achieve a glaze-like finish. They did so by painting pots after firing and decorating them with a clear, unknown wash – perhaps a kind of resin – that scholars call 'Péten gloss' due to its use by potters from cities in the Péten region.

In 1250–1521 Maya artisans in the southern highlands made and traded simple wares decorated with black and red designs on a cream or white base colour. Scholars call these pots 'Chinautla Polychrome'. Another distinctive development was the mixing of talc in clay, which produced a slightly reflective sheen and a cooking surface – on, for example, *comales* (tortilla griddles) – with certain non-stick qualities. Products made with this mixed clay were found throughout the highlands of the southern Maya region, where the Quiché and Cakquichels rose to prominence at this time.

IN AZTEC LANDS

One of the many aspects of the market in Tlatelolco that astonished the Spanish conquistadors was the vast display of beautifully finished ceramics. In the Aztec era, craftsmen produced a wide range of pottery for use in both sacred and utilitarian contexts. For sacred use they made incense burners, braziers, censers, urns, figures of gods and goddesses, goblets, votive vessels and model temples. For everyday use they made plates, cups, bowls, jugs, pitchers and other vessels.

Many of these utilitarian objects could also have had a sacred function, since they were included in offerings at the Templo Mayor, in graves at Teotihuacán, at Tollán or in other temple settings. The elite polychrome ceramics used in the *tlatoani's* palace and by members of the nobility were made in Cholula and parts of Oaxaca. Aztec-era potters also made fired-clay flutes and ceramic rattles.

FIGURES OF CLAY

Potters at Remojadas in the region of Veracruz produced very distinctive hollow clay figurines in the 8th–9th century (the late Classic Period). These craftsman, part of the 'Veracruz culture' associated with the city of El Tajín, were inheritors of an ancient Mesoamerican tradition. From as early as *c.*2500BC, at the beginning of settled village life in Mesoamerica, early craftsmen and women were making female figurines associated with cults of the land's fertility. One of these figures, dating from 2300BC, was found in a household fireplace at Zohapilco at the eastern end of Lake Chalco in the Valley of Mexico.

In the 2nd millennium BC, Olmec craftsmen made baby-face figurines called 'dolls' by some early archaeologists. These were beautifully produced hollow figures, with a surface coating of white, representing chubby figures with legs outspread and the face of a baby. The figures probably had some religious use associated with Olmec cults seemingly focused on the were-jaguar, a jaguar-faced human – often resembling a baby – thought by scholars to stand for the earth.

Olmec baby figurines were exported far and wide from centres such as La Venta and San Lorenzo using the Olmecs' extensive trading networks.

SHAMANIC RITES

About 1100BC, craftsmen made and used large numbers of handmade ceramic figures in the Valley of Mexico, in the villages of Tlatilco on the western side of Lake Texcoco and Tlapacoya beside Lake Chalco. Some were clearly used in association with shamanistic rites: they represented shaman-priests and weird two-headed creatures or three-eyed monsters that were perhaps the product of ecstatic visions and spirit-journeys following the consumption of mind-altering substances. Others were caught in such scenes of home life as mothers nursing babies or religious festivities and other celebrations involving cavorting acrobats, musicians and players of the sacred ball game.

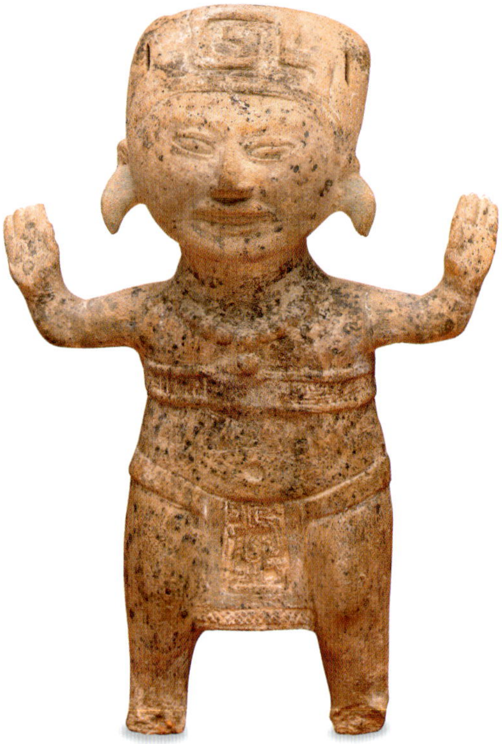

Above: This smiling boy (c.AD750–900) is typical of 'Remojadas figurines', with outstretched arms and wide, ecstatic grin.

Figurines such as this were produced in all parts of Mesoamerica in the Preclassic Period, but their use appears to have gradually died out towards the end of that era before reappearing in the mid-to-late Classic Period. Scholars have suggested that since the figurines were probably used in pre-temple religious rituals, they would not have been needed or welcome when formal religious life centred on temples became the norm. The new religious elite would probably

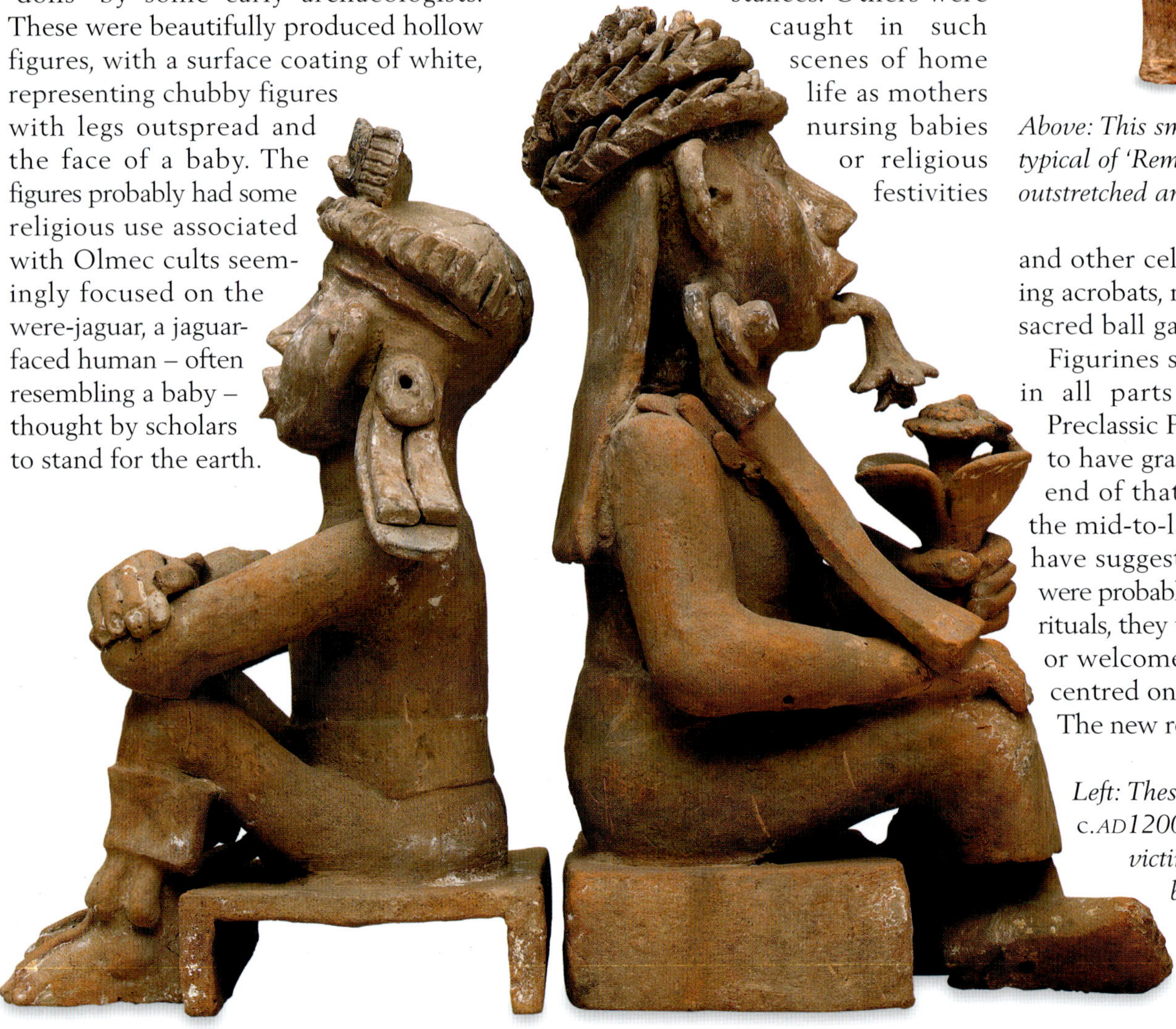

Left: These figurines made in Veracruz c.AD1200–1520 may represent ritual victims. The man (right) seems to be taking a hallucinogenic substance. Victims were drugged so that they seemed calm when going to their deaths.

have been keen to destroy all materials connected with rituals which they would have seen as outmoded. Archaeologists at Monte Albán, for example, report that hand-modelled figurines associated with household shrines disappeared from residential remains about the time that the building now called Mound X, identified as the city's first public temple, was erected some time after *c.*300BC. It is unclear precisely how and under what conditions the practice of making and using figurines resurfaced.

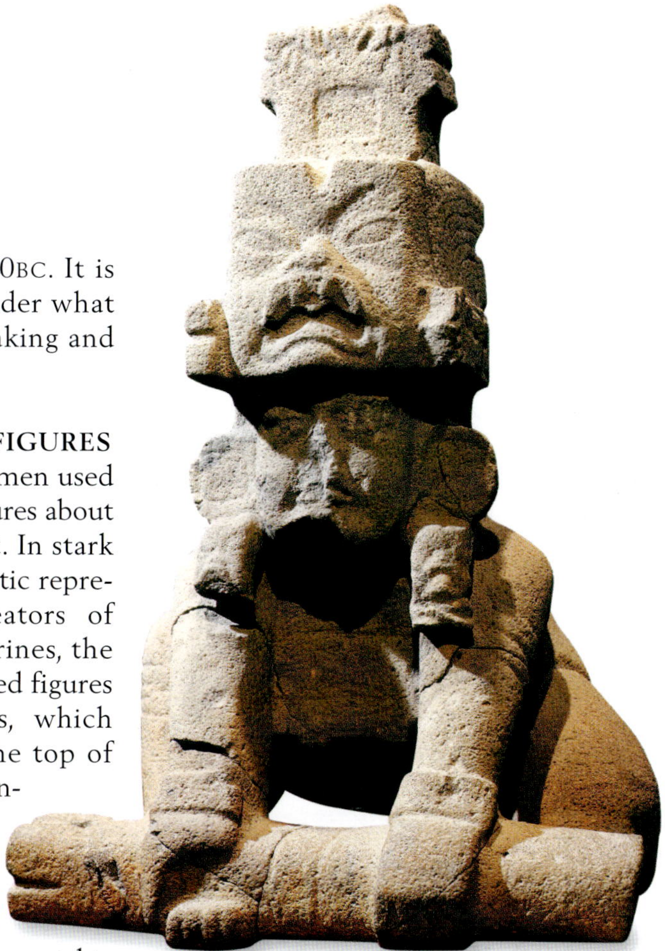

Above: *A Veracruz potter of* c.AD500–950 *fashioned this statue of a priest wearing a jaguar god headpiece and costume.*

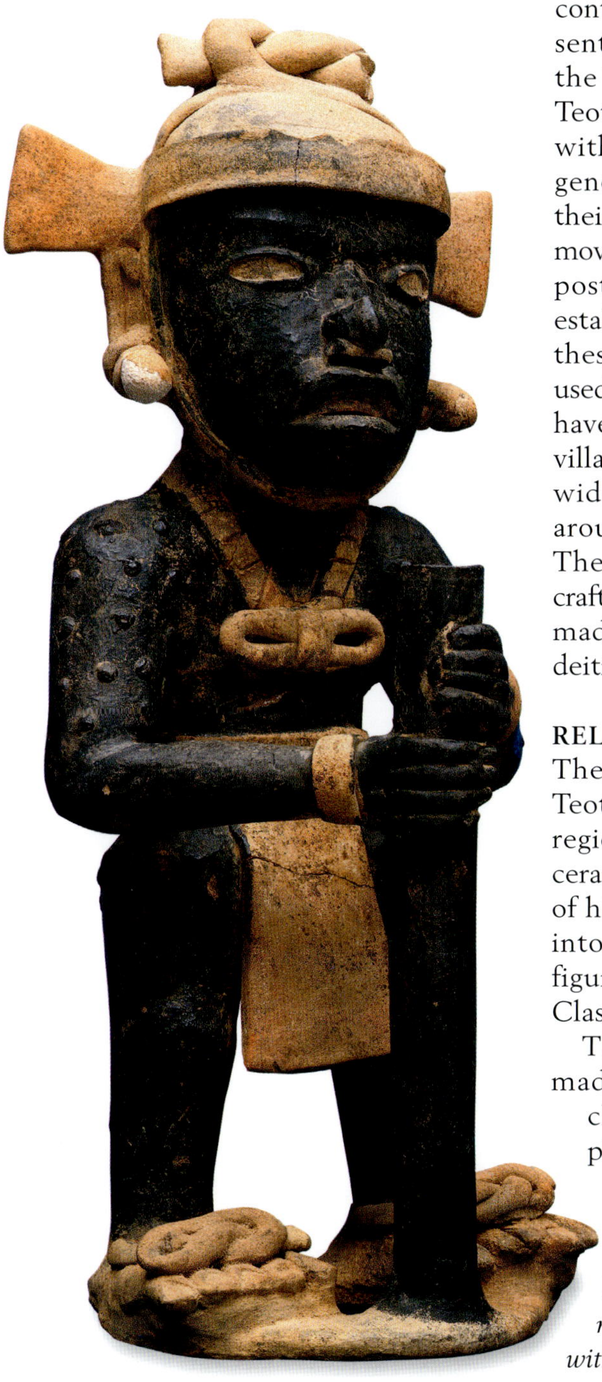

Left: Veracruz figurine c.AD250–500 *represents a club-wielding warrior with skin blackened for battle.*

STYLIZED TEOTIHUACÁN FIGURES

In Teotihuacán *c.*AD400, craftsmen used moulds to make articulated figures about 25–30cm (10–12in) in height. In stark contrast to the highly naturalistic representations of the later creators of the Veracruz Remojadas figurines, the Teotihuacános produced stylized figures with triangular-shaped faces, which generally have openings in the top of their heads. They also made non-moveable figures set in unusual postures. Scholars have not established a context in which these figures could have been used, beyond suggesting that they might have played a role in survivals of ancient village-based fertility celebrations in the wide spread of village communities around the metropolis of Teotihuacán. Then about AD650–700, Teotihuacáno craftsmen began to produce larger mould-made figurines representing nobles and deities on thrones.

RELIGIOUS ECSTASY

There was certainly significant Teotihuacáno influence in the Veracruz region, so the tradition of mould-made ceramic figurines in the great metropolis of highland Mexico might well have fed into the marvellous flowering of clay-figure moulding represented by the late Classic Period Remojadas craftsmen.

The gifted modellers at Remojadas made clay images of men, women and children, some attired as ball game players, some dressed as warriors. One distinctive form represented men – and more often women – with outstretched arms and elegant, wide-faced features, their mouths open and drawn in a broad smile or laugh, their teeth visible within their mouths.

The Remojadas potters produced highly naturalistic work. They decorated some figures with black asphalt paint to emphasize the features and details of the figures' often elaborate dress; other figurines they painted in many colours. Some scholars argue that the figures are in a state of religious ecstasy, having taken mind-altering substances. Others suggest that the laughing individuals are sacrificial victims whose unusual demeanour has been produced by swallowing hallucinogenic drinks intended to enable them to hide their terror and assume a joyful demeanour as they go to their deaths. The figures are typically about 30–45cm (12–18in) in height. The Toltecs at Tollán also produced mould-made clay figurines of people and animals, as did craftsmen at Xochicalco.

MODELS FROM THE WESTERN ISLE

Maya potters developed great artistry in moulding clay figurines in the middle to late Classic Period (*c.*AD400–900). A large collection of exquisitely modelled figures was found in graves on the limestone Island of Jaina, just off the west coast of the Yucatán peninsula.

The island was a flourishing sea-trading and fishing centre for many centuries. In addition to its port and trade facilities, it contained two modest ceremonial centres named El Zacpool and Zayosal, together with a ball court and cemeteries in which the clay figurines were found. The buildings were simple, made of an earthen core that was faced with an irregular pattern of stones, then plastered with stucco and painted.

RULERS' GRAVEYARD?

Scholars are uncertain whether the splendid clay figures and wealthy grave offerings were laid in the tombs of rich local merchants, of priests and sacerdotal assistants at the ceremonial centre or of nobles and rulers from inland cities such as Uxmal and Kabah. Because the island's ceremonial buildings were modest, it would appear most likely that cemeteries were the graves of elite groups from the mainland rather than of locals. Jaina lay just off the coast and could be reached by foot through swamps at low tide. Because the island was on the western coast of the peninsula, the sun dropped behind it each night as it sank into the underworld Xibalba. Accordingly, some scholars argue that Jaina might have been chosen as the site for an elite cemetery because symbolically it lay on the path to the underworld.

Older figures found at Jaina, dating from before AD650, are generally solid and hand-modelled. After *c.*AD650, potters began to produce hollow figures made using moulds, perhaps in emulation of the Teotihaucáno craftsmen who were making hollow-mould figures from *c.*AD400–500 onwards. Some of the later Jaina artisans were not happy to rely solely on moulds and combined the new technique with older traditions producing, for example, a figurine with a mould-made torso but a handmade head. Many of the figures are musical instruments. Some, with holes bored in the back, are whistles. Others contained clay pellets and could be used as rattles.

PORTRAITS IN CLAY

The Jaina figures are generally 20–30cm (8–12in) tall. Some figures are highly naturalistic portraits – perhaps of the nobles in whose graves they were buried. They depict proud warriors with scarred or tattoed skins, wise old men, beautiful maidens and elderly matrons. Other statuettes represent less than idealized figures taken from life such

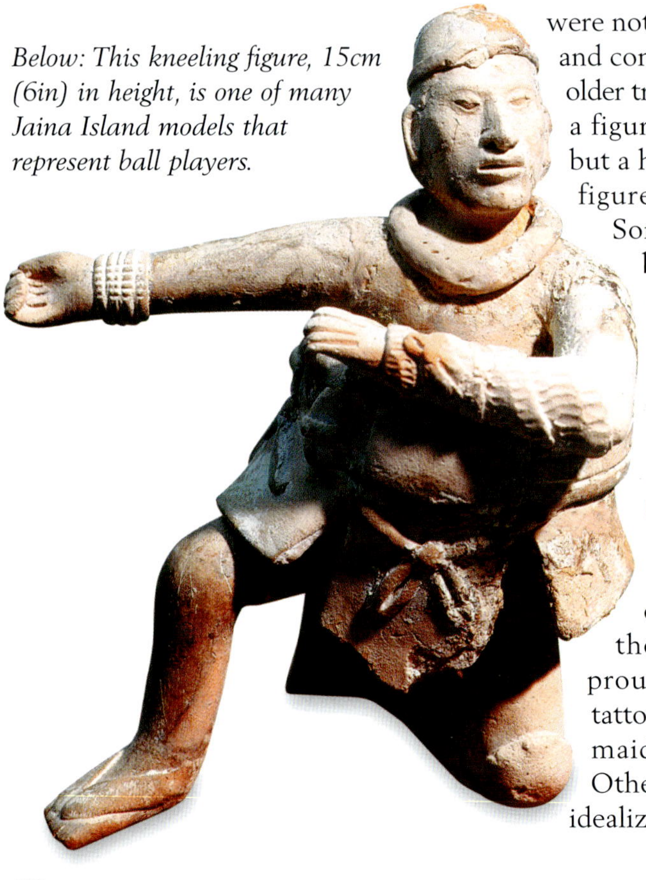

Below: This kneeling figure, 15cm (6in) in height, is one of many Jaina Island models that represent ball players.

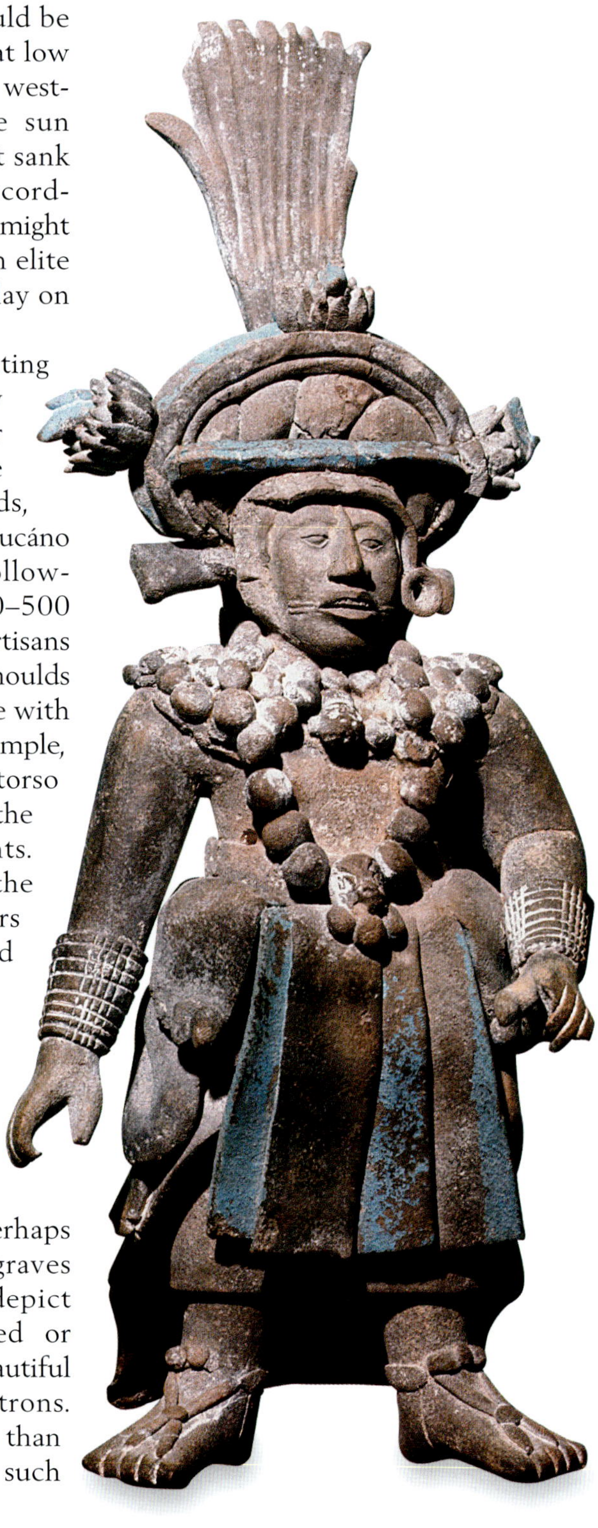

Below: The potters who made the Jaina Island models worked with great skill and delicacy, as evidenced in the attention to detail in the feather headdress, necklace, bracelets and ear decoration on this figurine.

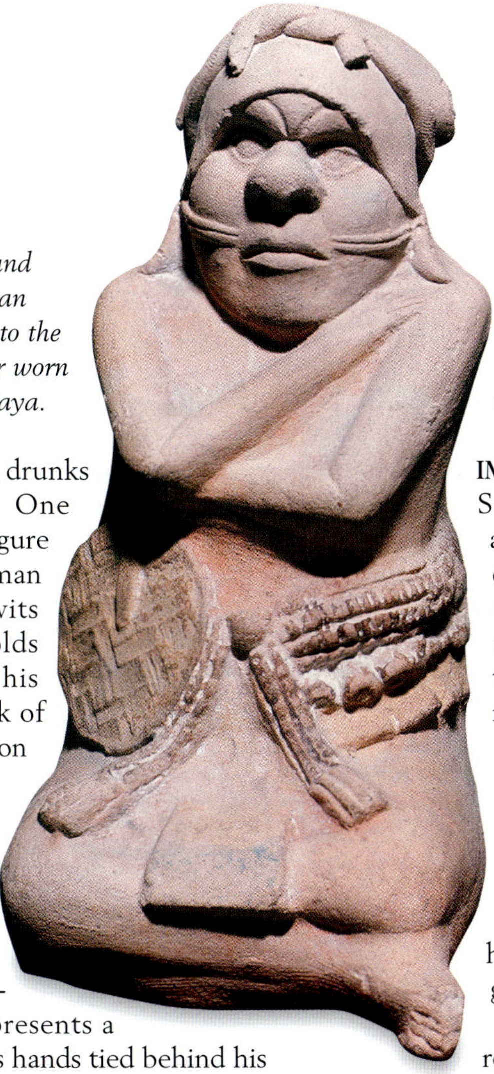

Right: The Jaina Island tomb figures give us an invaluable insight into the clothes and headgear worn by Classic Period Maya.

as invalids, dwarfs, drunks and hunchbacks. One 7th–9th-century figure represents an old man who has lost his wits to drink. He holds a flask beneath his arm and has a look of unseeing stupefaction on his face.

Some of these models are careful representations of figures involved in religious ritual. One such 7th–9th-century figure represents a naked man with his hands tied behind his back, who would appear to be a noble prisoner bound for ritual sacrifice following capture during a war campaign launched by a rival city against his own. Another figurine depicts a ball player wearing protective belt and holding the ball prior to the start of a ball game. Other Jaina Island figures represent a shaman or priest in a trance.

CERAMIC CULTURES

Fragments of pots, plates, bottles and jars generally provide the bulk of remains discovered by archaeologists when investigating living areas such as house platforms or household waste areas. In graves and temple offerings elite pottery forms are also well represented. The distribution of types of pottery and methods of decoration in different regions across spans of time gives a clue to the movements of people and influence. For this reason, archaeologists and historians often identify cultures by the type of pottery remains they left.

IMAGES OF GODS

Some figures show gods and goddesses – usually divinities associated with the underworld. One such statue-pair from the 8th–9th century AD represents an elderly, lecherous man who is trying to raise the skirt of a beautiful maiden: scholars identify the man as a treacherous underworld lord and his consort as the moon goddess Ix Chel.

Another statue-pair represent a woman who is standing behind and over a seated male, almost enveloping him in her cloak. This may be a celebration of the protective power of Ix Chel in her role as mother goddess. A deity who is represented several times among the Jaina models is a figure called the Fat God, a squat full-faced man with a feathered headdress and very tall helmet.

The Jaina Island figurines were painted in bright colours. Curiously, the potters did not work hard on reproducing the feet or hands of their subjects, which were often finished without attention to detail, but they put great effort into reproducing individual physiognomies and styles of clothing as well as adornment with jewellery, headdresses and body art such as tattoos.

The figures have been an invaluable source for historians seeking information about details of Maya court life – such as elite clothing. The finest of the figurines are the older, solid ones made before *c.*AD650. Experts declare them to be among the finest pieces of their kind in all the Americas. Because so many of the figures were of warriors, some argue that the island cemetery might have been reserved for members of the military elite, or for rank and file members of the army who had won particular glory in battle.

Below: Scholars believe that this cloaked Jaina Island figure with mysterious headdress may represent an elite priest.

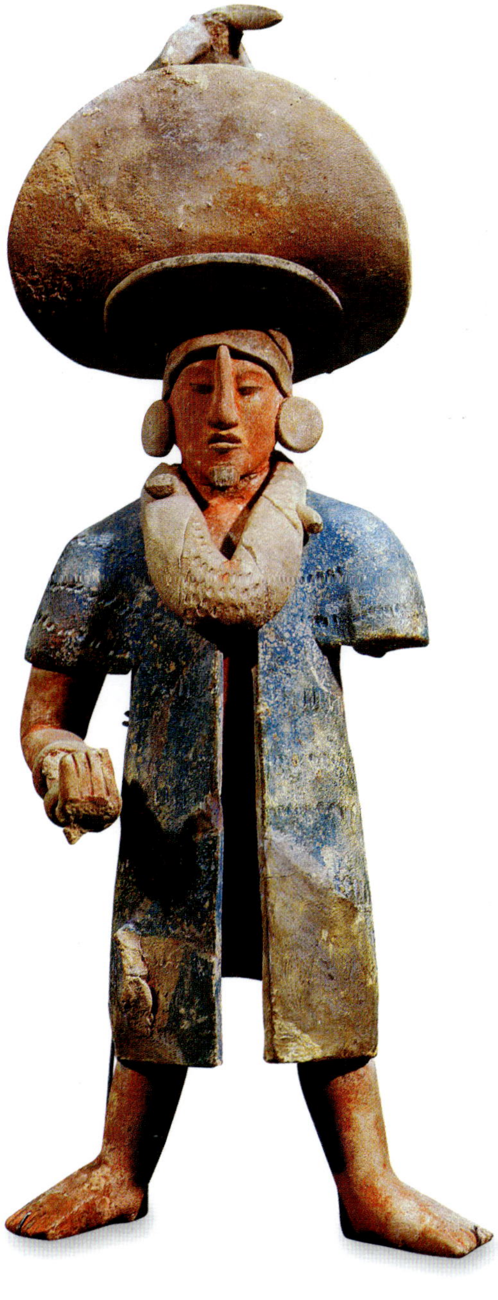

MANY-COLOURED SCENES OF COURT LIFE

The painted vases, plates, incense burners and drinking vessels produced in the Maya cities of *c.*AD550–800 in the late Classic Period were probably decorated by the highly educated noble artists usually referred to as scribes. Many of these vessels bore glyphic writing that gave the names and titles of the people represented and identified other elements of the image. Sometimes the glyphs provided an entire dynastic history for the ruler who was depicted sitting in state, conferring with his scribes and advisers, celebrating an anniversary of his accession or enjoying the chocolate drink.

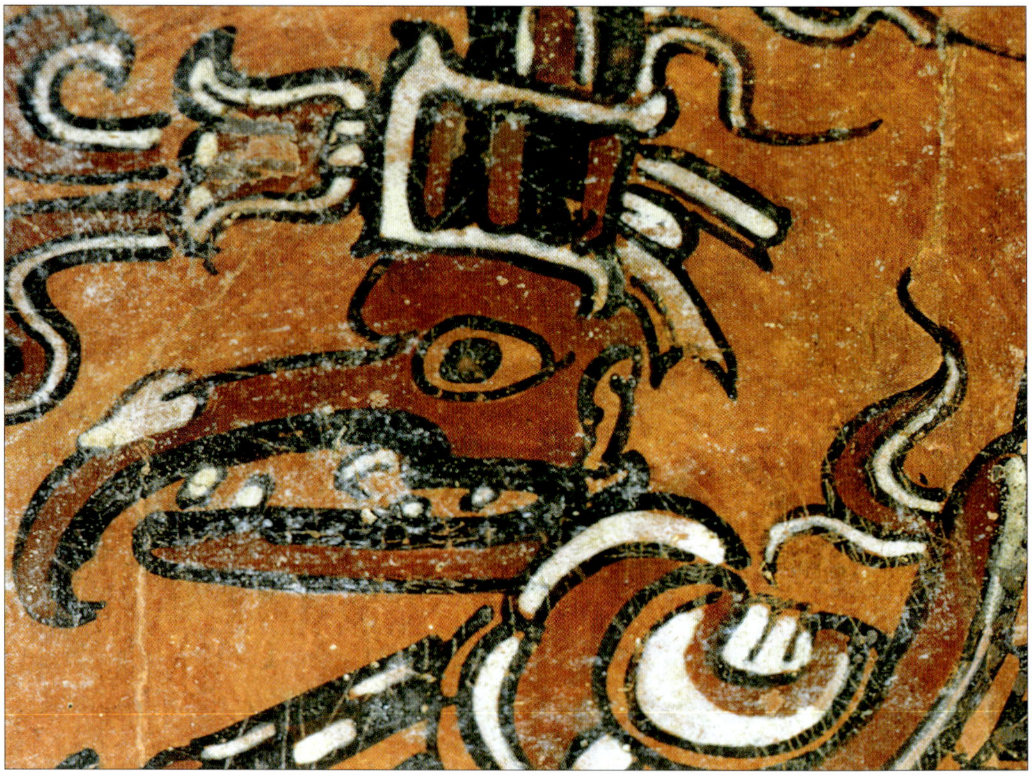

Above: Deities were often shown in attendance at the scenes of religious ritual and court life represented on vases.

EXPERT POTTERS

Some vases were incised with images and glyphs rather than painted, and in these cases the delicate lines were almost certainly cut by the same artists who were such skilled carvers of stelae and lintels.

We do not know whether specialist potters created the plates, cups and vases and then handed them over to be decorated or whether the scribal artists were also responsible for making the pots. Some of the surface effects and colouring on painted vessels were achieved by expert manipulation of oxygen levels during the firing of the pottery and in these cases the scribal artists responsible for the final appearance of the vessel must have been involved in its firing.

Below: Ceramics such as this painted vase from the Sula Valley, Honduras, accompanied elite burials in their tombs.

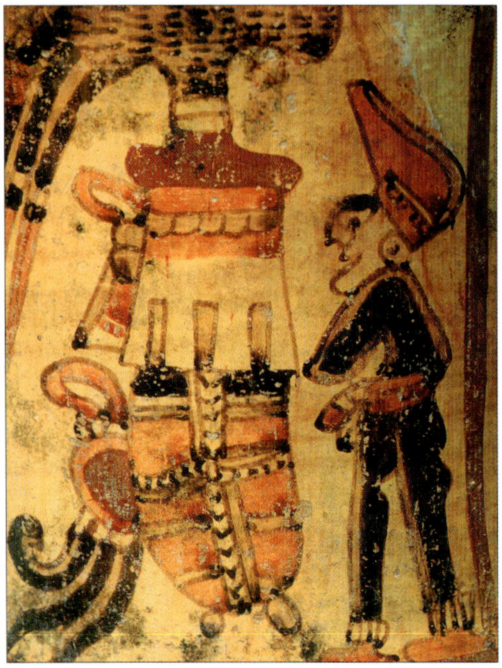

Scholars believe that many of the scenes depicted on pictorial vases were taken from screenfold books. The scribal artists must have developed an expert judgement in order to transfer the elegant proportions of composition and neat glyph-work to the curved surface of the vase being worked.

There is very little evidence that the scribes first marked out the designs before painting over them, for this would have left visible marks beneath the final design.

Scholar Michael Coe has suggested that the artists might have marked out the design in charcoal, which would have disappeared when the vessel was fired, but this can be no more than speculation.

ROYAL FUNERAL RITES

Examples of elegantly painted Maya ceramics of the late Classic Period include the vessel known to archaeologists as the Altar Vase, found in the Usumacinta-region city of Altar de Sacrificios. According to scholar R.E.W. Adams, the image painted on the vase represents a funeral held in AD754 following the death of a royal woman of middle age.

Six dancing figures on the vase are believed to represent three visiting dignitaries from other cities, each accompanied by a *way* or spirit companion. The visitors, who had travelled from nearby Yaxchilán, from mighty Tikal and from an unidentified city in the highlands of the southern Maya region, laid offerings of fine ceramics in the royal tomb. The Altar Vase itself was laid in the grave of a young woman sacrificed in honour of the deceased princess or royal wife.

An image on the vase of a young woman performing rites of autosacrificial bloodletting might be a portrait of this young victim, who was herself probably a junior royal.

At Uaxactún archaeologists found a magnificent cache of painted ceramics in a stone tomb containing the corpse of an elite figure, probably a king. The corpse, buried in the building known as Structure A-I, was laid along the sanctified north–south axis used for ceremonial centres, with its head to the north. Next to the skull was a vase painted in the 8th century AD with a scene of court ritual using black and yellow against a red-orange base colour. The scene shows a king enthroned beneath a feathered shade held by an attendant. The king faces two elaborately dressed visitors, their visible skin painted black, one carrying a spear and one holding a ritual object with three spikes that scholars call a 'knuckle duster'. A seated jaguar, mouth open in a roar or snarl, accompanies the two visitors.

In all, the tomb contained eleven exquisite pottery pieces, nine of them painted. A beautifully painted tripod plate depicting a dancer had a small hole bored in it – the result of a ceremony performed to free the soul of the plate so that it could travel with the spirit of the deceased king as he made his way to the underworld. Many other delicately painted ceramics were left as grave offerings in Tikal, Seibal, Altun Ha, Tayasal and other settlements.

HIGHLAND VASES

Painted vases of very high quality were also produced in the highlands of the southern Maya region. A vase found at Chama in the valley of the river Chixoy, Guatemala, depicts seven individuals in red, brown and black against a pink base. Two main figures face one another, both painted black, one wearing a jaguar skin. Individual features are represented in detail, suggesting that these were portraits executed from life. The black paint on the main figures might be intended to identify the two main figures as merchants by linking them to Ek Chuah, the patron god of that group.

Many vases, plates and cups were signed by the artists who painted them. For example, a cup for drinking chocolate was signed by Ah Maxam, the noble scribe from Naranjo who decorated it. The glyphs he inscribed in black paint on a cream base describe the function of the vessel and identify Ah Maxam as scribe and member of the royal household.

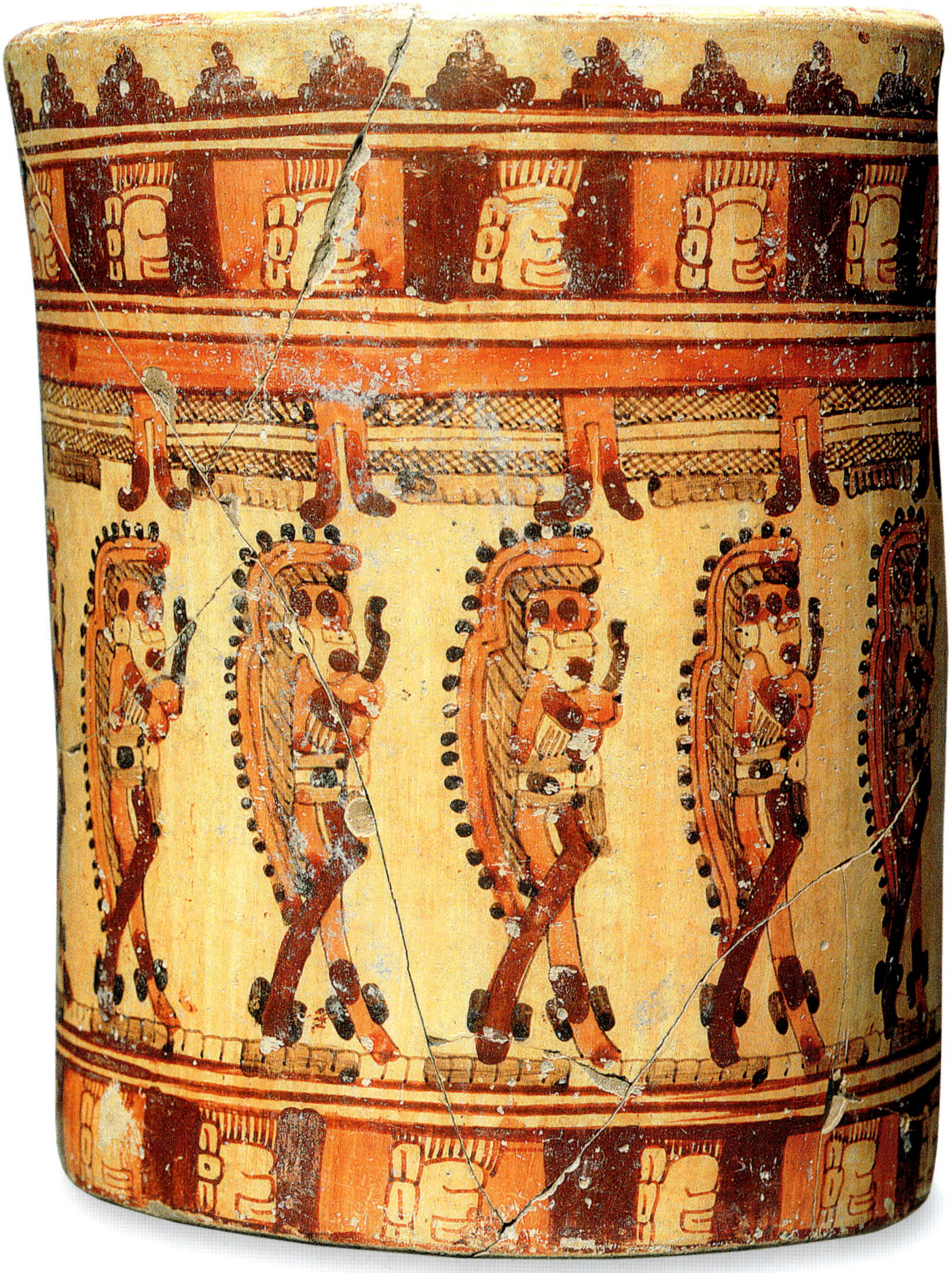

Right: Elaborately attired priests, warriors or gods ring a beautifully finished vase from Honduras, made c.AD600–900.

TENOCHTITLÁN'S LIFE-SIZE CERAMIC FIGURES

Aztec craftsmen produced remarkable fired-clay statues about 1.7m (5ft 4in) tall for the House of Eagles, a sacred precinct north of the Templo Mayor in Tenochtitlán. This was a notable development of the Mesoamerican tradition of making small clay figurines for use in worship. Aztec potters also followed this more modest path, making figures of deities such as Xipe Totec, perhaps 20cm (8in) tall. for use in domestic religious ritual and in temple offerings.

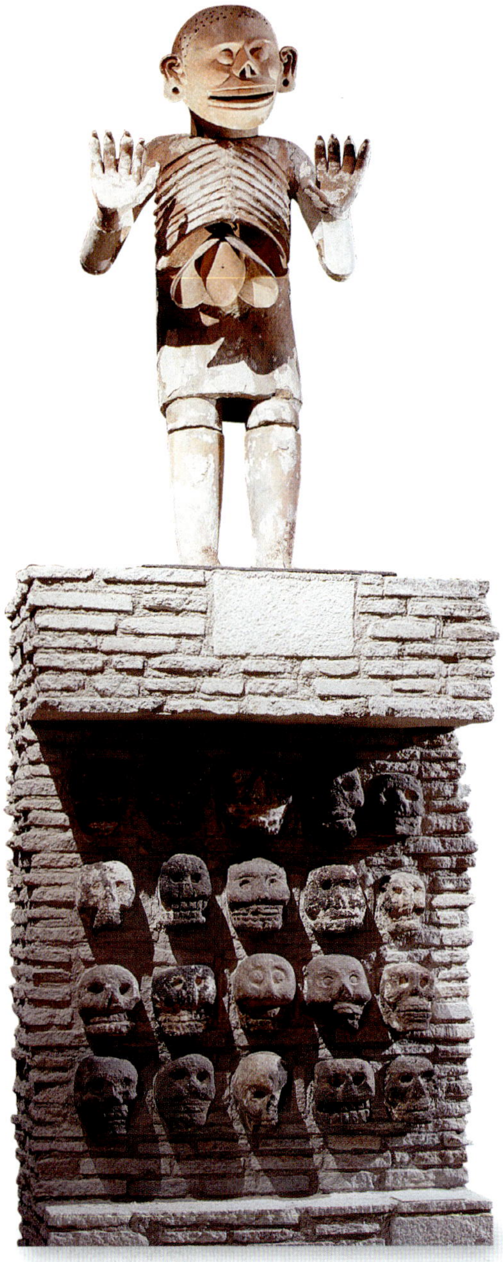

SUN COMPANIONS

A pair of life-sized statues representing eagle-warriors were mounted on a bench in the House of Eagles, which was used for penitential retreats and rites of autosacrificial bloodletting in which worshippers cut ears, cheeks or penis to offer blood to the gods. The statues were originally covered with stucco and decorated with a design in white paint that reproduced the eagle feathers worn into battle by these elite warriors. Each statue was made in four segments – the head and helmet; the torso and arms; the groin; and the lower legs. Archaeologists report that the eagle-warrior statues might have been images of the sun at dawn.

LORD OF THE UNDERWORLD

The House of Eagles also contained a pair of statues of Mictlantecuhtli, lord of the Aztec underworld Mictlán, also mounted on benches. One of the statues – 1.76m (5ft 7in) tall and 80cm (2ft 10in) wide – represented the hideous form of Mictlantecuhtli as a near-naked man with decaying flesh, bony torso and protruding liver, wearing a meagre loincloth, his hands vast claws, his mouth a terrifying grimace. Holes in the statue's skull would have held the dark curly hair associated with Aztec earth and death deities. Like those of the eagle-warriors, the statue was made in five pieces.

SKINNING OF THE MEN

Like their counterparts elsewhere in Mesoamerica during the Postclassic Period, Aztec craftsmen generally made smaller ceramic pieces using moulds. Four figures found in Tlatelolco in 1968 celebrated the gruesome rites of the festival of Tlacaxipehualiztli ('Skinning of the Men') held to honour Xipe Totec, god of vegetation and germinating seeds.

The clay statues, each about 15cm (6in) high, represented priests and worshippers. Two warriors were seated on a bench, while two priests or other participants wore the skins of flayed sacrificial victims. An intermediate-sized statue, 97cm (3ft 2in) tall, of a Xipe Totec priest wearing the puckered skin of a victim was found in 1975 in the fortified city of Tepeji el Viejo in the mountainous southern part of modern Puebla state. The sacrificial statue, which was very beautifully made, had in its turn been sacrificed by being smashed. Archaeologists have reassembled the pieces to recreate the work.

Left: One of a pair of ceramic figures (c.1480) of underworld god Mictlantecuhtli, shown with exposed liver and grimacing mouth. Traces of the original white stucco covering are still visible. Like the warrior figure, above right, he stood in the House of Eagles in Tenochtitlán's sacred precinct. Here he stands on a tzompantli *(skull altar).*

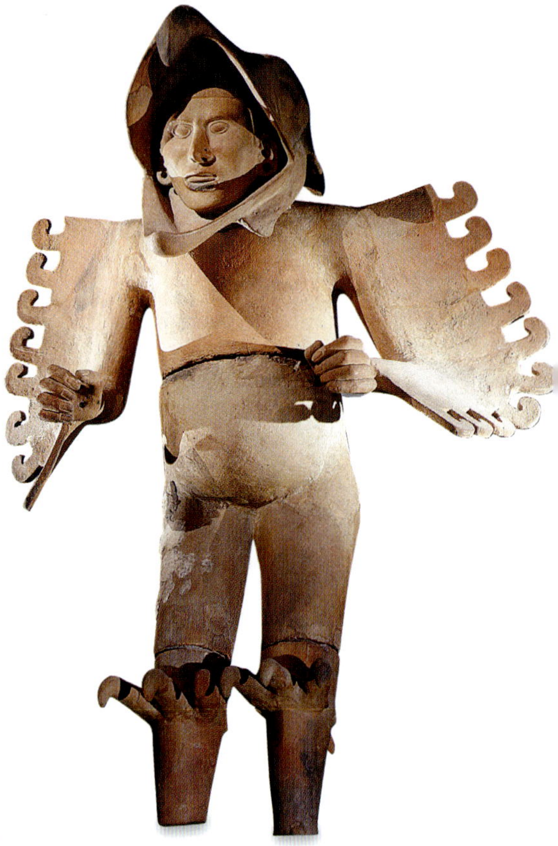

Above: One of two life-size ceramic figures of eagle-warriors who stood in the House of Eagles, this was made c.*1440–69.*

BASKETWORK, MATS AND FURNITURE

The lakeside reedbeds of Mexico and Guatemala kept Mesoamerican basket-workers well supplied with raw materials. The makers of baskets and reed mats were practitioners of an ancient craft tradition and users of skills developed thousands of years earlier. Archaeological evidence shows that even before the beginnings of village life in Mesoamerica, hunter-gatherer groups made baskets, mats and sandals from reeds. In the Classic and Postclassic Periods, most working householders probably knew enough about reed-weaving to make their own simple mats and baskets for every-day use, just as they had sufficient rudimentary pottery skills to make their own pots, plates and cups.

NAPATECUHTLI, PATRON GOD OF REED WEAVERS

The Aztec reed-weavers' patron god, Napatecuhtli, was represented wearing a tall headdress crowned with a *quetzalmiahuayo* ('gathering of sacred quetzal feathers'). A band of the bark paper used to soak up blood in rites of autosacrifice was wound around his head, with bark-paper ornaments suspended from it.

Doubtless because reed-weavers gathered their raw materials at the lakeside, Napatecuhtli was also a god of water and was associated with the rain deity Tláloc. For this reason Napatecuhtli's face was generally covered with a serpentine Tláloc mask, in which curling snakes formed eyes and upper lip. His robes were also made of bark paper and hung to his feet. He carried a reed sceptre or *oztopilli* in his left hand and sinuous snake-staff in his right hand. A delicately rendered fired-clay vessel of *c.*1500 representing Napatecuhtli was discovered in 1996 in Tláhuac, Mexico Federal District.

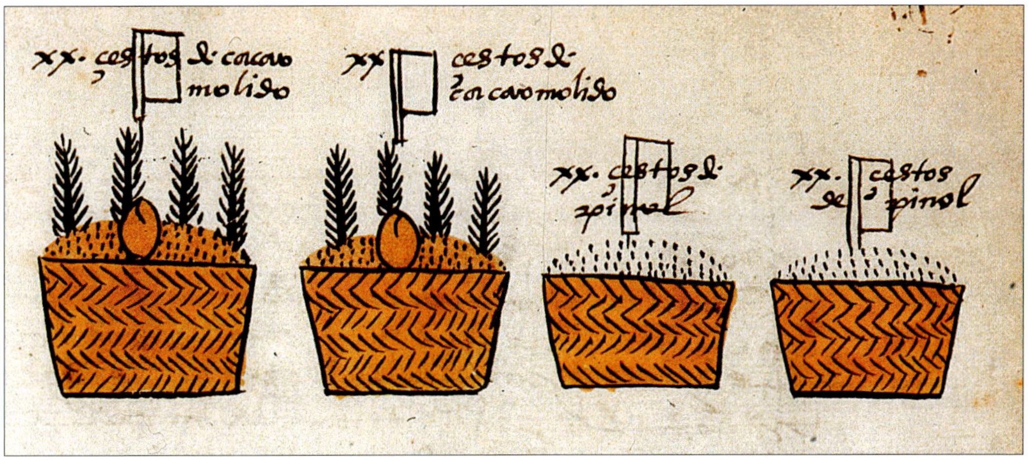

Above: A detail from the list of Aztec tribute due from Tlatelolco to Tenochtitlán shows woven baskets of cacao and chia.

Specialist basket-makers made and supplied finer quality goods to those who could afford to barter for them at market. In the Aztec era, the reed-workers also made use of palm leaf, slats of cane and the leaves of the maguey cactus. They fashioned baskets in many sizes and shapes that could be used on *chinampa* fields, in the marketplace, in the household and even in the temple precincts for moving goods, storing food, secreting valuables or ritual items and keeping clothes away from dust and dirt. Other reed-weavers made *petlatl* mats and seats in fine weave for supply to nobles. Seats and low tables were generally restricted to wealthy households, while other folk used mats on the ground.

MAYA MATS AND BASKETS

The Maya of the Classic Period certainly used mats and baskets, but none has survived. An image of a basket carved on Lintel 24 in the city of Yaxchilán reveals how intricate Maya baskets could be. It combines three decorative schemes – a featherwork pattern, a twill design and a combination of frets and small squares – in a single item. The imprint of a Postclassic Period mat has been found on the floor of the shrine discovered beneath the Temple of the Feathered Serpent at Chichén Itzá. The pattern of its weaving is the same as that of mats still produced in the locality.

Mats were conceptually associated with political power. In Aztec society the *tlatoani* was known as 'the one who takes this place upon the mat'. For the Maya, too, the mat was the locus of authority. The title *ahpop* assumed by Maya rulers meant 'the one who sits on the mat'.

Below: A typically wide-eyed and grimacing Veracruz clay figurine of c.AD*600–800 holds a woven basket full of produce.*

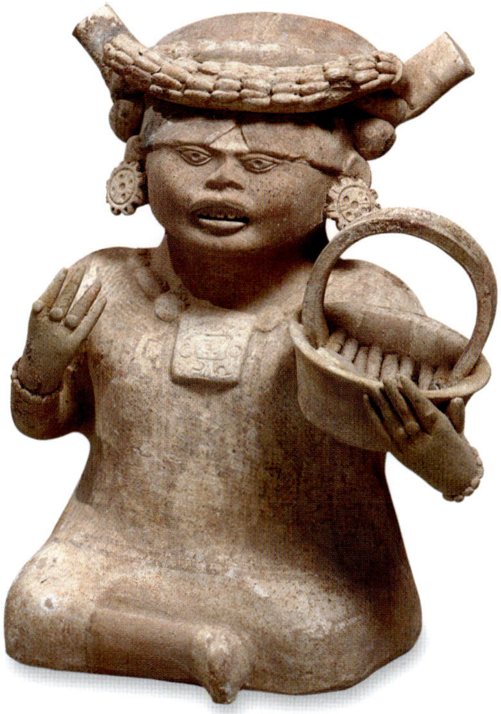

RICHLY DECORATED ROBES

From sculptures such as door lintels and stelae we know that the rulers and noble elite of Classic Period Maya cities wore cotton fabrics with a rich weave and elaborate embroidery. Weavers made large amounts of cotton cloth in a variety of patterns. Only a few fragments of cloth produced by the ancient Maya have survived. A cache of chipped flints buried in the 6th–7th century Copán temple known to archaeologists as the Rosalila structure was wrapped in disintegrating fabric. A few pieces of white cotton cloth were discovered with late Postclassic pottery of *c.*1250–1500 at Tenam, a site in the eastern part of Chiapas. When archaeologists dredged the *Cenote* of Sacrifice at Chichén Itzá, they found among the multitude of gold, silver and other precious offerings a few pieces of carbonized fabric with complex weaves.

Below: Toltec warriors wore quilted cotton battle dress. This stone soldier, carved at Tollán, reproduces the costume in detail.

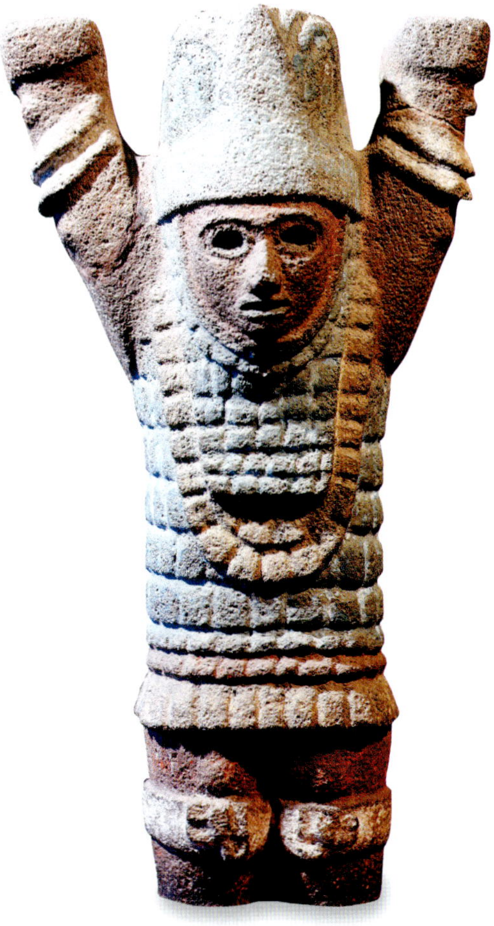

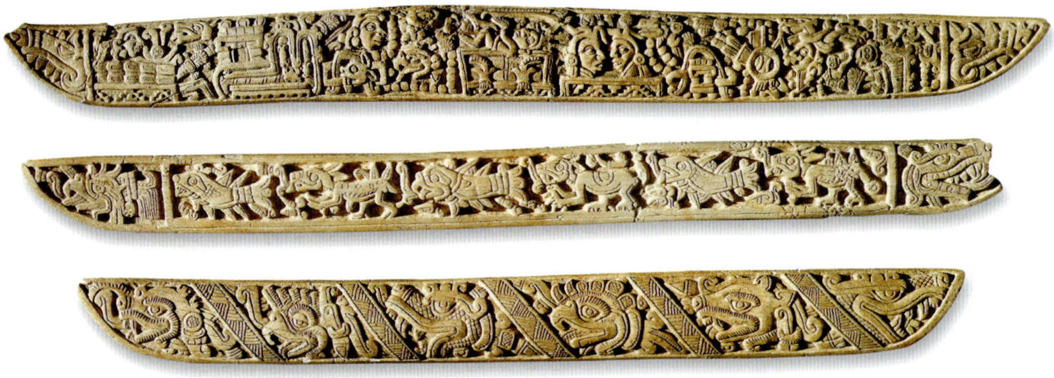

Above: Used by Zapotec artisans, these loom shuttles carved from bones of the regal jaguar were placed in Monte Albán Tomb 7.

AZTEC DESIGNS

In the Aztec empire, as in Maya lands, few pieces of cloth survived, but images in codices, in sculptures and in ceramics – together with the descriptions of Spanish invaders – reveal the rich variety of cloth and elegant decorative designs that were available.

As among the Maya, there were regionally distinctive designs. These were generally embroidered, woven, dyed or even painted on to the cloth. They were usually geometric designs, although some regions specialized in decorating with images of local animals or plants. The empire's finest textiles were those imported to Tenochtitlán from Veracruz. Huaxtec weavers, who were based in that region, produced highly prized white cotton cloth decorated with animal motifs.

Weavers made dyes from minerals, plants and animals. Red came from cochineal insects gathered in groves of nopal cacti – a useful sideline for agriculturalists. Blue clay and yellow ochre were other sources.

Purple came from the sea snail *Purpura patula*, found around the shores of Yucatán (see box). This snail was related to the Murex mollusc, found in the Mediterranean, from which the ancient Phoenicians made the 'royal purple' dye in classical Europe.

MAYA COLOUR CODE

Highland communities in modern Guatemala still follow ancient traditions in weaving practice, as far as historians can tell. These communities use handlooms to make cotton cloth and embroider this with cotton thread that has been dyed the required colour. Different communities have traditional designs. No two designs are identical, but they adhere to distinctive local patterns closely enough to be immediately recognizable. The meaning of the colours used also follows time-honoured ways. Red stands for blood, and blue sacrifice. Green-turquoise, the colour of the quetzal bird's magnificent tail plumes, is symbolic of royalty. Yellow, as the colour of maize, suggests food, while black stands for weapons – because it was the predominant colour of the obsidian used to make cutting blades for weapons. A deep purple colour derived from the sea snail *Purpura patula* found on the Pacific coast and carried inland by traders was highly esteemed.

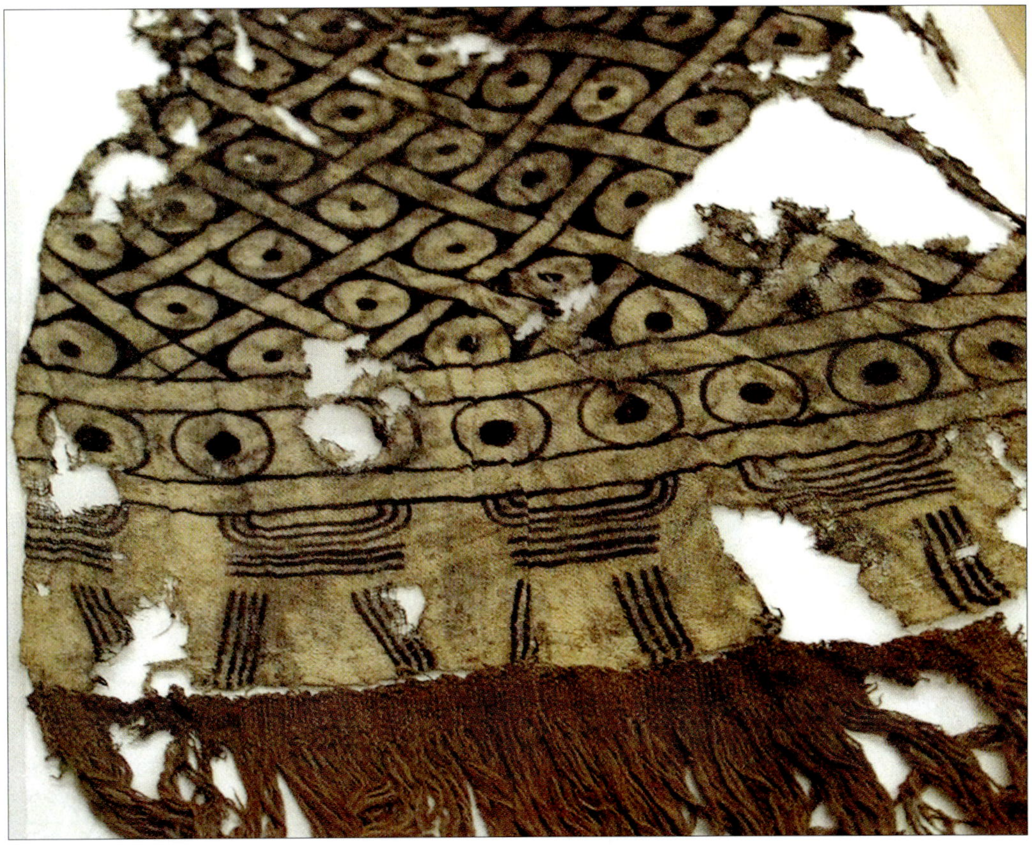

COLOURFUL BATTLE DRESS

A celebrated portrait in the 16th-century manuscript *Codex Ixtlilxochitl* of Netzahualcóyotl, ruler of Texcoco, shows the colourful costumes available to the noble elite in Aztec Mexico. The portrait shows Netzahualcóyotl in ceremonial battle garb, bearing a blue shield, with long red tassels, on his left arm and on his head a blue headdress with white and red horizontal bands. These colours were matched in the blue of his tunic and the red of the protective binding on his upper arms. On his lower half he wears a flowing kilt in horizontal colour bands of white, red, green, yellow, red and green once more.

A page from the *Codex Mendoza* (*c.*1541) also made clear the bright colours worn by elite warriors for ceremonial dress. It depicts a selection of colourful outfits with elaborate feather headdresses and coloured shields decorated by *amanteca* feather workers.

Below: A modern Mexican hooked rug uses an Aztec design, incorporating images of birds and animals, and plant motifs.

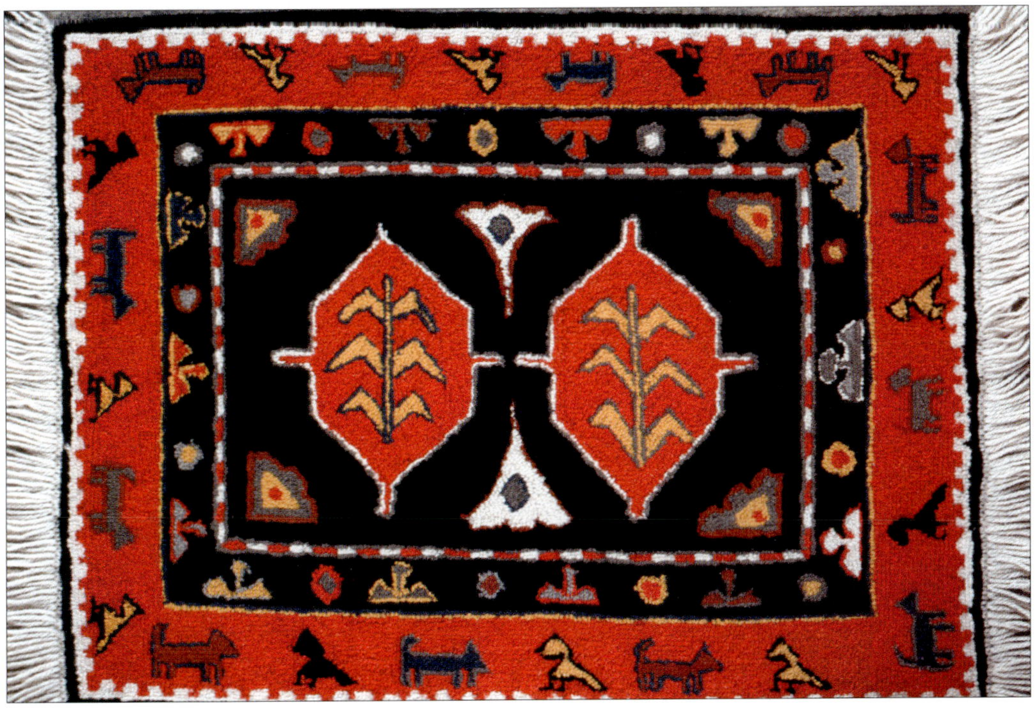

FESTIVAL COSTUME

Clothes played an important role in religious ceremonies. At festivals, priests and priestesses, prisoner-sacrificial victims or commoners selected for sacrifice wore costumes that identified them as the god or goddess being honoured.

The costumes were often elaborate and highly coloured and so added to the spectacle and drama generated by these public enactments of religious ritual. Colours and design elements added layers of religious meaning, a process well suited to representations of deities with many complex attributes, several of which they might share with other gods and goddesses.

Above: In August 2000, archaeologists excavating the Templo Mayor found this Aztec cloth in an offering to Tláloc.

For example, a celebrated statue of water goddess Chalchiúhtlicue (dated *c.*1500) found in Mexico City in 1824 wore the headdress that identified her as Chalchiúhtlicue, while her cape was embroidered with *chalchiuhtil* or jade symbols that were also essential elements of the goddess's outfit. However, she also wore a rattlesnake sash to hold up her lower garments and these associated her with maize goddesses and also with the earth goddess Coatlícue.

Statues like this one of Chalchiúhtlicue might have represented a deity or a priest/priestess impersonating a deity and showed details of festival dress. A few statues are naked or barely dressed figures and might have been dressed in brightly coloured real clothes as part of festival rites.

A GATHERING OF FEATHERS

Images in the *Florentine Codex* (1575–77) of Friar Bernardino de Sahagún depict highly skilled Aztec *amanteca* feather-workers at their job, sewing green quetzal feathers into elaborate headdresses for royal and priestly costumes, on to ceremonial shields and across temple banners. The emerald-green tail plumes of the male quetzal, gathered by specialist hunters in the tropical forests of Maya lands and imported to highland Mexico, could be 1m (3ft 3in) long. It made a great visual impact when sewn around a headdress or added to its crown to make a tall *quetzalmiahuayo* (gathering of quetzal feathers). The feather-workers also used feathers from macaws, parrots, spoonbills and a range of other birds and made elite items of clothing, bracelets and magnificent costumes for dancing.

From at least the prime of Teotihuacán, in *c.*AD500, the transport of feathers was a major component of Mesoamerican trade. Other images in the *Florentine Codex* depict Aztec traders at market sitting alongside brightly coloured feather displays. Feathers and feathered items were suitable offerings in temples because of their rarity and great worth. Quetzal feathers were additionally valued because of their length and, most importantly, because their colour resembled that of precious jade – the green of maize shoots and water, associated with Chalchiúhtlicue ('Mistress of the Jade Skirt'), and symbolic of life itself.

Below: Feather birds. These creatures on a painted terracotta brazier from Teotihuacán are stylized images of the sacred quetzal.

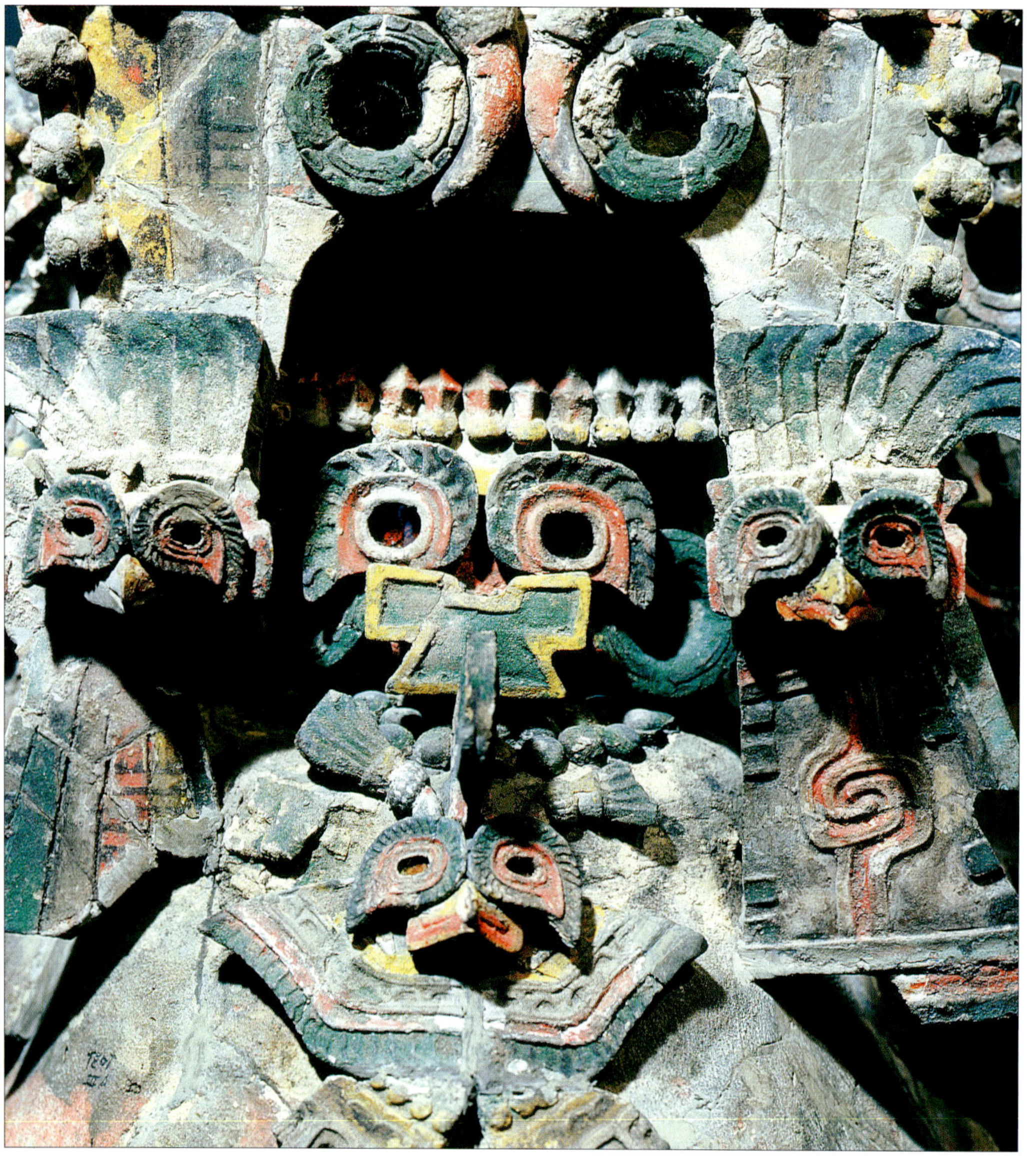

FEATHER-WORKING DEITY

The Aztec feather-workers, gathered in their own quarter of Tlatelolco, worshipped Coyotlinahual as their patron god. This deity was associated with Tezcatlipoca. In one version of the myth of Quetzalcóatl-Topiltzin as ruler of Tollán, when Tezcatlipoca arrived in the city of the Toltecs to bring about the fall of the Feathered Serpent through trickery and deception, he was accompanied by Coyotlinahual, who was identified as a magician.

EUROPEAN ADMIRATION

Feather-work was an unfamiliar craft to the Spanish invaders and one of the artistic achievements of the Aztecs and Maya that made the greatest impression on Europeans. (Although the conquistadors were keen to collect and send home Mixtec work in gold and silver, they admired it for its monetary rather than artistic worth and melted it down on its arrival in Europe.)

A magnificent example of the work of the most skilled *amanteca* was a *quetzalapanecayotl* ('quetzal-feather headdress') sent to King Charles V of Spain by Hernán Cortés in 1519 and now part of the collection of the Museum für Völkerkunde in Vienna, Austria. The vast headdress, which measures 1.16m by 1.75m (3ft 10in by 5ft 9in), contains 450 quetzal feathers adorned with gold appliqué and turquoise. It would have made a great impression, even from afar, when worn by priests of Quetzalcóatl in

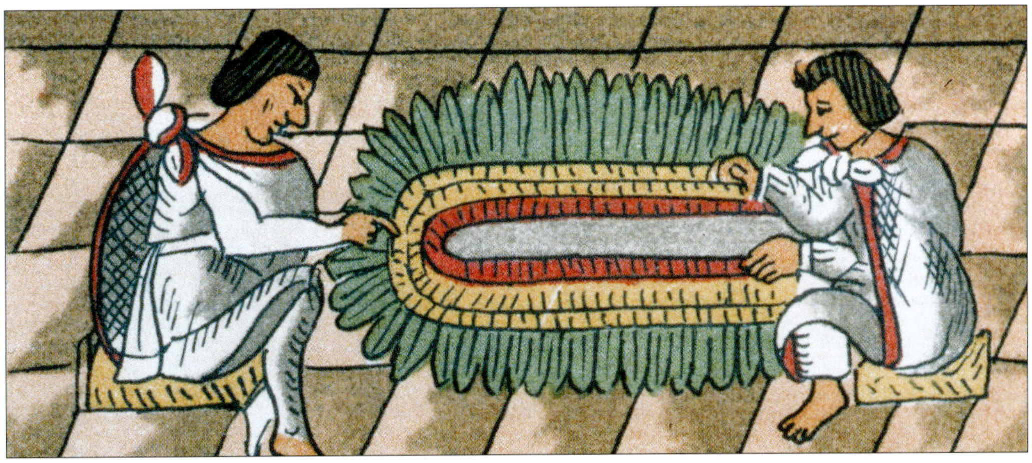

Right: The Florentine Codex *depicts highly regarded* amanteca *craftsmen lavishing attention on a feather costume.*

processions and sacrificial rituals. Cortés collected a good number of featherwork items and sent a large consignment of them to Spain in 1522 but the precious cargo was seized by pirates.

NOBLE ADORNMENT

The Museum für Völkerkunde also contains a large fan, 1.19m tall and 68cm in diameter (3ft 10in by 2ft 2in), made from quetzal feathers and gold appliqué in the last years of the Aztec empire. Fans were used by rulers, nobles and elite *pochteca* merchants. These most elegant of Tenochtitlán's citizens provided a regular demand for the feathered fans produced by the *amanteca* of Tlatelolco. Nobles could be seen carrying a brightly coloured fan – feathered, for example, with the plumage of parakeets and hummingbirds – in one hand, and a bunch of flowers in the other. The fans were usually made with carved wooden handles.

Another fine survival of Aztec featherwork was a striking ceremonial shield, 70cm (2ft 3in) in diameter of *c.*1500, that depicted a creature some scholars identify as a long-tailed water beast called an *ahuítzotl* ('water-prickle creature'). Aztec legend had it that the *ahuítzotl* lay in wait for an unwary wanderer on riverbanks and lakesides, caught the wanderer in its tail and pulled him down to the depths of the water where he drowned. The beast's name was taken by the *tlatoani* Ahuítzotl (*r.* 1486–1502), who led vast sacrificial rituals for the dedication of the rebuilt Templo Mayor in Tenochtitlán in 1487.

Other historians have suggested that the beast on the shield is a coyote, an animal form of the god Tezcatlipoca who was one of the patron deities of war, and that it might have been the mascot-symbol of an elite military order. The shield was made of reeds strengthened with lengths of wood and covered with animal hide. The craftsman stuck feathers of the spoonbill, oriole, macaw and cotinga to pieces of agave paper and glued these to the shield to create the design, adding quetzal plumes and more spoonbill and cotinga feathers around the rim. Strips of sheet gold emphasized the design.

MAYA FEATHERWORK

No examples of Maya feather-work have survived, but carved and painted images reveal the splendour of the capes, shields, headdresses, fans, spear pendants and other ornaments made by the Maya counterparts of the *amanteca*. At Piedras Negras, for example, Stela 12 depicts a ruler wearing both feather headdress and feather robe. Similarly, in Chichén Itzá's Temple of the Jaguars, wooden door lintels were carved with images of featherwork. The murals at Bonampak also provide evidence of elegant Maya featherwork designs.

IN THE CHRISTIAN ERA

The native craft of feather-work survived the Spanish Conquest, after which featherworkers' expertise in making priestly headdresses and costumes led to their contributing to the wardrobe and paraphernalia of Christian priests. The Bishop of Michoacán remarkable mitre was made in *c.*1530–60 from maguey paper and cotton cloth with a delicate mosaic of feathers from hummingbirds, macaws, parrots, cotingas, spoonbills, tzinitzans and starlings depicting events from Christ's Passion and the Last Judgement.

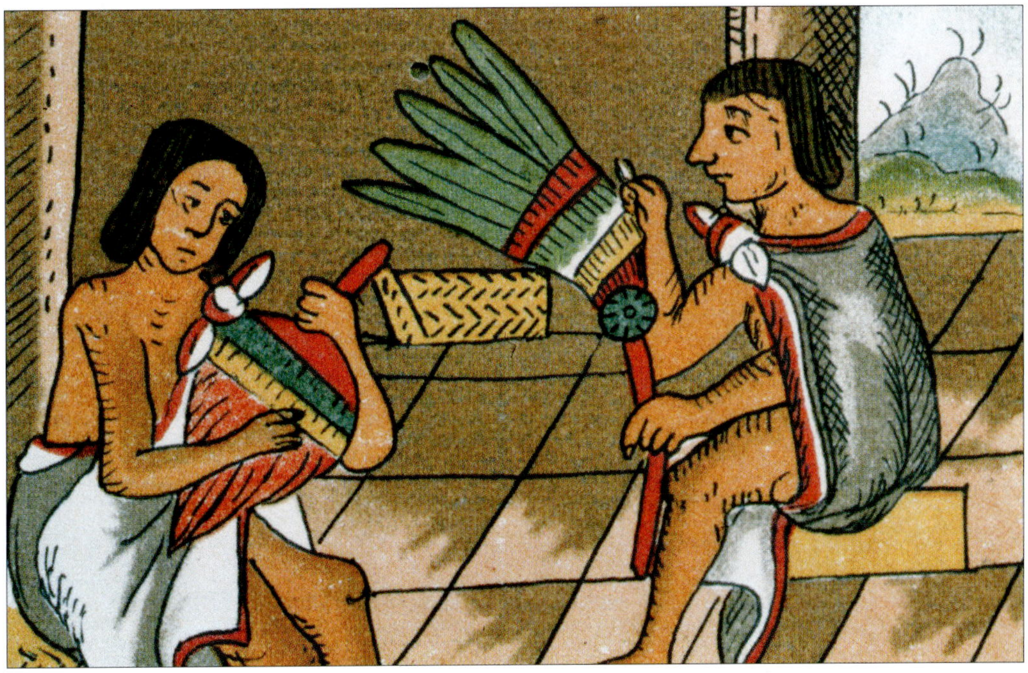

Right: Amanteca *had many commissions from Tenochtitlán's religious hierarchy for feathered costumes worn in sacred ritual.*

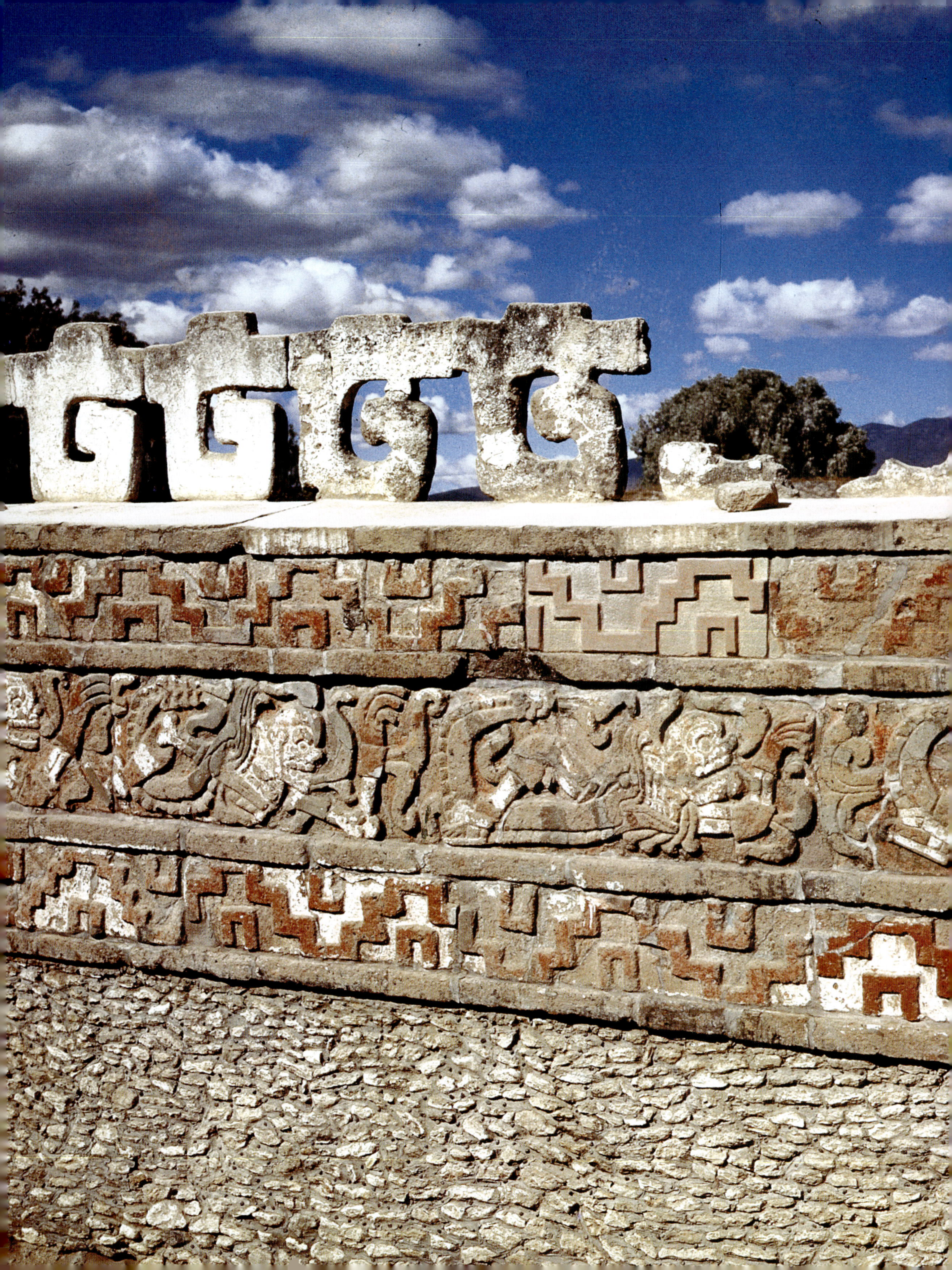

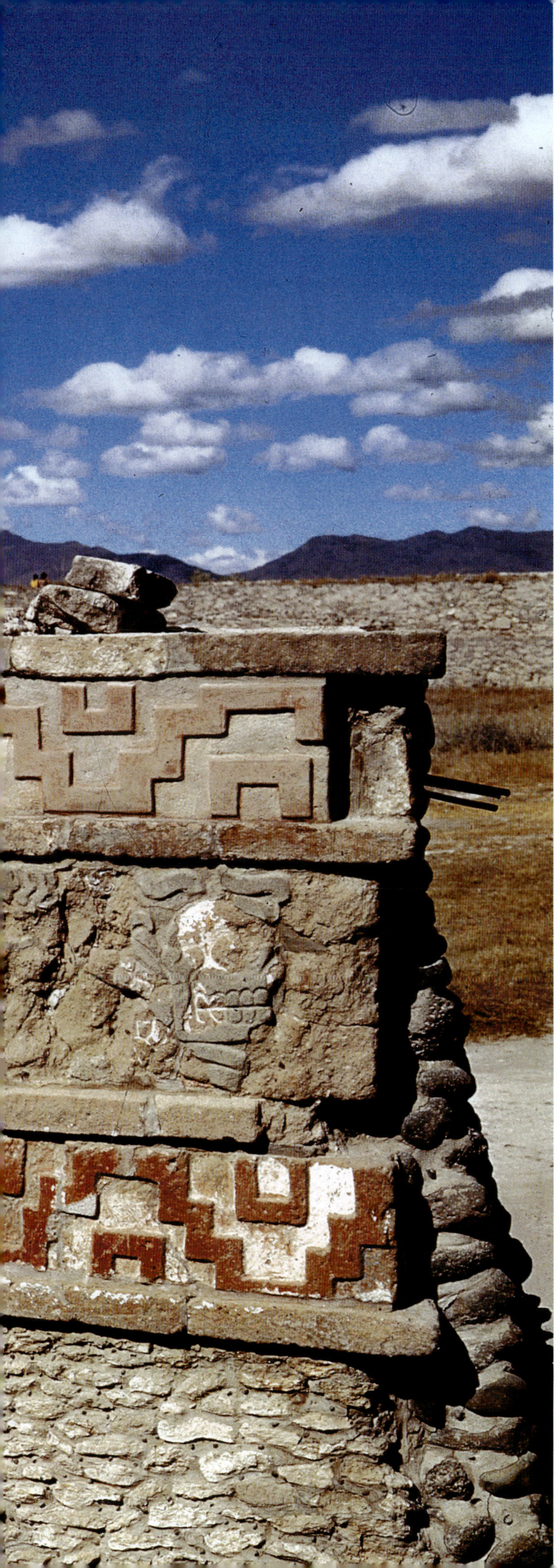

CHAPTER FOUR

THE CARVER'S ART

The monumental carved heads of Olmec kings in the 2nd–1st millennium BC were raised in rows in plazas or ceremonial areas, where their steady, inscrutable gaze would fall on any who approached. Likewise the carved stone pillars or stelae of Maya cities in the Classic Period stood in great public spaces, a statement of dynastic power. Sculpture in Mesoamerica took two main forms: free-standing monuments, such as Olmec heads or Maya stelae, and decorative elements on buildings.

In many cases carving on buildings was also for public consumption – for instance, the stucco deity masks that flanked access stairs on Maya pyramid-temples and the dynastic scenes carved on temple roof combs were both visible from the plazas below. In other cases – such as carving on door lintels at Yaxchilán or Piedras Negras or on stucco panels within temples at Palenque – these carved elements were intended for viewing close up and would have been seen only by members of the priestly and ruling elite. They still celebrated divine blessing on royal achievement and consolidated the standing of the dynasty, but did so by what historians call 'horizontal propaganda' within a single social level as opposed to 'vertical propaganda' from a higher level (of the rulers) to a lower level (of the commoners).

Left: The Toltecs developed the coatepantli *or serpent wall. At Tollán, it limited access to the main ceremonial area.*

THE KING'S HEAD: OLMEC MONUMENTAL CARVING

The craft of Olmec stonemasons appears to have burst fully formed into the history of Mesoamerican carving. Scholars know no precedent in the region for the monumental heads, three-dimensional figures, colossal royal thrones and early forms of stelae or pillars that the Olmec produced from the 2nd millennium BC onwards. The only three-dimensional representations in Mesoamerica before the rise of the Olmec in the Gulf Coast region were the small clay figures found at many sites including the villages around the lakes of the Valley of Mexico.

SYMBOLS OF ABSOLUTE POWER

Seventeen Olmec monumental heads have survived. They are remarkably similar, with fleshy faces and foreheads gathered in a frown. All wear a tight helmet or cap that comes down to just above the eyes. Some 2–3m tall (6ft 6in–10ft) and weighing up to 20 tons each, their size alone makes them deeply compelling, but they are also arresting in their naturalism; in the lifelike detail of thick, slightly separated lips, the pupils of the eyes and the folds of flesh on the cheek. Simultaneously, their emotionless gaze makes them seem withdrawn and superior and is expressive of authority and absolute power.

Below: Scholars believe that the Olmec could identify individual kings or the dynasties to which they belonged by interpeting emblems in their head dresses.

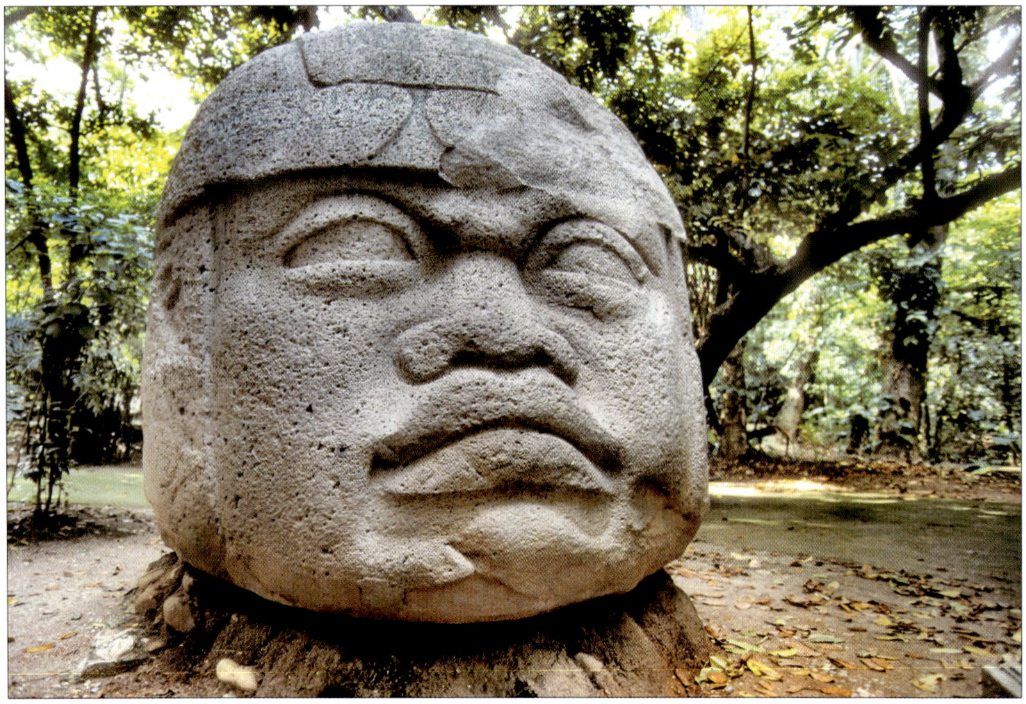

MONUMENTAL FEAT

The heads were carved from large, smooth basalt boulders that occur naturally in the Tuxtla mountains around 80km (50 miles) from the Olmec temple towns of La Venta, San Lorenzo and Laguna de Los Cerros. The boulders were probably carved *in situ* in the mountains, then carefully wrapped and transported by river-raft to the ceremonial centres of these settlements, where hundreds of labourers assembled to move and erect the vast structures in rows.

Scholars believe that the heads were portraits in basalt of Olmec kings, perhaps the reigning lord or his most recently deceased ancestor, probably commissioned to mark funerals, coronation rites or important anniversaries of these

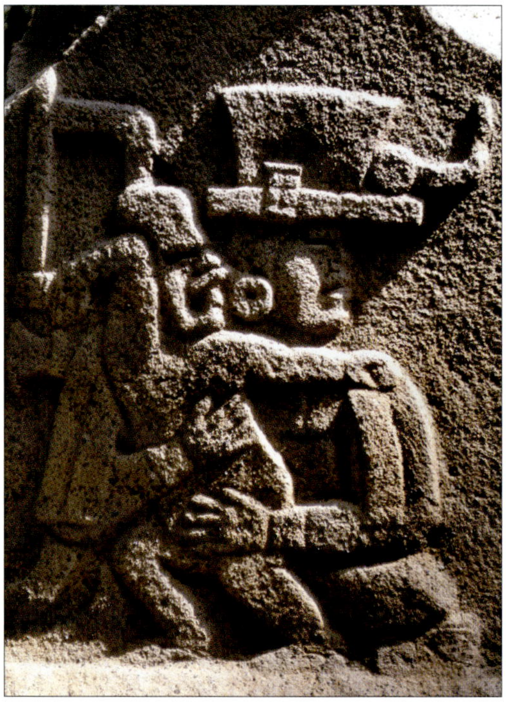

Above: La Venta Altar 5, marked with images of helmeted adults bearing 'were-jaguar' babies, was probably a royal throne.

Below: Olmec kings had power to deliver fertility, represented in this La Venta carving by the turtle shown above the ruler's head.

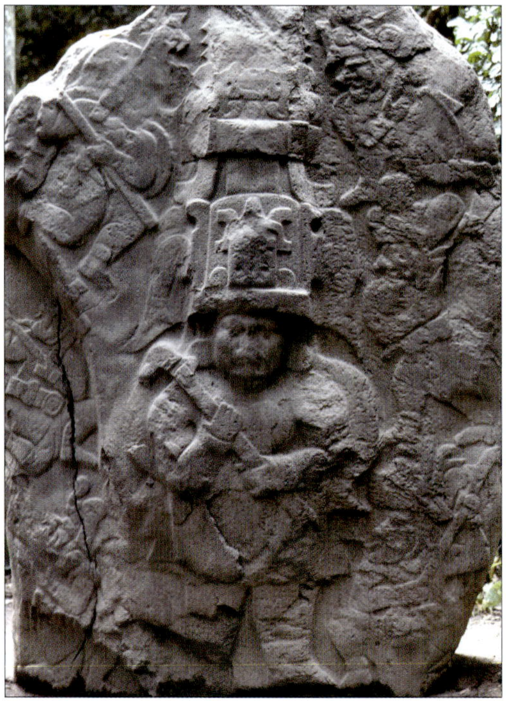

events. The headdresses are all different, marked with emblems that might have represented the king's name or that of the dynasty to which he belonged.

KNEELING BALL PLAYER?

Other notable Olmec stonework included a kneeling figure known as Monument 34 from San Lorenzo. Carved from basalt *c.*1100BC, the figure is 79cm (2ft 7in) high, with sockets cut at the shoulder that once held moveable arms and a carving of a concave mirror on his chest. Some scholars suggest that this kneeling male represents a player of the Mesoamerican ball game.

A statue carved at Laguna de Los Cerros *c.*1100BC is the only known standing figure carved by Olmec sculptors: the caped figure, nicknamed 'Superman' by scholars, stood 1.5m (5ft) tall.

More typical was a large greenstone statue of a seated man holding a baby that combined the features of a human infant with the square snout of a jaguar, an example of the 'were-jaguar' image commonly used by the Olmec and tentatively identified by scholars as an image of the rain god. This statue, found at Las Limas in Veracruz in 1965, is 55cm (22in) in height. On the knees and shoulders of the seated figure, the sculptor carved four profiled faces with distinctive features that may represent either four aspects of a deity or four distinct divinities.

Olmec craftsmen also carved several large stone thrones, which were once believed by archaeologists to be altars used in sacred ritual. Of these thrones, the most celebrated is the La Venta monument, which is known to archaeologists as Altar 4. This depicts a seated ruler in a bird headdress emerging from an opening in the front of the throne, holding a rope that connects him to a bound figure on one side of the stone. The same rope probably originally connected him to another figure on the other side, but this carving has been defaced. The rope might indicate that the king had taken the other figure captive, or that the two were bound by dynastic links.

Archaeologist David Grove identified a buck-toothed ruler portrayed on Head 4 at La Venta as one of the bound figures represented on a throne at San Lorenzo. This suggests either that the two sacred towns had been at war and that a San Lorenzo king had captured a La Venta king, or that the monument celebrated the kinship ties between the two ruling dynasties. On the La Venta Altar 4, a gaping jaguar's mouth was carved above the king suggesting that, in emerging from the niche in the stone, the king was coming forth from the heart of this regal predator.

Below: The posture and hand positions of this Olmec volcanic-stone statue led scholars to label him the 'standard bearer'.

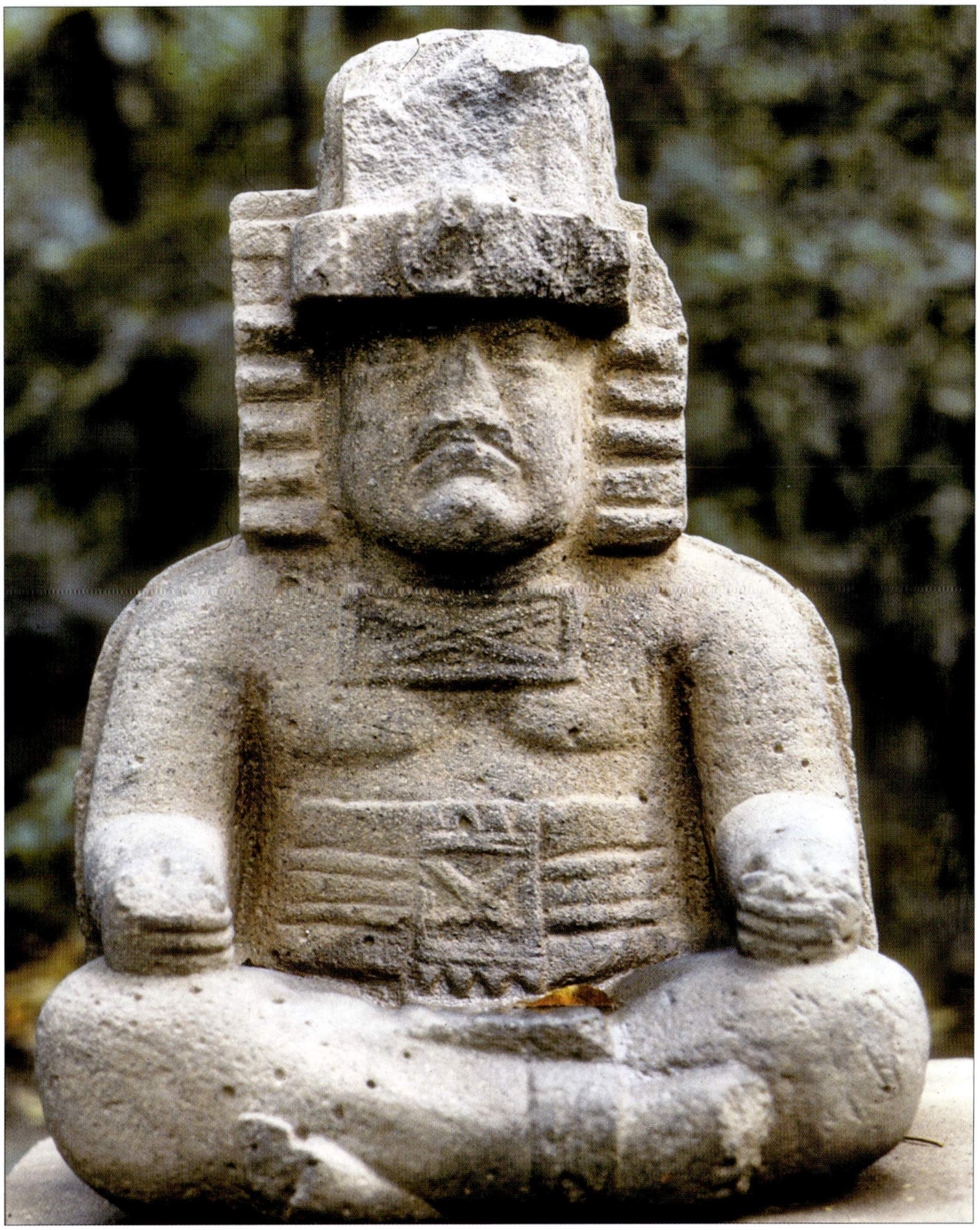

FROM THREE TO TWO DIMENSIONS: THE FIRST STELAE

After *c.*500BC, Mesoamerican craftsmen moved away from the three-dimensional carvings of heads and seated or kneeling figures produced by Olmec artisans to concentrate largely on relief carvings in two dimensions. For more than 1,000 years, although potters continued to make clay figurines, relief carvings on panels, and thrones, slabs attached to buildings and stone pillars or stelae were the norm.

From the 6th century AD onwards, sculptors at the Maya city of Toniná created an unusual group of stelae that were carved on all four sides of the block, almost like a statue. Then in the 9th century AD, with the rise of the Toltecs – and perhaps in the Chalcihuites culture of northern Mexico, which some scholars now identify as a source of many Toltec practices and motifs – craftsmen returned to making this kind of monumental three-dimensional statue.

The Toltec-Maya at Chichén Itzá and the Aztec inheritors of Toltec power at Tenochtitlán were also enthusiastic practitioners of three-dimensional sculpture.

Below: The skeletal figure on this late Preclassic stone fragment from Izapa represents the underworld god of the dead.

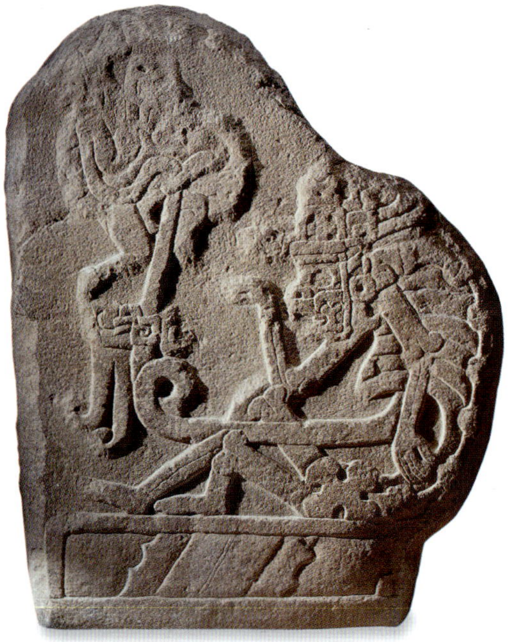

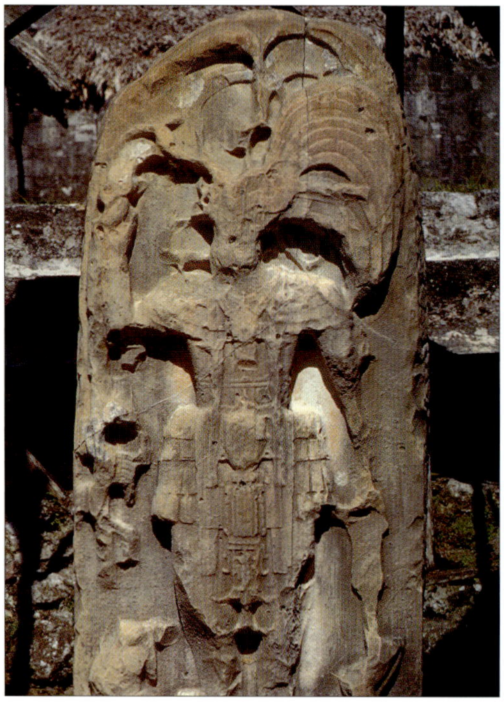

Above: The deep relief carving of King Curl Head on Stela 10 (c.AD527) from Tikal has been eroded by time. Stela 10 stood on the North Terrace facing the Great Plaza.

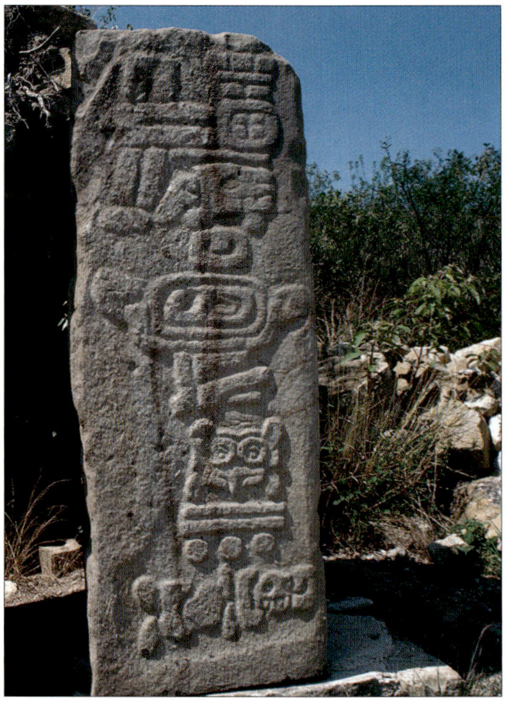

Above: Some Monte Albán stelae celebrated the achievements of individual rulers. They were carved with dates believed to be birthdates taken by the kings as their names.

CHALCATZINGO CARVINGS

The Olmecs had already demonstrated a great capacity for relief carving, evidenced in their high-relief work on stone thrones, in rock carvings and also in stone pillars or stelae. As early as 1100BC, craftsmen who were themselves Olmecs or who were working in the Olmec style cut elaborate reliefs in rocks at the trading centre of Chalcatzingo in the Amatzinac valley, to the south-east of the Valley of Mexico. One, dubbed 'El Rey' by historians, represents a king wearing an elaborate headdress, seated on a throne and holding a bar bearing a scroll design identical to the one carved on his throne, within a monster-mouth or cave believed to represent the entrance to the underworld. Art historian Esther Pasztory notes that the focus is on the importance of costume, equipment and location, as distinct from the monumental heads, which celebrated the power of the physical form.

Olmec stelae similarly celebrated rulers in elaborate costume. The monument labelled Stela 2 at La Venta, for example, represents a figure in ceremonial attire apparently holding a sceptre, weapon or bat. Historians suggest that the image may depict a player of the ball game – perhaps a royal ball game player. The stela, 2.46m (8ft) tall, was carved *c.*1100BC.

RECORDING THE CYCLES OF TIME

The Olmecs' contemporaries in Oaxaca also excelled at relief carving. At San José Mogote, Zapotec craftsmen carved a stone slab representing a fallen figure and set it in the doorway of a ceremonial building where people would tread. In the carving, known to archaeologists as Monument 3, skilled and learned stonemasons cut the day sign 1-Earthquake from the 260-day ritual calendar between the feet of the figure, perhaps to record the name of the person represented or the date on

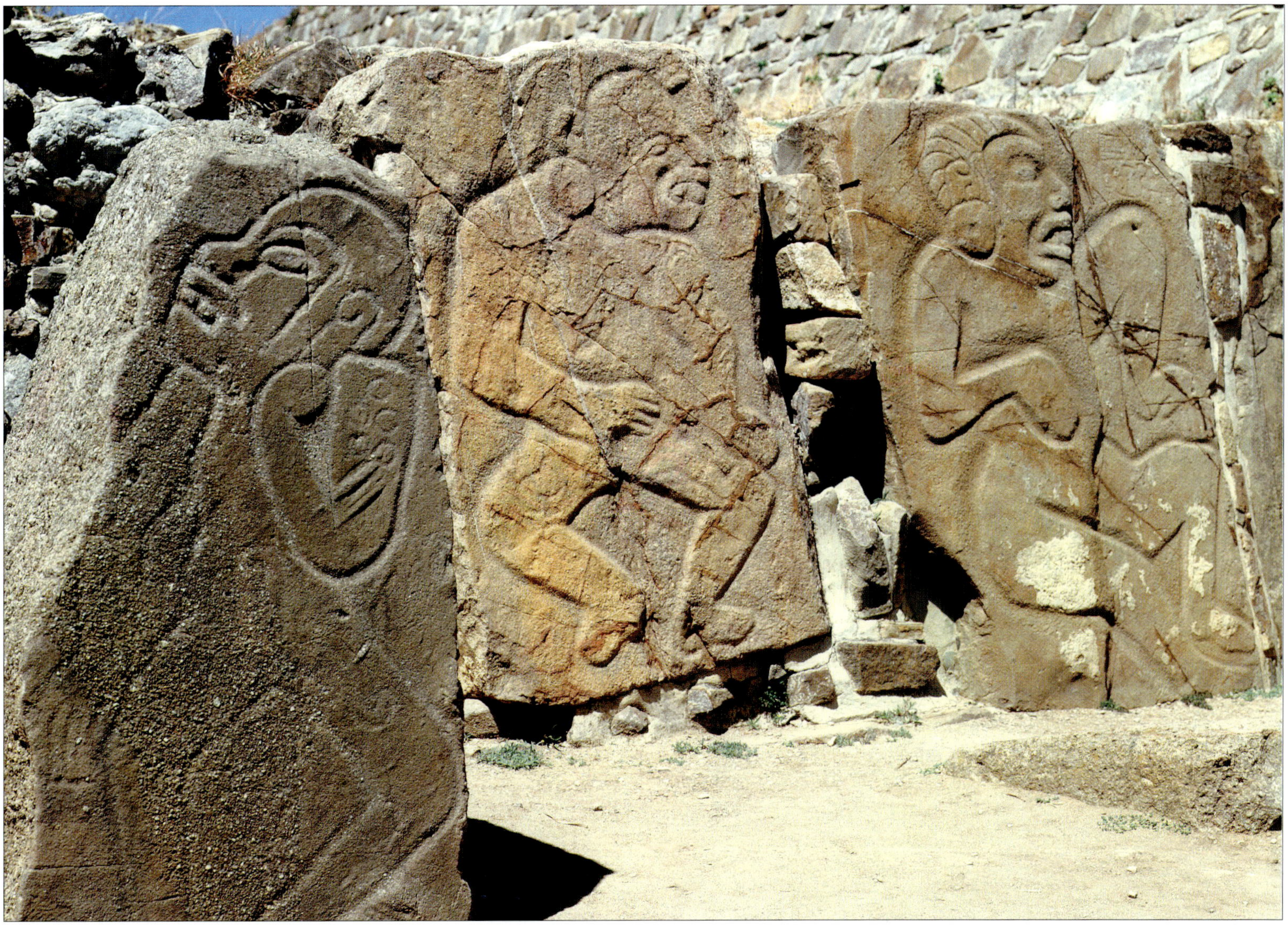

Above: Danzantes. Some 300 carvings of ritual victims or prisoners – once thought to be dancers – were displayed on Building J as a statement of Monte Albán's might.

which he was killed or sacrificed. Cut c.700–500BC, this is the oldest evidence we have for the use of the 260-day calendar in Mesoamerica.

Shortly afterwards, in c.500–200BC, Zapotec artisans at nearby Monte Albán carved loose-limbed figures on the structure now called Building L or the Temple of the Danzantes. Slabs bearing these carvings were probably arranged along the side of the building. The fluid carving of these figures – believed to be prisoners of war or sacrificial victims – includes scrolls emanating from the groin, probably representing the flow of sacrificial blood after the priests had mutilated the victims' sexual organs, or possibly celebrating rites of autosacrifice in which the depicted figures had cut their own sexual organs to offer their blood. Scholars note that the stonemasons here represented victims rather than rulers, and as at San José Mogote, exhibited a concern with marking the place of the images within the cycles of time.

STELAE IN MAYA LANDS

At Izapa on the Pacific coastal plain of Chiapas, in the southern Maya region, craftsmen developed a highly influential style in carving stelae from c.300BC onwards. They cut images of scenes from religious narratives, in which human-animal figures interact in making offerings.

Scholars identify Stela 21 at Izapa (cut c.100BC–AD100) as the first representation in Mesoamerican carving of the act of sacrifice. The pillar depicts a standing figure holding the head of a newly decapitated victim, whose lifeblood pours forth in long scrolls both from the head and the prostrate body, while in the background a ruler or noble passes by in a sedan chair carried by two porters. Another roughly contemporary stela, number 25, represents a man or hero from religious narrative standing on the ritually important right-hand side of a scene, holding a staff on which a magnificent bird perches and facing a crocodile with its nose in the ground and tail vertically in the air. The stone-carver gave the crocodile an explicit likeness to a tree and indeed added a bird in the 'branches' of its tail. Scholars cannot fully explain the scene, but the crocodile, normally an image for the earth, may be a representation of the ceiba cosmic tree connecting underworld and heavens through the terrestrial plane.

Craftsmen also cut stelae in this period at Kaminaljuyú in the Guatemala valley. They carved rulers, generally portrayed walking in profile wearing elaborate garb and headdress and holding objects of ceremonial or ritual significance.

SET IN STONE:
THE POWER OF MAYA KINGS

Craftsmen in settlements such as Izapa, Kaminaljuyú and Abaj Takalik in the southern Maya region were cutting glyphic inscriptions that probably included calendrical dates in the years *c.* 100BC–AD250 (the late Preclassic Period). Fragments of what might originally have been dated monuments survive, but none of the dates themselves have been found.

CHANGING PERSPECTIVE

In these early years, Maya sculptors represented rulers with feet, legs and head in profile, but the torso turned towards the viewer with both arms visible. At Tikal, sculptors began to experiment with the position of the figure. Stela 4, dated AD378 and recording the accession of King Curl Nose, is the oldest known pillar to show a figure turned entirely towards the viewer. Another Curl Nose monument, Stela 18 of AD396, is the oldest known Maya image of a seated figure facing the viewer. Another early carving of a figure looking straight out of the pillar, Stela 26 at Uaxactún, is dated AD445. This position was then found on stelae throughout the Classic Period, at sites including Palenque, Yaxchilán, Piedras Negras and Seibal.

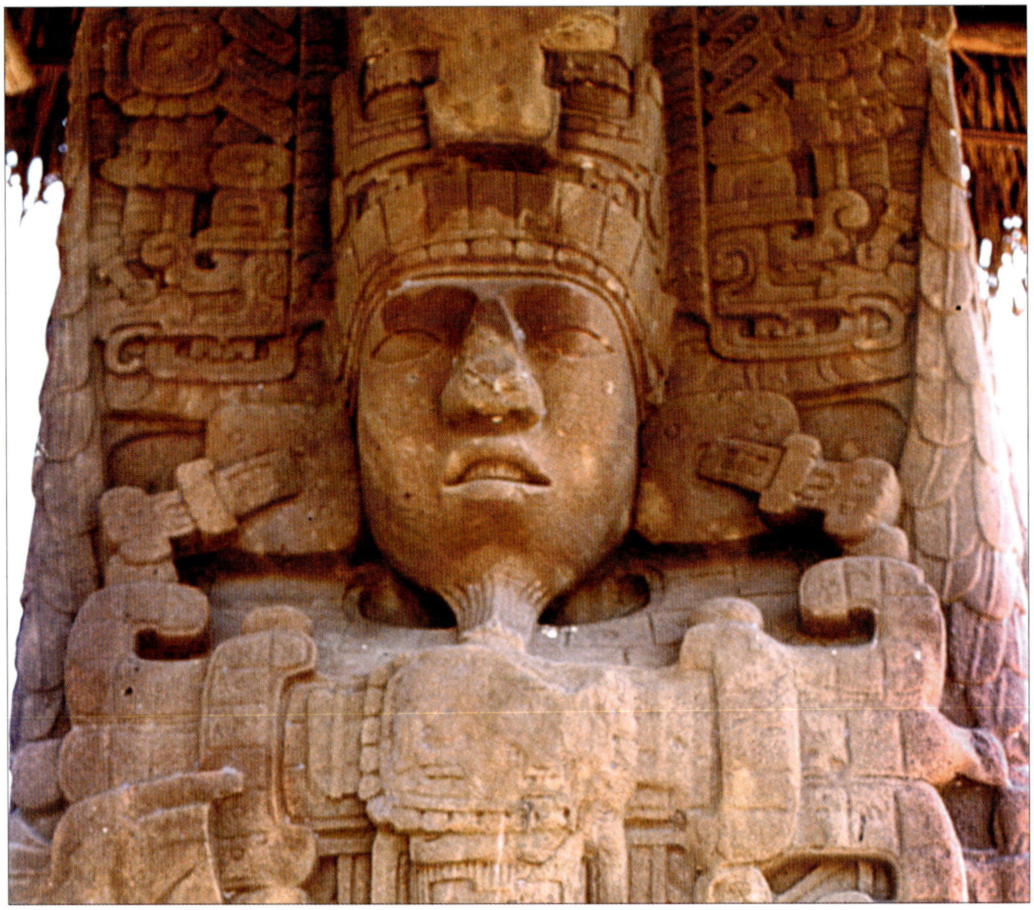

Above: At Quiriguá, Stela D is one of several in the Main Plaza bearing the face of King Cauac Sky (r. 724–84).

Below: Intricate Puuc-style carving surrounds a standing figure of the king on this monument from Kabah in Yucatán.

KINGS AND QUEENS OF CALAKMUL

The city of Calakmul, in south-eastern Campeche, contains 113 stelae – more than at any other Maya city. Some of these are unique in the Maya world in that they were raised in pairs that bear male and female portraits, understood to be the king and his queen. The first of these paired portraits were Stela 29 and Stela 28, raised by the city's second king in AD623. Another set, Stela 24 and Stela 23, were erected in AD702 by Calakmul's fifth king on the western edge of the city's Central Plaza.

Four stelae at Piedras Negras depict a newly inaugurated king in the position adopted on the celebrated Olmec Altar 4: seated cross-legged in a recess, facing the viewer. These four stelae were Stela 25 (dedicated in AD608), Stela 6 (AD687), Stela 11 (AD731) and Stela 14 (AD761). Each was an advance on its predecessor in terms of the success with which the carving was achieved, using progressively deeper recesses that permitted fuller development of the seated figure.

DEEP RELIEF

Images of kings facing out of the stela were most successfully developed by craftsmen at Copán and Quiriguá. At Copán, the carving on Stelae H (AD730)

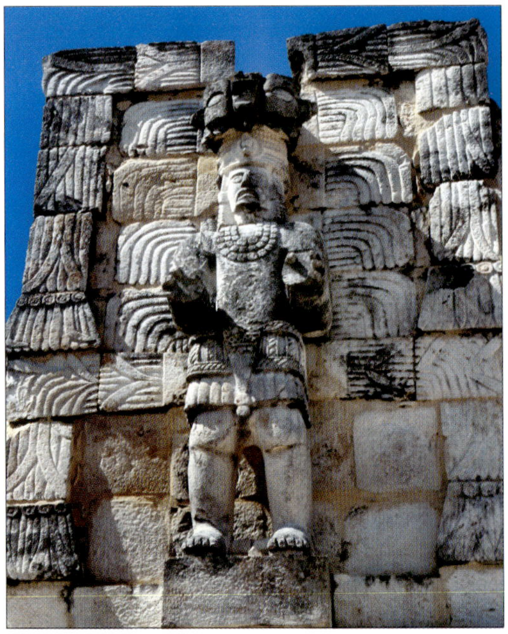

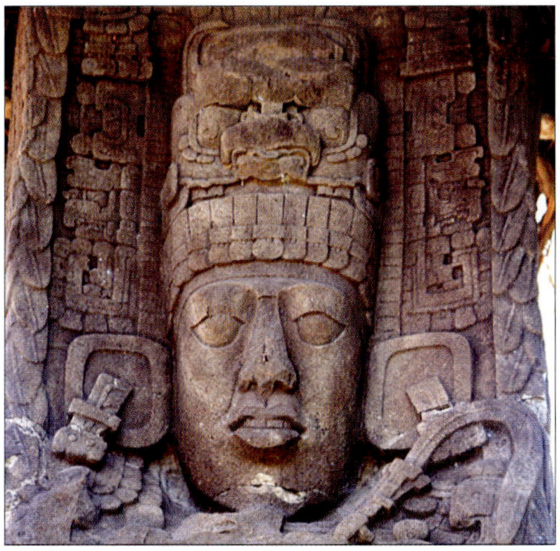

Above: Quiriguá. The image of Cauac Sky on Stela E – which stands 10.7m (35ft) tall – is more than three times life size.

and Stela A (AD731) is extremely ornate and in very deep relief. At Quiriguá, Monument 5 (also known as Stela E and dated AD771) bears a splendid high-relief portrait of King Cauac Sky commemorating his victory over Copán. The largest known Maya stela, it measures 1.5m (5ft) wide by 10.7m (35ft) high and has an estimated weight of 65 tons.

CARVING THE GODS

Sculptors at Quiriguá moved on from stelae to carve large, unquarried sandstone boulders, subsequently known as zoomorphs, with images of sky divinities, earth creatures and kings.

One of these, Zoomorph P (also known as Monument 16), depicts a young ruler seated in the open jaws of a serpent representing the underworld and holds a shield with a sun god portrait and a sceptre of rulership. More than 3.4m (11ft) wide and 2.1m (7ft) high, the vast structure was typical of Maya sculptural aesthetics in its combination of natural and grotesque supernatural figures and the refusal to leave any space plain. The zoomorph was dedicated in AD795 and might have been cut to celebrate the accession of King Jade Sky.

ALL-ROUND CARVING AT TONINÁ

The stelae at Toniná, a city 50km (30 miles) south of Palenque, were unique in the Maya world in that they were carved in the round like statues. They were also unusually small, about 2m (6ft 6in) tall rather than the average for Maya stelae of 2.5–3m (8–10ft). Another carved structure at Toniná, known as Monument 122, features more conventional carving. It bears an image of King Kan Xul II of Palenque as a captive. Toniná's third ruler, who acceded to the throne in AD688, achieved a great coup in capturing Kan Xul II in AD711. Art historian Linda Schele suggests part of the tribute involved the despatch to Toniná of an elite sculptor from Palenque who was forced to carve an image of his defeated king.

Below: Many believe the deep-relief carving on Copán stelae to be the finest in the Maya world. Animal masks and complex regalia contrast with the serenity of the face.

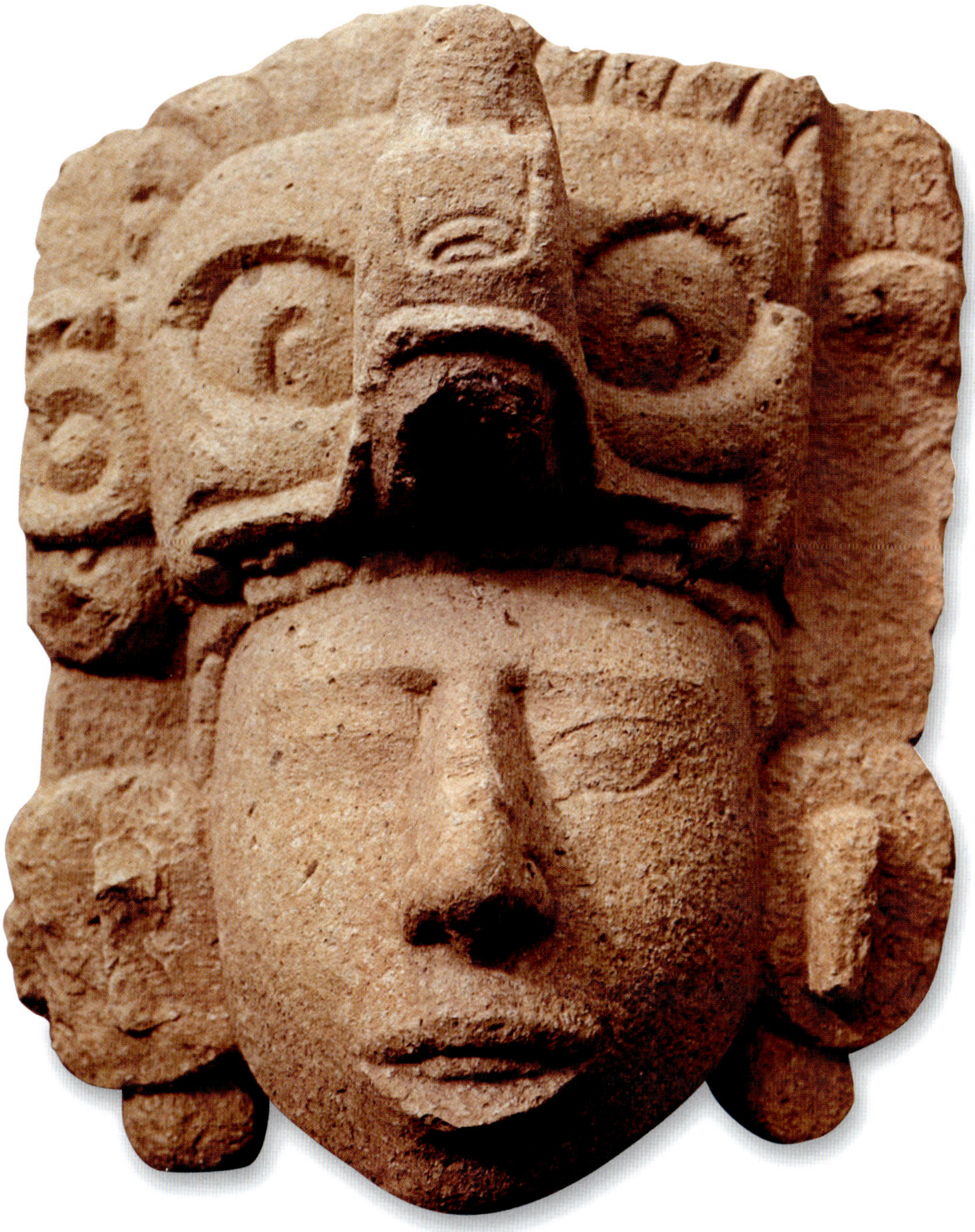

THE WORK OF MAYA STONEMASONS

Maya carvers worked the rock that was locally available. For most this was limestone. At Quiriguá, Altar de Sacrificios, Toniná and a few other sites, stonemasons had access to sandstone, while at Copán they used a volcanic rock called trachyte. With a fine grain and predictable texture, trachyte was easy to carve and its availability at Copán was one important reason why that site rose to such prominence as a centre of the sculptor's art. The only drawback of trachyte was that it sometimes contained very hard flint lumps. These were either hacked off, creating small depressions in the monument's surface, or left in place, forming small lumps. Elsewhere, stonecutters needed to work limestone and sandstone shortly after it had been quarried, for the rock was soft when first exposed but grew harder the longer it was in contact with the air.

THE RULER'S ORNATE SCEPTRE

Maya kings were often represented on stelae and in other carvings holding 'the manikin sceptre', an ornately decorated staff symbolic of royal power: an example can be seen on Monument 16 at Quiriguá (carved in 795). Some centuries earlier, the influence of Teotihuacán on Maya sites had been seen in part by the carving of a Teotihuacano-style weapon, the spear thrower, on royal images: Stela 4 at Tikal celebrated the accession of King Curl Nose in 378 by depicting the king holding a spear thrower on his left arm beneath an image of the divine Maya patron of royalty, Bolon Tza'cab. Scholar Clemency Coggins demonstrated that the manikin sceptre symbol was formed by combining an image of Bolon Tza'cab with a carving of a spear thrower.

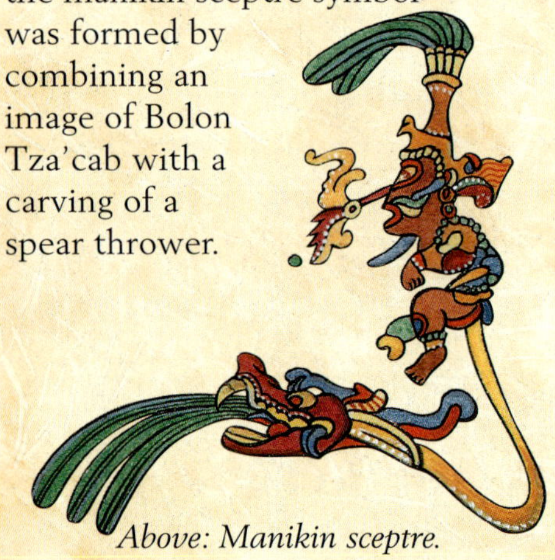

Above: Manikin sceptre.

ANCIENT QUARRYING

Labourers quarried rock by digging along the sides and ends of an oblong shaft of stone suitable for a stela. Then, probably using tree trunks as rollers and creepers as ropes, they hauled the shaft to the site where it was to be erected. There they dug a receiving hole and lined it with masonry, then pulled the shaft upright into the hole, probably by building a ramp of logs behind the shaft and using an A-frame fashioned from wooden beams to raise it. Once the shaft was in place, they built platforms around it on which skilled carvers set to work. They used round-handled, single-edged stone chisels 5–15cm (2–6in) and hammer stones up to 7cm (2¾in) across.

After the carvers were finished, their work was rubbed smooth using sand and water, then plastered and painted. Most stelae were painted a dark red or blue mixed with copal resin. This produced a long-lasting coating with a varnish-like finish. In some places, particularly where the relief carving was deeper, the paint remains visible, more than 1,000 years later.

WALL PANELS AND LINTELS

In addition to stelae, Maya sculptors excelled in cutting wall panels, thrones, stone lintels and decorative elements on buildings. Some of the finest examples of wall panels and thrones were carved at Piedras Negras, roughly midway between Yaxchilán and Palenque on the river Usumacinta. A wall panel carved in the year 9.16.6.9.16 (AD757) adorned a nine-level mortuary monument now called Structure O-13 by archaeologists. The panel represents the fourth king of the Piedras Negras dynasty making a ritual designation of his son as the royal heir.

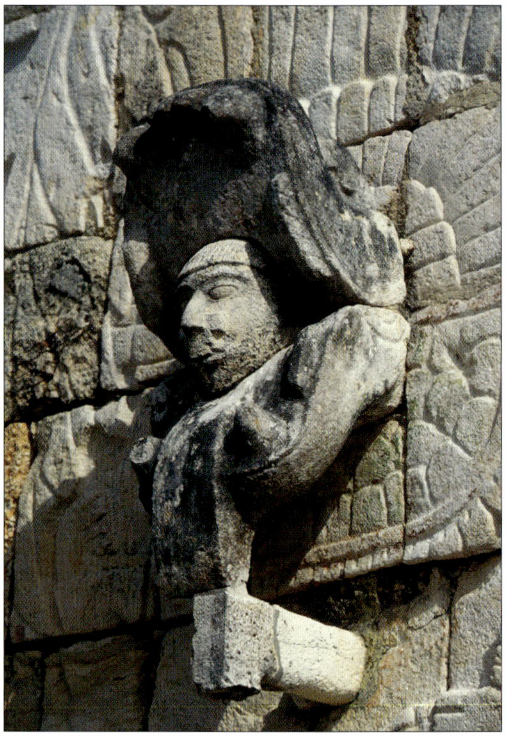

Above: Serpent warrior. On the Temple of the Warriors at Chichén Itzá, a soldier emerges from the jaws of a sacred snake.

Below: This limestone chacmool, *inlaid with shell and obsidian, was originally painted. He performed service as an offering stone for ritual victims' hearts at Chichén Itzá.*

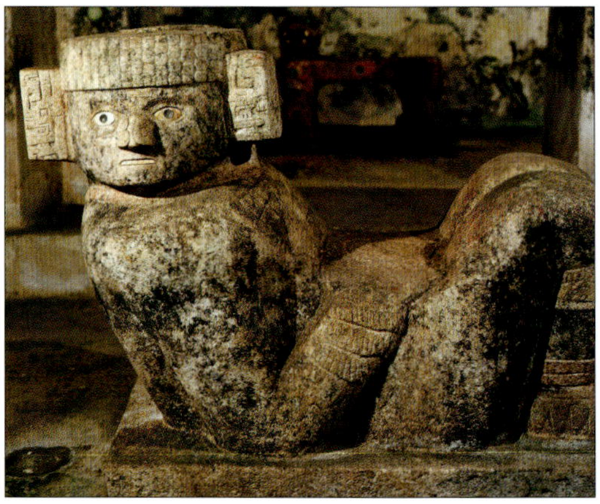

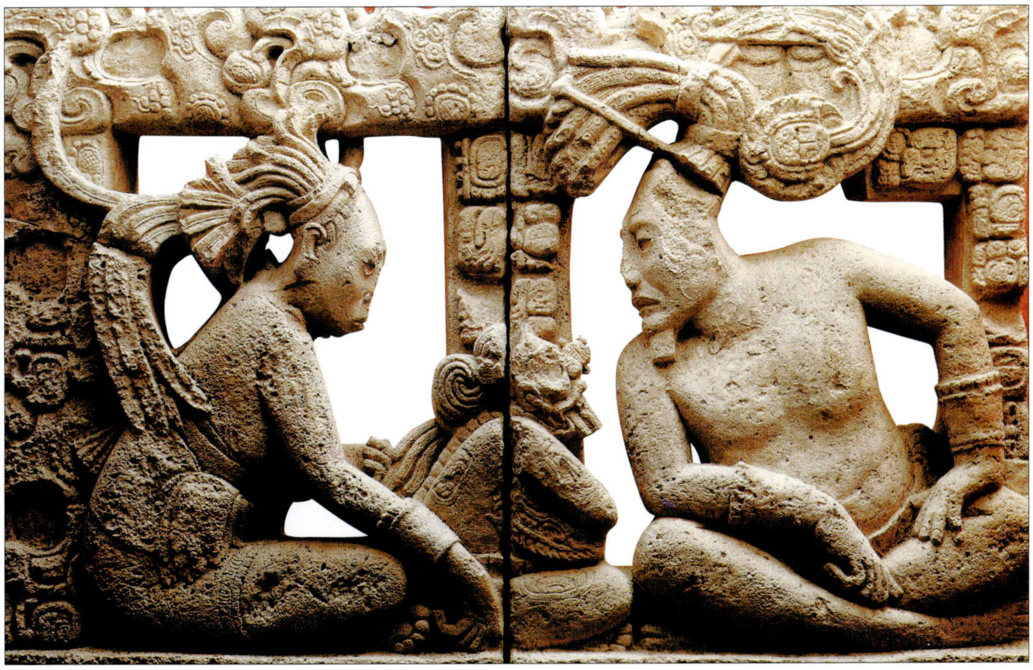

Above: Delicate limestone carving of courtly consultation adorned the back of a royal throne dated AD*747 and found in Chiapas.*

The king is depicted on his throne, with his son and two other boys standing on his left and three elite visitors from Yaxchilán, including King Bird Jaguar, on his right. Piedras Negras stonecarvers also created a magnificent, bench-like throne that was placed in the main room of the palace in a position where it could be seen by subjects standing in the courtyard before the palace. The stonemason-scribes carved glyphs on three sides of the throne's front legs; the inscriptions reveal that the piece was dedicated to royal use in 9.17.15.0.0. (AD785).

The finest carved stone lintels in the Maya world were the depictions of King Shield Jaguar and his wife Lady Xoc on Lintels 24, 25 and 26 at Yaxchilán. These images of Lady Xoc performing autosacrifice by drawing a thorn cord across her tongue, of Lady Xoc experiencing a vision and of the king dressing for battle ,were raised in Temple 23, dedicated to the queen and the gods in AD726.

At Copán, stonemasons excelled not only in carving stelae and altars or thrones, but also in providing elaborate decoration for architectural elements such as stairways and a platform with monumental stairway that archaeologists call a 'reviewing stand'. On the Hieroglyphic Stairway, which was dedicated in AD756, they cut more than 2,000 glyphs recording the city's dynastic history. The 63-step structure stood more than 20m (65ft) high and was 10m (33ft) wide, including its balustrades.

THE SEAT OF THE JAGUAR

In the 9th–10th centuries AD, rulers in the cities of the northern Maya region stopped commissioning carved monuments, instead employing stonecarvers to make decorative elements for sacred buildings. Artists at Uxmal produced an image of a head emerging from a serpent's jaws that was mounted in the façade of the base of the pyramid known as the House of the Magician. They also carved a new type of royal seat, the jaguar throne: a life-sized jaguar with flattened back on which the ruler sat. A jaguar throne has also been found at Chichén Itzá. Also at Chichén Itzá, under Toltec influence, stonemasons carved the reclining *chacmool* figures that were set before temples. The arched figures each include a vessel into which the heart of a sacrificial victim was placed.

The carvers also made standard bearers, seated figures about 1m (3ft 4in) tall that held a feather banner, and the upright warriors that archaeologists now call 'Atlantean figures'. These were used to provide the support necessary for door lintels and daises.

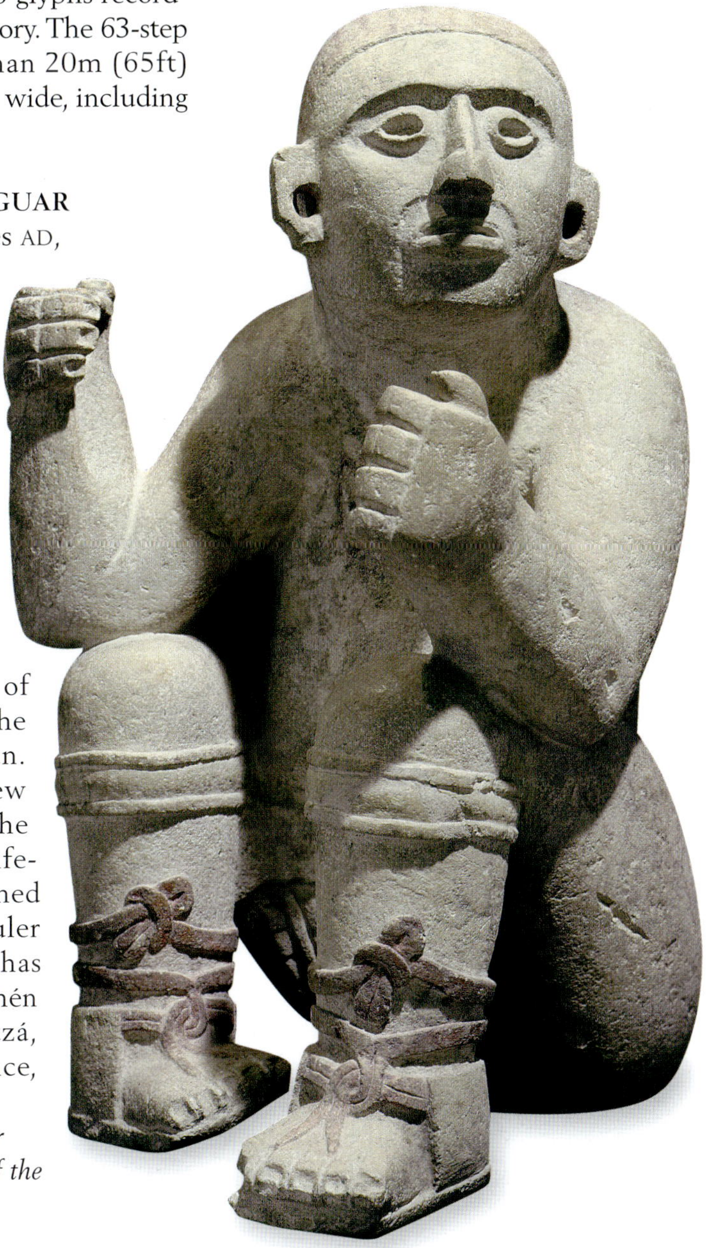

Right: This standard bearer was made for the Temple of the Warriors in Chichén Itzá.

INTRICATE CARVING IN STUCCO

There was a long tradition in Maya lands of carving in stucco or plaster. From the late Preclassic Period (400BC–AD100), builders used carved stucco as a decorative element on sacred buildings.

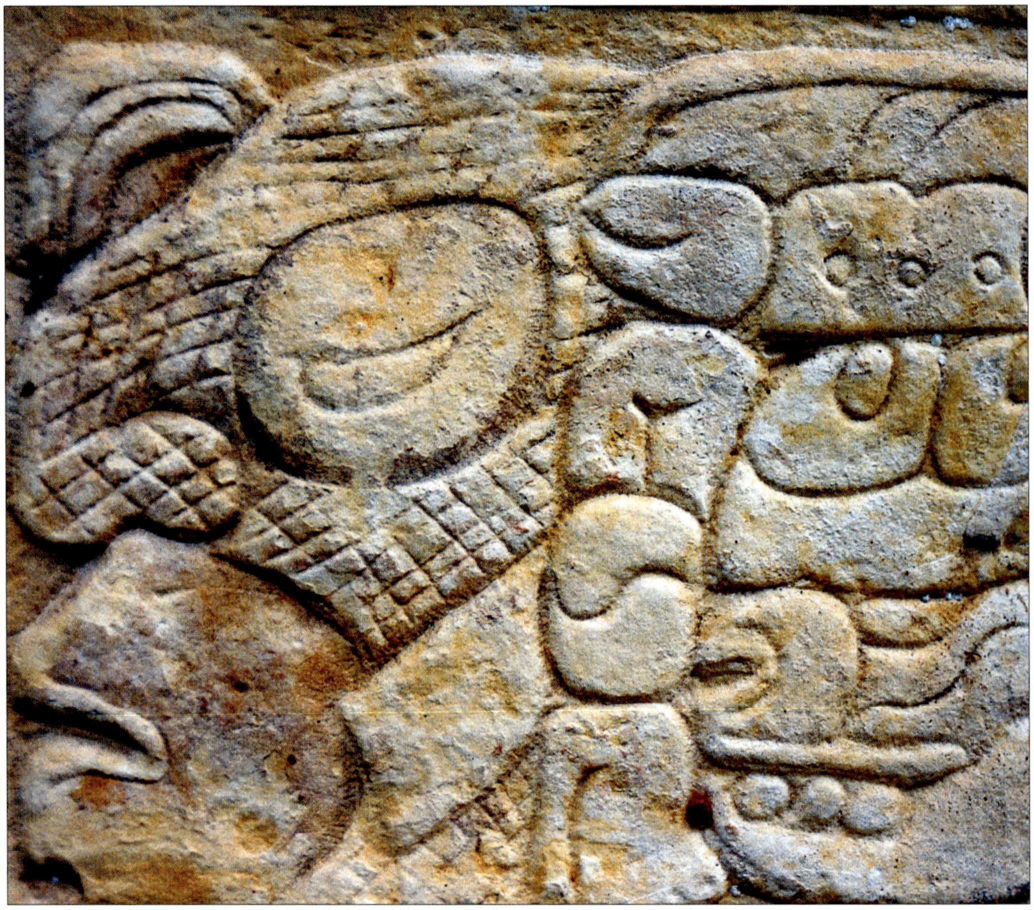

Above: Best known for murals, Bonampak also provides evidence of the well developed Maya art of stucco carving. A series of 130 stucco glyphs, like this one at Bonampak, were carved in Temple 18 at Palenque.

PLASTER MASKS

At Cerros, in Belize, a temple-platform known as Stucture 5C-2 and built *c.*50BC included a long stairway flanked by four large painted plaster masks, one pair representing the rising and setting sun and the other depicting the planet Venus as morning and evening star.

At Uaxactún, a temple platform (H-sub 3) erected about the same time had a similar decorative layout. Four large masks representing the sacred mountain monster of Maya belief flanked the central stairway on the western face of the platform. In the lower two, the mountain was shown rising from the waters. The upper pair showed the mountain giving issue to the Vision Serpent that the Maya believed conducted shamans and initiates on spirit journeys along its many coils.

Below: Awe-inspiring lord of day. This stucco mask from Kohunlich is of the sun god Kinich Ahau, a form of Itzamná.

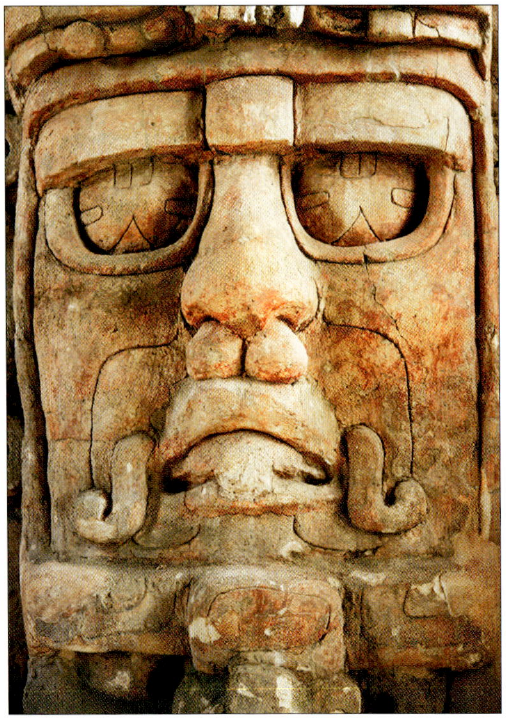

At the same site, the modestly sized platform known by archaeologists as E-VII-sub had a total of 16 stucco masks on its four faces. These masks represented the sun and Venus, as at Cerros. The platform served as an astronomical observatory in an arrangement of sacred buildings that historians call Group E, laid out to align with sunrise on winter and summer solstices. Similar masks were carved on sacred buildings at Tikal, Kohunlich, Lamanai and El Mirador in the late Preclassic Period.

RELIEF AT PALENQUE

The Maya tradition of decorative stucco carving continued into the Classic Period. It probably reached its apogée in the elegant relief panels and heads carved at Palenque in the 7th century AD. Here,

FROM STUCCO TO STONE

In the reign of King 18-Rabbit of Copán (695–738), when the centre of the city was transformed with the rebuilding of many structures and the erection of several monuments and much of the Acropolis took its final form, the king ordered the transition from stucco to carved stone for decorative elements on buildings. In their original form the stone carvings were covered with plaster and then painted. The underlying stone proved a much more durable material than plaster.

relief panels and other decorations took on the role, played by stelae in many other cities, of recording royal history and transmitting dynastic propaganda. The Group of the Cross temples built by Chan-Bahlum, son and successor of the great King Pacal, contained three large stucco relief panels. These represented scenes rich in religious detail celebrating the transfer of power from the deceased king to his son. On the roof of the Temple of Inscriptions, beneath which King Pacal was buried in a hidden crypt, stood a wide, five-doored temple. On its roof comb were stucco reliefs that similarly portrayed the new king being granted the right to rule by his father.

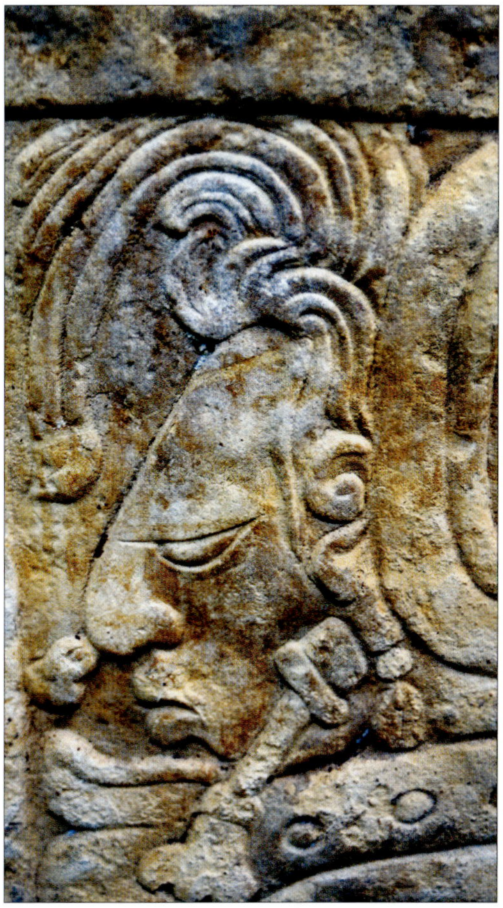

Right: A noble profile carved in stucco at Bonampak shows the nose built up to join the forehead in line with the Maya ideal.

STUCCO MASTERPIECES

The crypt in which King Pacal was laid to rest was adorned with beautiful stucco reliefs representing nine figures variously identified by scholars as the nine lords of the night, the nine gods of the underworld or nine of the king's divine ancestors. On the crypt floor beneath the king's sarcophagus were two masterpieces of stucco carving: life-sized twin portraits of the king, one in his youth and the other in mid-life maturity. The heads, about 40cm (16in) high, portray an idealized image of the king. In line with Maya ideas of youthful beauty, the bridge of the nose of the youthful portrait is built up to connect to the forehead. However, the second head, of the middle-aged king, elegantly combined the ideal with the truth, for it reproduces the long face that the king had in other representations.

Scholars believe that Pacal's successor, Chan-Bahlum, probably ordered his carvers to produce actual rather than idealized portraits. An image of Chan-Bahlum on a stucco tablet from Temple IV shows him with a thick lower lip, an outsized nose that went far beyond the Maya ideal and an expression of nervousness that is far different to the serenity accorded to Pacal. Similarly, fine stucco panels carved in House D in the Palenque palace complex during Chan-Bahlum's reign appear to show more realistic than idealized portraits.

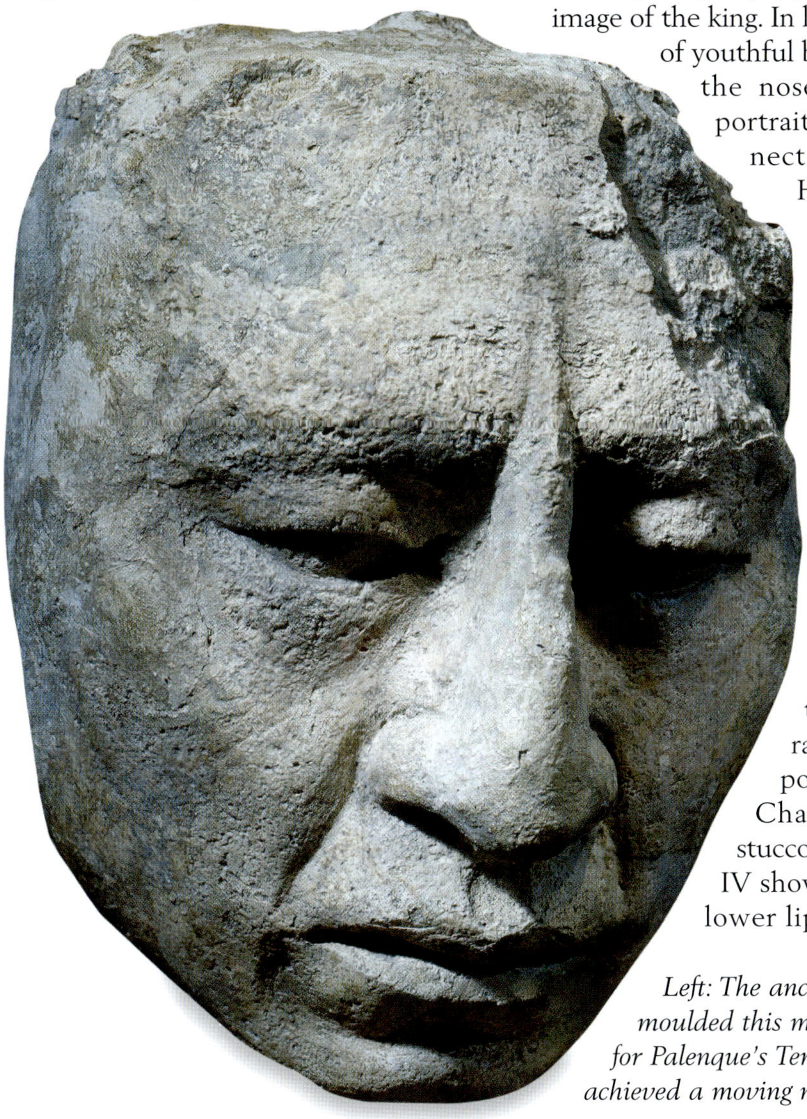

Left: The ancient sculptor who moulded this melancholy portrait for Palenque's Temple of the Sun achieved a moving naturalism.

ROSALILA MASKS

At Copán, stucco carvers reached great heights of achievement. Early buildings in the area later called the Acropolis were covered with elaborate stucco masks, but these were destroyed when the buildings were enclosed by later development. Nearby in the mid-6th century AD, a temple now called Rosalila by archaeologists was erected, its façade covered with fine stucco carvings. When, after many years, the building was encased by the next phase of construction, the masks and other elements were carefully preserved.

MEN AND GODS IN STONE:
AZTEC STONE CARVING

The years after *c.*AD900 in Mesoamerica saw a return to free-standing sculpture, an art that had not been practised since the time of the Olmec. Peoples of the northern Mexican Chalcihuites culture, the Toltecs of Tollán and those influenced by them at Chichén Itzá and elsewhere made three-dimensional Atlantean figures that supported temple roofs and door lintels, seated standard-bearer statues and reclining *chacmool* figures which were used to display and store human hearts in sacrificial ritual.

The Huastecs, a Maya-speaking people who inhabited the Gulf coast in northern Veracruz, also made monumental seated and standing statues that were a major influence on Aztec sculptors. Many of these anthropomorphic stone statues bore a second figure on its back, thought by scholars to represent an ancestral spirit companion. The Huastecs, who were particularly associated with the worship of Quetzalcóatl in his form as wind god Éhecatl, also built circular temples that might have inspired the building of the circular Caracol at Chichén Itzá and which were certainly forerunners of the circular Éhecatl-Quetzalcóatl temple in the Aztecs' main ceremonial centre in Tenochtitlán. Having conquered the Huastecs *c.*1400, the Aztecs imported these styles in sculpture and temple architecture among the spoils of war.

GODS IN STONE

The Aztecs carved many stone figures of gods and goddesses with detailed iconography. This served to identify the deities and to suggest the complex attributes that they shared with other gods.

An 80cm (2ft 6in) stone statue of Xiuhtecuhtli, patron of the rulers or *tlatoque* (plural of *tlatoani*), depicted him wearing the *tlatoani's* costume: a diadem, *xicolli* ceremonial waistcoat, triangular loincloth that signified warrior status and sandals adorned with sun-rays at the heels. His mouth gave issue to fangs that were a symbol of the god's great age: Xiuhtecuhtli was so old that he had lost his real teeth. Xiuhtecuhtli was also a god of fire and associated with the sun: he was the Aztec form of the ancient god Huehuetéotl ('The Old One').

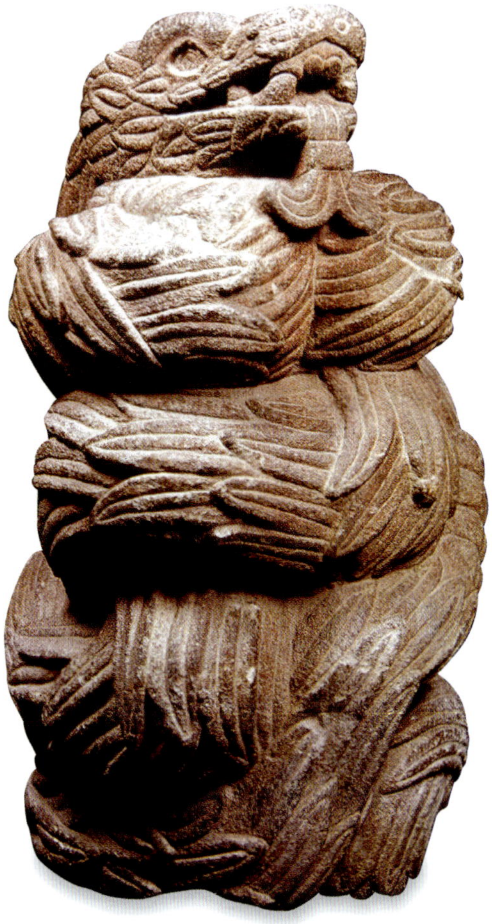

Above: This Aztec sculpture of Quetzalcóatl in his form as a coiled rattlesnake was cut from a single block of stone.

Below: The Tizoc stone celebrates the military triumphs of the tlatoani *Tizoc, who took 14 towns for the expanding empire.*

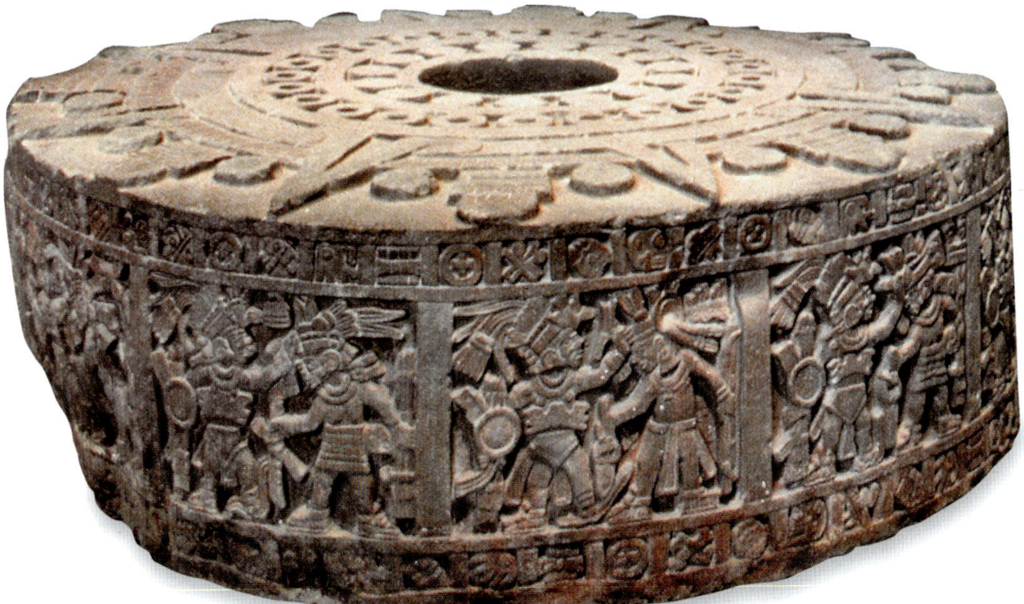

Such statues combined inconographic detail with naturalistic verve and a mastery of the human form. Seated statues of flower god Xochipilli depict a near-naked youth wearing only mask, loincloth and sandals. One, 115cm (4ft) tall, had flowers cut as if tattooed on the arms and legs. Some scholars suggest that these were images of plants with mind-altering properties used in divinatory rites. The statue was found in the 19th century in the village of Tlamanalco on the side of the sacred volcano Ixtaccíhuatl.

THE HUMAN FORM

Aztec sculptors also made beautifully realized statues of ordinary men and women. A female nude statue dated

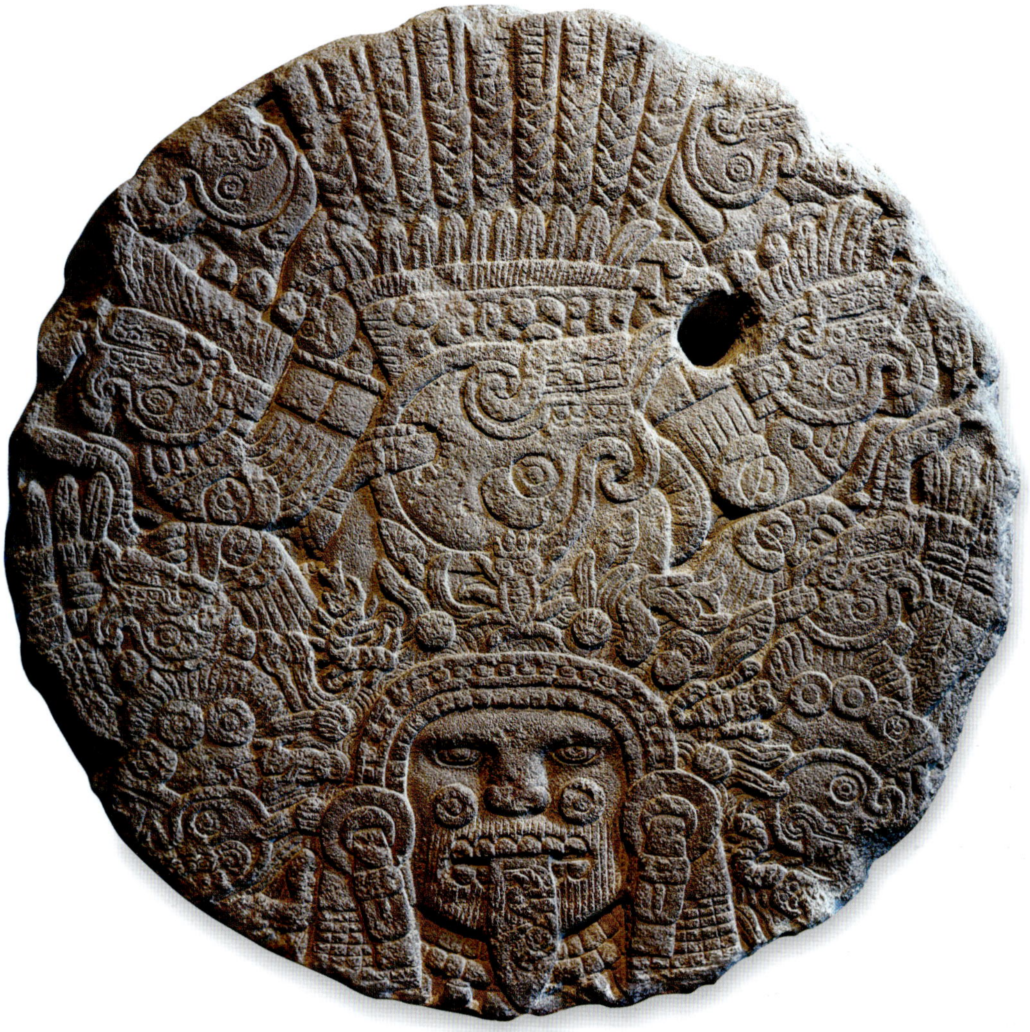

Right: This cuauhxicalli *or eagle vessel, used for storing sacrificial victims' hearts, was sacred to Huitzilopochtli.*

*c.*1500 found in Texcoco and once called the 'Venus of Texcoco', together with several seated and standing statues of *macehualtin* commoner young men either naked or wearing loincloths, celebrated the youthful human form. Such statues might have been dressed in ritual costume that identified them as particular deities at festival time. A seated 33cm (13in) statue of a hunchback made *c.*1500 exhibited the sculptors' delight in naturalism and might also have been a tribute to Nanahuatzin, the disfigured and deformed god who rose to become the sun in the religious narrative of the first days at Teotihuacán. Hunchbacks and other people with physical deformities were well cared for in Tenochtitlán, but at times of solar eclipse might be chosen for human sacrifice because their bodies marked them out as the children of the sun god.

ANIMAL CARVINGS

Sculptors also represented the natural world, producing statues of dogs, coyotes, rabbits, jaguars, insects, lizards, fish, snakes, eagles, toads, pumpkins, squash and cacti. Many, while exhibiting the craftsmen's great naturalistic skill, had powerful sacred symbolism, since many gods and goddesses took animal form. Stone solar discs were carved and celebrated as symbols of the sun god Tonatiuh and of the current world age, which came under his rule and protection.

Aztec craftsmen reproduced Toltec forms such as Atlantean figures and *chacmools*. Archaeologists found a sculpted *chacmool* figure in front of the Tláloc shrine atop the early version (*c.*1390) of the great pyramid of the Templo Mayor in Tenochtitlán. The rather crude effigy was carved with Tláloc symbols, as was a later and more expertly carved *chacmool* *c.*1502–20. A series of five stone warrior figures roughly 1.2m (4ft) tall found in Tenochtitlán possibly functioned as roof supports in the style of Toltec Atlantean figures. The five statues represented four male soldiers clutching spear throwers and wearing the triangular loincloth of the warrior and one female, wearing a skirt of arrows. Scholars suggest that they might have stood in the four cardinal points: males at east, south and north and the female in the west, a direction associated with women. The fourth male would have stood in the centre, the position of the world tree and the current world age, the spot occupied in Aztec cosmology by the great Templo Mayor itself.

TRIUMPHAL MONUMENTS

The Aztecs also produced monumental stone carving that celebrated the power of the gods, of the *tlatoani* and of the state. The celebrated Sun Stone, carved from basalt in the reign of Axayáctal (1469–81) with a diameter of 3.6m (12ft), commemorated the myth of the five world ages, the glory of the sun god and the power of the *tlatoani*. The Tizoc stone, a great cylinder 2.65m (8ft 8in) across and carved in 1481–86, celebrated the military triumphs of the Aztec army and in particular the *tlatoani* Tizoc (*r.* 1481–86) was depicted 15 times around the stone gripping a battle-weary victim by the hair, with a glyph beside each victim identifying the place of conquest. Another similar stone, 2.24m (7ft 4in) in diameter, was carved to celebrate the victories of Moctezuma I (*r.* 1440–69).

The Teocalli stone, carved in the shape of a pyramid-temple with front steps flanked by date glyphs, bore a 'temple' at the top carved with a sun disc and images of Huitzilopochtli to the left and Moctezuma II (*r.* 1502–20) to the right, both preparing to offer their blood in rites of autosacrifice. The stone, 1.23m by 92cm by 99cm (4ft by 3ft by 3ft 3in), was probably used as a royal throne. It was carved to celebrate the new fire ceremony that marked the beginning of a new 52-year cycle in 1507.

CARVING IN WOOD

The Maya called their stelae 'stone trees', suggesting that in the great cities of the Classic Period, dynastic monuments might once have been carved from tree trunks. There was certainly a flourishing Maya woodcarving tradition, as is evidenced by the few examples of wooden door lintels and beams that have survived.

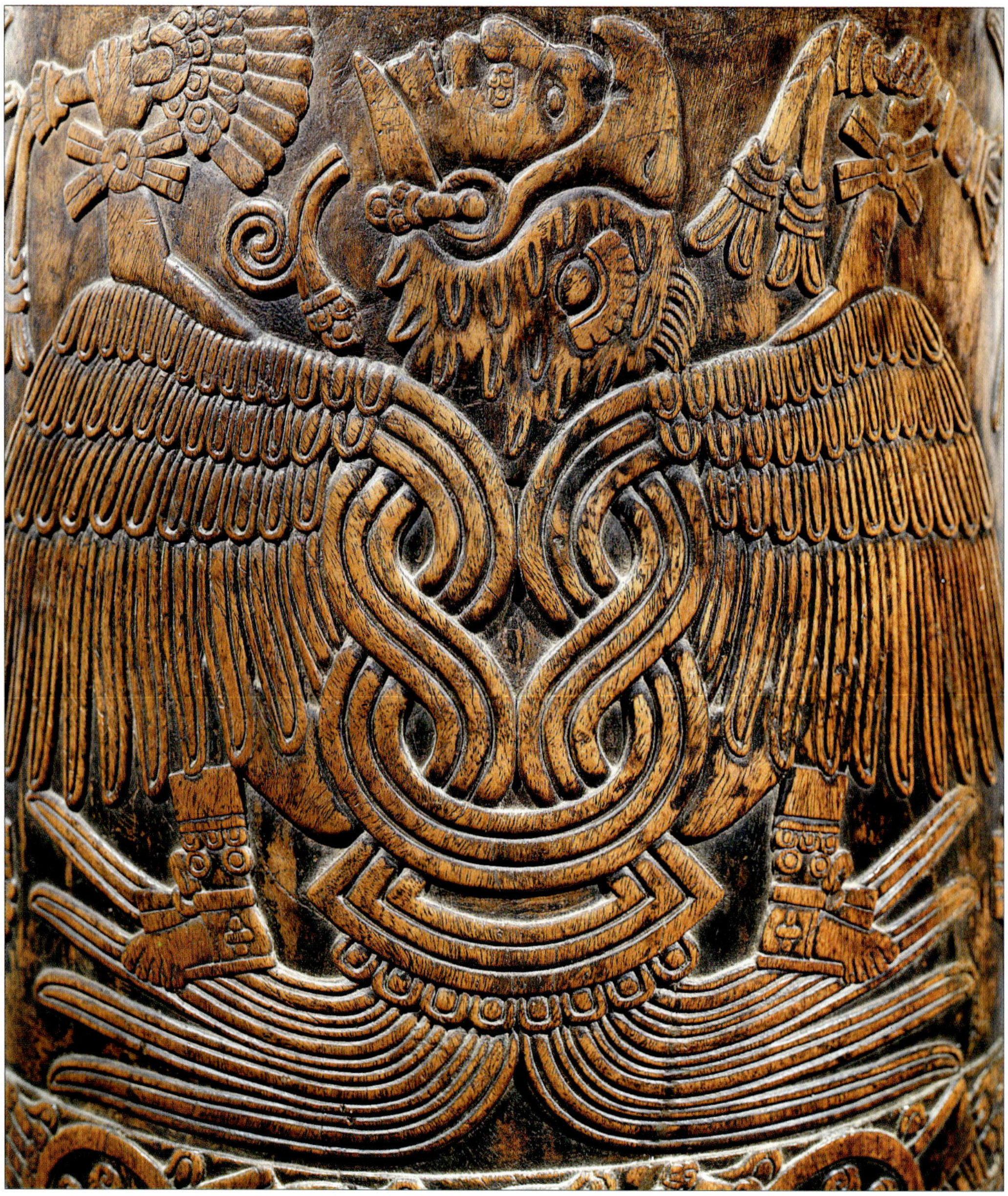

Above: *A detail of an Aztec wooden drum of c.1500 shows an eagle-warrior who stands for the sun god Tonatiuh.*

DOOR LINTELS

The temples of Tikal were once graced by wooden door lintels. One of the surviving lintels, which once spanned a doorway in the building known as Temple IV, was carved from sapodilla wood with an arched serpent in the mid-8th century AD. From the serpent's mouth emerged an ancestral spirit, who might represent the dynastic founder, while above the serpent was the sacred quetzal bird of the Maya, its wings outstretched. Beneath the serpent's arched back was King Yax Kin (*r.* AD734–46), enthroned in splendour. The glyphic inscription declares that the king was shown celebrating a military triumph for Tikal on 26 July AD743. A slightly older lintel survives from Temple I, depicting King Ah Cacau (AD682–734) on the throne of Tikal, with a deity – perhaps his ancestral spirit – above him and a glyphic text celebrating military triumph over Calakmul on 5 August AD695.

Later wooden lintels survived in temples at Chichén Itzá and Uxmal. In the Temple of the Jaguars at Chichén Itzá, a carved lintel depicts a human figure surrounded by a feathered serpent and another figure within a spiked circular design representing the sun. US traveller John Lloyd Stephens (1805–52) discovered a carved sapodilla beam in the Governor's Palace at Uxmal and took it with him when he returned to the USA. Unfortunately, it was destroyed in a fire, much to the dismay of later scholars, who might have been able to use the beam to date the beautiful building in which it was found.

SKILL OF THE WOODCARVERS

The beauty, detail and precision of the glyphic carving in wood was remarkable. The scribes carved the hard sapodilla wood while it was still green, for once

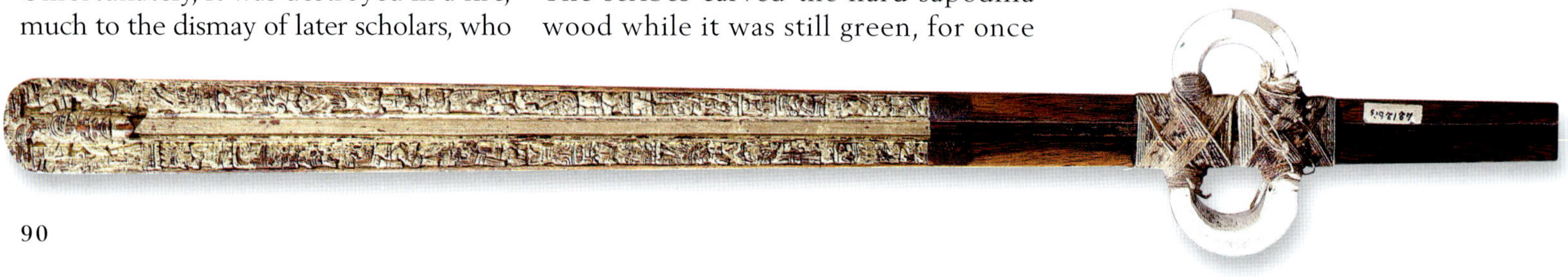

Below: *Woodcarvers received military commissions for ceremonial weapons, such as this gold-covered spear-thrower.*

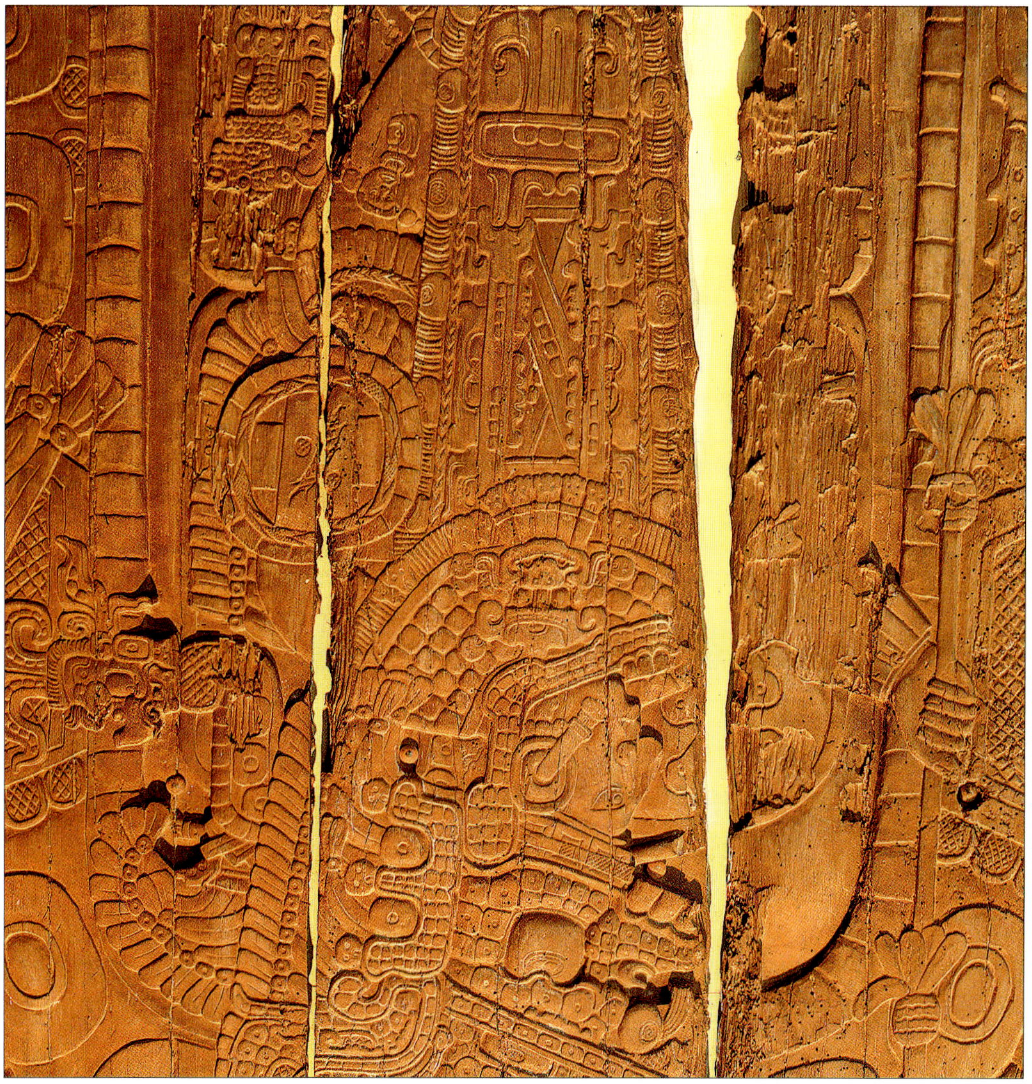

cured it became as hard as metal. Scholar Michael Coe has suggested that the scribes first painted the symbols on the wood before cutting them with obsidian blades. Another surviving piece that demonstrates the skill of Maya glyphic carvers is a wooden box celebrating the memory of a late 7th century AD king of Tortuguero, a settlement near Tikal. The style of the glyphs closely resembles that on the Tikal lintels.

Maya woodcarvers almost certainly also made figures of gods and goddesses from wood, but none have survived, for they would have been easily and enthusiastically destroyed by Catholic churchmen. Images in the *Madrid Codex* depict the gods themsleves at work fashioning masks and figures from wood. This would seem to provide evidence that the craft was practised in Maya workshops.

A few examples of wooden figures of Aztec deities have survived. A seated statue of Macuilxóchitl of *c.*1500 depicts the god of music and gaming wearing his trademark crested headdress. Traces of paint show that the statue was originally red, but the inlay from the eyes and the ornament that once adorned his mouth are missing.

The statue was found in a cave, where atmospheric conditions were favourable to its survival. The same was true of a cedarwood fertility goddess figure of *c.*1500 which was discovered still in use for worship in a cave near the Toluca valley, Veracruz, in the 19th century. The figure wore the hairstyle which was conventionally adopted by married women and held her hands up to support the weight of her breasts, emphasizing her maternal role. Wooden statues of deities were called *cuauhximalli* by the Aztecs.

WOODEN DRUMS

Elaborately carved examples of both *huehuetl* upright drums and *teponaxtli* oblong drums have survived. A *huehuetl* drum, 98cm (3ft 2in) tall and elaborately carved with war symbols, was found in Malinalco – one of the mountain-top temples of the eagle- and jaguar-warrior elite – in the latter part of the 19th century. The carver cut the symbol for the current world age, Nahua Ollin (4-Earthquake), between an eagle-warrior and a jaguar-warrior. The glyph for war, *teoatl-tlachinolli* ('fire water') arises from the warriors' mouths. On the opposite side of the round drum the craftsman cut an image of an eagle-man that was almost certainly intended to be the sun god Tonatiuh himself. The lower part of the drum base was adorned with images of eagle- and jaguar-warriors in warlike procession.

A *teponaxtli* drum of *c.*1250 carved in the form of a jaguar was found in Puebla state in the late 19th century. Making these drums was the work of highly skilled specialists, who first hollowed the wood by burning, then finished the interior with chisel work. The top of the horizontal drum was split into two tongues and played with a hammer to produce a two-tone note.

Yet another example of a beautifully finished drum of *c.*1500 was carved in the shape of a reclining warrior from Tlaxcala shown with a copper-bladed axe.

Above: A sapodilla-wood door lintel from Tikal Temple IV celebrates a military victory of King Yax Kin in July AD*743.*

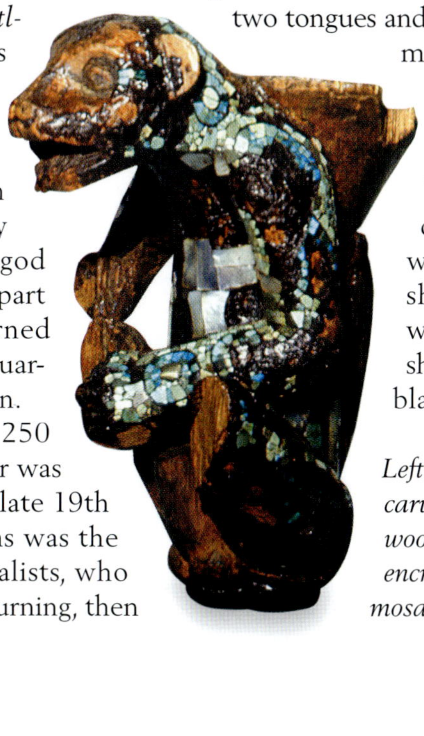

Left: Mixtec craftsmen carved this delicate wooden jaguar and encrusted it with fine mosaic in c.*1400–1520.*

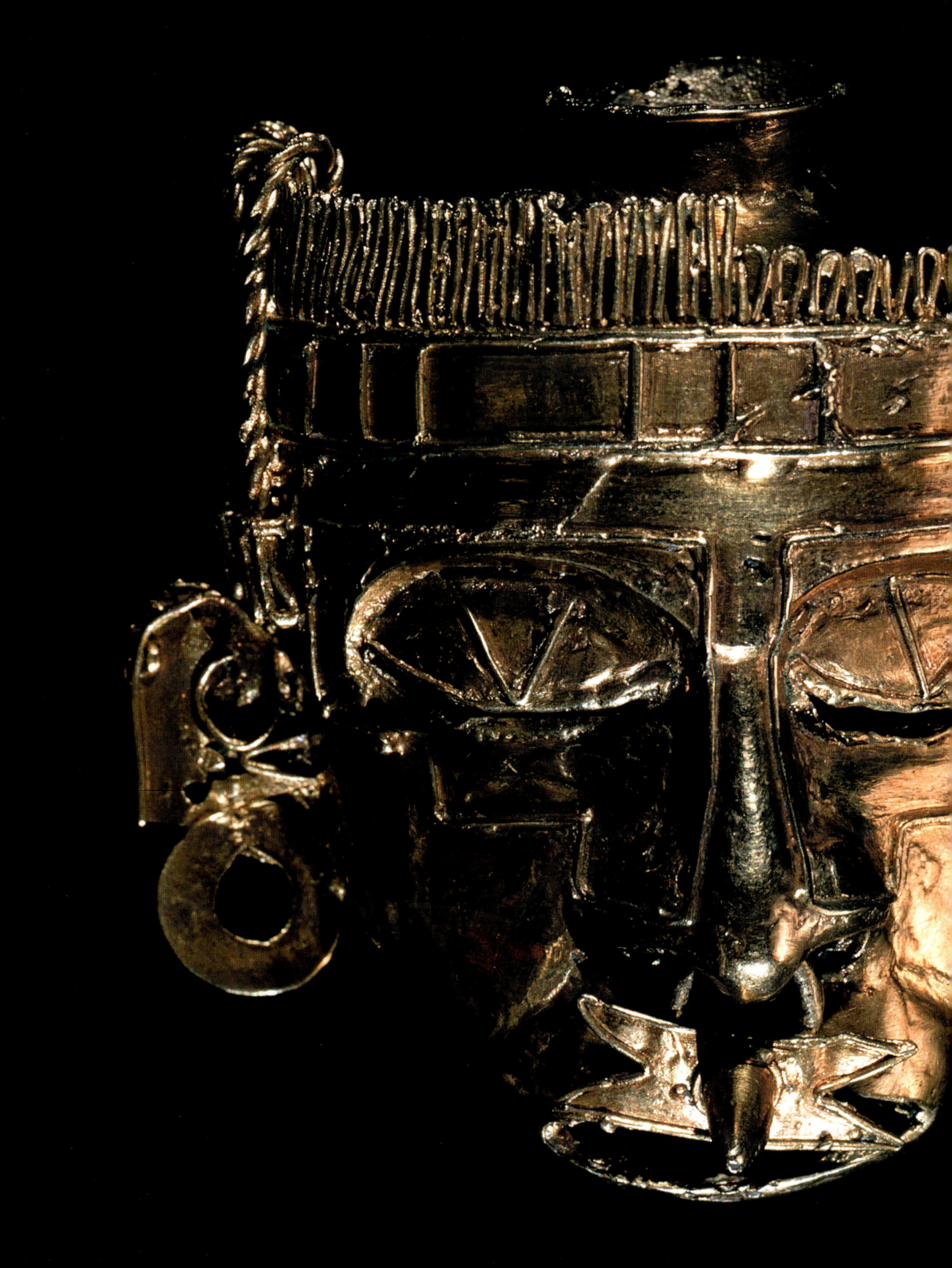

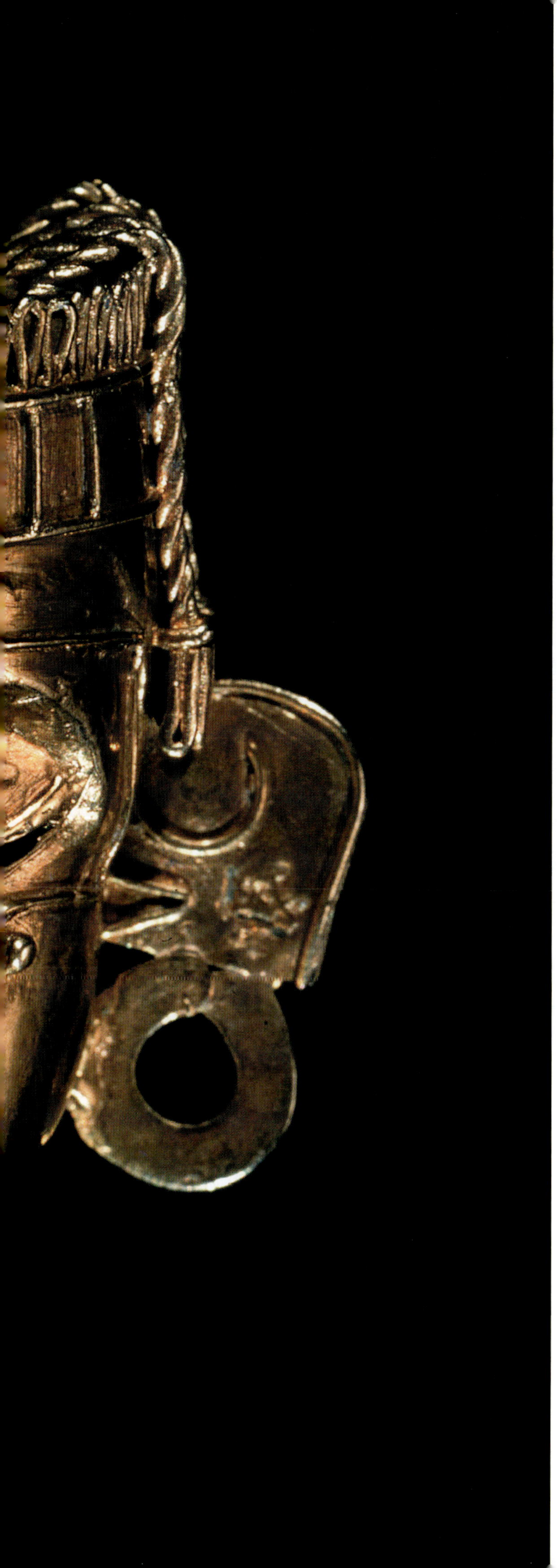

CHAPTER FIVE

PRECIOUS WORK

In April 1519 Moctezuma II sent magnificent gifts of gold and silver to Hernán Cortés and his conquistadors. The collection – which included a solid gold disc as big as a cartwheel, together with an even larger disc of silver – was intended to honour the newcomers and to impress the Aztec emperor's power and wealth upon them. The gift also made a religious statement, for the gold and silver discs represented the sun and moon and celebrated the pre-eminence of the Aztecs – self-styled 'People of the Sun'.

The Spaniards, versed in a different culture, could not be expected to understand the religious message: the gift served only to fan their lust for Aztec riches. Some members of the invading group, including Cortés himself, certainly admired the craftsmanship of the pieces – he wrote to Charles V about Aztec jewellery that 'nowhere in the world could a smith have done better'. But many Europeans could not see beyond the dazzling monetary value of the silver and gold; predictably, the discs did not survive – they were melted down for their metal, the fate that awaited the great majority of gold and silver ritual items, ceremonial jewellery and other pieces sent back to Europe by the conquistadors. Cortés despatched several loads of Aztec precious metalwork, and these were among the items that astonished German artist Albrecht Dürer, who declared them to be 'strange and wonderfully worked objects' that thrilled his heart.

Left: God of spring and goldsmiths. This exquisite gold mask of Xipe Totec was an offering in Tomb 7 at Monte Albán.

AN IMPORTED CRAFT: METALWORK IN MESOAMERICA

On 6 January 1932 Mexican archaeologist Alfonso Caso made a breathtaking find in a tomb at the Zapotec mountaintop city of Monte Albán. The grave had originally been laid out *c.*AD 500–750 with a large fore chamber leading into two rooms aligned east–west. These contained a stone carved with Zapotec glyphs and a number of funerary urns. The grave had then been reopened in the late Postclassic Period (*c.*1250–1500) by local Mixtec mourners, who buried nine skeletons with a magnificent tribute-cache of metalwork and jewellery. The grave, known as Tomb Number 7, contained no fewer than 121 golden objects, 24 silver objects and a large number of rings, necklaces and pendants. This find provided ample evidence of the Mixtecs' astonishing skill in metalwork and making jewellery.

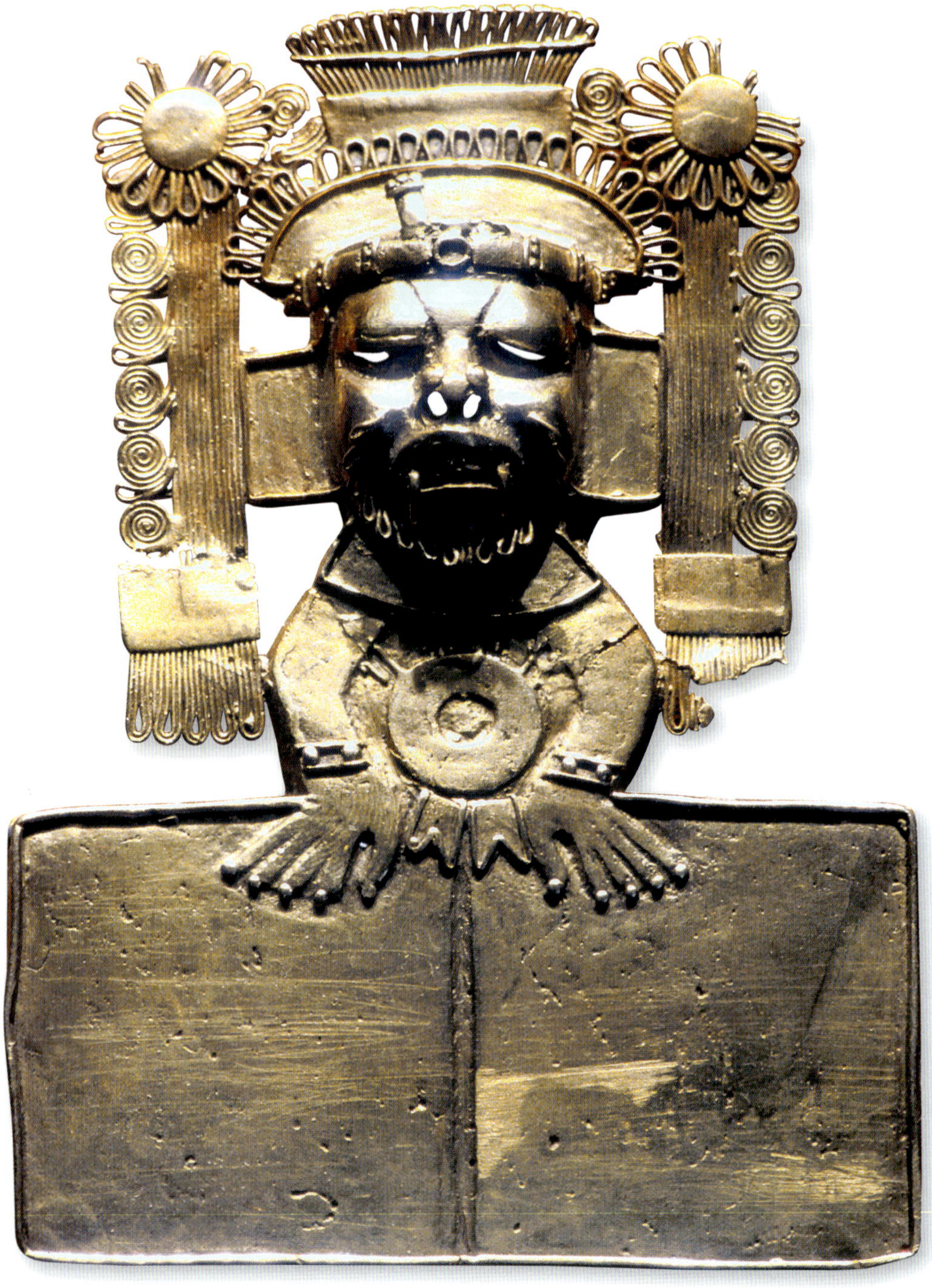

LATE STARTERS

When compared to their South American neighbours, Mesoamerican craftsmen were late starters in metalwork. Native Mesoamericans did not make jewellery, ritual items, weapons or tools from metal until after *c.*AD800. As early as 2000BC, the inhabitants of the Andes mountains in South America had begun to develop metalworking techniques that slowly travelled northwards along marine and land trade routes. These techniques took almost 3,000 years to reach Mesoamerica, probably arriving roughly simultaneously in two separate areas: the northern Maya region of the Yucatán peninsula and, hundreds of miles to the west, coastal settlements in western Mexico.

Among the oldest metal objects in Mesoamerica is a small claw, *c.*AD550 in Panama. It is made of the alloy of silver, copper and gold known as tumbaga, and was buried in the ceremonial centre of Altun Há, on the coastal plain north of modern Belize City. Later, a hollow figure of a gold-copper alloy was deposited as part of a cache of valuables beneath Stela H at Copán. The stela was dedicated in AD782, although archaeologists cannot rule out the possibility that the cache was buried after this or added to at a later date. Only the legs of the figurine remain, but expert analysis of the casting and alloy suggest that it was imported from a site in the southern parts of Central America such as Panama or Costa Rica.

BEGINNINGS IN MEXICO

Archaeologists have established that in the earliest days of Mesoamerican metalworking, during the 9th century, artisans working with copper in western Mexico were producing the same items in the same way as their counterparts in

Left: One of the finds in Tomb 7 was this Mixtec gold pectoral or breast ornament representing the 'old fire god' Xiuhtecuhtli.

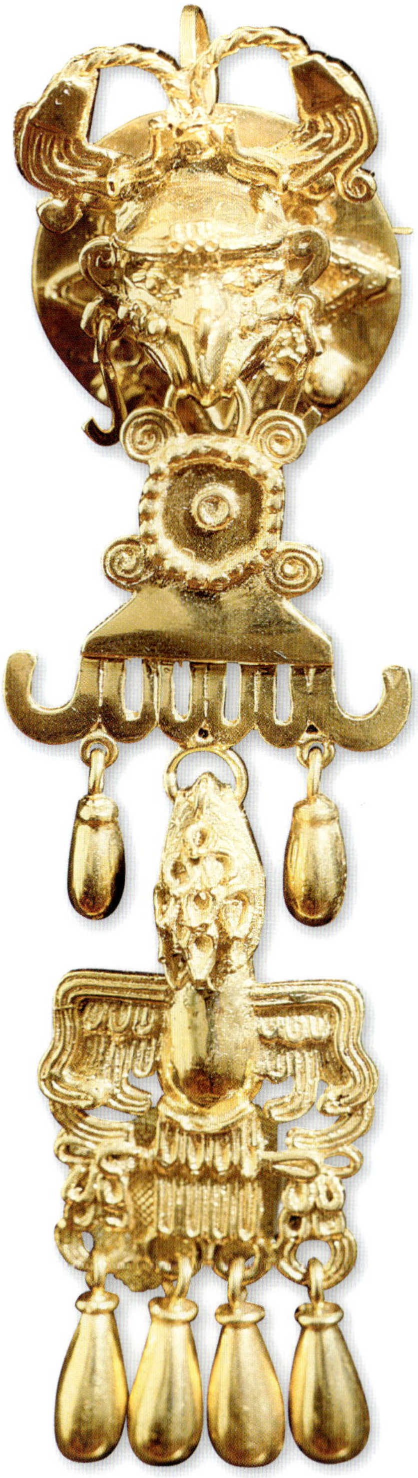

Ecuador. They were making needles, rings, tweezers, fishhooks, axe-heads for wooden-handled weapons and the sharply pointed pricking instruments known as awls. There is evidence that smelting and metalwork were carried out on the coast of Guerrero by *c.*AD900. In a settlement at Zihuatanejo, archaeologists uncovered slag pieces (the refuse separated from metal when it is smelted) and many bronze and other metal pieces in a find dated *c.*AD900–1100. The metal pieces included rings, bells and sheets of gold.

Left: This Mixtec gold earring was one of the hoard buried in Tomb 7 at Monte Albán. The Mixtecs' exquisite gold jewellery and other fine metalwork was admired and highly influential across Mesoamerica.

Another metalworking centre was established at Amapa, Nayarit, about 50km (30 miles) inland from the Pacific coast, on the river Santiago. Here artisans made copper rings, knives, needles, pins, axe-heads, beads, plaques, bells and awls.

In Michoacán the Tarascans worked local copper to produce small ritual figures, tweezers, open rings, needles and a large numbers of bells. They also made copper axe-heads that were used as a form of money.

In Oaxaca the Mixtecs began developing their metalworking expertise after AD900. They became the pre-eminent metalworkers of the Aztec age, when some Mixtecs worked as producers of jewellery and precious-metal items in Tenochtitlán, while others worked in their own centres in Oaxaca. Méxica/Aztec craftsmen centred in Azcapotzalco also produced metalwork in the Mixtec style. They worked in gold, silver and tumbaga.

In the northern Maya region, metal-workers developed great expertise in repoussé work, hammering designs into a sheet of metal from the reverse side. Many repoussé pieces hammered from both gold and copper were found among the objects cast into the *Cenote* of Sacrifice at Chichén Itzá. They depicted scenes of conflict between Maya soldiers and warriors of the invading wave of 'Mexicanized' merchants.

THE GODS' GOLD

Gold was identified as *teocuitlatl* ('the gods' excrement') in the Nahuatl tongue, probably because it was found in nuggets, like the droppings of animals. Its colour meant it was also associated with the sun. Images of the gods sometimes represented them wearing the gold jewellery worn by rulers, warriors, nobles and priests. A stone casket of the late 15th century that belonged to the *tlatoani* of Tenochtitlán, Ahuítzotl (*r.* 1486–1502), depicted the god Tláloc wearing a necklace carved with the symbol for gold. A statue of Xochipilli of *c.*1350–1500 shows the god of flowers and music wearing a gold necklace.

Below: This Mixtec painted vase is of a human head laden with jewellery with pierced earrings and an elaborate headdress.

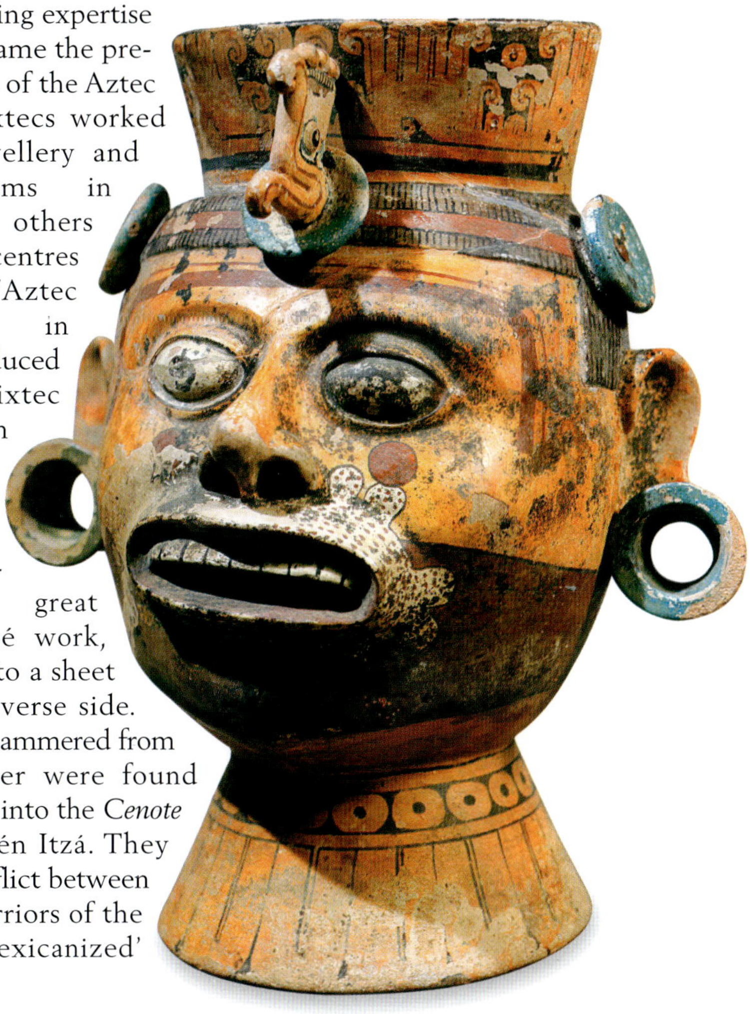

GOLDEN ORNAMENTS

Among the gold, silver and other precious items found in Tomb 7 at Monte Albán was a remarkable gold pendant, some 22cm (8.5in) long, made by Mixtec craftsmen *c.*1200–1500. This elaborate piece, an earring, was cast by the lost-wax process and consists of four detailed images set horizontally and beneath them four pendant elements. The four images represent, from the top: two gods playing the Mesoamerican ball game on an I-shaped court; a solar disc; a butterfly set in a square border that some identify as an image of a flint knife; and the crocodile earth monster. Some scholars interpret these as levels of the universe: the celestial realm of the gods, the sun, the moon (represented by the butterfly/knife) and the earth. Mixtec craftsmen were the masters of jewellery-making in the Aztec age.

JEWELLERY IN A SINGLE STYLE

The wearing of jewellery was strictly regulated in Aztec lands. Only elite warriors and members of the nobility were permitted to wear lip, nose, neck or ear ornaments in social intercourse, although gold and silver finery was also used as part of the sacred costumes worn by priests. Jewellery was made in a single style across the Mesoamerican region – except among the Tarascans of western Mexico, who kept the Aztec world at bay. Scholars call this pan-Mesoamerican jewellery the South Mexican International Style. This style had three distinguishing features. First, its decorative elements were similar to the style of the codices or bark-paper books painted by the Mixtecs. Second, it was of very high technical quality, made by artisans expert in lost-wax casting and wirework. Third, its artisans favoured composite designs that combined metal and precious stones, more than one type of metal or that added pendant elements to pectorals or rings.

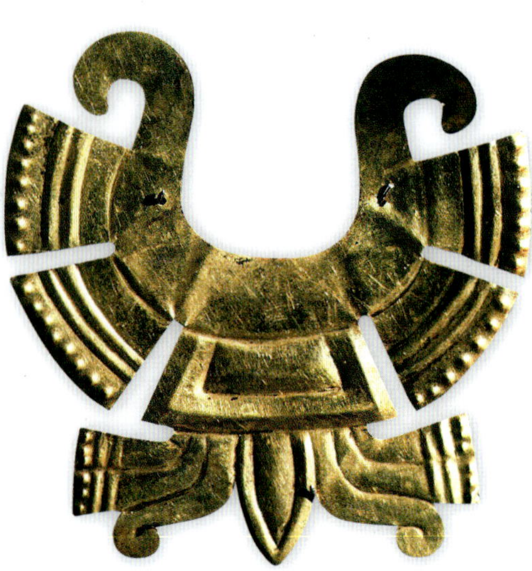

Below: This Aztec butterfly nose-ring was probably worn by a statue of moon goddess Coyolxauhqui in the Templo Mayor.

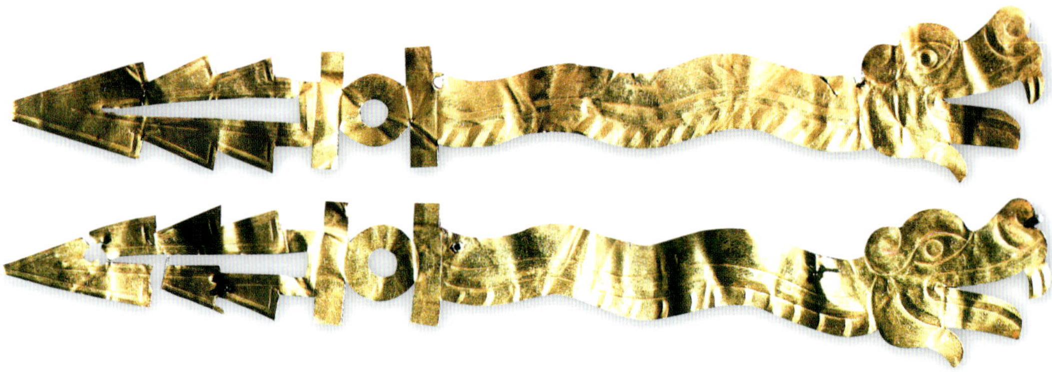

Above: Aztec beaten gold arrows represent the xiuhcóatl *or fire snake wielded by Huitzilopochtli. They end in serpent mouths.*

ANIMAL SIGNIFICANCE

A pair of 6cm (2.4in)-long ear ornaments, made by Méxica/Aztec or Mixtec craftsmen *c.*1400–1521, represent bird heads emerging from solar disks and giving issue from their mouths to tassels and bells. Experts identify the birds as *coxcoxtli*, a woodland species associated with Xochipilli, god of flowers, music and games. A 15th-century gold finger ring made by Mixtec craftsmen is adorned with the head of an eagle crowned with an intricately reproduced feather diadem. The eagle's beak probably once held a pendant element or a bell. The body of the ring takes the form of a delicately imagined serpent. This ring is typical of Mixtec output in representing common animals that had powerful sacred significance: the eagle is an image of Huitzilopochtli and the snake of Quetzalcóatl. Another Mixtec ring (*c.*1200–1521) represented both a jaguar head and a double-headed serpent, summoning the qualities of those powerful creatures for the wearer. Such rings were worn by members of the noble elite, in these cases perhaps by leading military figures, since the jaguar and the eagle both had important martial associations as the symbols of elite warrior groups.

Some jewellery represented the gods. A 6cm (2.4in)-long Mixtec gold pendant of *c.*1500 depicts Xiuhtecuhlti, patron of rulers and fire god, with the cylindrical elements in his headdress that were his

USING AND DISPOSING OF JEWELLERY

Jewellery was worn by members of the Aztec and Maya ruling and noble class for display and as part of ritual costumes in religious ceremonial. Precious items were offered in sacrifice, cast into the Sacred *Cenote* at Chichén Itzá, laid in a temple offering or provided as part of a cache interred during dedicatory rites for a building or stela. The best offering was the most precious: blood, the force of life. Jade, the colour of Chalchiúhtlicue and closely associated with life in the form of green maize shoots, was considered even more precious than gold or silver.

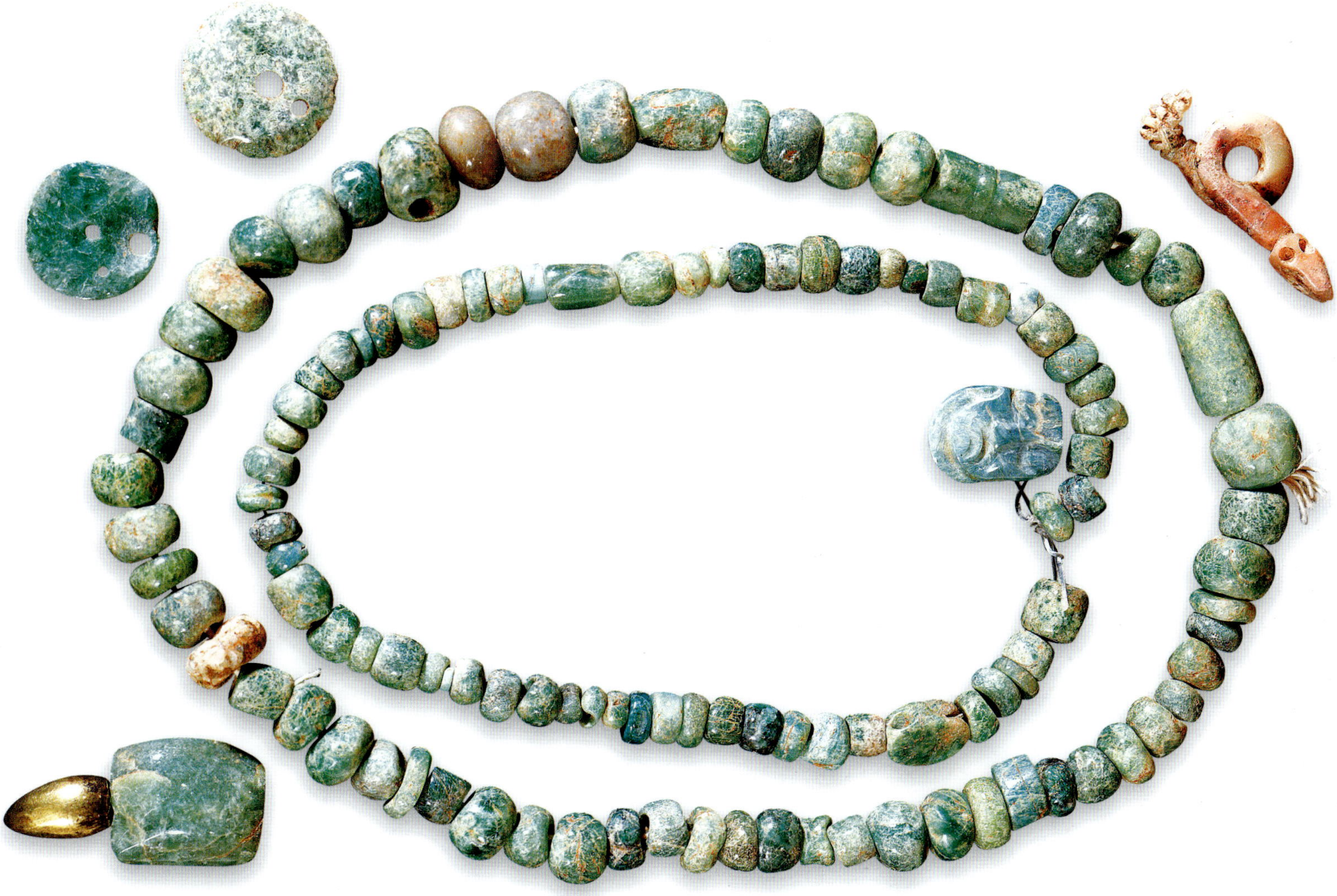

trademark; such cylinders were the sticks used to start a fire. The god's face bears a beard and from his mouth emerge two fangs, features that mark him as a primordial deity who has lost his teeth through age. From his ears hang two large circular ornaments that end in solar rays. These are appropriate as Xiuhtecuhtli also had solar associations and was identified as the Aztec counterpart of the Mixtec sun god Iha Ndikandii. A Mixtec pectoral brooch of *c.*1500 also depicted Xiuhtecuhtli/Iha Ndikandii with these characteristic elements of fangs, beard and headdress with vertical cylinders.

LIP ORNAMENTS

Mixtec goldsmiths made elaborate lip ornaments for the Aztec warriors and nobles. A cast-gold lip plug in the shape of an eagle's head made *c.*1500 shows remarkable detailing in the feathers and beak of the bird. The plug was worn on the lower lip: its shaft was inserted through a hole in the skin and gum and held in place by a plate worn inside the mouth. Eagle lip plugs were probably worn by leading members of the eagle-warrior society. Such plugs must have been heavy. Another example, made *c.*1400–1500, had a cast-gold eagle head and gold plug for securing the ornament in the mouth, but the connecting piece was fashioned from rock crystal to make it lighter.

Above: Sacred jade had connections to fertility. These jade-bead jewellery pieces were found in a tomb at El Otero, Mexico.

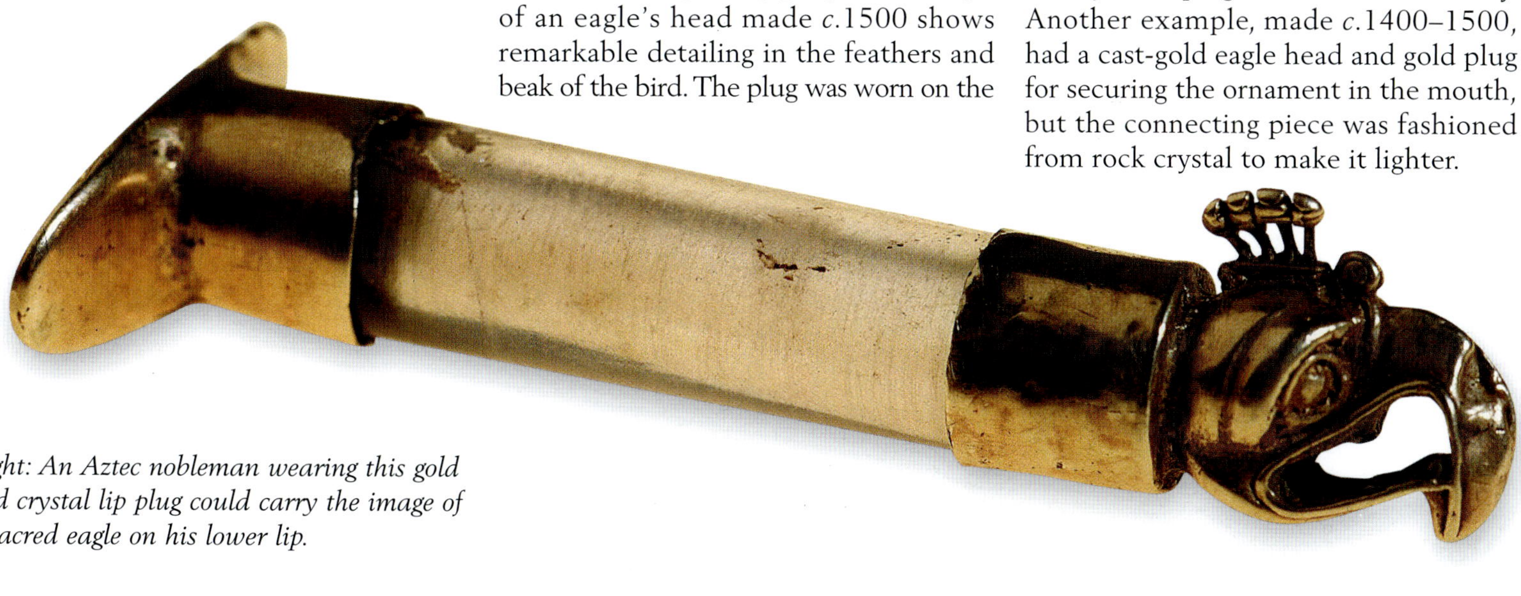

Right: An Aztec nobleman wearing this gold and crystal lip plug could carry the image of a sacred eagle on his lower lip.

WORK OF THE GOLDSMITHS

In his *General History of the Things of New Spain*, Friar Bernardino de Sahagún gave a lengthy inventory of the astounding wealth of gold, other rare metals and precious stones stored in Moctezuma II's treasury as items for ornamenting dancers and their costumes. These included gold models of plants, pelicans, sacred eagles and the *xiuhcóatl* fire serpent wielded by Huitzilopochtli. There was a turquoise disc set in gold, an eagle fashioned from greenstone and mounted in gold and a cylindrical crystal lip plug with feathers from the cotinga bird, also set in gold. The store also contained many articles made from jade and amber.

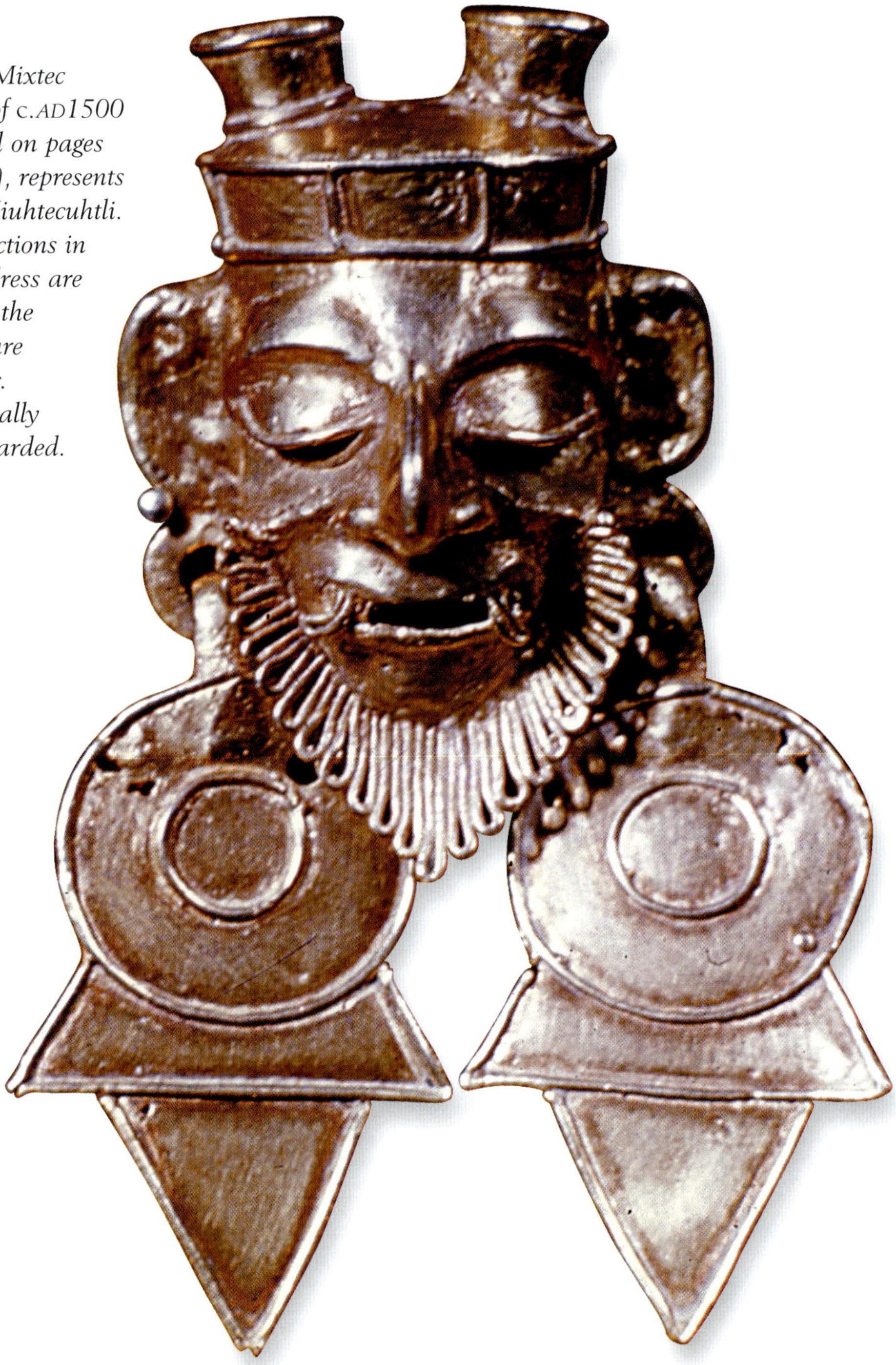

Right: A Mixtec pendant of c.AD*1500 (described on pages 220–221), represents fire god Xiuhtecuhtli. The projections in his headdress are firesticks; the earrings are solar rays. He is usually shown bearded.*

CELEBRATING WARRIORS

In wearing pendants or other images of warriors, an Aztec indicated that he or she was of good birth and a leading member of the nobility. A number of gold items have survived that celebrate or represent elite warriors. An exquisite pendant bell in the shape of an eagle warrior, made *c.*1500 by Aztec goldsmiths using the lost-wax technique, was worn on a chain or necklace. The bell, 9cm tall and 7.5 cm across (3.5in by 2.9in), consists of a hollow, pear-shaped gold vessel containing a copper pellet with eagle claws at the base. At the top of the pear shape, the warrior's head is enclosed in a battle helmet in the likeness of an eagle's beak, open to reveal the soldier's stern face. His arms are thin and feathered, giving them the appearance of wings. The left arms is bent to the front across his chest, where the soldier wears a pendant plaque in the warrior style. The right arm is raised beside his head and grasping a small, feather-trimmed shield, three dart-like spears and a staff – perhaps an *atlatl* (spear-thrower). Above the head there is a rectangular frame fashioned from gold wire. On the back of the helmet, two loops were used to mount the pendant on a chain when the piece was worn by a member of the fraternity of eagle-warriors in Tenochtitlán.

A Mixtec pendant of *c.*1200–1521 depicts another elite warrior in remarkable detail. The cast-gold figure, 8cm tall and 4.5cm across (3.1in by 1.7in), was worn on the chest or as a lip pendant. The figure wears a decorated headband and long, dangling earrings, together with a nose ornament, warrior-plaques on his chest and a lip plug from which a victim's head and three bells are suspended. His left hand holds a ceremonial shield, while his right grasps a pole that perhaps represents an *atlatl* spear-thrower or a staff of authority.

Another precious-metal warrior figure is a free-standing figurine made from tumbaga (a gold-coloured alloy of silver, copper and gold). The curious piece was

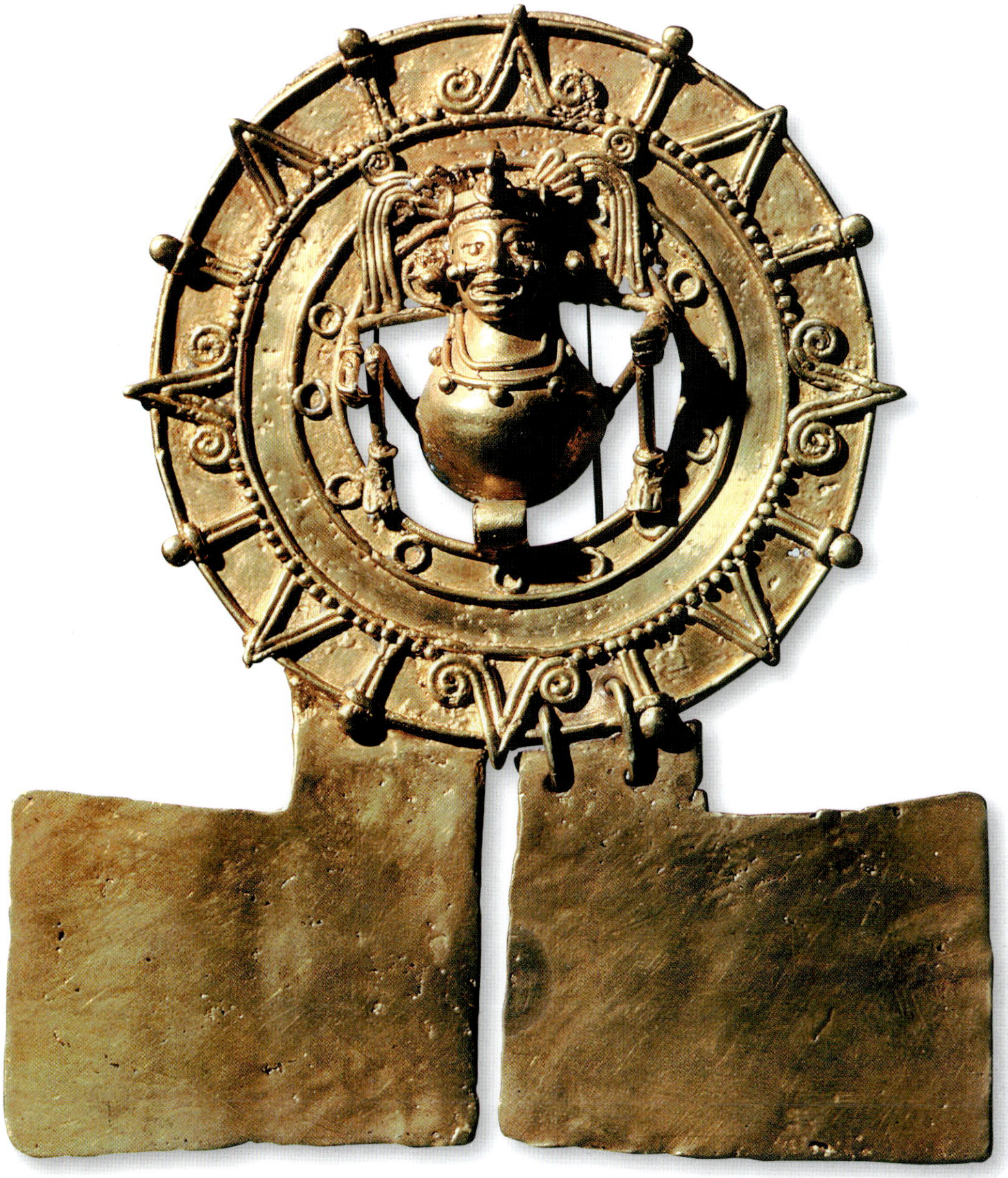

found in a cache of gold objects in Texcoco. The figurine, made by Aztec metalworkers after 1346, stands 11.2cm tall and measures 6.1cm across (4.4in by 2.4in). The figure wears ornaments in the lip, ears and nose, together with a splendid headdress. His warrior's loincloth is covered with a skirt of pendant bells. In his left arm he carries a shield and weapons and in his right hand he holds a ritual object and another pendant bell. Cavities in his chest and the back of his head almost certainly once held precious stones. The eyes, now empty, were probably also inlaid with obsidian and shell. The glyphs 2-Rabbit and 3-Water, marked on his back, have puzzled scholars, for they have no obvious relevant meaning. Scientific tests on the metal suggest that it was cast in the period 1346–1570.

GOLD AS TRIBUTE

Mixtec and Méxica/Aztec craftsmen used gold that had been supplied as tribute from subject regions of the empire. In regions such as Soconusco in western Chiapas, it was washed down from the hills and mountains in rivers and collected in the form of nuggets from the riverbeds. In workshops in the valley of Mexico, the metal was smelted at very high temperatures produced by craftsmen-labourers blowing through long tubes on to charcoal fires. Some goldsmiths worked in Moctezuma's palace in Tenochtitlán, producing goldwork exclusively for the *tlatoani* and his inner circle of nobles. These artisans were valued so highly that they were exempt from paying tax.

GOD OF THE GOLDSMITHS

Xipe Totec, worshipped by the Aztecs as the god of regeneration and of the green shoots of spring, was the patron deity of the Mixtec goldsmiths. Scholars believe that his cult, adopted by the Aztecs from the Mixtecs, had in turn been taken by the Mixtecs of Oaxaca from the region of Guerrero where some of western Mexico's very earliest metalworking centres were established in the 9th century AD. The breaking open of seeds in spring

Above: Golden deity. Mixtec goldsmiths produced delicate, lightweight pieces with intricate decorative and figurative elements. This breast ornament appears to make use of solar symbolism.

Xipe personified was perhaps considered to be like the breaking of moulds when goldworkers used the lost-wax method for casting.

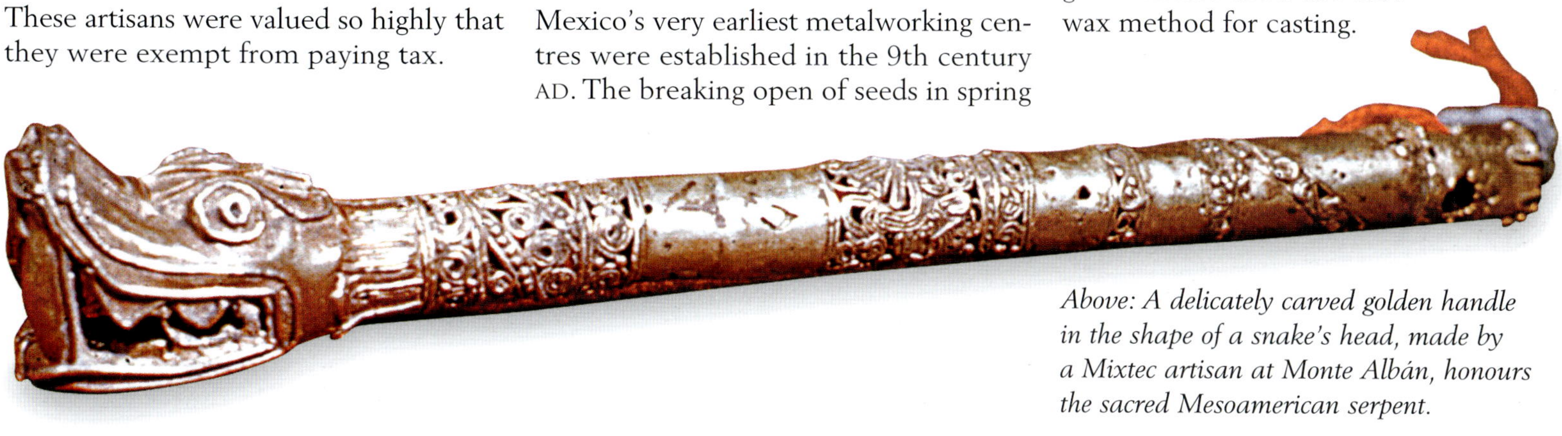

Above: A delicately carved golden handle in the shape of a snake's head, made by a Mixtec artisan at Monte Albán, honours the sacred Mesoamerican serpent.

BELLS AND REPOUSSÉ DISCS

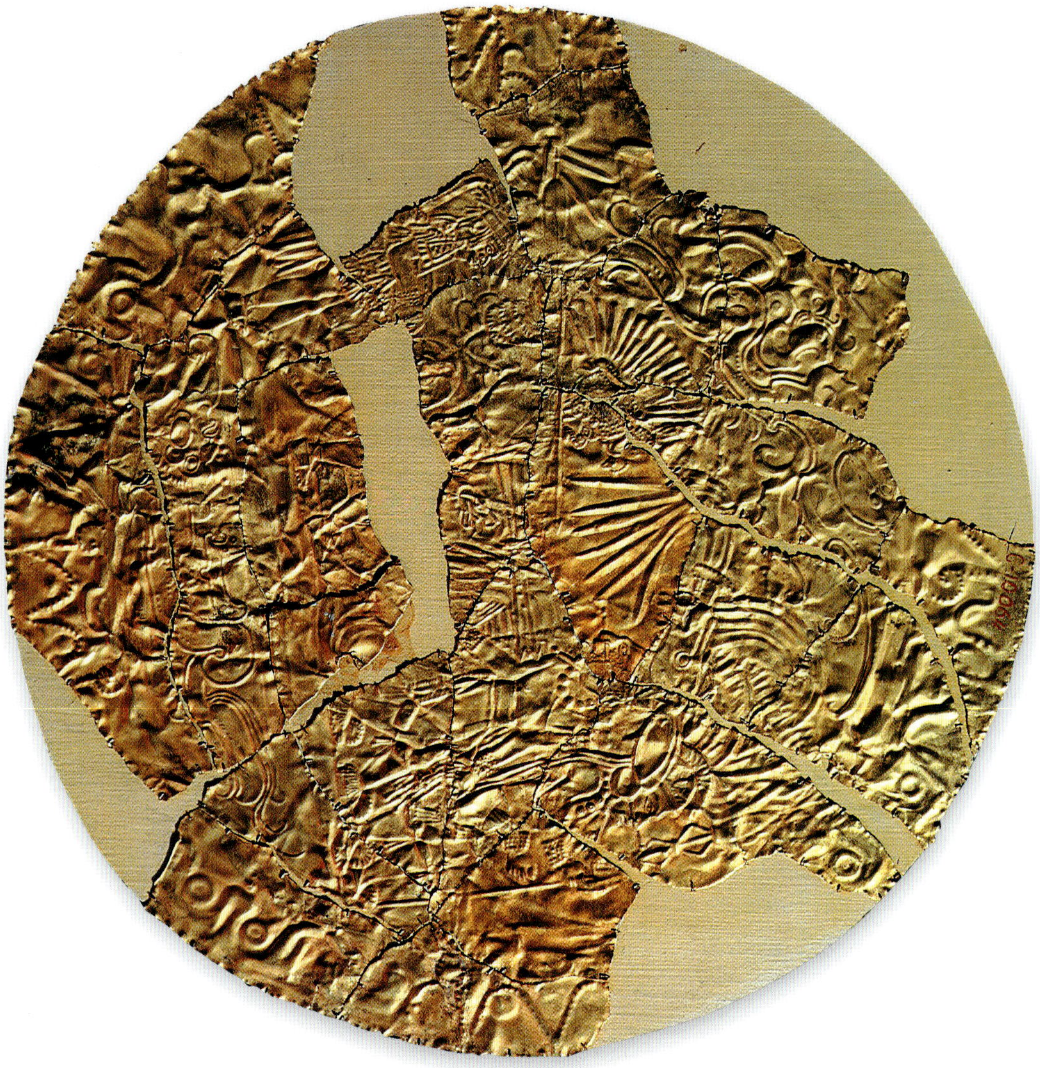

Above: The skilful repoussé work can still be seen in remains of a gold disc recovered from the sacred cenote at Chichén Itzá.

Among members of the Aztec nobility, metal bells with a good sound and a pleasing colour were highly prized. Many of the bells made by metalworkers were sewn on to nobles' outfits, so their resonance was highly valued. The creation of a good sound when walking was an important part of the overall impression that a nobleman made.

The colour of the bells was also significant, with silver and gold the preferred colours. The association of these colours with the moon and the sun had been established from ancient times among South American metalworkers and was passed into Mesoamerican belief and cultural patterns along with the metalworking techniques.

Metalworkers learned to make silver-coloured bells and other items by adding a little arsenic to copper and to make gold-coloured metal for artefacts by combining copper with tin.

Hernán Cortés reported on the widespread use of bells in costumes and other artefacts in his first despatch from Mexico. He described a bluestone mosaic headdress with many bells and gold beads, and a collection of animal heads with coloured skins that were hung with bells.

Small copper bells were widely made and distributed in Maya lands. They were worn by the death god Yum Cimil, who is also known to archaeologists as God A and are found on their own because they were probably hung on images of the god that have since been broken or disintegrated. The inhabitants of Quiriguá were using copper bells and ornaments in the period after *c.*AD800. These were almost certainly locally made.

SKILLED HAMMERWORK

Metalworkers in the northern Maya region developed particular skill in repoussé work, hammering intricate raised designs into copper, silver and gold from the reverse side of the disc. The work is stylistically close to the murals and carved reliefs of the early Postclassic Period at Chichén Itzá (AD1000–1250). One repoussé disc bears the image of a ruler with elaborate nose ornaments seated on a stone. He is wearing a magnificent feathered headdress and leaning forward in the direction of his extended left hand, which holds a pair of darts or small spears, while his other hand holds a ritual object. Several repoussé discs portray scenes of conflict between defeated Maya warriors and victorious warriors wearing and using Mexican-style equipment. One, 22cm (8.75in) in diameter, depicts two Mexican or Toltec-styled warriors driving Maya footsoldiers forward at the point of a feathered spear. The Maya warriors have the built-up upper noses characteristic of their people and wear long nose ornaments, together with elaborate feathered headdresses. On the ground by the feet of the Toltec warriors, a sacred serpent, perhaps a representation of the god Quetzalcóatl, rears to give his blessing while the outer rim of the disc is decorated with a serpentine motif that also appears to incorporate the goggle eyes of rain god Tláloc. Another disc represents the mouth of a sky-serpent yawning to give issue to a Toltec-styled warrior. Some discs show sacrificial scenes, representing the highland Mexican rite of tearing the

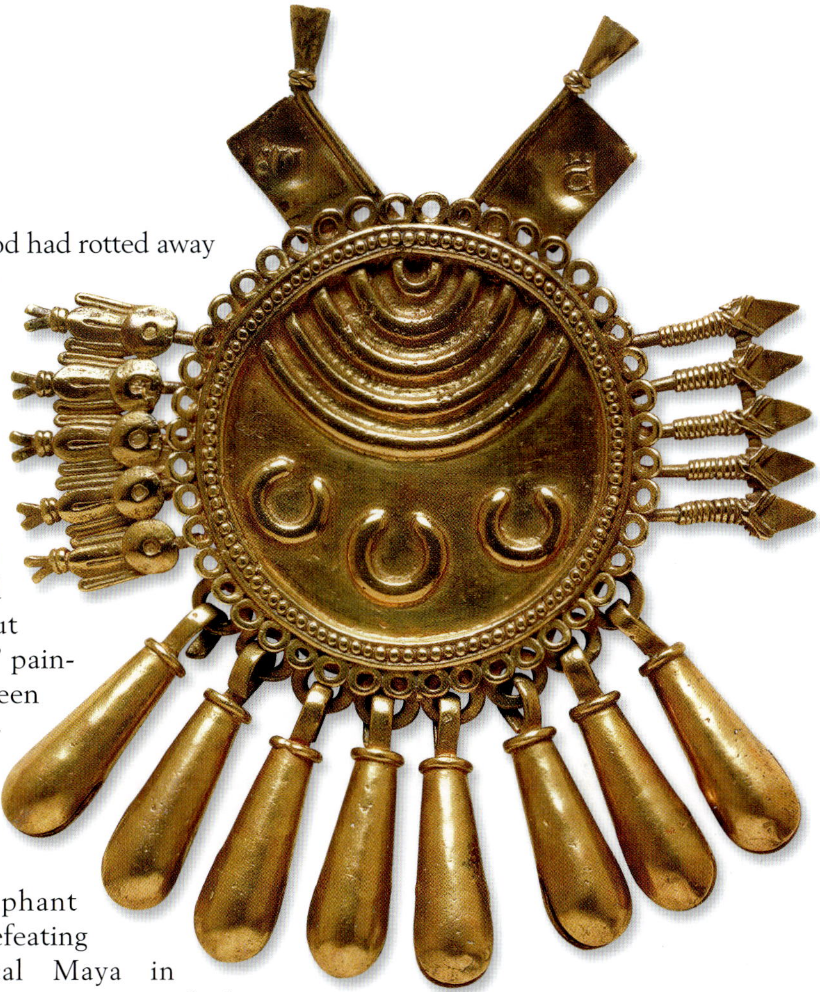

Above: *Recovered from the waters. This gold shield pendant was part of a hoard of Aztec gold, probably looted by conquistadors from the palace of Axayácatl, then lost at sea and found in 1975 in deep water near Puerto de Veracruz. Eight bells hang from its base. It was cast by the lost-wax method. The horseshoe-like marks on the lower part are representations of a half-moon.*

CASTING BY THE LOST-WAX METHOD

Mesoamerican metalworkers used the lost-wax or *ciré-perdu* method to cast objects. To cast a statuette, a craftsman would first make a clay model then, after dusting this with charcoal, he would brush the shape evenly with melted wax. Once the wax had hardened, he would dust the surface again with charcoal before adding a second layer of clay. He would invert the object and heat it until the wax melted and poured out. Then he would set the mould right way up before filling it with molten metal. He would set the whole aside to cool. Later he would break the mould to reveal the cast-metal object.

Some objects in two metals were produced by two-stage casting, An example is the ornament historians call the Pectoral of Teotitlán del Camino, which is now held in Mexico City's National Museum. This combines gold and silver. The gold segment was cast first, then the silver part afterwards.

victim's heart from his chest. These were made in northern Yucatán using metal reworked from imported items.

OFFERINGS IN THE CENOTE

Archaeologists found a large number of metal offerings in the Sacred *Cenote* at Chichén Itzá. These include bracelets, necklaces, pendants, rings, bells, beads, earplugs, masks and disks decorated with scenes in elaborate repoussé work. They are made of copper and gold. The archaeological team also uncovered decorative metal elements from wooden objects such as ritual masks and ceremonial shields, in cases where the wood had rotted away leaving only the metal. Many items had been broken or damaged as part of a rite designed to free the spirit of the object before it was offered. One gold sheet was rolled into a ball, but through academics' painstaking work has been restored to a condition in which it can be viewed and copied. It is decorated with an image of a triumphant Mexican warrior defeating two hapless local Maya in the course of the invasion of the Yucatán peninsula.

Many of the metal objects found at Chichén Itzá were imported items made in South America, the southern countries of Central America and the metalworking regions of western Mexico. Scientific analysis of the items dredged from the Sacred *Cenote* revealed that some of the pieces were made in Chiapas, Oaxaca, and the valley of Mexico, in Honduras, Panama and Colombia.

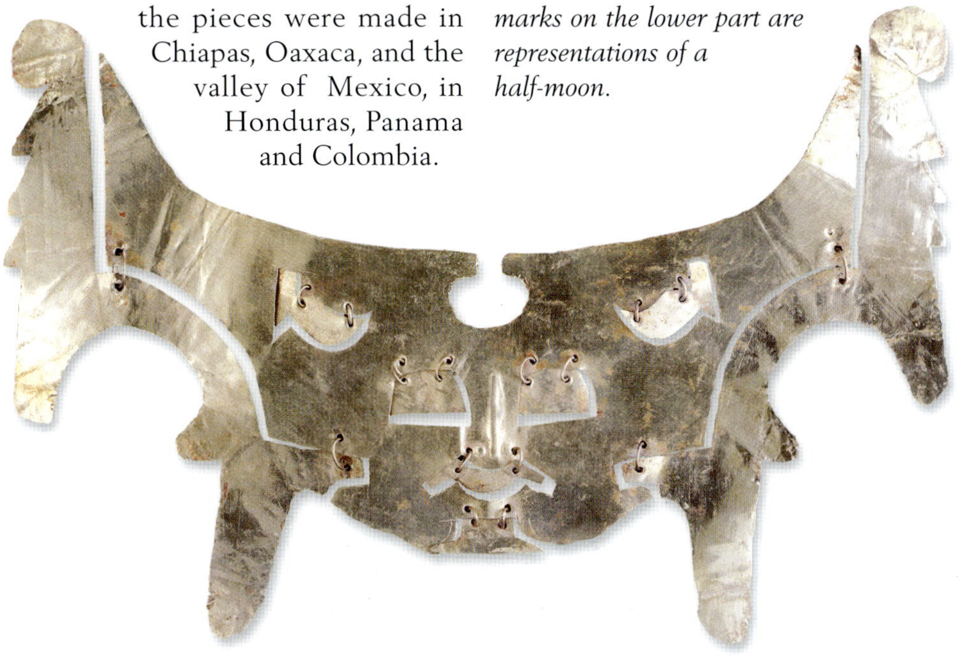

Right: This delicate beaten gold nose ornament was found at Colima, Meixco.

FACES OF GODS AND KINGS

An important strand of Olmec art was the carving of masks in greenstone, jade and other precious stones. Some have regular human features that scholars believe might have been portraits of rulers. Many others represent fierce animal faces with a snout. These may have been connected to the cult of the 'were-jaguar' that scholars identify as a possible image of the rain god. Members of the Olmec elite wore these fierce deity masks on their chests and in their headdresses during both religious and secular ceremonies. After death, rulers were laid to rest wearing these masks over their faces.

ANCIENT SHAMANIC RITES

Many scholars believe that the carving and wearing of animal-featured masks probably predated the Olmec to the people of the first villages in Mesoamerica. Shamans might have worn such masks during religious and divinatory ceremonies: the shamans were understood to take the form of fierce, snouted creatures such as the jaguar during their religious experiences. Perhaps the masks were worn more generally by the people during community festivities and gift-giving ceremonies in which wealthier members of the community – the members of a developing ruling class – redistributed some of their wealth as a way both of establishing their own status and satisfying the needs of the poor. The Olmec rulers apparently appropriated the tradition, commissioning and wearing masks of the most precious materials such as jade and greenstone. These were highly valued because of their green-turquoise colour, which had such powerful associations for Mesoamericans with fertility and life-giving waters.

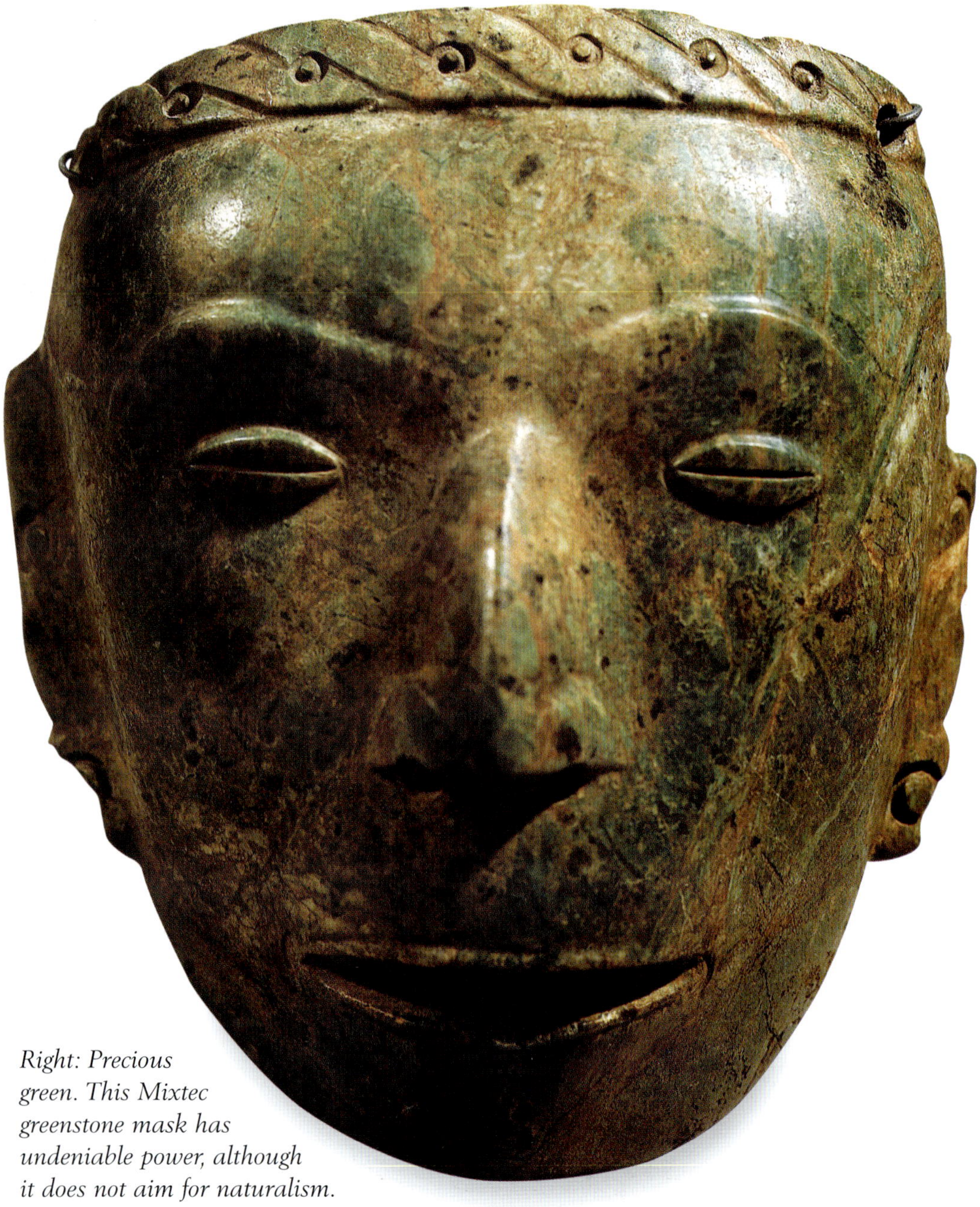

Right: Precious green. This Mixtec greenstone mask has undeniable power, although it does not aim for naturalism.

MYSTERY OF THE MASKS

In Teotihuacán, carvers of serpentine, greenstone and other precious stones represented serene-looking human faces in masks. The masks often had eyes inlaid with shell, iron pyrite and other materials. They were certainly not portrait masks, for they had regular, slightly abstracted features.

Archaeologists have uncovered hundreds of these masks in the ruins of the ancient city. They were not worn during ritual or placed in graves, but might have been mounted on clay busts or bodies made of perishable materials. The busts or bodies were dressed in splendid costumes and worshipped as ancestors or as nature deities. Some authorities suggest that the masks were attached to corpse-bundles containing mummified bodies and venerated in a sacred setting.

In the same period, craftsmen in Maya regions were also carving masks of jade and other precious stones to be placed in elite graves. At Calakmul an elite figure identified from glyphs by scholar Joyce Marcus as Long-lipped Jawbone was

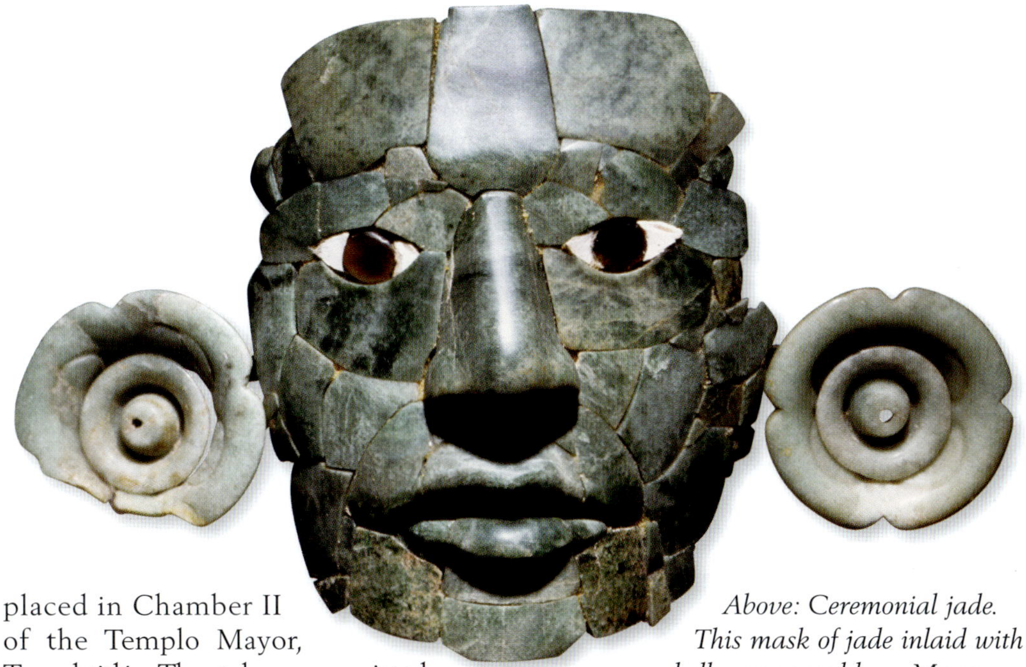

buried before c.AD500 wearing a jade-mosaic mask, with a second laid on his chest and a third worn on his belt. A life-sized jade mask with inlays of shell and pyrite was buried at Tikal in the grave known to archaeologists as Burial 160 in c.AD527. A jade mosaic mask was laid over the face of King Pacal's corpse in his tomb at Palenque (*d.* AD683). It was found in pieces but has been painstakingly remade by art historians.

OLMEC HEIRLOOMS

Many Olmec portrait and deity masks were placed in graves and preserved throughout Mesoamerican history. In Aztec times they were treasured possessions passed down the generations as heirlooms. The Aztecs also collected Teotihuacáno and other masks and often reused them as grave offerings, sometimes adding their own mosaic work to the original artifact before placing it in a tomb.

Some 88 painted greenstone masks carved in the abstract style identified by archaeologists as Mezcala were collected and placed in Chamber II of the Templo Mayor, Tenochtitlán. The style was associated with a culture that flourished near the Mezcala river in the region of the modern Mexican state of Guerrero from c.AD100–650, contemporary with Teotihuacán. Masks and figurines made by Mezcala craftsmen tended to have abstract features, indicated by circles, lines or depressions and raised areas in the surface. Some of the buried masks had the attributes of Tláloc, and scholars believe that the large offering was made to honour the rain god's helpers, the *tlaloque*.

The Aztecs themselves carved many masks in greenstone, obsidian, jade and other stones. Priests, priestesses and other impersonators of deities wore the masks in temple ceremonies.

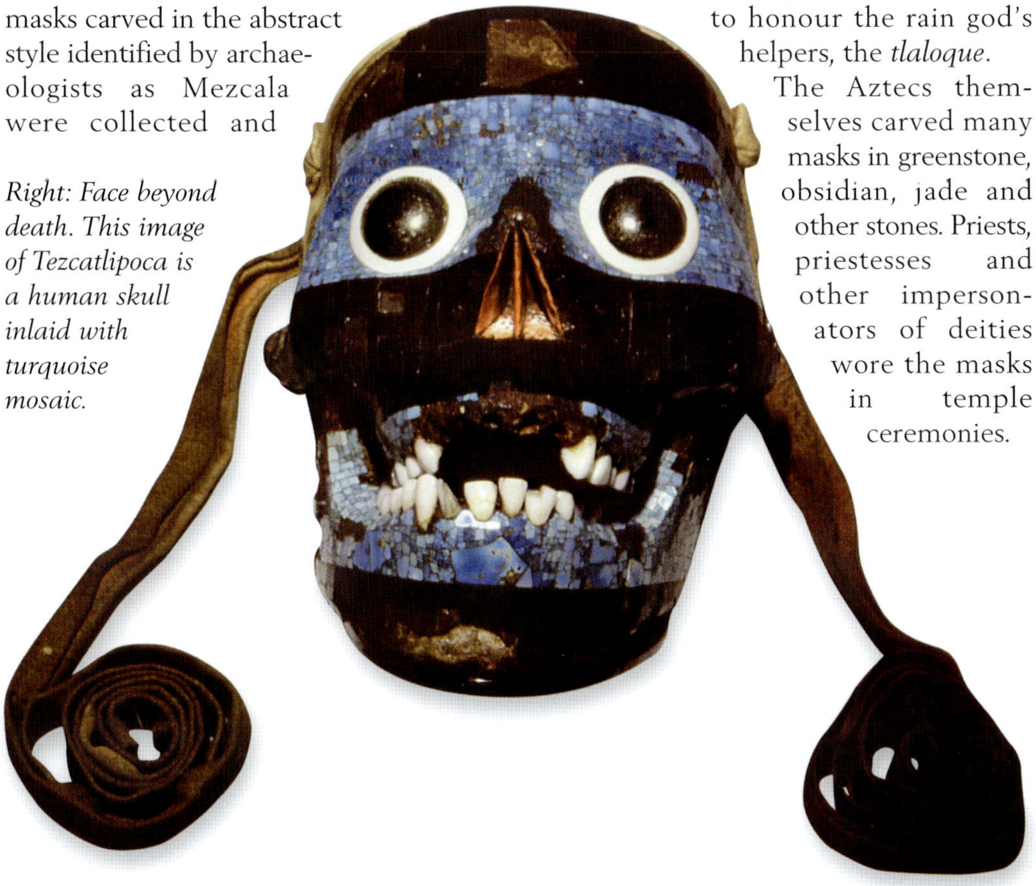

Right: Face beyond death. This image of Tezcatlipoca is a human skull inlaid with turquoise mosaic.

Above: Ceremonial jade. This mask of jade inlaid with shell was carved by a Maya artisan in the Classic Period.

Sometimes, as in Teotihuacán, the masks were attached to sacred bundles, to represent the face on the divine body. A splendid Aztec greenstone mask of Coyolxauhqui, moon goddess and sister of Huitzilopochtli, was probably decorated with ornaments and worn on the chest during ritual performances. The mask, made c.1500, was carved with images of bells on the cheeks that celebrated the goddess's name ('Lady with Bells on Her Face'). A diorite mask of Chalchiúhtlicue, carved c.1500, was probably attached to a sacred body. It included carvings of a quetzal-feather crown, marks representing face paint on the cheeks and, on the rear, an engraving of the glyph '8-Grass', one of the goddess's names in the ritual calendar.

DEATH MASKS

Craftsmen in Tenochtitlán and other cities also made masks that were buried with the deceased, presumably to provide individuals with a face for the spirit world after the cremation of the corpse. A very fine stone portrait mask carved c.1350–1500 and representing the features of a fresh-faced young man was dedicated to Quetzalcóatl in his guise as wind god Éhecatl by an image of the seated wind god together, with a carving interpreted as '9-Wind', one of the god's names in the ritual calendar.

SHELL AND PRECIOUS STONE DECORATION

Mesoamerican craftsmen excelled in fine mosaic work using turquoise, onyx, mother-of-pearl, malachite, jade, marine shells and other forms of inlay. From Olmec times, deity and funerary masks carved from precious stones were sometimes decorated with mosaic covering or inlaid with obsidian, onyx and shell to represent the eyes.

A magnificent Teotihuacáno mask of *c.*AD450 was covered with turquoise across most of the face, with inlays of shell for the eyes and obsidian for the eyeballs. Red spondylus or mollusc shell added a geometric nose ring, outlined the eyebrows and added a central forehead glyph that scholars believe once identified the person or deity celebrated in the mask itself.

This mask was found in an ancient grave in Malinaltepec, modern Guerrero province, in 1921. It was probably carried there by traders from Teotihuacán.

*Below: At Palenque artists made exquisite mosaic masks, such as this late Classic Period jade piece (*c.*AD600–900).*

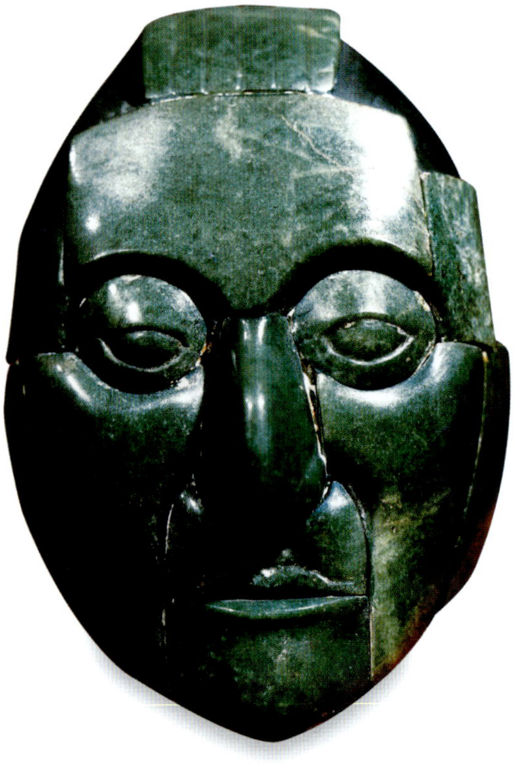

TIKAL TREASURES

Two superb Maya jade mosaic vessels were buried at Tikal in the 8th century AD. One was laid with the body of King Ah Cacau (*r.* AD682–734) and a rich selection of jade jewellery, shells, pearls and jaguar skins in the grave known as Burial 116 beneath Temple I. The vessel was constructed from jade pieces tacked with jade pins around a cylinder of wood; its lid bore a portrait believed to be of the king himself. A second, similar vessel was laid in the grave now called Burial 196, within the comparatively modest Temple 73 at the south-western corner of Tikal's Great Plaza. Other items in the tomb, including the inscribed spine of a stingray and a named drinking cup, suggest that the tomb was associated with Ah Cacau's successor, Yax Kin (*r.* AD734–46). However, many scholars argue that the tomb is too modest to be that of so great a king as Yax Kin and that it might be that of his far less celebrated son (AD766–68), known to scholars only as the '28th Ruler'.

In the 14th–16th centuries, Mixtec craftsmen were renowned for their mosaic work as well as for their metalwork. One of Moctezuma II's tribute lists reveals that each year Tenochtitlán received ten turquoise-mosaic masks made by skilled artisans in Oaxaca. Tribute of turquoise-mosaic ceremonial shields was also sent from Oaxaca to Tenochtitlán each year.

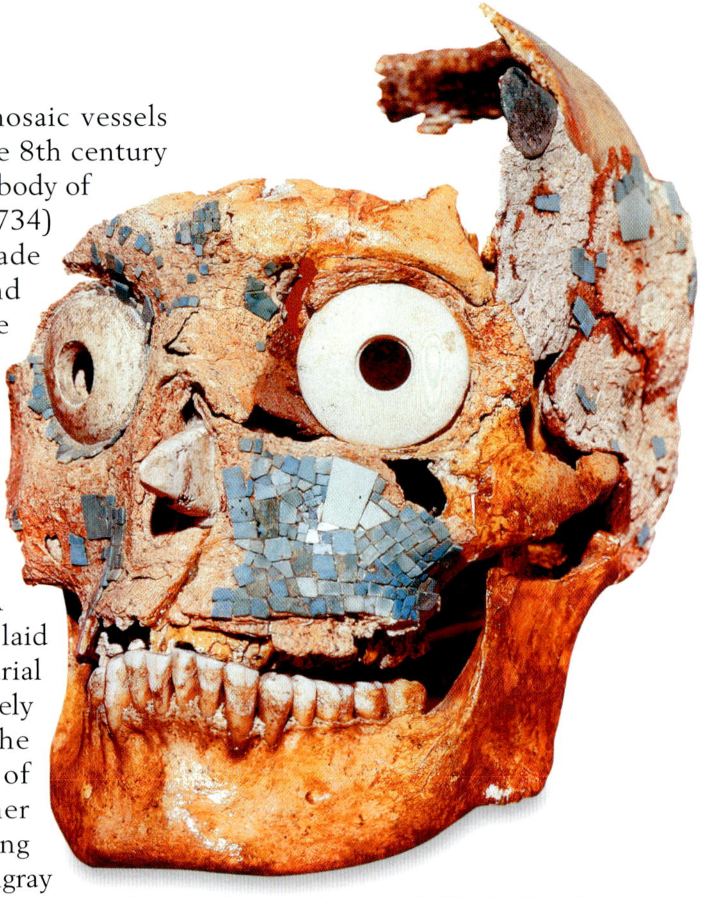

Above: A human skull inlaid with turquoise and ivory mosaic was among the gold offerings found in Tomb 7 at Monte Albán.

FACE OF THE GODS

A number of Aztec-Mixtec mosaic-encrusted deity masks have survived. One celebrated example is a mask of the god of darkness and fate Tezcatlipoca. This was fashioned *c.*1400–1521 from a human skull with a mosaic of turquoise and lignite inlaid in bands across the front, and eyes filled with white shell and black discs of iron pyrite. The inner part of the skull was lined with leather and the lower jaw hinged so that it could be moved when the mask was worn by a priest during religious ceremonial.

A turquoise-mosaic mask with serpents encircling the eyes and mosaic representations of feathers on either side of the eyes was made, probably by Mixtec specialists, on a cedar-wood base *c.*1400–1521. The mask was intended for priests of Quetzalcóatl or of Tláloc. The serpent eye-goggles were traditionally a symbol of Tláloc, while the feathers suggested the plumed serpent Quetzalcóatl. The mask, 17.3cm high and 16.7cm wide (6.8in by 6.7in), closely matches the description given by Bernardino de Sahagún of a turquoise-encrusted mask despatched as a gift by Moctezuma II to Hernán Cortés in 1519. Sahagún reported that the mask would have been worn with a tall plume of quetzal feathers.

Another Tláloc mask, of *c.*1500, is made of turquoise, malachite, mother-of-pearl, jade and red and white shell laid on a wooden base. The mask, with the rain god's elongated snout and tall head-dress, was 29cm (11.4in) tall. Scholars suggest that this sacred Tláloc likeness formed the top of a priest's staff or ruler's sceptre.

A magnificent Aztec wooden pectoral covered with turquoise mosaic and shell inlay represents the double-headed sky serpent that was one of the symbols of the feathered serpent god Quetzalcóatl. The pectoral, made *c.*1400–1521, measures 20.5cm by 43.3cm (8in by 17in)

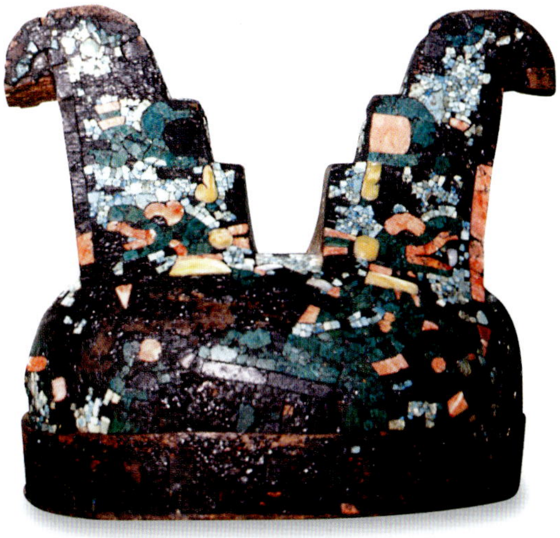

Above: This Aztec helmet decorated with mosaic of precious stones was probably made by a Mixtec artist c.AD*1400–1520.*

and was worn by priests of the feathered serpent god Quetzalcóatl or by the ruler himself – Quetzalcóatl was one of the patrons of Mesoamerican kingship. Its eye sockets, now empty, were probably once inlaid with shell and iron pyrites. Some scholars suggest that the pectoral was worn during ritual celebration of the birth of the Aztecs' tribal god Huitzilopochtli, whose birthplace Coatepec ('Serpent Mountain') was represented by the towering bulk of the Templo Mayor in Tenochtitlán.

In the Aztec era, mosaic craftsmen also applied their expertise to the making of elaborate handles for sacrificial knives. The handle of one splendid knife depicts an eagle-warrior in a mosaic of turquoise, shell and malachite laid on wood; the blade is of chalcedony. The crouching warrior holds the handle or *ixcuac* between extended hands, while his face emerges from the open bird's beak.

MOSAIC ON WOOD

Throughout Mesoamerican history, artisans probably also cut deity and portrait masks from wood and then added fine mosaic overlay. Few of these precious objects have survived. Some, made by Aztec-Mixtec craftsmen in the 14th–15th centuries and preserved in desert conditions near Tehuacan in the modern Mexican state of Puebla, give an indication of the style and quality of the work.

One of the masks found in Puebla retains all its original turquoise covering, and part of the onyx inlay in the eyes and mouth. The find in Tehuacan also contained several once-splendid mosaic ceremonial shields, some with all the mosaic decoration now sadly worn off.

Below: On this unique double-headed Aztec serpent pectoral, turquoise mosaic is attached to the wooden base using resinous gum. White and red shell mark the mouth.

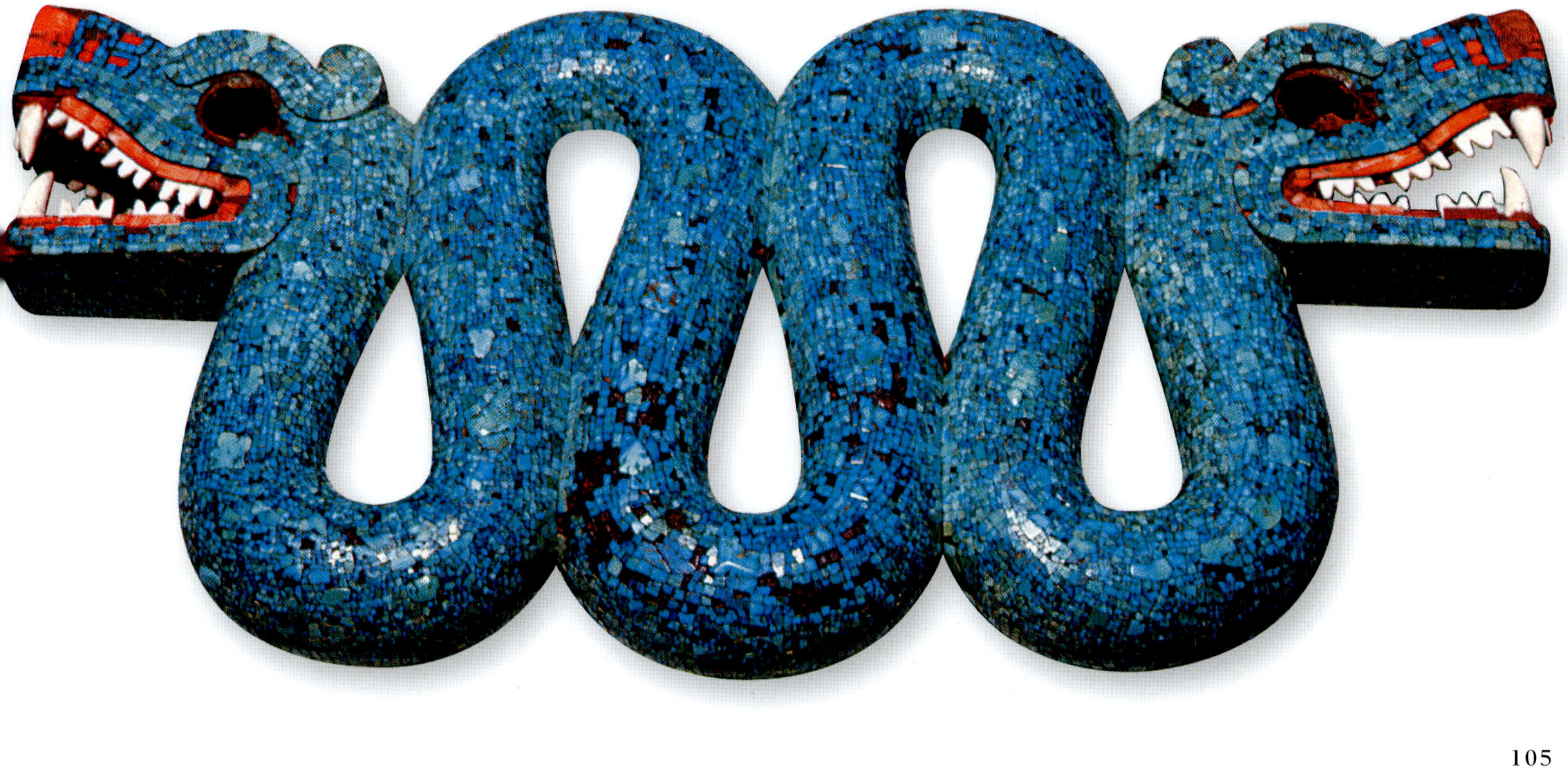

CHIPPED AND CARVED STONES:
ELABORATE OFFERINGS

Maya artisans chipped and cut stones, blades and flints with elaborate skill. Obsidian and flint blades and the remarkable decorative chipped flints known by scholars as 'flint eccentrics' were sacred objects, buried in large caches beneath temples and monuments.

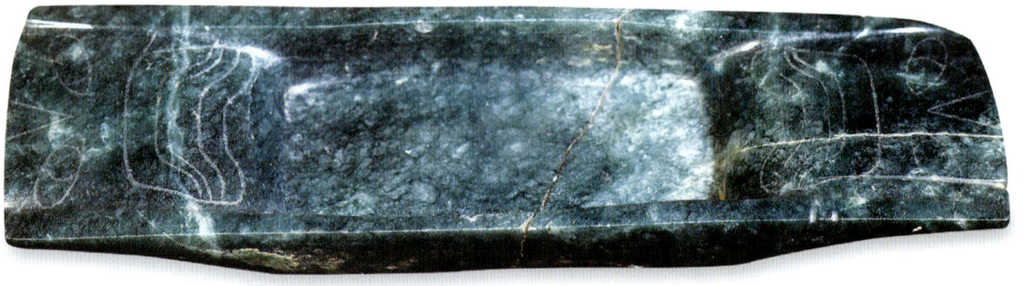

Above: An Olmec jade piece was carved in the form of a canoe c.500BC. Sacred markings are visible at the ends.

FLINT ECCENTRICS
Some eccentrics are fashioned to represent human heads in profile. A number of chipped flints found at El Palmar, Quintana Roo, were probably once the heads of ritual staffs. One represents a human figure, with elaborate headdress, protruding lips perhaps intended to suggest a lip plug and a large ornament on the back. The 6th-century Copán temple that archaeologists call the 'Rosalila structure' contained a large cache of chipped flints, including a number of human profiles. Scholars believe that these may once have been the heads of the 'manikin sceptres' carried by Maya rulers as a sign of authority. Other flints are chipped to represent leaves or the form of the symbols of office called 'knuckle dusters' by scholars and held by notable court attendants in murals and painted scenes on vases.

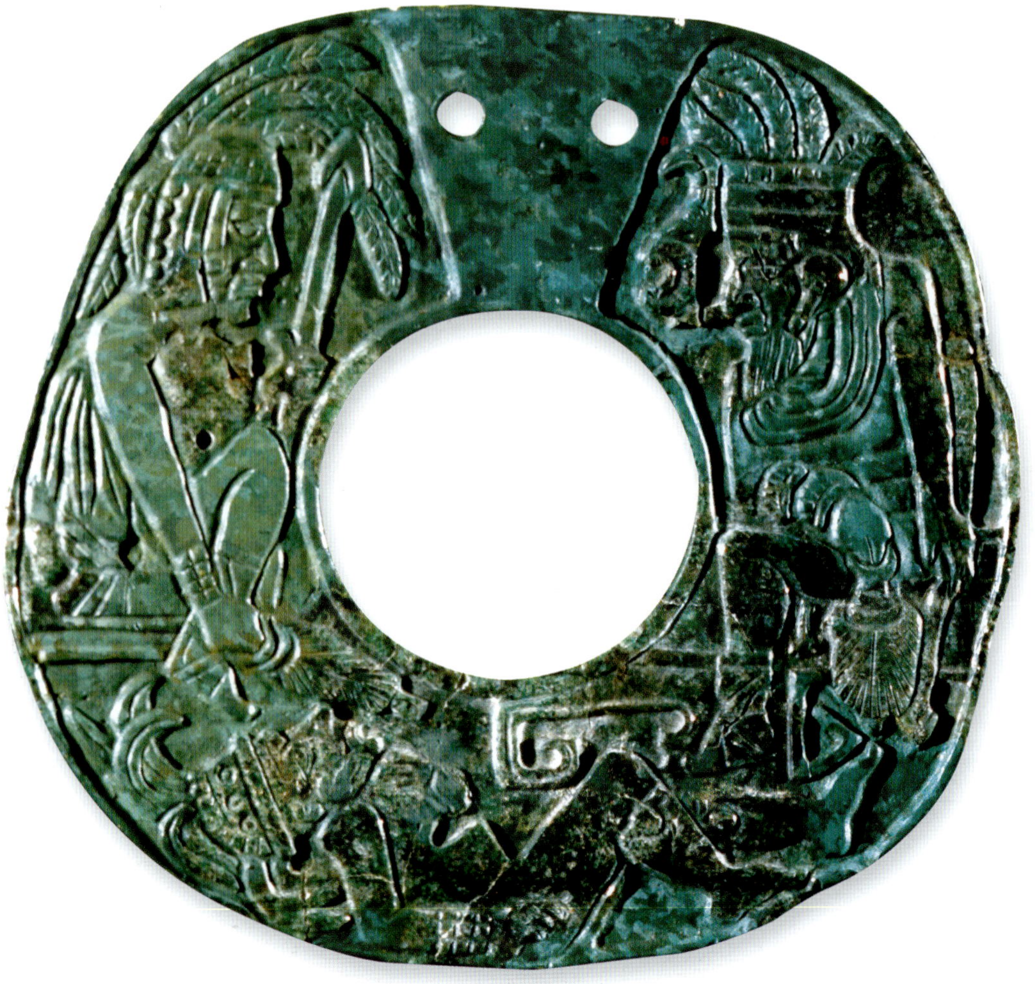

Below: This carved Maya jade pendant, 12cm (5in) across (c.AD850–1250), was found in the Sacred Cenote *at Chichén Itzá.*

CARVED FIGURES AND PLAQUES
From the days of the Olmec, Mesoamerican craftsmen cut small pieces of jade and other stones with remarkable delicacy and precision. An Olmec jade bead found in Chiapas was fashioned in the shape of a human head, while another small jade found at Necaxa in modern

WORKING JADE

Technically, Maya jades are jadeite, a very hard mineral with a chemical composition distinct from that of nephrite, the material carved in Chinese jades.

Mesoamericans gathered jadeite from streams and rivers in the form of pebbles, rocks and even sizeable boulders. Skilled craftsmen used a sawing motion with cords to cut and deepen lines in the hard rock, drilling holes with bones or pieces of hardwood, in both cases using water and sand or tiny stones to aid in cutting. The precision, delicacy and artistic flair of their work is astonishing.

Partly because the rock was found in streams, but more significantly because of its typical mottled green to blue-green colouring, jadeite was associated with water and fertility among the Aztecs, and with water and rain deities such as Chalchiúhtlicue and Tláloc.

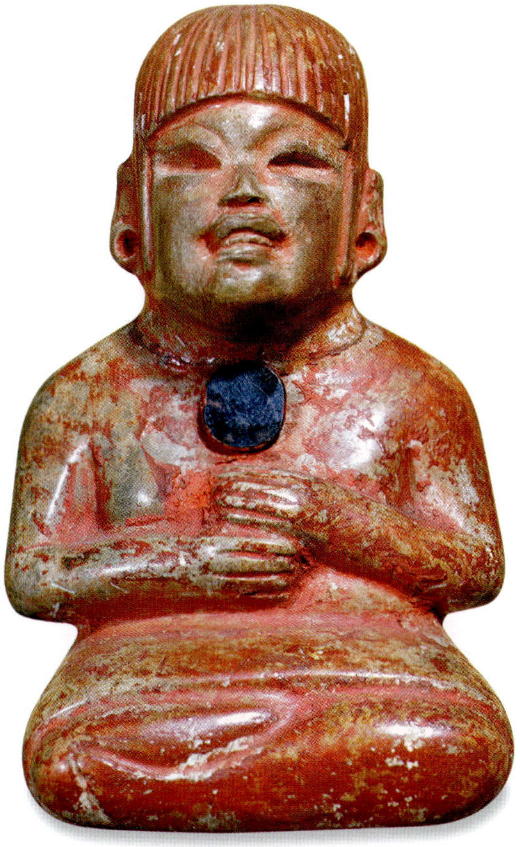

Above: An Olmec jade figurine, found at La Venta and made c.*1200–200*BC*, is believed to represent the god of the maize plant.*

Puebla state was cut in the shape of a crouching tiger. In Maya lands, archaeologists found several delicately carved figurines in jade and other similar stones during excavations at Copán, Chichén Itzá, Uaxactún and other sites.

The small, carved heads were often worn as pendants. One found at Chichén Itzá bore a date in the Maya Long Count equivalent to AD674. Scholars believe that traders brought it to Chichén Itzá from Piedras Negras, its probable place of origin. A cross-legged human figure beautifully fashioned from fuchsite, a stone similar to, but softer than jade, was deposited in an offering at Uaxactún beneath a stairway at the structure archaeologists call Temple A-XVIII. The figurine had linked forearms, rounded belly, rectangular eye sockets originally painted red and a large left ear – its right ear was apparently damaged. Holes drilled in the stone probably gave such ornamental pieces ritual meaning.

At Palenque, a carved jade figurine of the Maya sun god Kinich Ahau was placed within King Pacal's sarcophagus in the royal tomb beneath the Temple of the Inscriptions. A substantial jade head of the same god, found in a king's tomb at Altun Há in Belize, weighed 4.42kg (9.7lb), making it the largest Maya sculpture in this precious stone.

CELTS, PLAQUES AND PECTORALS

A 4th-century jade celt or implement, probably worn as a belt decoration, was carved with the Maya Long Count date 8.14.3.1.12 (17 September AD320) and with a full-length portrait of Tikal ruler Moon Zero Bird. The celt, known by scholars as the Leyden Plaque, celebrated Moon Zero Bird's 'seating' or accession to the throne of Tikal on the marked date in AD320. It depicts the king, in full ceremonial costume with celts and deity masks hanging from his belt, trampling on a captive depicted in a style similar to that used for images of captives on Tikal monuments. The plaque, one of the oldest dated Maya artefacts, was probably taken from King Moon Zero Bird's tomb at Tikal in ancient times. It was found in 1864 at Puerto de Barrios near the river Motagua in Guatemala.

A blue-green jade plaque, 30cm (12in) tall, was carved by a leading jade-craftsman of the late Classic Period Maya world. It represents a king on a throne, his body facing forwards but head in profile, wearing a serpent headdress from which emerges a figure with an unsettling, grotesque face. Before the throne a second figure kneels in supplication, while a speech scroll coming forth from the king's mouth indicates that he is declaring his identity and mighty achievements or else offering prayers to the gods on behalf of his people. The beautifully worked piece, found in Teotihuacán, was perhaps offered as an elite gift or else traded for valuable goods.

A splendid jade pectoral cut by Mixtec craftsmen *c.*AD1000 bears witness to the continued popularity of this precious stone for ceremonial and sacred objects.

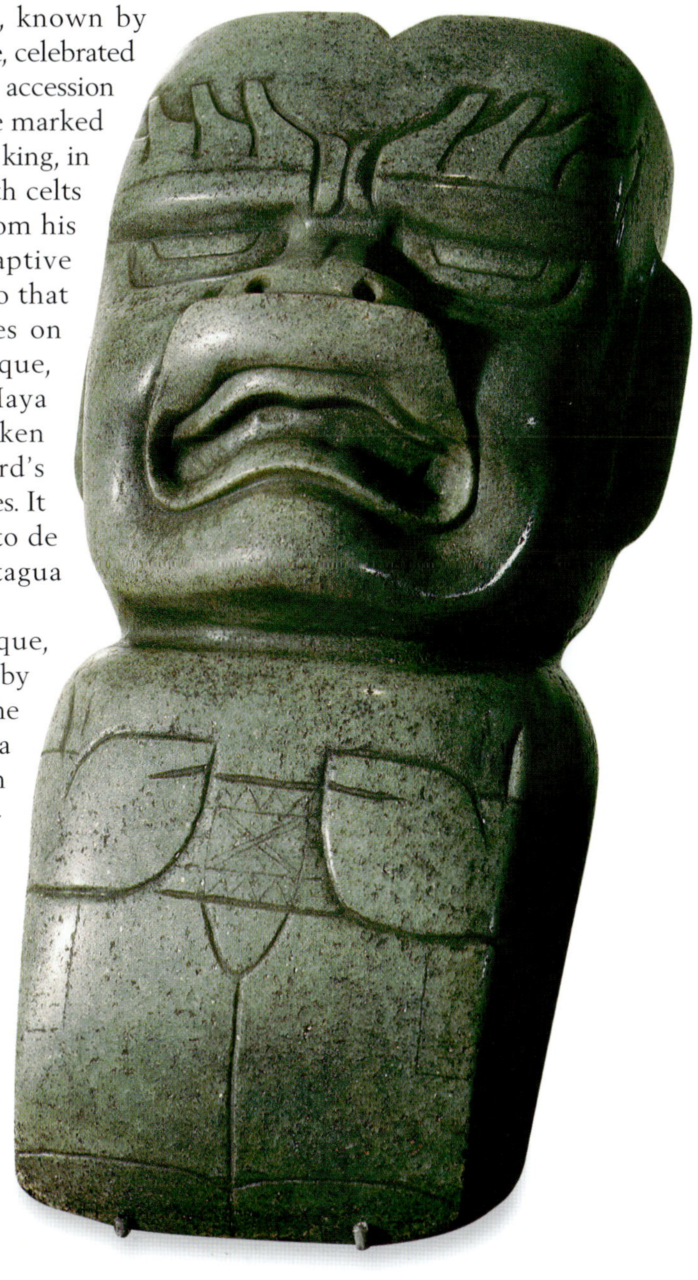

Right: An Olmec adze, or type of axe, from Veracruz is carved with the features of the sacred jaguar.

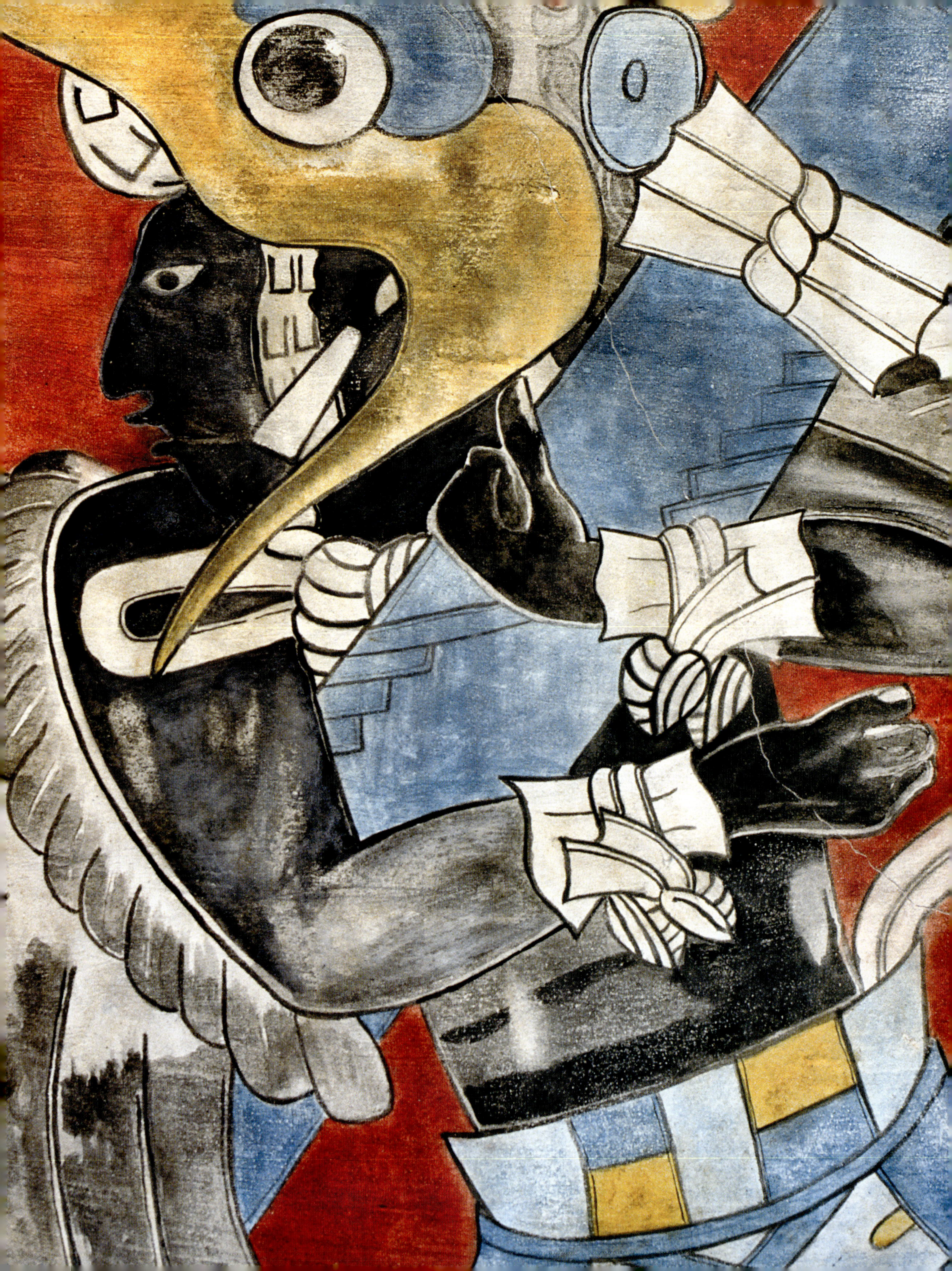

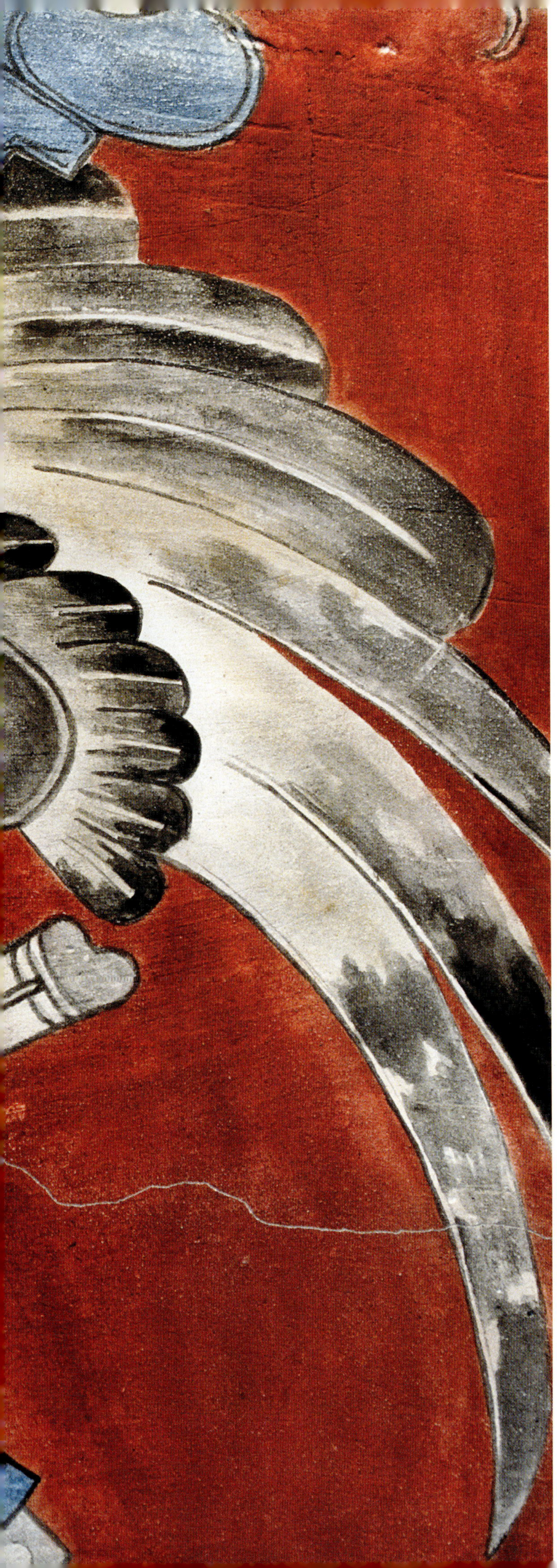

CHAPTER SIX

IMAGES, SYMBOLS AND WORDS

Mesoamerican wall paintings are filled with religious and political meaning. Sometimes accompanied by explanatory hieroglyphs, they are sacred statements, often dense with complex symbolism, intended to be 'read' and interpreted: celebrations of the gods' goodness in guaranteeing the fertility of the earth, of the power of the king and his ancestors or of the movements of time as evidenced by astronomical cycles.

Classic Period Maya-painted scenes include the humiliation or sacrifice of a defeated ruler, victory in battle, ceremonies of dynastic consolidation or acts of ritual bloodletting. Images represent action and carry narrative, while glyphs provide meaning and permanence by giving names and by setting the events in time.

In a parallel tradition, beginning in Teotihuacán and also finding expression in murals at Cacaxtla and in Caribbean Yucatán in the 13th–16th centuries, artists created symbolic religious scenes connected with the underworld, fertility and the cycles of the stars rather than dynastic or military events. In this tradition, glyphic writing played a much smaller role – there were no glyphic inscriptions at Teotihuacán. But scholars are convinced that religious symbols such as the five-pointed half-star Venus sign could be 'read' as part of a 'symbolic writing' by residents of Teotihuacán or Cacaxtla.

Left: Solar symbolism. A mural in Cacaxtla shows a man with eagle beak and wings who may represent the sun by day.

THE DATING OF EVENTS

The desire to record and celebrate the patterned movements of sacred time might have been the impetus that drove Mesoamericans to develop their glyphic system of writing. Many historians agree that the complex 260-day and 365-day calendars evolved before the earliest forms of writing, somewhere around the mid-first millennium BC.

CYCLES OF THE CALENDAR

As far as we know, written language was first used to identify people or to mark military triumphs by placing them within the cycles of the calendar.

The carvings often cited as the oldest piece of Mesoamerican writing are the hieroglyphs cut in the threshold of Monument 3 at San José Mogote *c.*600BC. These record the date 1-Earthquake from the 260-day calendar alongside an image of a prostrate figure.

The symbol is interpreted either as identification of the figure who, like many later Mesoamericans, had taken his name from the date of his birth, or as a record of the date of the victory in which he was taken captive or the day on which he was sacrificed.

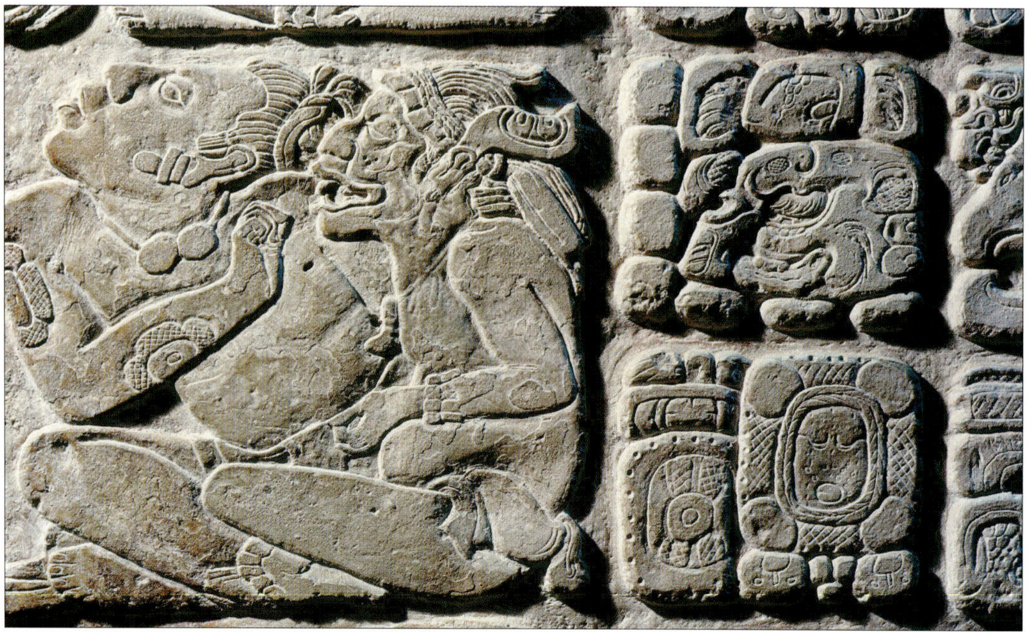

Below: Intricate calendrical hieroglyphs in the Palace at Palenque date the events depicted to AD644, during Pacal's reign.

Scribes or stonemasons using the dates of the 260-day and 365-day calendars could place an event precisely within a hallowed cycle of 52 years that the Maya called the Calendar Round. (This longer period represented the time that elapsed before a day in the 365-day year and a day in the 260-day year coincided: 18,980 days, or 52 solar years of 365 days.) Scribes who wanted to date events within longer spans of time needed a different measure. The dating system used on stelae of Maya cities in the Classic Period, known as the Maya Long Count, identified events both within the Calendar Round and within a span of years beginning on 13 August 3114BC. Historians do not know the significance of this date, but some have suggested that it marked the creation of the current world cycle, according to religious narrative.

The Long Count organized days in units of 20: *kin* (one day), *uinal* (20 days), *tun* (360 days), *katun* (7,200 days) and *baktun* (144,000 days). Given that the system was vigesimal – it used units of 20 rather than units of 10, as in decimal calculation – the *tun* count should have been 400 (1 *kin* multiplied by 20 multiplied by 20), but the developers of the Long Count amended this to 360 to make it closer to the length of the solar year.

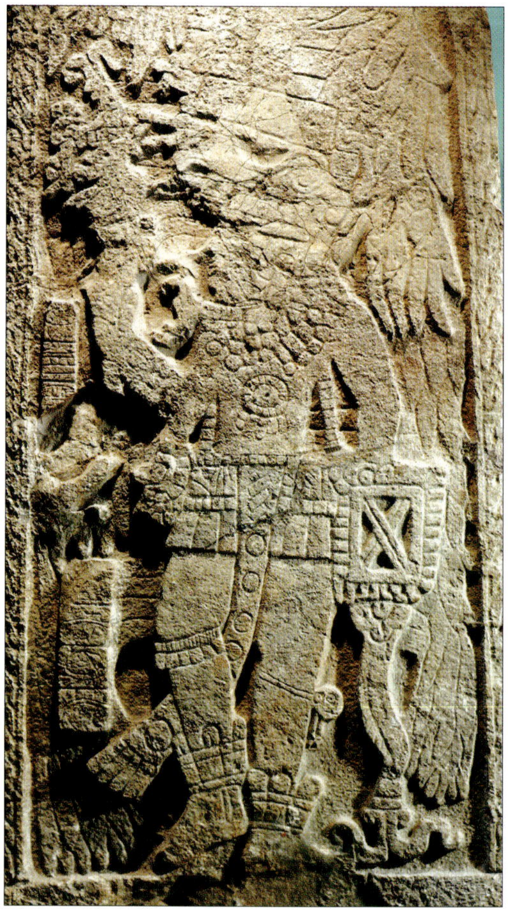

Above: Stela at Sayil, dated AD800–950. Contemporaries could interpret details of the king's stance, costume and equipment.

WRITING NUMBERS

Before creating the Long Count, the Maya must first have developed the concept of zero, so that some units in the count could be marked empty. Scribes and stonemasons indicated numbers by using dots for units up to four and a horizontal bar for the number five. They could write numbers up to 19 (three bars and four dots) using this system. For larger numbers they used the same symbols in horizontal layers, representing

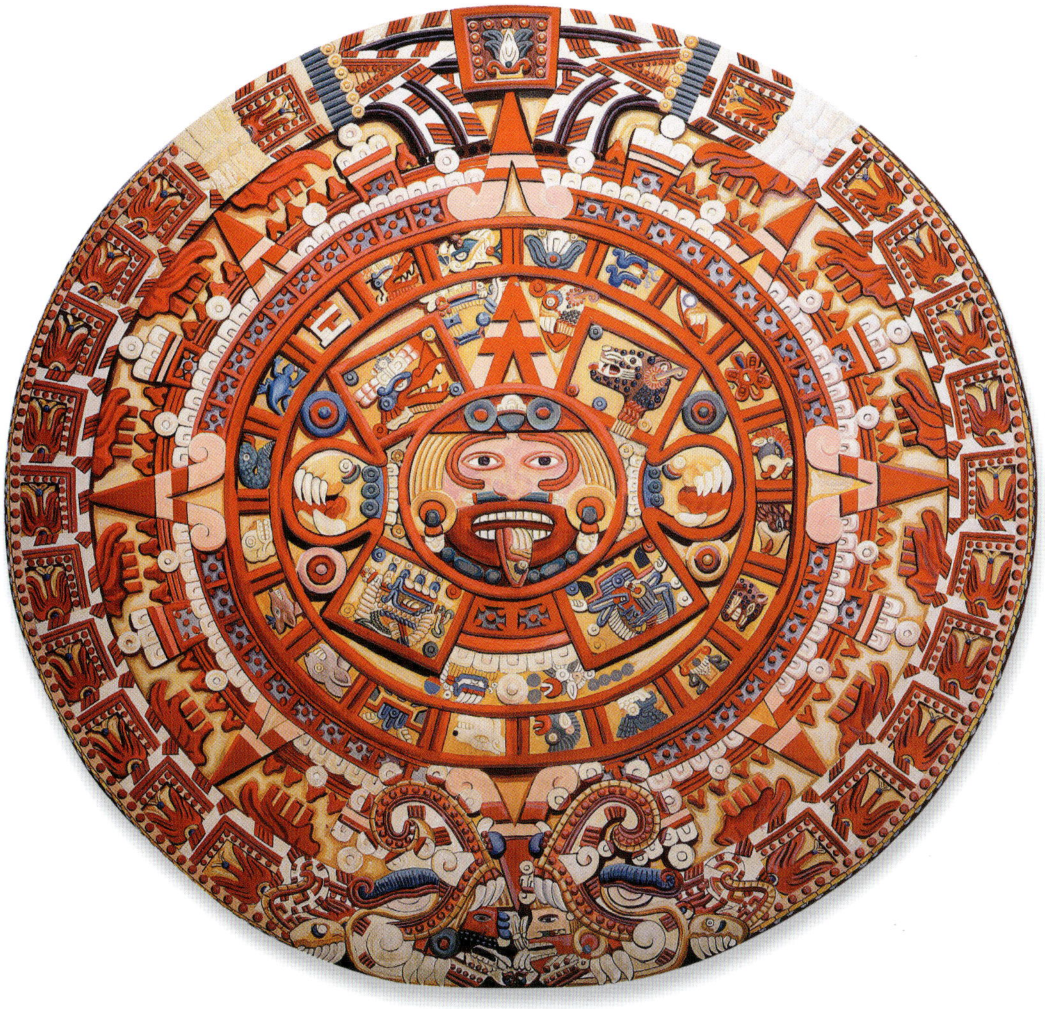

Above: *Divinely ordained cycles of time were plotted in calendrical charts. This is a modern reconstruction of an Aztec calendar.*

units of 20. The lowest layer showed the number of units (1–19), the second showed the number of 20s, the third showed the number of 400s (that is 20 units of 20) and the fourth the number of 8,000s (20 units of 400).

On stelae, sculptors carved dates in vertical columns to be read from bottom to top, beginning with the largest unit.

The Long Count date on Stela 29 at Tikal used no zeros and was cut with the figures 8.12.14.8.15, meaning 8 *baktuns*, 12 *katuns*, 14 *tuns*, 8 *uinals* and 15 *kins* after the initial date of 13 August 3114BC, giving a date for the stela of 8 July AD292. Almost exactly 400 years later, in the same city, a mason cut the date 9.13.0.0.0. on the stone throne or altar associated with a twin-pyramid group set up by King Ah Cacau. This meant 9 *baktuns*, 13 *katuns*, 0 *tuns*, 0 *unials* and 0 *kins* after 13 August 3114BC: 18 March AD692.

Twin-pyramid groups were raised by Maya rulers in this period to celebrate the ending of *katun*-periods, which explains why the date in the inscription fell so precisely at the end of the 13th *katun*.

Below: Stela 9 at Tikal celebrates King Kan Boar. Both narrow edges of the monument are carved with an inscription that ends with his name glyph and that of Tikal.

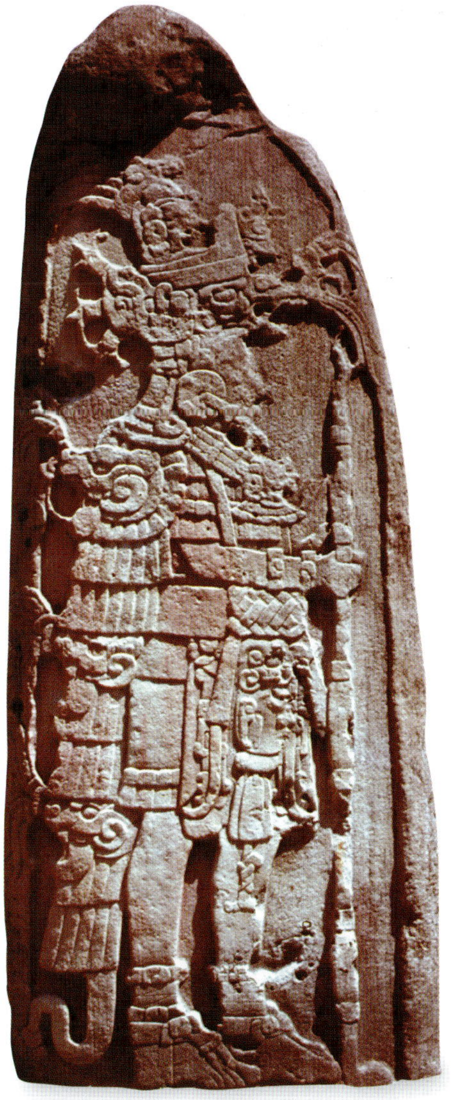

DID THE OLMEC USE WRITING?

A tall column of basalt known as the Ambassador's Monument was found at the Olmec holy town of La Venta. Some historians claim this bears the very first evidence of writing in Mesoamerica.

Some time between *c.*1150BC and 500BC, stonemason-scribes carved one end of the column with the image of a walking bearded man (likened by scholars to an ambassador) alongside three signs (which appear to be glyphs) and one of which, a bird's head, might represent his calendar name. Olmec potters and carvers of ceremonial implements in precious jade and serpentine also incised symbols which might be glyphs, but scholars have been unable to break the code of the symbols.

Linguists suggest that Mesoamerican writing probably originated in a lowland environment like that occupied by the Olmec or the people of the central Maya region rather than the highland surroundings of the Zapotecs in Oaxaca. The glyphs represent predominantly lowland creatures such as the crocodile, the jaguar and the monkey.

REFERENCE BOOKS FOR PRIESTS

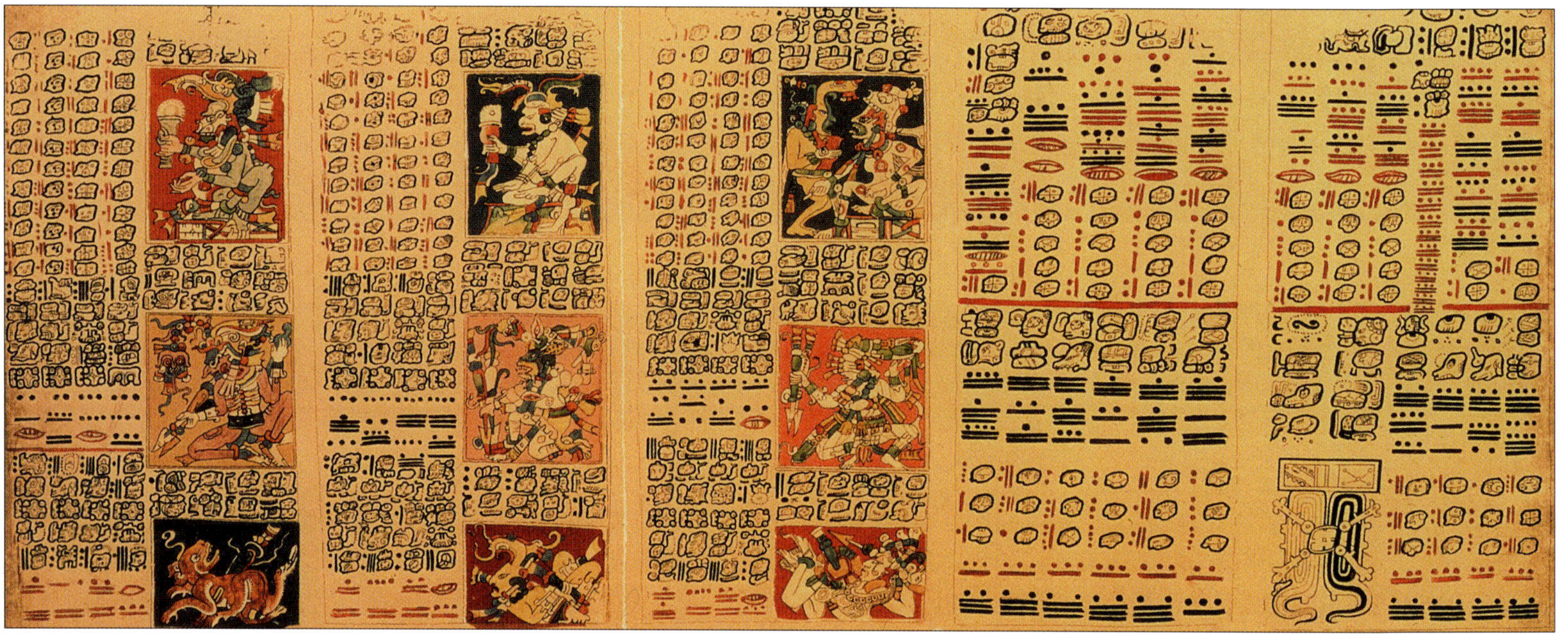

Above: Gods, days and rituals. The intricately covered almanac pages of the Dresden Codex *are dense with meaning.*

The chief scribes of Maya cities in the Classic Period were in charge of large libraries, containing a wide range of books written on bark paper or deer skin recording genealogies, arcane ritual and astronomical knowledge, medical information, and compendia of herbs, plants and animals. A mere handful of these books have survived natural decay over several hundred years and the book-burning zeal of the Spanish, who believed the sacred and even secular literature of the Maya and Aztecs to have been tainted by its association with sacrificial religion. Of the four surviving Maya codices, three date from the years before the Spanish Conquest, with one probably made in the 17th century. The finest of the three pre-Conquest books is the *Dresden Codex* , so named from its location, since 1744, in the Royal Library in Dresden, Germany.

THE DRESDEN CODEX

Consisting of 39 pages of *amate* paper, with writing and images on both sides, the *Dresden Codex* contains almanacs of the 260-day calendar, with details of presiding deities and appropriate rituals, mathematical tables, descriptions of new year ritual celebrations and detailed charts of solar eclipses and cycles of the planets Venus and Mars. Its scribes used very fine calligraphy, particularly in the Venus chart, which has tiny, delicate glyphs as small as 4mm (0.15in) high and 5mm (0.19in) across. According to the scholar Michael Coe, this is the most delicate fine-line work of any world manuscript, and it was written with a quill or with a reed pen rather than with the brush used for other Maya manuscripts.

The book was written by more than one hand. Variant scholarly accounts identify five or even eight distinct calligraphic styles across the 39 pages. In particular, the section on new year ceremonies on pages 25–28 of the manuscript is in a quite distinct and 'broader-brush' style, with glyphs more than three times wider than those in the Venus Table. Some scholars date the *Dresden Codex* to as early as AD1250. Others place its composition in about 1345.

Some scholars believe the book to be a copy of a codex produced during the Classic Period. It was in Vienna in the 16th century, having perhaps been found

THE 'WRIGHT CODEX'

The earliest known codex is not a book at all, but a ceramic vase around 25cm (10in) in height, which was discovered in a private American collection in 1991. On each of the four sides of the rectangular vase an artisan incised hieroglyphs and religious figures that appear to be reproductions of pages from a codex. Probably made in Guatemala *c.* AD600–900, the vase – known to scholars as the *Wright Codex* – is as much as 700 years older than the most venerable existing Maya codex previously known. Its illustrations represent a man taking part in religious ceremonies, perhaps associated with his way or spirit companion. Scholars have hailed the vase as physical proof of their contention that the Maya used books throughout the Classic Period.

by Hernán Cortés in 1519 on the island of Cozumel. The shrine of moon goddess Ix Chel on Cozumel was an important pilgrimage site, and the book might have been brought there as an offering from an important city.

WORK OF A PROVINCIAL SCRIBE

The oldest surviving Maya codex is the *Grolier Codex* of *c.*AD1230. It is so named because, following its discovery in Mexico in 1965, it was first exhibited at the Grolier Club in New York City in 1971. The codex is a 10-page section of an original, probably twice as long, dealing with the 584-day cycles of the planet Venus. Its screenfold pages are painted on one side only. It contains little information beyond details of the day signs and deities associated with each phase of the planet's cycle and it was written without great care, perhaps in haste or by an unskilled scribe in a provincial setting.

One account of its provenance suggests that it was found in a wooden box with a sacrificial knife and a mosaic mask in a dry cave near Tortuguero, in the modern state of Chiapas. The book might have been used for reference by a provincial priest in the region of Chiapas or Tabasco, some distance from such contemporary centres of ritual religion and learning as Chichén Itzá.

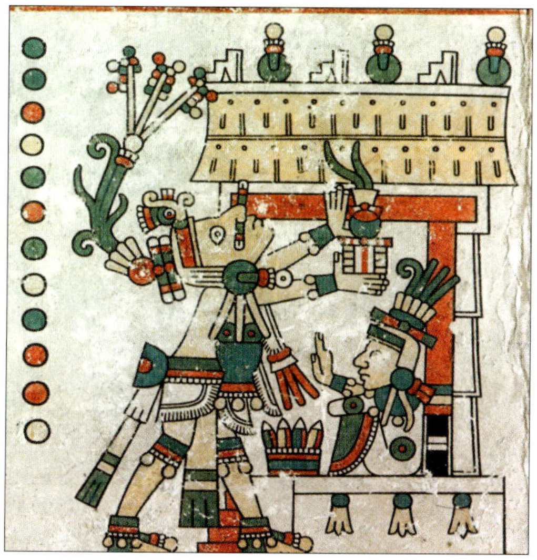

Left: In the Codex Ferjérváry-Mayer, *a maize plant in the form of Chalchiúhtlicue is blessed by Tláloc, lord of the rains.*

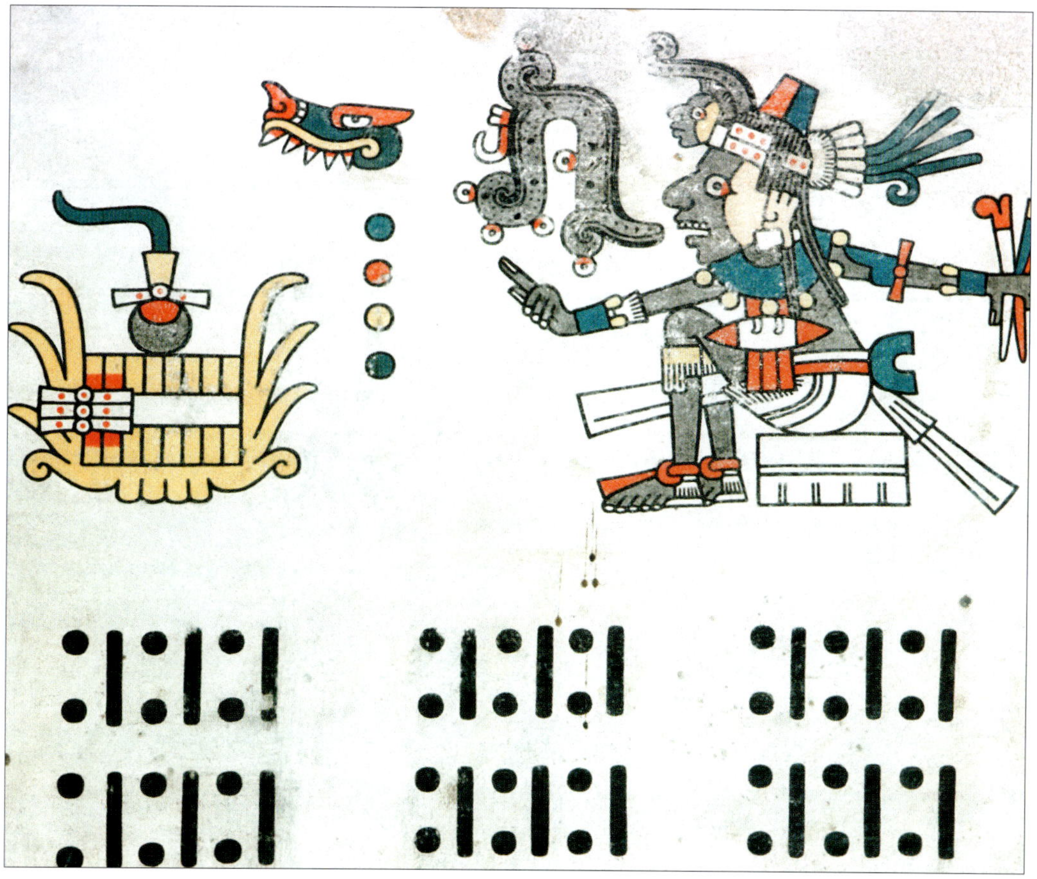

Above: The Codex Ferjérváry-Mayer *is one of only nine* tonalamatl *reference books to have survived the Spanish Conquest.*

CEREMONIES OF YUCATÁN

The *Paris Codex*, which takes its name from the French capital where it has been stored since 1832 in the Bibliothèque Nationale, probably dates to *c.*1450. According to historian Bruce Love, it might have been produced in the Itzá city of Mayapán. Analysis shows that its 11 double-sided pages were all written by one scribe. It contains information on cycles of *katuns* (periods of 7,200 days) and of *tuns* (360-day years) and on the importance of the larger 13-*katun* period, (containing 93,600 days or roughly 260 years), after which a new cycle of history was expected to begin, probably bringing a repetition of events in the previous 13-*katun* period. It also provides details of the gods presiding over the *katuns*, of the Year Bearers in the ritual calendar and of new year celebrations, as well as almanacs of astronomical cycles.

The fourth Maya codex is the *Madrid Codex*, which was probably produced in the 17th century in Yucatán.

CALENDAR OF FESTIVALS

In Aztec lands, some fifteen pre-Conquest codices survived destruction in the early 16th century.

One example is the *Codex Cospi*. Written by Mixtec scribes in the period 1350–1500, it takes its name from its later European owner, the Marchese Ferdinando Cospi. Its 13 screenfold pages, made of coated deerskin, are painted on both sides and contain details of the ritual calendar and the Venus cycle as well as of sacrificial rites appropriate to the worship of different deities.

The *Codex Fejérváry-Mayer*, made before 1521 and also named after later European owners, is a *tonalamatl* reference book on the 260-day and 365-day calendars. It contains 22 double-sided pages of animal skin covered in white lime and painted with interpretations of the calendars. It also contains accounts of variously presiding deities, including the nine lords of the night and details of tribute in goods and labour which were required at different times of the year.

RECORD OF A VANISHING CULTURE

The majority of surviving codices were produced after the Spanish Conquest in the 16th century either by Spanish churchmen or by young Mexicans educated in colonial schools.

Many of these were based on eyewitness accounts or were reworkings of pre-Conquest manuscripts. Among the most celebrated and useful to scholars is the *Codex Mendoza*. This was composed in the period *c.*1525–41, following a commission by the first Spanish Viceroy, Don Antonio de Mendoza. It is made of European paper and contains 72 pages written by a Mexican scribe in Nahuatl. Translations and interpretations have been added in Spanish by a bilingual author.

The first section starts with the building of Tenochtitlán and then describes the lives of nine Aztec rulers up to and including Moctezuma II, ending with an account of the Conquest. The second part contains an exhaustive tribute list of goods claimed by Moctezuma II from the empire of the Triple Alliance. A third section details customs of daily life among the Aztecs, including birth, marriage, education, state obligations, law and justice.

Below: Hieroglyphs are inscribed on the scales of the feathered serpent Quetzalcóatl in this detail from the Madrid Codex.

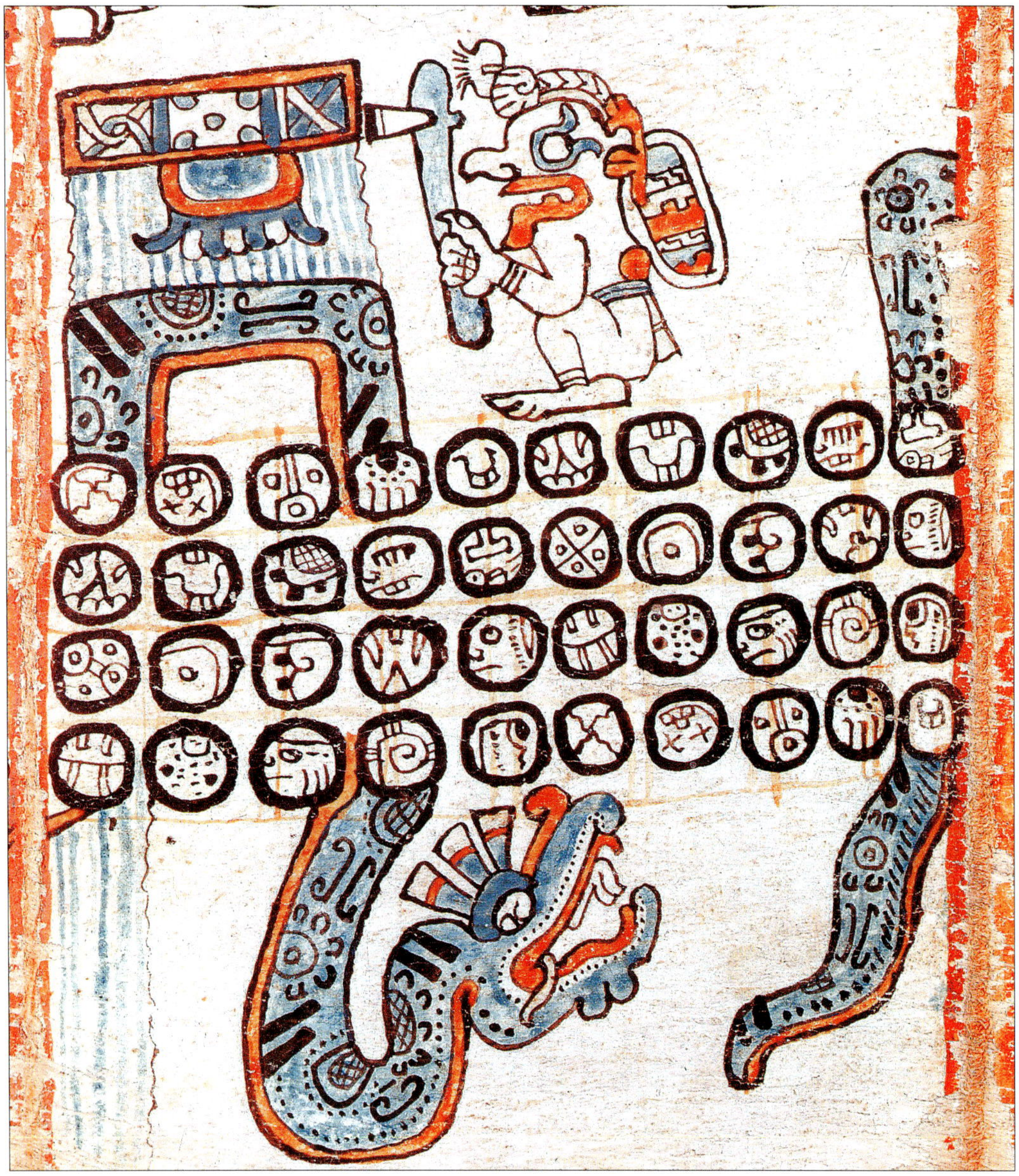

COPIED MANUSCRIPTS

A number of post-Conquest books appear to be copies of Aztec manuscripts. The *Codex Magliabechiano*, produced *c.*1521–1600 on European paper, includes illustrations of ritual outfits, a *tonalpohualli* sacred calendar and details of the sacred monthly festivals, together with images of funeral and sacrificial rites, autosacrificial bloodletting and ritual cannibalism. The *Codex Telleriano-Remensis*, written and illustrated by Mexican scribes and artists in Tlatelolco in 1555–61, combines an account of sacred festivals, a *tonalamatl* book of days used for divination and a chronicle of Aztec history.

The *Codex Ríos*, written and illustrated by Mexican Dominican friar Pedro de los Ríos *c.*1570–95, contains additions in Italian by another author which explain the ceremonies and religious traditions of the Aztecs. Its first section retells religious narratives and gives accounts of Aztec cosmology, while the second includes a *tonalpohualli* 260-day ritual calendar with a *xiuhpohualli* 365-day solar calendar. The third part details sacrificial and mortuary rites and provides information about calendrical day-signs, while the fourth contains post-Conquest historical accounts.

The style of drawing in the Ríos and the Telleriano-Remensis codices is very similar. Scholars believe they were both copied from a single pre-Conquest source.

ACCOUNTS BY CHURCHMEN

Two other important post-Conquest books classified as codices are the accounts of Aztec history and customs written by Spanish churchmen, the *Codex Durán* and the *Florentine Codex*. The *Codex Durán* is the name applied to the *History of the Indies of New Spain*. This

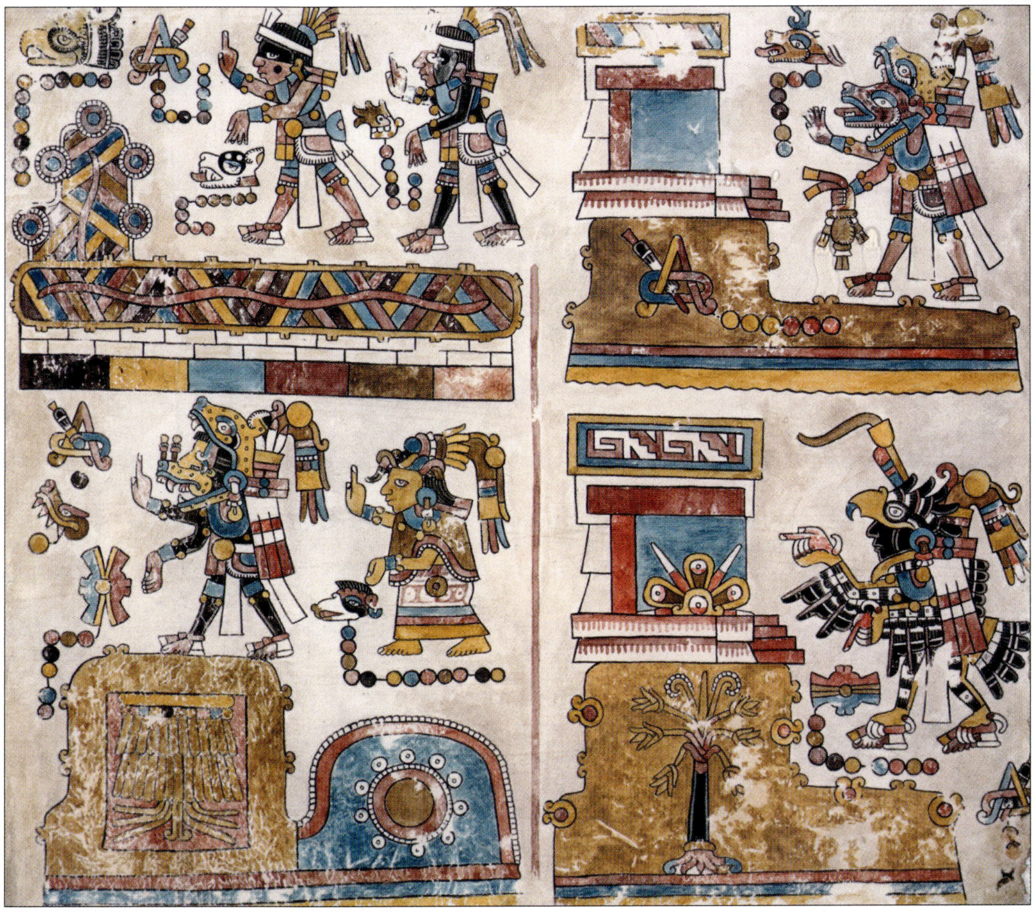

Above: A page from the Vienna Codex, *also known as the* Codex Vindobonensis. *Walking figures are gods or kings in action.*

was written in Spanish in 1570–81 by Dominican missionary Diego Durán. Spanish Franciscan friar Bernardino de Sahagún's *General History of the Things of New Spain*, also known as the *Florentine Codex* because of its association with libraries in the Italian city of Firenze (Florence), was written by scribes in Tlateloclo in 1575–77 in Spanish and Nahuatl. Both the Florentine and Durán codices contain detailed accounts of Aztec religious traditions, sacrificial rites, history and daily customs composed by their European authors on the basis of information gathered over many years among local survivors of the Spanish Conquest.

MAYA BOOK OF RITUAL

In Maya lands, one of the four surviving Maya codices is post-Conquest in date. This is the *Madrid Codex*, so called because it is kept in the Museo de América in the Spanish capital. It was long considered to be two separate manuscripts known as the *Troano* and the *Cortesianus*, but in 1880 Frenchman Léon de Rosny established that the two were sections of a single manuscript. The *Madrid Codex* contains 56 leaves, all except the first painted on both sides, making a total of 111 codex pages.

The *Madrid Codex* combines details of Maya beliefs about the four cardinal directions and their presiding deities with information about new year celebrations and detailed almanacs of the 260-day calendar. Like the *Grolier Codex*, it was apparently written in haste or by a lesser scribe, as it contains grammatical errors and careless penmanship. Scholar Michael Coe argues that as the *Madrid Codex* contains a piece of recycled Spanish paper among its bark-paper leaves, it must have been produced after the Spanish Conquest of Yucatán in 1542 that it was perhaps written in Tayasal, which retained its independence until 1697. Martin de Ursua, Spanish Governor of Yucatán, took Tayasal as part of a road-building project to link Guatemala and Yucatán.

Accounts of the history and religious traditions of particular Maya groups based on ancient sources were written down in the post-Conquest period. The *Popol Vuh* ('Book of Advice') contains a wealth of Maya religious narrative and astronomical knowledge including detailed accounts of the myth of the ball-playing Hero Twins. It was transcribed from sources written in hieroglyphs into the Roman alphabet by senior members of the Quiché Maya *c.*1554. It was then translated from the Quiché tongue into Spanish by Franciscan friar Francisco Ximenez in the 18th century.

The *Books of Chilam Balam* recorded the history and traditions of groups of Maya from north-western Yucatán and were named after a Maya shaman-seer of the late 14th century. They were written in the Roman alphabet and Yucatec tongue from hieroglyphic sources from the 16th century onwards.

Below: Stone workers hewing and crafting stone from Bernardino de Sahagún's General History of the Things of New Spain, *also known as the* Florentine Codex.

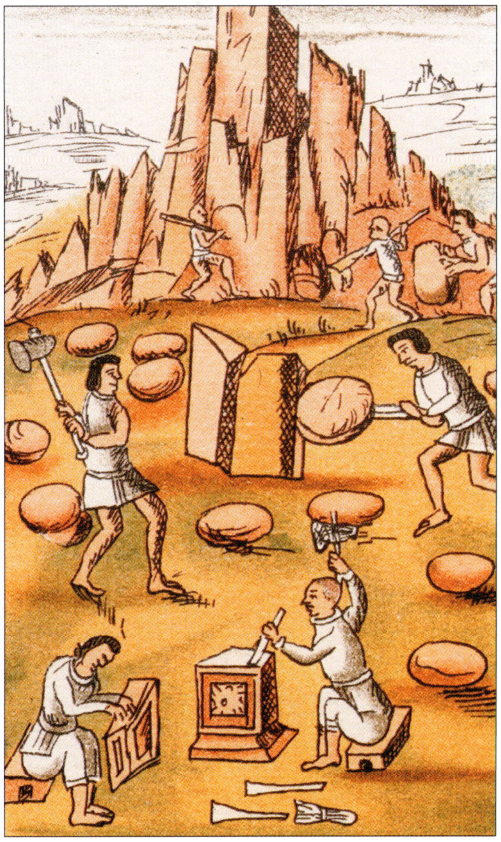

GLYPHS AND IMAGES

Sculptors of Maya stelae embedded their meaning in the image. Viewers were expected to understand the hieroglyphs in conjunction with the image portrayed. The image could be of a king with his defeated rival or of a ruler performing sacred rites of bloodletting. The hieroglyphs placed the event in the cycles of time and named the protagonists.

TYPICAL INSCRIPTIONS

A typical stela inscription began with detailed calendrical information, giving the precise day on which the event celebrated in the image took place. First it named the patron god or goddess of the month, then it gave the Long Count date and transcribed this same date into the 260-day ritual calendar, naming the god among the nine lords of the night who controlled that day and the phase of the moon that applied.

After this, an inscription might specify an event or anniversary of ritual significance that applied to the depicted activity, such as a *katun*-ending, then name the king and any other protagonist who had been involved.

Sometimes the glyphs giving the identity of the king would also name his ancestors or his offspring. At other times they would provide evidence of recent heroic activity. For example, various glyphs identified the king as lord of five, ten or even twenty captives. Following glyphs might give dates for subsequent events such as the king's partaking in ritual bloodletting or sacrificial worship. The second date in an inscription would be given only in the 260-day calendar, since the historical context within the Long Count had already been established.

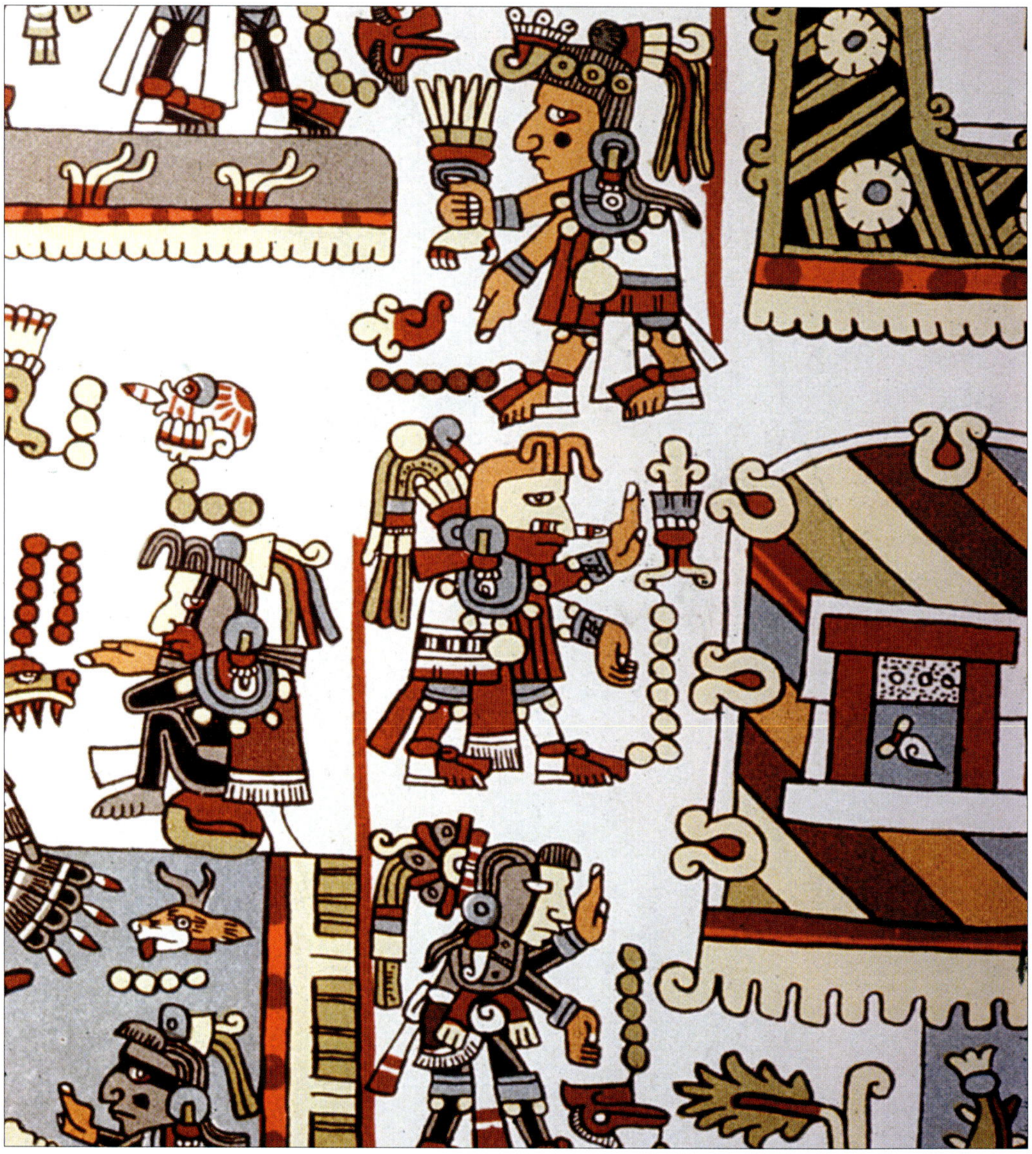

Above: Meaning in action. Divine rulers and gods adopt abstract postures in Mixtec-style codices. This page is from the Codex Zouche-Nuttall, *which may have been a gift from Moctezuma II to Hernan Cortés.*

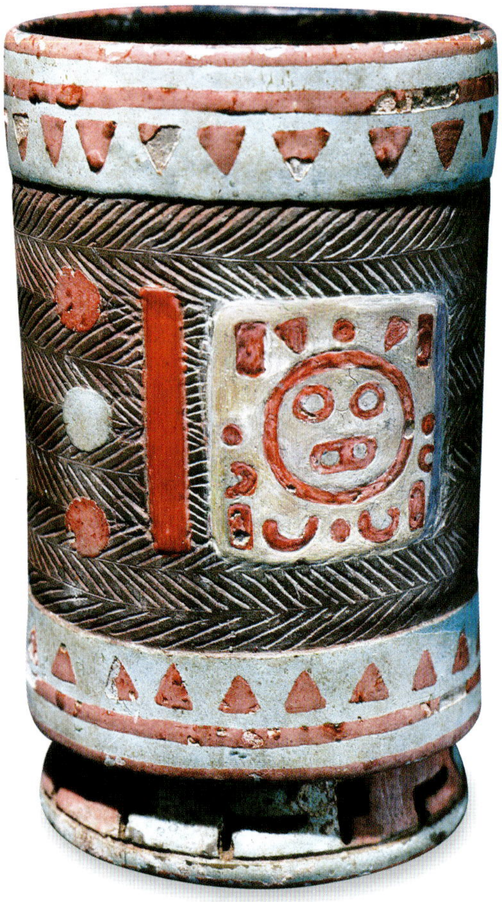

Above: This cylindrical vase from Uaxactún is marked with a symbol and date that may record the owner's birth-date and name.

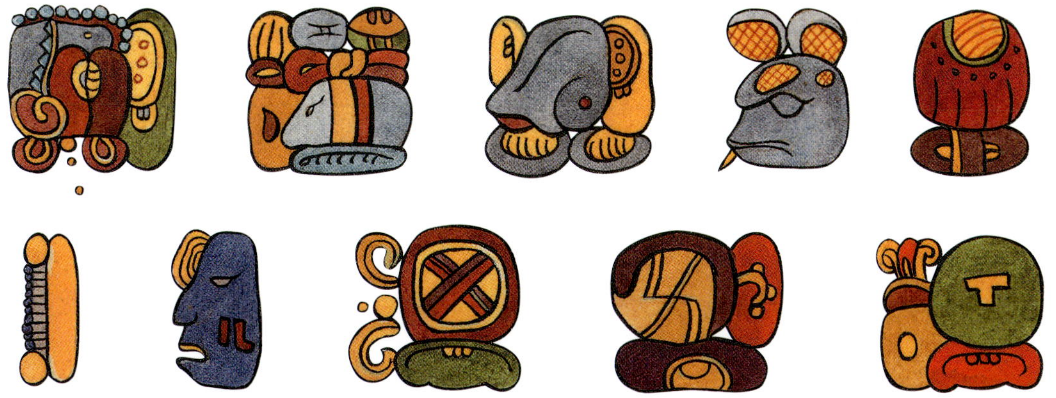

Above: The Maya used these glyphs to convey historical and dynastic information. From top left – 'was born'; 'acceded to throne'; 'event of taking captive'; 'taker of captives'; 'taken captive'; 'he'; 'she'; 'wife'; 'ruler's number in dynastic line'; 'king or queen died'.

NAMING

Some scholars liken the glyphs naming kings and dating their stelae to the name tags that the Maya inscribed on sacred and everyday items such as incised bones, ear ornaments and drinking vessels.

The practice of name-tagging was discovered by scholar Peter Mathews in 1979 when studying an ear flare from Altun Há, Belize. The ornament was inscribed with the phrase *u tup* ('this man's ear flare'), together with the name of the owner, who was a member of the royal family. Name tags were subsequently identified on incised bones from the tomb of King Ah Cacau in Tikal, and on plates, dishes and vases.

Scholar Michael Coe found a repeating pattern of hierogylphs on elaborately decorated polychrome vases of the late Classic Period. This pattern, named the Primary Standard Sequence, amounted to a formula for naming and dating vases.

Generally painted around the outer rim of the vase or bowl or sometimes placed in a vertical column, it included up to 22 glyphs, always in the same order, but often with some missing and sometimes with as few as three glyphs. The sequence begins with several initial glyphs, sometimes including the head of the god Pawahtún, a four-fold god of the directions. This is thought to have functioned as a dedication of the vessel. Then came glyphs indicating whether the pot was carved or painted and identifying its shape, its use (perhaps for drinking or serving cacao), its owner and the artist who produced it. Sometimes the sequence also includes a date in the Calendar Round, which unusually referred to the date the object was made rather than the date on which the depicted events took place.

WORDS IN CODICES

In codices and in murals – just as in the inscriptions on stelae, stone thrones, zoomorphs and ceramics – words functioned to identify names and provide calendrical information, while images represented the activity that was being celebrated. In such pre-Conquest Mixtec books as the *Codex Zouche-Nuttall* or the *Codex Cospi*, illustrations were not designed primarily for aesthetic effect but to convey meaning.

Glyphs generally identified three key facts: dates, places and names. The human figures took a limited number of stylized postures, usually walking, standing or seated in profile and deity figures were usually shown in a flat, full frontal position. There was no attempt to achieve the naturalistic effects found in Classic Period Maya murals, stucco-work and polychrome vases and in Postclassic statuary.

Below: The highly prized role of the scribe could be taken by royal or noble women as well as by top-ranking men. This Maya ceramic shows a female scribe at work.

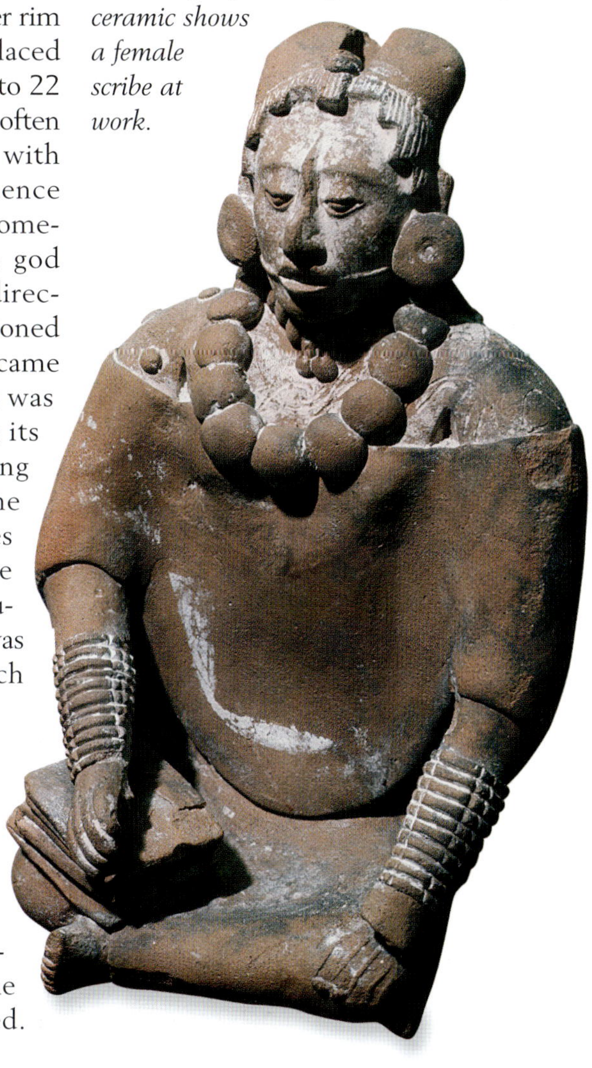

THE AGE OF BOOKS

In the Postclassic Period, the artistic style of Mesoamerica derived largely from that of codices. Ceramic decorations, mural images, representations on monumental state sculpture and decorative symbols in jewellery are all similar to illustrations in the codices. Because the largest number of surviving codices were written and painted by Mixtec scribes working near the city of Puebla, scholars call this the 'Mixteca-Puebla style'.

The style was not regional but far-reaching and even international. In Tenochtitlán, images carved on state monuments resembled pages from a codex. In Oaxaca, delicate jewellery figures and fine murals at Mitla had the 'codex style'. On the Caribbean seaboard at sites such as Tulum in eastern Yucatán and Santa Rita Corozal in northern Belize, 15th-century murals closely mirrored the appearance of Mixtec codices.

SCENES OF RELIGIOUS LIFE

Murals were painted at Cholula in the Puebla region of Mexico *c.*AD100–400, when the settlement was pre-eminent in its area and had close ties to both Teotihuacán and Monte Albán in Oaxaca. The earliest images are similar to some Teotihuacán wall paintings. They represent stylized insects with very large heads painted in red and yellow against black and other backgrounds.

THE DRINKERS

A more significant Cholula mural is one known to scholars as 'The Drinkers' and apparently representing scenes of ritual intoxication. Some 60m (200ft) across, the painting depicts a succession of humans – all wearing loincloths and some with headdresses or masks of fabulous creatures – together with several large drinking jars.

The figures are painted a light-orange flesh colour against a red background and rest on a blue-green band, beneath which are decorative elements including rhombuses. Some of the figures lift the vases up as if to pour out libations for nobles at a banquet, others hold drinking bowls. The drinking was probably of *pulque* (maguey cactus liquor) as part of a religious ritual. The figures are in loose, relaxed positions, probably because of the effects of the *pulque*, while their masks might be intended to represent the animal spirit companions that a shaman or spiritual adventurer would expect to meet during spirit voyages facilitated by *pulque* or other psychotropic substances. The mural was painted on the west-facing façade of a mortuary pyramid in which archaeologists found the rich burial of a man with Maya facial features.

Below: Staple food. In the Red Temple at Cacaxtla the muralist painted a maize plant that gives issue to human heads.

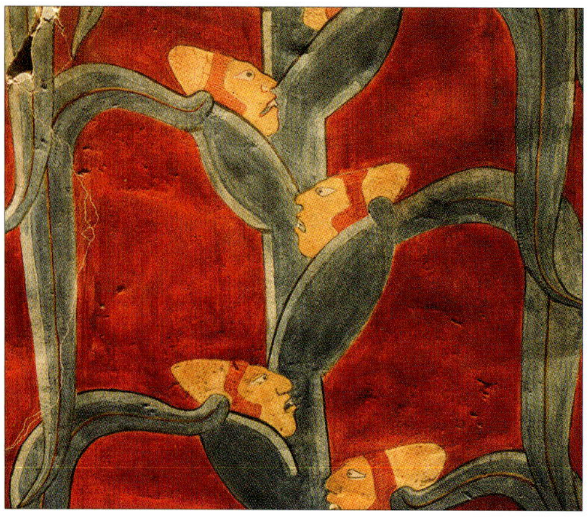

Another Cholula mural, in a structure known to scholars as Building 2, represented shells and five-pointed stars, imagery found both at Teotihuacán and Cacaxtla and thought to be associated with fertility and the planet Venus.

A SYMBOLIC BATTLE?

A magnificent series of murals were painted in the hilltop settlement of Cacaxtla, above the Tlaxcala valley, *c.*AD655–835. These remarkable pictures, some of the finest in Mesoamerica, were discovered by looters in October 1975.

Overlooking the ceremonial area, the elongated structure known as Building B contains brightly coloured murals of battles or perhaps ritualized conflicts between two groups of warriors, who are clearly identified by their battledress. Some scholars focus on the geographical and cultural affiliations of the two groups. They identify the first group as Mexicanized Maya, who exhibit the influence of Teotihuacán in their battledress and equipment and who probably come from the Mexican Gulf Coast. They identify the second group as warriors from Maya lands farther east.

Other historians suggest that the conflict might be symbolic. The Mexicanized warriors sport equipment with jaguar symbolism while the central Maya wear nothing except bird helmets and body ornaments. The clash might be between night (represented by the jaguar, fearsome night predator and the form taken by the sun when it journeyed through the underworld during the hours of darkness) and day (represented by the birds of the air). The images exhibit great naturalistic skill and painstaking attention to detail in their depiction of headdress and costume.

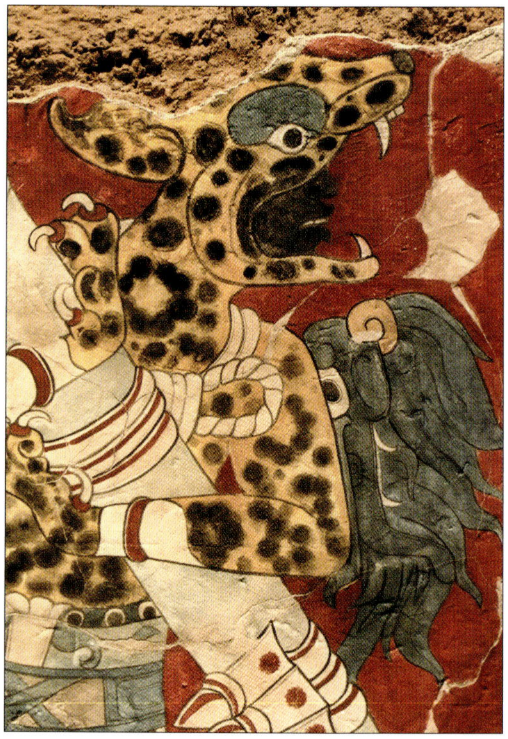

Above: At Cacaxtla drops of rain fall from a serpent sceptre wielded by a jaguar man. He is thought to represent the moon.

GODS OF THE SKY

Murals with complex religious symbolism adorn Building A at Cacaxtla, which is reached via a short stairway from Building B. These images consist of four large standing figures. On the south doorjamb of the entrance looms a black-skinned man, apparently dancing, who holds a conch shell from which a head emerges bedecked in jewels. On the south wall, another black-skinned man in eagle costume stands on a blue-green feathered serpent, holding a bright blue-green serpent sceptre from which flames emerge. On the north doorjamb of the entrance is a man with jaguar paws and skin, his head emerging from the open jaws of the jaguar. He wears a serpent headdress and holds a serpent in his left hand while, using his right arm, he upends a large jar decorated with the symbols of the rain god from which life-giving blue-green waters fall. From his belly emerges a maize or water-lily plant, bearing flowers.

On the north wall of the building another jaguar man holds a brilliant blue-green rain sceptre from which waters fall on to the body of a creature that is both jaguar and serpent. The scholar Maria Teresa Uriarte has identified these complex figures as images of the night sun (or moon) on the north wall and the sun by day on the south wall, with images of the rain god Tláloc/Chac on the north doorjamb and of Pahuantún or god N, a deity with links to the four directions and the underworld, on the south doorjamb. The main north and south wall images might represent the Hero Twins of Maya religious narrative as moon and sun, for in some accounts the twins rose to become these celestial bodies.

A third richly coloured mural adorns the structure at Cacaxtla dubbed the Temple of Venus by scholars. Artists painted a pair of blue-skinned figures, one to each side of the doorway. One badly damaged mural represents a female figure, with one breast visible, and the wall disintegrated where the other breast and her head would be. The other depicts a standing male with black hair, large protruding eye and arms upraised. Both wear jaguar-skin skirts beneath large, five-pointed half-star symbols of the planet Venus that hang from their waists. Both have bare feet, with white cloths tied around their ankles. One of the man's hands is not visible due to wall damage, but the other is in the shape of a jaguar's paw and in it he holds a five-pointed half-star. Behind him a scorpion's tail is visible and his arms are segmented like the tail. The images represent dual aspects of the planet Venus. Maria Teresa Uriarte suggests they might celebrate an astronomical conjunction between the planet Venus and the scorpion constellation. The visible part of the Venus cycle had associations with the rainy season, so the planet and its deity therefore had links to water and fertility.

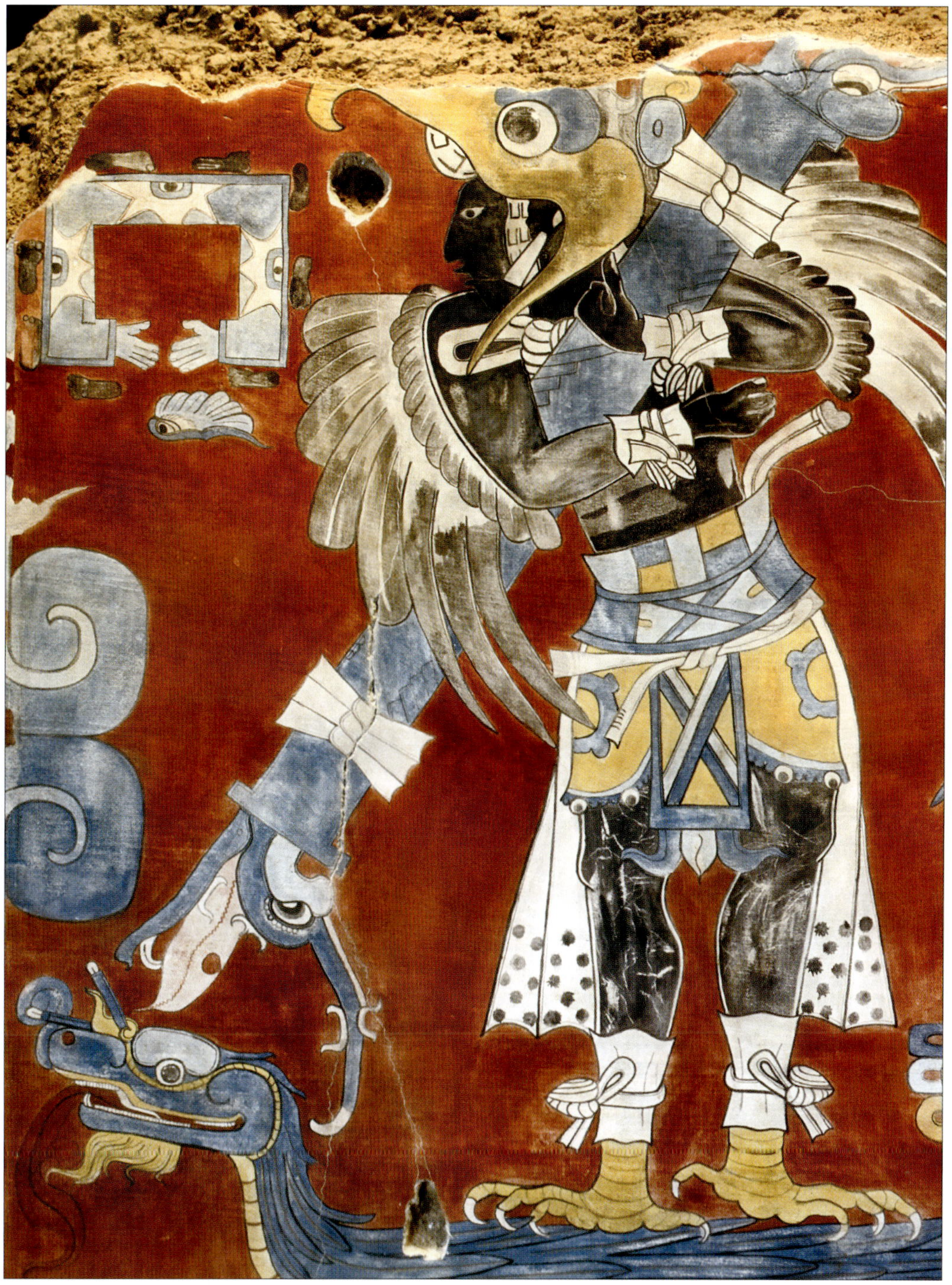

Above: The opposing Cacaxtla image depicts the sun – an eagle man holding a fire-serpent and standing on an earth-serpent.

GOD OF THE UNDERWORLD

Another remarkable set of murals adorned the building known as the Red Temple at Cacaxtla. The muralists decorated the east and west walls of the temple, either side of a staircase. On the east wall they painted a feathered serpent rising behind a human figure who stands against a terracotta background over a bundle that might represent the travelling pack of a merchant, while before him grow a cocoa plant and blue-green maize plants that give issue to human heads. Among the plants is a toad with a blue-green body. The mural's border consists of serpentine figures and watery images in turquoise and yellow. Scholars suggest that the figure might be god L or the Old Black God, lord of the Maya underworld.

THE BONAMPAK MURALS:
A PRINCE IN LINE

The famous murals in the Maya city of Bonampak, on the River Lacanjá in the Chiapas region, were painted in the building now known as Temple 1 in the late 8th century AD. They celebrated the designation of the royal heir to King Chan Muan, a prolonged ritual that took place over 20 months from 14 December AD790 to 6 August AD792. Bonampak was greatly influenced by the larger centre of Yaxchilán, 30km (18 miles) to the north. The two centres may have been connected by a *sacbé* (sacred causeway) that archaeologists have discovered departing Bonampak and heading north. Alongside King Chan Muan and his heir, Yaxchilán royals are depicted taking part in the ceremonies as allies or overlords.

The murals adorn three rooms in the temple. They are painted on both the walls and the inner roof, with a band of hieroglyphs running between them. The hieroglyph section contains Long Count dates giving precise dates for the events depicted. The artists probably intended the images to be viewed from the benches that are laid out on the floors of these rooms.

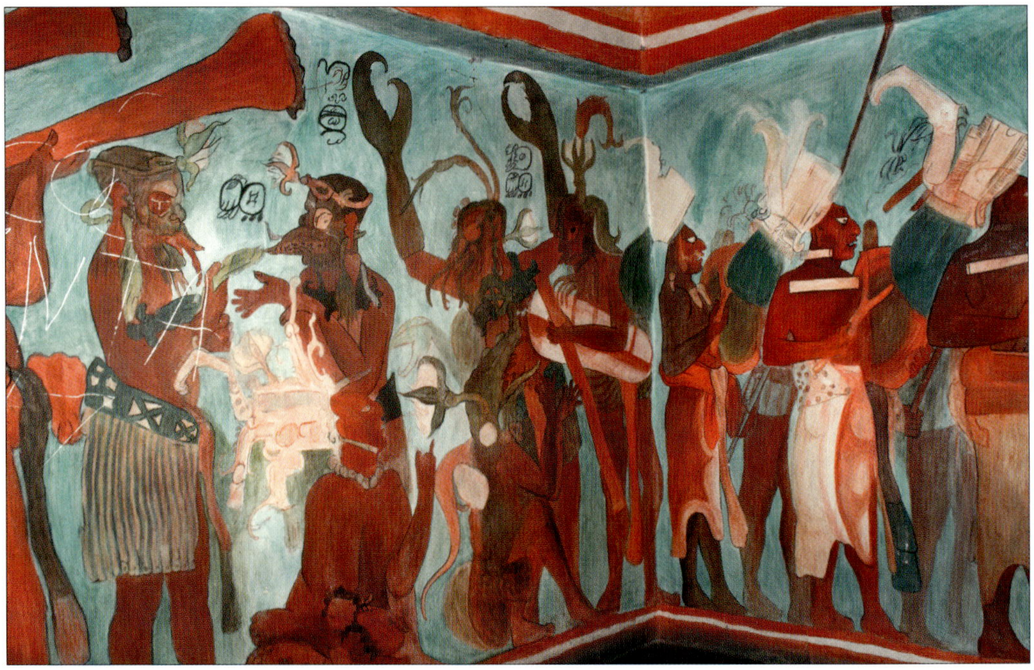

Above: On the lower north wall of the first room, musicians and elaborately dressed gods or priests celebrate the heir's accession.

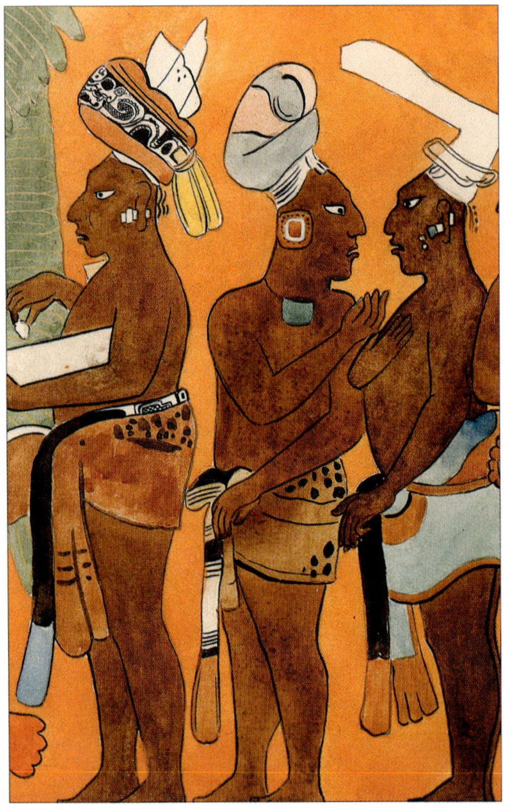

Below: A detail from the celebration scenes depicts senior figures from the court of King Chan Muan in intimate conversation.

PRESENTATION OF THE HEIR

In the first room, the painting on the vault of the west wall depicts the young royal heir being presented to 14 white-robed noblemen of the court while his royal father and mother look on approvingly from a wide throne-stone. The vault of the north wall shows the king wearing a vast feather headdress, a jade pectoral and ear plugs. He is accompanied by two splendidly attired lords, apparently preparing for a ritual held, according to the hieroglyphic inscription, 336 days later than the initial presentation of the prince. The lower walls appear to depict this celebration, showing a band of musicians playing a wooden drum, trumpets, flutes, turtle shells and rattles, as well as a procession of masked and elaborately costumed members of the court, or perhaps priestly figures. One figure appears to have crayfish pincers in place of arms. One wears the costume of the maize god, while a third is robed to represent a crocodile. Two members wear flowers in their headdresses.

VICTIMS FOR SACRIFICE

The second room depicts a battle fought to secure prisoners for ritual sacrifice, an important part of the heir-designation ceremony. The south, west and east walls are covered with battle scenes that vividly depict the chaos and carnage of conflict, with elaborately dressed soldiers fighting hand-to-hand, grabbing one another by the hair and thrusting spears forward threateningly. King Chan Muan is shown holding a jaguar-skin spear and a prisoner by the hair while standing alongside an allied ruler that scholars identify as King Shield Jaguar II of Yaxchilán. Both kings sport magnificent headdresses, wear jaguar-skin clothing and are protected from possible injury by a cadre of proud warriors. On the vaults above these walls,

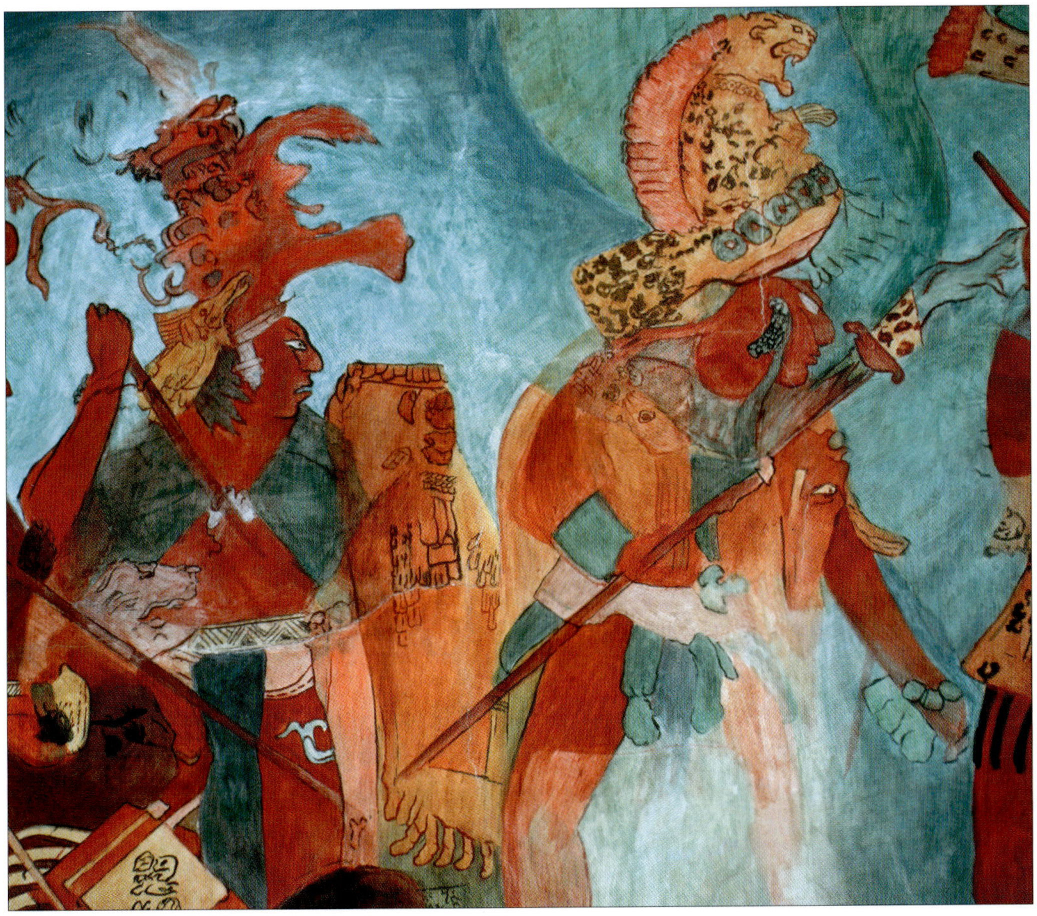

Above: A battle scene from the second room shows fierce soldiers with extravagant headdresses facing down the enemy.

images represent the astronomical alignments that were found to be propitious for this great battle. On the southern vault, a turtle with three stars on its shell stands for the constellation of Orion. Other images represent different stars and the planet Venus.

The north wall of the second room depicts King Chan Muan presiding over the painful torture of captives destined for sacrifice to sanctify the heir-designation. One prisoner has already been killed and decapitated; his head lies on one of the platform-steps. Several nobles and two royal ladies flank the king at the top of the steps, standing beneath glyphs of their names. One of the women is Queen Green Rabbit from Yaxchilán. At the foot of the steps, warriors stand guard over the prisoners.

SACRED BLOODLETTING

Unfortunately, the murals of the third room have sustained quite serious damage, but enough is visible to reveal that they represent further royal scenes in the heir-designation ritual. In one painting, king and nobles in elaborate costume stand on a pyramid while musicians and dancers perform sacred rites in the plaza below them. A second painting depicts the royal family on a throne or dais within the palace performing autosacrificial bloodletting as a way of seeking the gods' blessing on the prince of Bonampak. The king cuts his tongue with a spiked cord and collects the blood on bark paper. He will later burn the paper, both as an offering and as a way of summoning the Vision Serpent, along whose coils he might travel to encounter his way spirit companion, great royal ancestors or even the god and goddesses themselves.

The murals at Bonampak are valued for the insight they give, through their colourful and naturalistic representations of court ritual, into royal and religious life in Maya cities of the late Classic Period. Although they are an unusually complete survival, they are typical of the wall decoration used in many Maya palaces, religious and ceremonial structures. It was common practice to commemorate religious, dynastic and military events through wall painting.

Below: On the north side of the second room, King Chan Muan takes centre stage, wearing jaguar skin and holding a spear. At his feet prisoners of war endure torture at the hands of their captors.

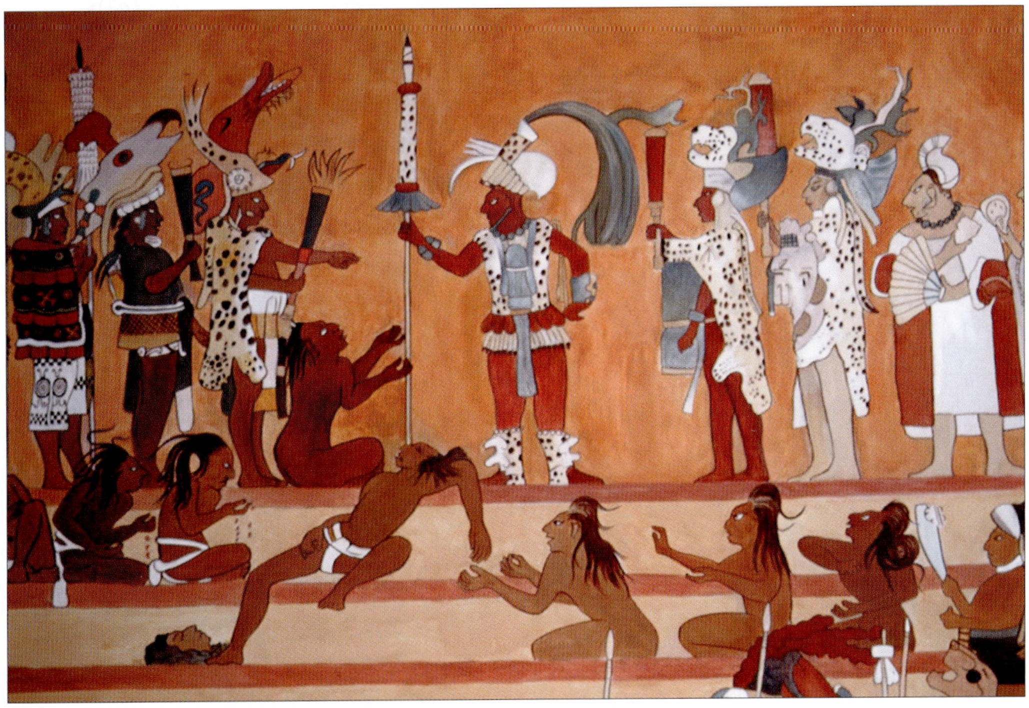

WALL PAINTINGS AND MURALS

Fragments of murals survive at many Maya sites. At Tikal, small parts of murals dating to the 4th century AD have been found in the buildings architects call Group 6C-XVI, just to the south of the Lost World complex. One represents a human figure alongside a black circle marked with a glyph that has underworld associations. A second mural, known as 'The Mural of the Gamers', depicts eight human figures in two groups of four, walking in profile. Those whose heads are undamaged wear ribbon headdresses. Some authorities suggest that the figures in both murals are ball players.

At Xelhá near the coast of Quintana Roo, a mural in the substructure of the buildings called Group B depicts flying parrots and macaws. These images date to *c.*AD400–600. At Uaxactún, artists painted a mural *c.*AD450–550 to adorn a room in the building called structure B-XIII. They depict scenes of noble life, showing groups of standing figures with fine headdresses and adornment. One group is seated within a building. Associated hierogylphs probably provide dates or names.

At Palenque, in House E of the royal palace, mural images of four-petalled flowers and geometric decorative designs have survived, along with a profile head of a noble or king wearing a splendid headdress containing a fish. These date from the 7th century AD.

At Yaxchilán only a single figure in profile and a few patches of colour remain of wall-paintings that once covered the interior of Temple 40, built during the reign of King Bird Jaguar (*r.* AD752–68).

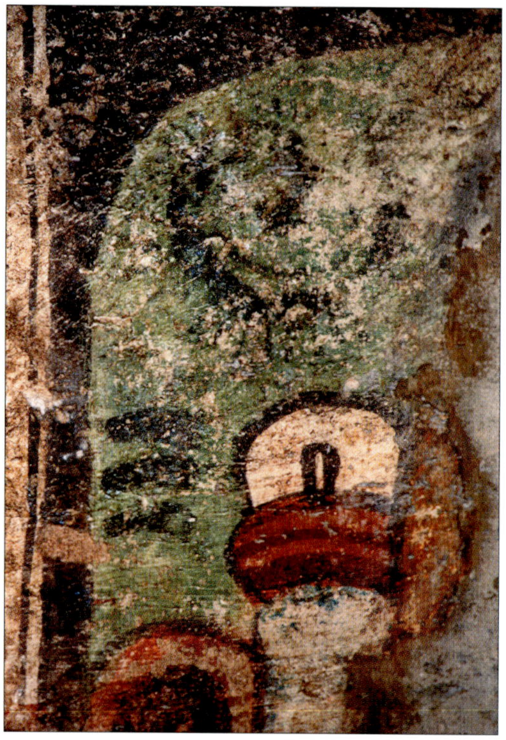

Above: Mayapán's rulers commissioned murals in order to add to their city's status as it rose to eclipse Chichén Itzá.

Below: This damaged mural from Tulum appears to be an image of the rain god, worshipped as Chac by the Maya.

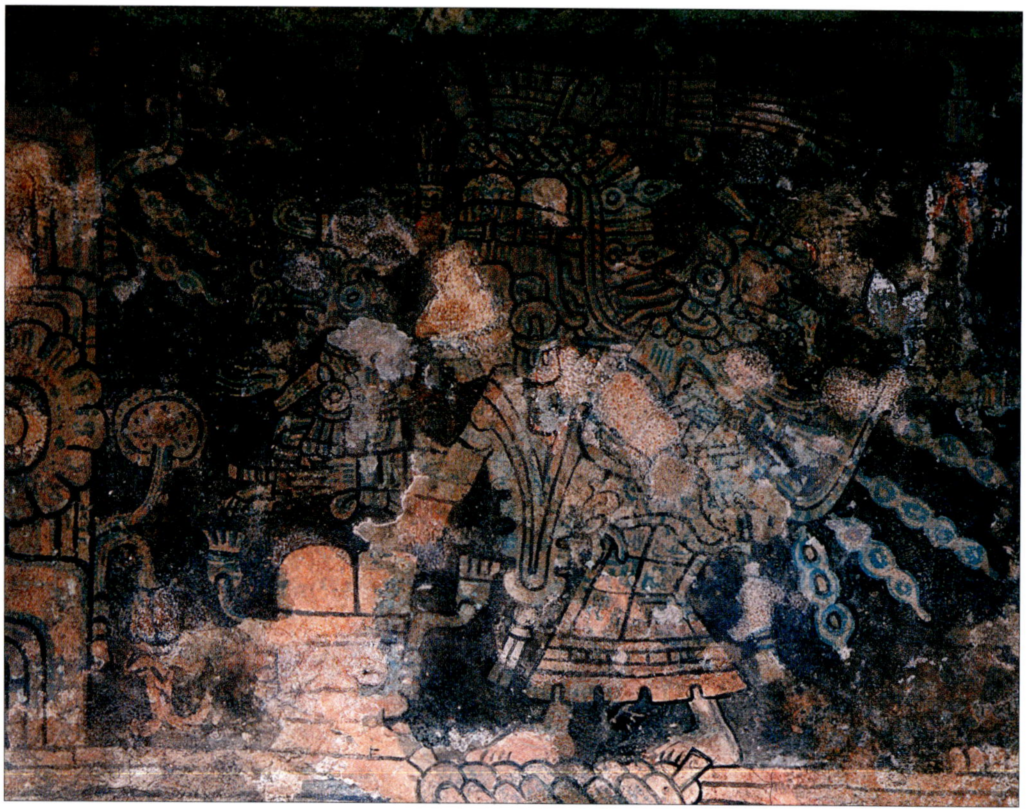

MAYA TOMB PAINTINGS

From an early period the Maya painted the walls of tombs. A tomb dated to *c.*50BC in the North Acropolis at Tikal (Burial 166) has a mural with a red background and black outlines depicting standing figures with feather headdresses and deity masks, probably representing divine ancestors of the king or nobleman buried in the tomb. These are identified as the most venerable painted images yet discovered in Maya lands.

Several other Tikal tombs had paintings and glyphic inscriptions: Burial 48 is dated to AD457. Near-contemporary images in Tomb 1 at Río Azul in Guatemala, represent deity masks, serpents and watery features, and they can be dated to AD417 by a Long Count date in the accompanying inscription. At the same site, Tomb 19 (*c.*450–550) bears paintings said to represent the Jester god linked to the ruler's glyph 'ahaw'.

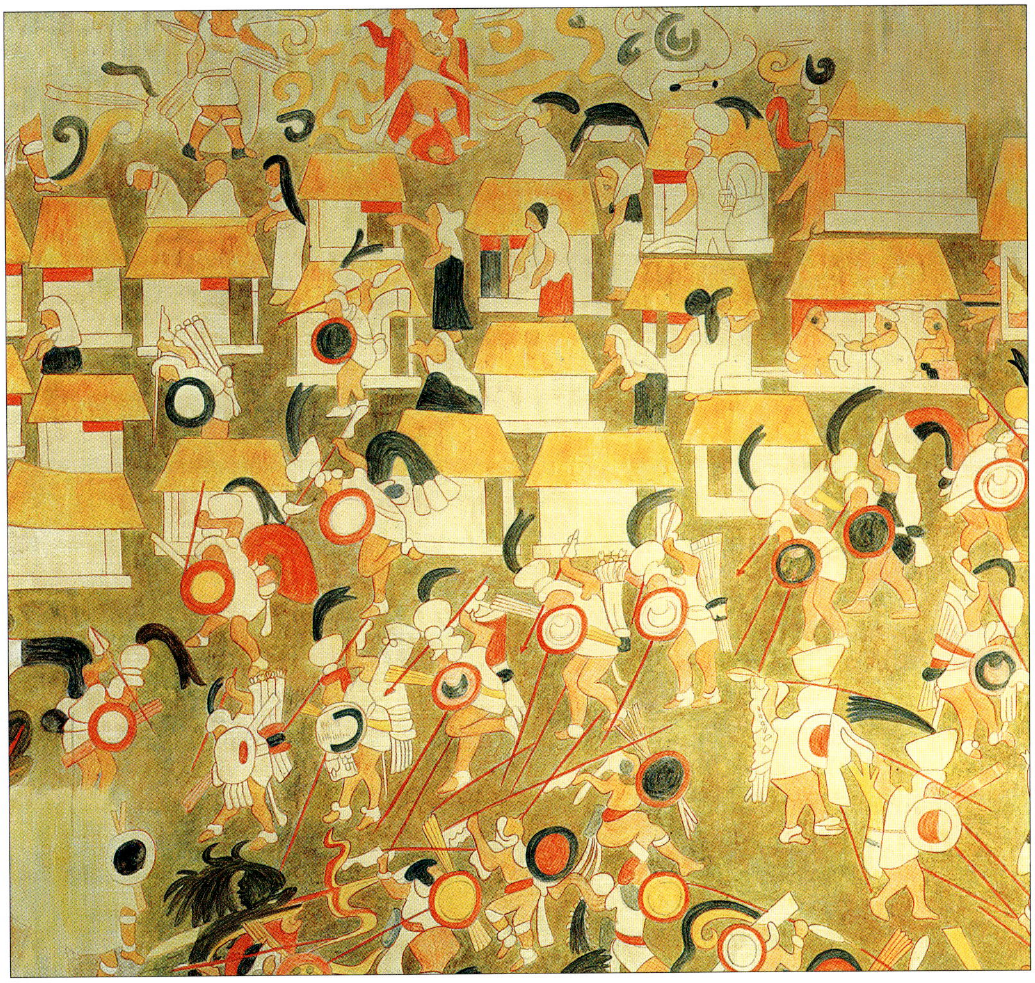

Above: War machine. In a mural from the Temple of the Jaguars, Chichén Itzá, the city's rampaging army engulfs a village.

HIGHLAND MEXICAN STYLE

At Chichén Itzá, fragments of mural were found on rubble pieces that once formed the inner walls of the Temple of the Warriors. They have been reconstructed to form two murals, one representing a military attack on a town and the capture of prisoners, the other depicting life in a coastal village. These are painted in a quite different style to the fluid, expressive naturalism of Maya mural painting that reached its apogée at Bonampak; instead, they are flat, two-dimensional and almost schematic. They apparently form part of the wave of Mexicanized culture and artefacts also represented by the appearance at Chichén Itzá of sacred furniture such as *chacmool* sacrificial figures and skull racks, of serpent-columns on buildings and of atlante carved warriors. The same schematic style, though with rather more movement, is apparent in murals of fighting soldiers painted within the Temple of the Jaguars.

Below: Murals at Tulum and other cities of Postclassic Yucatán apparently return to the style and subjects of Teotihuacán art.

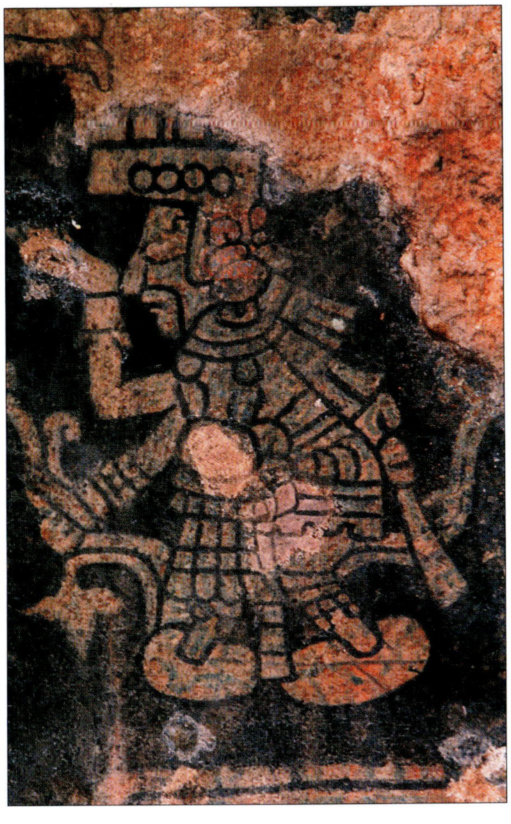

Wall paintings were also commissioned by the rulers of the city of Mayapán, which succeeded Chichén Itzá as the pre-eminent city of northern Yucatán after *c.*1250. Fine paintings discovered in 1997 in the buildings known as Structure Q160 and Structure Q80 exhibit a style reminiscent of the codex art of contemporary Maya and especially Mixtec painter-scribes. In Structure Q80, serpents are combined with geometric designs while anthropomorphic figures adorn Structure Q160.

INFLUENCE OF BOOKMAKERS

Murals at many sites on the Caribbean coast of Yucatán – including Tulum, Xelhá, Cobá, Rancho Ina and Tancah – exhibit this same codex-influenced style in the years after *c.*1250. They are different from earlier Maya murals in subject matter as well as in style. They do not represent scenes of military glory, dynastic succession and ritual sacrifice, but focus instead on themes of agriculture and the fertility of the earth, rebirth and astronomic cycles in an apparent return to the mural subjects of Teotihuacán style.

At Tancah, for example, within the building called Structure 12, a mural represents seven deities performing an agricultural rite in the company of the young maize god, who wears an ear of corn as a headdress. In Structure 1 at Cobá, a mural of the Postclassic Period shows a similar agricultural rite performed by deities included the maize god, the rain god Chac and the creator god Itzamná. Murals at Tulum adorn the Temple of the Frescoes and the Temple of the Diving God. In the latter, another scene of agricultural ritual represents two pairs of gods separated by the linked bodies of serpents. The mural is divided into the three cosmic levels of heavens, terrestrial plain and underworld.

SYMBOLISM AND NATURALISM

The artists of Teotihuacán produced representations in murals, pottery, masks and figurines that exhibited little interest in naturalism and far more in religious symbolism. Humans were anonymous members of a mass group: in masks, human features were often reduced almost to geometric shapes or hidden behind nose bars. Murals tended to represent people in profile, often in procession, moving towards a goddess or god figure who was shown full frontal. Many scenes were of animals, plants and deities, often involved in rites associated with fertility. These images did not glorify the military and political achievements of rulers, apparently focusing instead on deities and religious symbols.

In contrast, many Maya muralists, stucco sculptors and ceramicists of the Classic Period (AD250–900) excelled in naturalistic representations of the human face and body. At Bonampak, for example, the suffering of prostrate prisoners of war was depicted with deft and feeling naturalism in Room 2 of Temple 1. Images of court life on polychrome vases and stucco carvings of King Pacal or King Chan Bahlum at Palenque are accurate and fluid representations of human expressions and gestures. (This is distinct from the much more stylized representations of royal figures produced by stonemasons on stelae and stone thrones.)

Images in Maya murals, ceramics and stucco focused on the beauty of the human body and face and of ceremonial attire such as the headdresses and costumes that also glorified the gods through sacred symbolism. Artists celebrated an ideal of human beauty in the stucco heads of King Pacal at Palenque and in the young maize god at Copán; in images of kings and courtiers on polychrome vases and in murals. This ideal consisted of a serene face with wide eyes, the bridge of the nose built up to join the forehead, full lips and smooth cheeks.

ROYAL PORTRAIT CONVENTIONS

Maya muralists and other artists generally stayed within established conventions of representation. They usually showed royal figures as exemplars of ideal beauty, not prone to ageing, in elegant costume and standing formally or occupying a regal seat. Artists had more leeway when it came to scenes of battle or those involving prisoners. The muralists at Bonampak took full advantage in representing an intense battle and subsequent presentation of prisoners to King Chan Muan in Room 2 of Temple 1. They showed soldiers and prisoners in many lifelike postures and expressions, prone and sitting, striding and thrusting, grimacing with pain and rolling their heads as if about to lose consciousness.

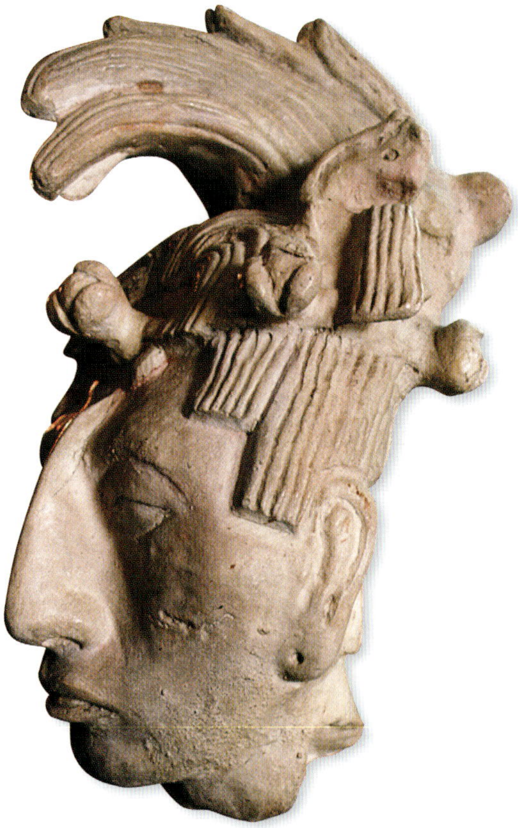

Above: Stone beauty. Maya sculpture probably reached its apogée in work such as this elegant head found at Copán.

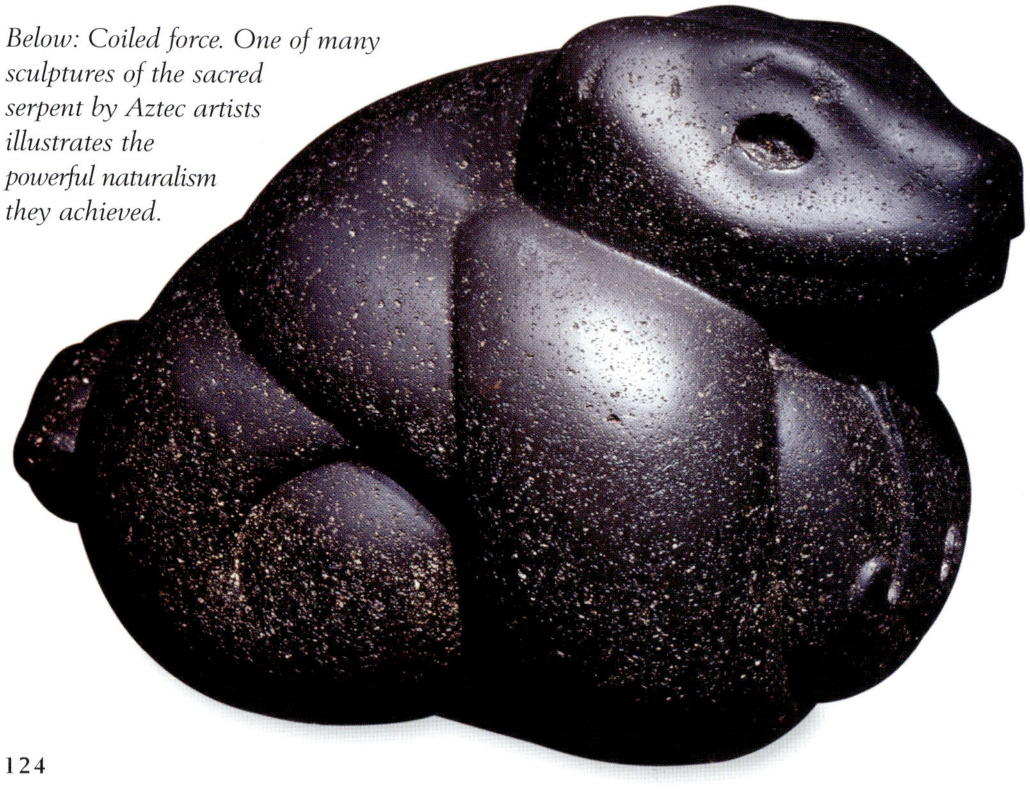

Below: Coiled force. One of many sculptures of the sacred serpent by Aztec artists illustrates the powerful naturalism they achieved.

THE SHAPE OF A KING

Artists at Palenque made a limited departure from the tradition of idealizing the physical appearance of the ruling family. Doubtless on royal orders, they appear to have emphasized physical abnormalities peculiar to the ruling dynasty of King

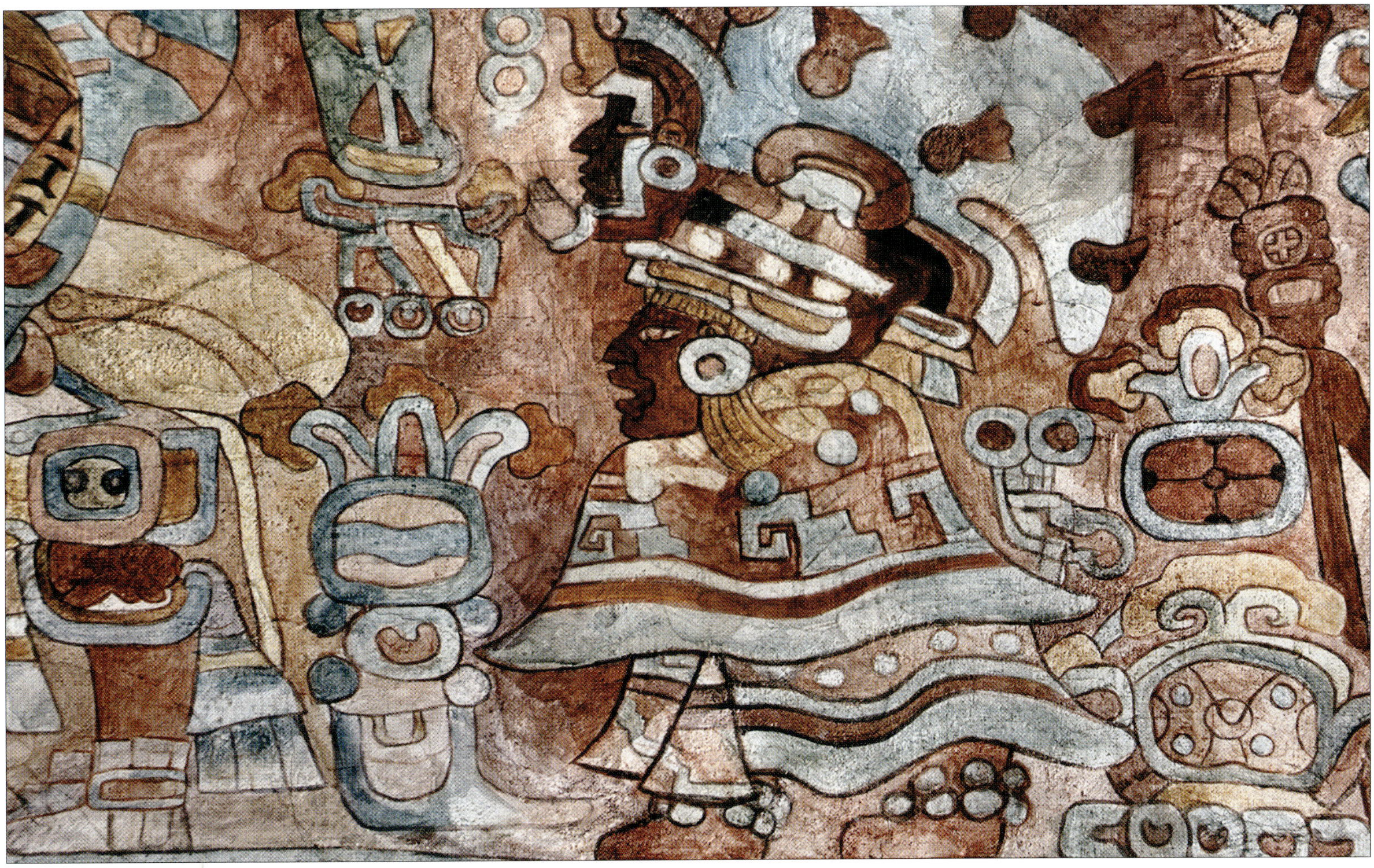

Pacal. These included an outsized head and jaw, signs of the pituitary disorder known as acromegaly, seen in images of Pacal's mother Lady Zac-Kuk. Depictions of Pacal's son, Chan-Bahlum, on the Temple of the Inscriptions show him with six fingers on the left hand and six toes on both feet. One of Pacal's uncles had a club foot, and scholars believe that Pacal himself might have inherited this. In images Pacal's foot was stylized as a serpent, and from the early 10th century AD, a god with serpent feet, Bolon Dz'Acab, became established as patron of kings. King Chan Bahlum appears to have encouraged his sculptors and artists to pursue a more realistic style in portraiture, as evidenced by a portrait head of the king in Temple XIV which depicts him with natural features at odds with the Maya ideal.

These dual strands of Maya naturalism and Teotihuacáno symbolic art had a joint flowering in the remarkable murals of Cacaxtla, in Tlaxcala, which were painted in the 7th–9th centuries AD. Artists combined concern with representing the human body in action (for example, in the Mural of the Battle in Building B) with a commitment to near-abstract scenes dense with religious symbolism (such as the murals possibly representing the sun and moon in Building A).

Artists of the Aztec era enthusiastically pursued naturalism in some statuary, but in painted work on vases and in codices followed the tradition of Teotihuacán.

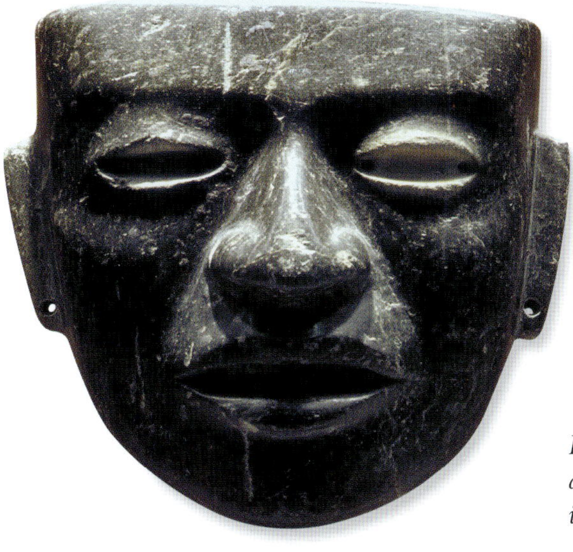

Above: The artists who painted this mural in Tomb 105 at Monte Albán used symbolism reminiscent of Teotihuacán.

The codex art of the Mixtecs and Aztecs was reminiscent of Teotihuacáno murals in representing humans in profile in flat, almost schematic scenes. It differed in that it was often focused on the recording of dynastic history and the achievements of rulers, while Teotihuacáno art was intent on celebrating fertility through religious symbols.

The murals of cities such as Tulum, Xelhá and Cobá on or near the Caribbean coast of Yucatán in the 13–16th centuries returned to the religious-artistic themes of the Teotihuacános. It used a decorative style that was close to that of the Mixtec codices to celebrate fertility and astronomic themes using images of deities and religious symbols.

Left: The evocative impact of Teotihuacáno art is evident in this jade mask, probably intended for funerary use.

INDEX

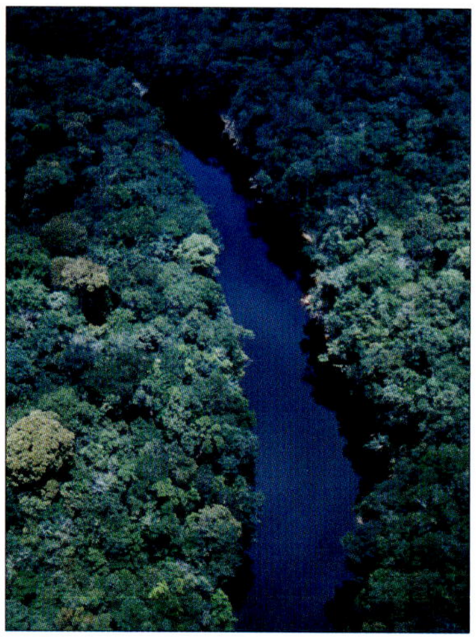

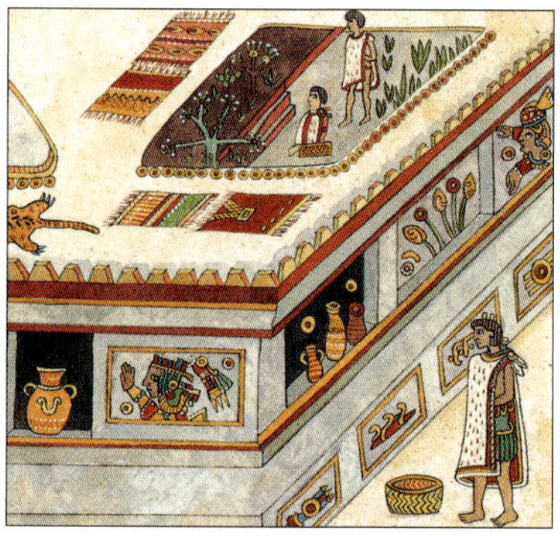

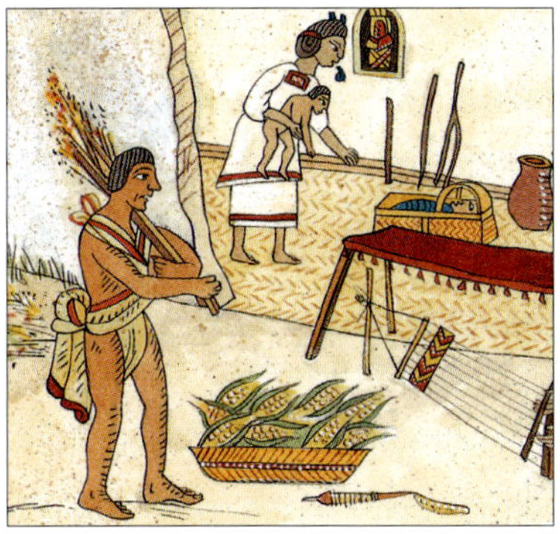

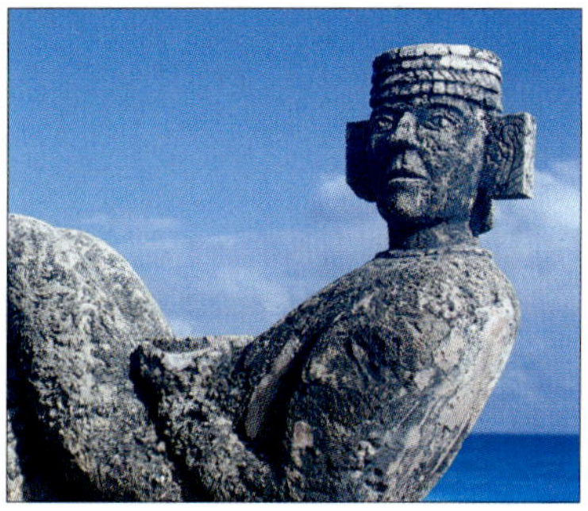

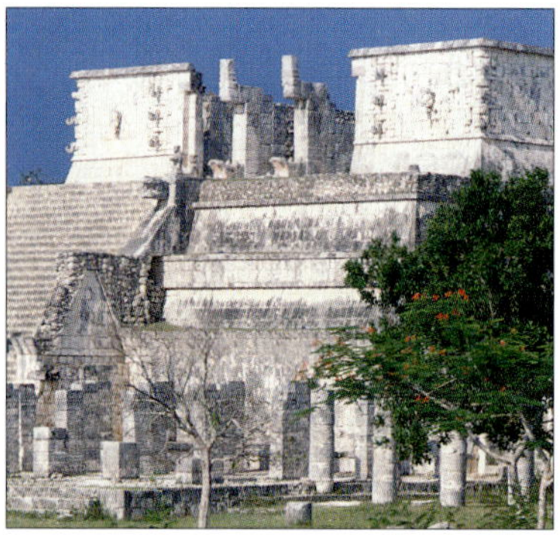

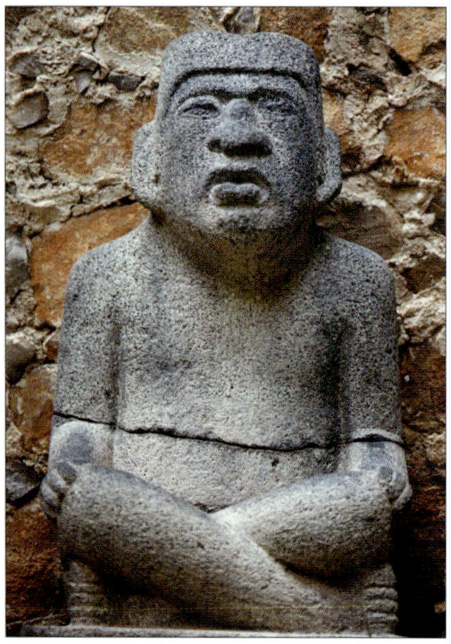

PICTURE ACKNOWLEDGEMENTS

The Ancient Art and Architecture Collection Ltd: 5bl, 7t, 13b, 28t, 30t, 82t, 83t&b, 88t, 91b, 98, 99b, 103t&b, 105t&b, 111b, 116t, 124t&b.

The Art Archive: /Antochiw Collection, Mexico/Mireille Vautier: 75t&b; /Archaeological and Ethnological Museum, Guatemala City/Dagli Orti: 5.3, 60–1, 116b, 120b; /Biblioteca Nacional, Madrid/Dagli Orti: 59bl; /Biblioteca Nacional, Mexico/ Dagli Orti: 8–9, 11t, 25t; /Bodleian Library, Oxford: 35t, 71t; /British Museum, London/Eileen Tweedy: 4, 107b; /Museo de America, Madrid/ Dagli Orti: 114; /Museo Ciudad, Mexico/Dagli Orti: 59br; /Museo Ethnografico Pigorini, Rome/Dagli Orti: 90b; /Museo de Jiquilpan, Mexico/Dagli Orti: 97t; /Museo Regional de Antropologia, Merida, Mexico/Dagli Orti: 85b; /Museo Regional de Oaxaca, Mexico/Dagli Orti: 5.5, 72t, 92–3, 95tl, 104tr; /Museo Regional, Puebla, Mexico/Dagli Orti: 18t, 85t; /Museo del Templo Mayor, Mexico/Dagli Orti: 70l&r; /Museo de Teotenango, Mexico/ Dagli Orti: 90t; /Museum San Pedro de Sula, Honduras /Dagli Orti: 7b, 68b, 69; /Museum für Völkerkunde, Vienna/Dagli Orti: 97b, 102; /National Anthropological Museum, Mexico/Dagli Orti: 3, 27b, 66bl, 67br, 72b, 74, 80b, 87b, 89, 95b, 96t&b, 99t, 100, 104b, 106t, 110t, 111t, 123t; /Dagli Orti: 2, 5.4, 19t&b, 20t, 21t, 23t&b, 25b, 27t, 29t, 32t&b, 33t, 38t, 41t, 45b, 50t, 51t&b, 52t&b, 56t, 57t, 76–7, 81, 84br, 110b; /Nicolas Sapieha: 41b; /Mireille Vautier: 106b, 115b, 122t&b, 123b; /Franceso Venturi: 91t; /Xalapa Museum, Veracruz, Mexico/Dagli Orti: 39b, 65t.

The Bridgeman Picture Library: /Baluarete de Santiago, Veracruz, Mexico, Banco Mexicano de Imagenes, INAH 101t; /British Museum, London 101b; /Museo Nacional de Antropologia, Mexico City, Mexico/Giraudon: 107t; /Private Collection: 10t, 112; /Private Collection, The Stapleton Collection: 10b.

Corbis: 49; /Paul Almasy: 33b; /Bowers Museum of Cultural Art: 62, 63b, 64b&t, 65b; /Richard A Cooke: 43t; /Sergio Dorantes: 55t; /Macduff Everton: 30b, 47, 55b; /Werner Forman: 35bl, 66r, 67t, 113t&b, 117b; /Angelo Hornak: 57b; /Jacqui Hurst: 73b; /Kimbell Art Museum: 63t, 71b; /Robert Landau: 22b; /Otto Lang: 38b; /Danny Lehman: 28b, 39t, 56b; /Charles and Josette Lenars: 24t, 34t, 40t, 48b, 80tr, 120t&t; /Craig Lovell 48t; /Gianni Dagli Orti: 12, 14t, 15b, 42b, 43b, 115t; /Della Zuana Pascal/Corbis Sygma: 121b; /Reuters; 73t; /Gian Berto Vanni: 31b, 80tl, 86b; /Vanni Archive: 31t; /Francesco Venturi: 22t; /Peter M Wilson; 5.1, 16–17.

South American Pictures from Tony and Marion Morrison: /Fabienne Fossez: 86t, 87t; /Robert Francis: 29b, 44, 78bl, 84t; /Tony Morrison: 11b, 78br, 79; /Iain Pearson: 54t&b; /Chris Sharp: 5.2, 5.6, 6t, 13t, 18b, 36–7, 53b, 68t, 78t, 82b, 88b, 94, 108–9, 118t&b, 119, 125t&b; /Karen Ward: 26t.

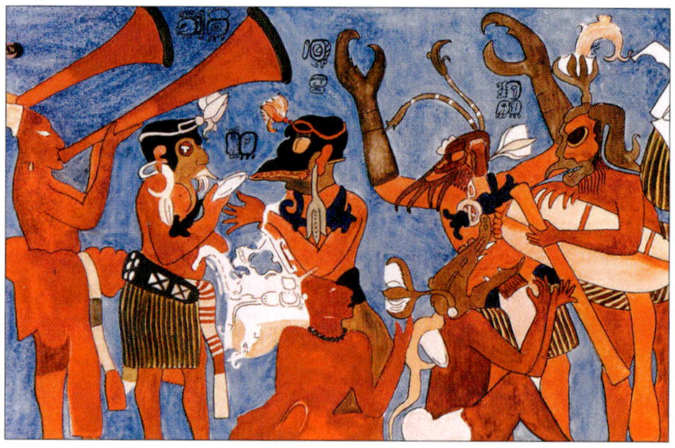